TRIAL ADVOCACY
IN A NUTSHELL

FIFTH EDITION

By

PAUL BERGMAN

Professor of Law, Emeritus
University of California, Los Angeles

WEST.®

A Thomson Reuters business

Mat #41326388

COPYRIGHT © 1989 WEST PUBLISHING CO.
© West, a Thomson business, 1997, 2006
© 2013 Thomson Reuters

       610 Opperman Drive
       St. Paul, MN 55123
       1-800-313-9378

Printed in the United States of America

ISBN: 978–0–314–28439–6

DEDICATION

With Gratitude For My Family

PREFACE

This Fifth Edition continues its predecessors' focus on both the technical skills of courtroom advocacy and effective persuasive strategies.

My review of the Fourth Edition revealed several portions of text in which the didactic value of analytical subtleties was substantially outweighed by the risk of unfair complexity. Under the editorial equivalent of Federal Rule of Evidence 403, unnecessary analytical subtleties have been stricken from this Fifth Edition

One added feature in this edition consists of analyses of "trial transcripts" taken from classic courtroom movies. For example, you will find analyses of the opening statements from *Philadelphia*, a direct examination of an expert witness from *My Cousin Vinny*, and Atticus Finch's closing argument in *To Kill a Mockingbird*. The carefully-chosen scenes are realistic yet concise enough to provide useful and interesting learning opportunities. Moreover, while you might not be able to watch great trial lawyers of the past in action, you can enhance your learning by combining the analyses with viewing the scenes. And if this Nutshell foments your interest in watching courtroom films, my co-authored book *Reel Justice: The Courtroom Goes to the Movies* (2006) has descriptions and folksy analyses of over 200 films. Also, the

Nutshell concludes on a light note by mentioning memeorable courtroom movie "lawyer pranks." For further information on this subject, see my essay entitled *Pranks for the Memory*, 30 University of San Francisco Law Review 1235 (1996).

Chapters 9 and 10 greatly expand the previous editions' attention to the process of laying foundations for the introduction of evidence. Even the most rhetorically-gifted litigator has to know how to perform such basic yet crucial trial tasks as demonstrating relevance, authenticating electronic messages (emails), eliciting opinions, satisfying the Original Writing (Best Evidence) Rule and establishing the elements of hearsay exceptions. The new materials explain and illustrate crucial trial skills such as these.

Civility among litigators, or more accurately the lack thereof, is a frequent agenda item at bar association meetings. Chapter 1 includes a short introduction to this sadly-necessary conversation.

My goal as always is to produce a book that is clear and reader-friendly. To that end, I have reviewed and edited the Fourth Edition text in its entirety. I hope you enjoy reading the book and find it helpful.

PAUL BERGMAN

Los Angeles
November 2012

ACKNOWLEDGMENTS

The people whose contributions are reflected throughout this book know who they are. However, apparently this was not good enough for them. Thus, I publicly acknowledge and give gratitude to my long-time and valued UCLA colleagues David Binder and Albert Moore, whose ideas permeate the text. Among the many practicing litigators who have been kind enough to provide feedback and suggestions, I want to especially thank Randy Even, a longtime friend and excellent litigator. Randy proves that the values of decency, public service and private advocacy can co-exist in one person.

Thank you also to Professor Sander Goldberg of the UCLA Department of Classics for background information on the trial of Euphilitis. And I am grateful to UCLA Professor Edward Geiselman, who testifies frequently as an expert witness in eyewitness identification and who contributed greatly to the book's discussion of expert witnesses.

To anyone who's gotten a draft of the manuscript with a request for feedback, you can now delete the draft.

OUTLINE

PREFACE V
ACKNOWLEDGMENTS VII

Chapter 1. An Approach to Trial Advocacy 1
A. Argument-Centered Narratives 2
B. Trial by Inference 5
C. Trial Skills in an Age of Settlement and
    Alternative Dispute Resolution 7
D. Truth and the Adversary System 8
E. Civility 9

PART 1. STRATEGIES FOR
DEVELOPING ARGUMENT-CENTERED
NARRATIVES

Chapter 2. Persuasive Legal Narratives 14
A. Why Stories Are Effective 14
B. Timelines 17
C. Attributes of Argument–Centered Narratives .. 21
    1. Substantively Critical Events 22
    2. Inferential Evidence 23
    3. Credibility Evidence 24
    4. Explanatory Evidence 25
    5. Contextual Details 26
    6. Emotional Evidence 29
    7. Visual Aids 30
    8. Defense Stories 31
D. Conclusion 33

Chapter 3. Inferential Arguments **34**
A. Definition of Inferential Arguments 34
B. Factual Propositions 35
C. Marshal Evidence Around Factual
    Propositions 39
D. Undermine Adversaries' Inferential
    Arguments 42
E. Normative Inferential Arguments 43

Chapter 4. Credibility Arguments **48**
A. Importance of Credibility Arguments 48
B. Focus on Important Disputes 49
C. A Credibility Model 50
D. "Story" Credibility Factors 52
    1. Consistency With Everyday Experience 52
    2. Internal Consistency 58
    3. Consistency With Established Facts 62
E. Source Credibility Factors 63
    1. In General 63
    2. Specific vs. General Credibility Evidence ... 64
    3. Lying or Mistaken? 66
    4. Expertise 67
    5. Motive or Bias 68
    6. Reason to Observe or Recall 72
    7. Demeanor 73
    8. Character for Honesty 76
F. Case Example: The *Hillmon* Case 78

Chapter 5. Silent Arguments **84**

PART 2. COURTROOM PRESENTATION STRATEGIES

Chapter 6. Opening Statements **92**
A. Contents of Effective Opening Statements 92
    1. A Roadmap to Roadmaps 93
    2. Argument–Centered Stories 95
    3. Themes 99
    4. Bottom Lines 101
    5. Substantive Rules 103
B. Effective Presentation Strategies 104
    1. Level of Detail 104
    2. Separate Chronologies 107
    3. Don't Talk Like a Lawyer (or Like How
        You Think Lawyers Talk) 107
    4. Effective Performance Techniques 109
    5. Visual Aids 111
    6. "The Evidence Will Show . . ." 112
    7. Opening Statement Boilerplate 113
C. Follow the Rules 114
    1. Argument 114
    2. Inadmissible or Unavailable Evidence 116
    3. Evidence Solely Within an Adversary's
        Control 118
    4. Vouching 119
    5. Prima Facie Cases 121
D. Common Judgment Calls 121
    1. Volunteering Weaknesses 121
    2. Defense Opening Statements 123
    3. Bench Trials 125
E. Opening Statement Example 1 125
F. Opening Statement Example 2 135

Chapter 7. Direct Examination **139**
A. Overview 139
B. Follow the Rules 141
    1. Witness Competency 142
    2. Personal Knowledge 145
    3. Do Not Testify............................... 146
    4. Housekeeping Rules 147
        a. The Well............................... 148
        b. Sitting and Standing 148
        c. Converse in the Triangular 149
C. Forms of Questions.............................. 151
    1. Open Questions 151
    2. Closed Questions 155
    3. Narrative Questions..................... 157
    4. Leading Questions........................ 162
        a. Leading Questions Defined................ 162
        b. Legitimate Uses of Leading
           Questions........................... 164
        c. Leading Questions and Credibility.... 171
D. Getting Started................................... 172
    1. Background Questions 172
    2. Scene–Setting Questions 175
E. Argument-Centered Stories............................. 180
    1. Importance of Argument-Centered
        Direct Examinations 181
    2. Atypical Chronologies 183
F. Emphasis Techniques........................... 185
    1. Front Load Important Events 185
    2. Layered Questioning 188
    3. "No, No, No" Technique............... 190
    4. Points of Reference ("Loops")..................... 192
    5. Bases of Conclusions and Opinions.......... 194
    6. Exhibits...................................... 196
    7. Verbalizing Gestures.................. 197

8. Silent Arguments 200

G. Concluding Direct Examinations 201

H. Redirect Examination 202

I. Sample Direct Examinations 204

J. Common Judgment Points 226

K. Witness Preparation Strategies 233

L. Final Tips 237

Chapter 8. Cross Examination........................ 240

A. The Mystique of Cross Examination 240

B. Follow the Rules 245

    1. Stay Within the Scope of the Direct.......... 245

    2. Avoid Argumentative Questions 246

    3. Base Questions on a "Good–Faith
       Belief" 248

    4. Comply With the "Collateral Evidence
       Rule" 249

    5. Quote Testimony Accurately 250

C. Essential Questioning Strategies 251

    1. Rely on Leading Questions 251

    2. Ask Single–Item Questions 253

    3. Don't Ask "Why" 255

    4. Avoid the "One Question Too Many"......... 257

    5. Avoid Asking Questions You Do Not
       Know the Answer To 260

D. A Cross Examination Safety Model 262

    1. Highly Safe Questions................................ 263

       a. Witness' Provable Prior Statement 263

       b. Consistency With Established
          Facts 267

    2. Medium Safe Questions 268

       a. Consistency With Everyday
          Experience....................................... 268

       b. Assumed Testimony of an
          Unavailable Witness....................... 276

        3. Unsafe Questions ("Fishing") 280
E. Argument–Centered Questioning..................... 286
F. Impeachment With Prior Inconsistent
        Statements... 290
        1. Evidentiary Rules....................................... 290
        2. Impeachment Options................................. 291
        3. "I Don't Remember" Testimony 293
        4. Effective Impeachment Strategies 294
        5. Omissions Impeachment............................. 299
G. Character Evidence Impeachment.................... 302
H. Impeachment—Other Bases............................. 307
        1. Bias.. 308
        2. Contradiction 312
        3. Testimonial Impairment............................. 313
I. Emphasis Strategies... 315
        1. "No, No, No"... 315
        2. Ultimate Conclusion Questions................. 316
J. Selective Use of Open Questions....................... 319
K. Order of Questioning... 320
L. Forgoing Cross Examination 321
M. Responding to Evasive Answers 323
        1. Repeat the Question.................................... 324
        2. "I Didn't Ask X, I Asked Y" 324
        3. Move to Strike and Repeat a Question 325
        4. Judge's Instruction to Answer................... 325
        5. Avoid Arguing With Witnesses................... 326
        6. "May" and "Might"....................................... 327
N. Responding to Explanations.............................. 327
        1. Refuse Requests to Explain 328
        2. Ignore and Repeat 328
        3. Interrupt an Explanation 329
        4. Move to Strike 330
        5. Implausible Explanations........................... 331
        6. Pre–Instructing Witnesses 333

7. "Closing the Door" 333
O. "Cross" Examination? 335
P. "Your Story" Cross Examination 336
Q. Preparing Witnesses for Cross Examination... 337
R. Protecting Your Witnesses 340
   1. "Objection, argumentative" 340
   2. "Objection, counsel is not allowing the
      witness to finish answering" 341
   3. "Objection, counsel is badgering
      (harassing) the witness" 341
   4. "Objection, counsel is misstating the
      evidence (misquoting the witness)" 342
   5. "Objection, asked and answered" 342
   6. "Objection, beyond the scope of direct" 343
   7. "Objection, assumes facts not in
      evidence" 343

**Chapter 9. Satisfying Foundational
Requirements for Non-Tangible
Evidence** **344**
A. Inter-Personal Communications 345
B. Recollection Refreshed 348
C. Lay Witness Opinions 353
   1. Two Prongs for Admissibility 353
   2. Inebriation 357
   3. Character for Truth-Telling 360
D. Habit 362
E. Mercy Rule Evidence 363
F. Non-Character Uses of Other Acts 365
G. Character Evidence in Sexual Assault Cases.. 368
H. Courtroom Demonstrations 369
I. Hearsay Statements 372
   1. Opposing Party Statements 373
   2. Present Sense Impressions 377
   3. Excited Utterances 378

4. Medical Hearsay 380
5. Unavailability 381
6. Dying Declarations 385
7. Forfeiture by Wrongdoing 387

**Chapter 10. Satisfying Foundational
Requirements for Tangible Evidence 390**
A. Real vs. Demonstrative Exhibits 390
B. Benefits of Exhibits 393
C. Follow the Rules 396
   1. Mark Exhibits 397
   2. Authenticate Exhibits 399
   3. Satisfy Foundational Requirements 401
   4. Leave Admitted Exhibits in the
      Courtroom 402
   5. "Publish" Exhibits 402
   6. Handle Exhibits Effectively 404
D. Foundations for Common Tangible Exhibits .. 404
   1. Real Evidence 405
   2. Chain of Custody Questions 408
   3. Photographs 411
   4. Diagrams 413
   5. The Original Writing (Nee Best
      Evidence) Rule 419
      a. Original Writings 420
      b. Duplicates 421
      c. Original Writing Excused: Contents
         Not in Issue 422
      d. Original Writing Excused: The
         Original Is Lost 423
      e. Original Writing Excused: The
         Original Was Innocently
         Destroyed 426

6. Authenticating Signed or Handwritten
    Documents.. 427
7. Business Records...................................... 431
8. Public Records 433
9. Computer Records 436
10. Faxed Writings 437
11. Texts and Tweets.................................... 439
12. Recorded Recollection............................. 441
13. Live Exhibitions 443
14. Professionally–Prepared Exhibits........... 447

Chapter 11. Expert Witnesses........................ 449
A. Experts' Varied Roles 450
B. Follow the Rules 452
    1. Personal Knowledge 452
    2. Otherwise–Inadmissible Evidence............ 453
    3. Compensation 454
    4. Relaxed Testimonial Rules 454
    5. Reliability of a Field of Expertise.............. 455
    6. Experts' Qualifications.............................. 457
    7. Hypothetical Questions............................. 458
    8. Ultimate Issues 459
C. Direct Examination Strategies 460
    1. Background Testimony (Establishing
        an Expert's Qualifications) 460
    2. Explain the Field 467
    3. Eliciting Opinions...................................... 469
D. Cross Examination Strategies.......................... 480

Chapter 12. Closing Argument 485
A. Follow the Rules 486
    1. Facts Outside the Record........................... 486
    2. Draw Reasonable Inferences 488
    3. Puffing... 489
    4. Voucher Rule 490

5. "Send a Message" Arguments 492
6. Miscellaneous Forbidden Arguments 493
B. Argument Strategies 493
C. Effective Oral Presentation Techniques 494
D. Content of Persuasive Closing Arguments 496
1. Introductory Remarks 497
2. Organization 499
3. Consider an "Evidence Review" 500
4. Presenting Inferential Arguments 502
5. Presenting Credibility Arguments 503
a. Lying or Mistaken? 503
b. "Falsus in Uno, Falsus in
Omnibus" 505
c. Arguments Supporting Credibility 507
6. Undermining Silent Arguments 509
7. Normative and "Pseudo–Normative"
Arguments 510
8. The Bottom Line 511
E. Additional Argument Strategies 513
1. Two–Sided Arguments 513
2. Analogies 519
a. Developing Analogies 519
b. Responding to an Adversary's
Analogy 524
3. Legal Principles 525
a. The Burden of Proof 526
b. Other Jury Instructions 527
F. Arguments in Bench Trials 530
G. Argument Excerpts: People vs. O. J.
Simpson (1995) and Citizens of Athens vs.
Euphiletus (circa 400–380 b.c.) 530
1. Introductory Remarks 532
2. Roadmaps 533

3. Adversary's Failure to Offer Promised
    Evidence 534

4. Use of Visual Aids 534

5. Puffing... 535

6. Silent Arguments 535

7. Analogies.. 537

8. Responding to an Adversary's Analogy..... 538

9. Credibility Argument: *Falsus in Uno,
    Falsus in Omnibus* 539

10. Inoculation 539

11. Inferential Arguments 540

12. Two–Sided Arguments 541

13. Preemption... 541

14. The Result.. 542

15. Send a Message Arguments..................... 542

16. Pseudo–Normative Argument 543

H. Argument Analysis: To Kill a Mockingbird..... 543

Chapter 13. Odds and Ends............................. **549**

A. Excluding (Sequestering) Witnesses 549

B. Stipulations.. 551

C. Making Objections... 554

1. Motions *in Limine* 554

2. Tactical and Ethical Considerations 558

3. Objections Procedures................................ 559

4. Continuing Objections................................ 562

5. Offers of Proof... 563

6. Beyond Objections 567

7. Common Grounds for Objection 568

D. Responding to an Adversary's Objections........ 575

1. You Concede the Point 575

2. Arguing Objections...................................... 576

3. Offering Evidence for Limited Purposes... 577

4. The Adversary's Objection Is Overruled... 577

5. The Adversary's Objection Is Sustained ... 577

E. Judge or Jury Trial? 578
F. Jury *Voir Dire* 582
G. Jury Instructions 591
H. Subpoenas 593
I. Packing for Trial 594

J. Miscellaneous Customs and Practices 597
    1. Sitting and Standing 597
    2. Promptness 598
    3. Approaching the Bench 598
    4. Converse in the Triangular 598
    5. Observe Courthouse Etiquette 599
    6. Handling Client Distractions 599
    7. Note–Taking 600
K. The Tricks Hall of Fame 601
INDEX 607

TRIAL
ADVOCACY
IN A NUTSHELL

FIFTH EDITION

CHAPTER 1
AN APPROACH TO TRIAL ADVOCACY

Influenced by films, TV shows and news media reports focusing on courtroom disputes, theatrics and strategies, you may have embarked on law school with the goal of becoming a litigator. Perhaps the most visible and enduring symbols of the American legal system, adversarial trials (in popular culture, almost always with juries present) are also one of its most important. Trials are the mechanism by which individuals and institutions enforce the rights that legislatures and judges create, and are at the center of the popular self-conception of the American public that the United States is "a country of laws, not of people."

For law students and novice litigators, however, the mythology of the courtroom can be intimidating. Popular culture images, in combination with lawyers' war stories describing courtroom triumphs and tragedies, tend to suggest that effective courtroom advocates must possess:

* the story-creation skills of a Pulitzer Prize-winning novelist;

* the performance skills of an Academy Award-winning thespian;

1

* the forensic skills of a debate champion; and

* an unfailing knack for ferreting out mendacity.

    (For example, consider barrister Sir Wilfrid
    Robarts' "monocle test" in the classic courtroom
    film, *Witness for the Prosecution.* Sir Wilfrid
    determined clients' honesty by studying their
    facial expressions closely as they answered his
    questions while trying to fend off the light re-
    flected into their eyes from his monocle.)

Like all enduring myths, these concerning trial
lawyers contain kernels of truth. For example, sto-
ry-construction and oral rhetorical skills are indeed
important components of effective courtroom advocacy. However, much of the "art" of trial advocacy consists of techniques and strategies that you can apply
as skillfully as principles of addition, subtraction and
the Rule Against Perpetuities—well, of addition and
subtraction anyway. Of course, you will have to in-
fuse these strategies and techniques with your common sense and judgment in the context of specific
cases. The purpose of this Nutshell is to provide you
with a solid foundation for doing so and for persona-
lizing and building on these tools for persuasion as
you gain experience.

A. ARGUMENT-CENTERED NARRATIVES

In law schools and legal treatises, legal analysis (or
"thinking like a lawyer") generally focuses on "legal
complexity." Legal complexity arises when you devel-

op arguments about the meaning and applicability of abstract legal rules based on factors such as prior court decisions, social policies and case-specific facts.

The subject of this book is "thinking like a *trial* lawyer." Thinking like a trial lawyer extends the scope of legal analysis to "factual complexity." The reason is that at trial, before judges and jurors can apply rules to facts, they first have to decide what happened. In a world of factual complexity, effective story-telling is your principal method for influencing judges' and jurors' factual conclusions.

Many story-tellers can achieve success merely by telling stories that arouse emotions such as sadness, joy or fear. But as a trial lawyer, your success depends on whether the stories you elicit convince judges and jurors that historical events entitle your clients to legal relief (or prevent adversaries from obtaining legal relief). Persuasive trial stories are *argument-centered*. Argument-centered narratives have three principal characteristics:

1. *Chronology*. Like most stories, argument-centered narratives generally unfold chronologically. You have to exercise professional judgment to decide when a story begins and ends. Moreover, you may want to deviate from chronology when marshalling different items of evidence that bear on the same legal issue. Nevertheless, chronology tends to help judges and jurors understand and give credence to events.

2. *Legally salient facts.* Argument-centered narratives emphasize the evidence that substantive rules clothe with legal meaning. From voir dire through witness examinations to closing argument, your argument-centered narratives emphasize the substantive evidence that supports your clients' legal claims and undermines adversaries' claims. For example, the story you present on behalf of a plaintiff in a medical malpractice case should emphasize the doctor's actions that fell below a reasonable standard of professional care.

3. *Credibility.* Argument-centered narratives emphasize credibility evidence that supports the accuracy of helpful evidence and undermines the accuracy of harmful evidence. For example, if you are a prosecutor whose witness identifies the defendant as the culprit, the story you elicit should emphasize evidence bolstering the accuracy of the identification.

Part 1 of this Nutshell (Chapters 2-5) explores strategies for developing argument-centered narratives. These strategies relate to all types of cases, no matter what substantive law applies, civil or criminal.

Starting in childhood with such stories as *Goldilocks and the Three Bears* and *Dante's Inferno*, you will have been exposed to many stories by the time you read this Nutshell. You know that the effectiveness of stories depends not just on their content but also on the manner of telling. In the same way, clear and competent presentation of argument-centered narratives enhances effectiveness. Part 2 of this Nutshell (Chapters 6–13) describes and illustrates strategies and techniques for effective courtroom presentations.

B. TRIAL BY INFERENCE

Argument-centered narratives typically consist primarily of circumstantial evidence, the probative value of which relies on inferences. Circumstantial evidence predominates at trial because stories give legal meaning to substantively critical events by explaining what took place before and after those events occurred. And such "before and after" events constitute circumstantial evidence.

For example, assume that the prosecutor in a bank robbery case offers evidence that the defendant walked around the bank's interior for about fifteen minutes the day before it was robbed without transacting any business. This "before" evidence is circumstantial, as the prosecutor offers it to support an argument that the judge or jury should infer that the defendant was in the bank in order to "case" it in preparation for robbing it.

In the same case, assume that the defense attorney offers evidence that the day after the bank was robbed, the defendant kept an appointment with his probation officer. This "after" evidence is also circumstantial, as the defense attorney offers it to support an argument that the judge or jury should infer that the defendant would not have visited a law enforcement officer had he robbed a bank a day earlier.

Of course, trial stories often include direct evidence, which proves or disproves a legal issue without the need of an inference. But disputes at trial often focus on the credibility of direct evidence, and evidence that pertains to credibility is a type of circumstantial evidence.

For example, in the same bank robbery case, assume that a bank customer identifies the defendant as the robber. This is direct evidence of the defendant's guilt; no inference is needed to connect the customer's testimony to the legal element of "identity." But to bolster the credibility of the testimony, the prosecutor may elicit testimony that the customer observed the robber from a distance of only 15 feet. To attack the credibility of the testimony, the defense attorney may elicit testimony that the customer observed the robber from the rear and off to the side, while crouching behind a poster display. Both attorneys offer circumstantial evidence, as the credibility of the customer's identification rests on inferences.

Thus, whether evidence pertains to a disputed legal issue or to witness credibility, argument-centered narratives consist primarily of circumstantial evidence.

C. TRIAL SKILLS IN AN AGE OF SETTLEMENT AND ALTERNATIVE DISPUTE RESOLUTION

Trial advocacy skills might seem an anomaly in an era when statistics suggest that well over 90% of civil and criminal cases never make it to trial. Most litigants manage to settle their disputes, either voluntarily or "in the shadow of the courthouse," often with the aid of court-ordered mediation. Indeed, the popularity of alternative dispute resolution has created such a need for mediators that the most appropriate answer to the question, "What do you call a litigator with 20 years of experience?" may be, "A mediator." Moreover, many disputes that may have formerly entered the formal justice system and resulted in jury trials are resolved through binding arbitration. Thus, litigators today may have little actual trial experience, somewhat like the admirals of Gilbert & Sullivan operettas who never went to sea.

Even in an Age of Settlement, however, if you are a litigator you should be comfortable with your trial advocacy skills. For one thing, persuasive and legally compelling stories affect not only trial outcomes, but also the outcomes of settlements, mediations and arbitrations. Moreover, only if you are comfortable in courtrooms can you be confident that a recommendation of settlement is based on a client's best interests, not on your own discomfort with trial.

D. TRUTH AND THE ADVERSARY SYSTEM

The continued social legitimacy of the adversary system is tied to the popular belief that judges and jurors can distill truth from the clash of opposing stories. Advocates generally recognize the epistemological limits of this conception. After all, trial lawyers do not engage in a neutral and unfettered search for truth but rather seek and select admissible evidence to prove that propositions favorable to their clients are true. The need to resolve disputes reasonably speedily, the restrictions on investigation and proof imposed by legal regulations and clients' pocketbooks, doubts about whether even the most honest and unbiased witnesses can observe and recollect accurately, and judges and jurors necessarily filtering evidence through their own prisms of beliefs and experiences make further inroads on the truth-finding image of trials. The legal system explicitly recognizes these weaknesses by making trial outcomes turn not on certainty but rather on probabilities such as "a preponderance of the evidence" and "beyond a reasonable doubt."

While some observers might claim that lawyers' rhetorical strategies are an improper overlay on an already dubious mode of truth-seeking, at the end of the day those strategies probably promote rather than interfere with accurate fact-finding. With objective reality un-provable, effective trial strategies are necessary if you are to convince judges and jurors that your narratives and arguments are accurate.

E. CIVILITY

Canon 7 of the American Bar Association Model Code provides that "A lawyer should represent a client zealously within the bounds of the law." Many bar association leaders blame an over-zealous reliance on Canon 7 for what they consider a rising tide of "lawyer incivility" (or bullying) that characterizes modern litigation. Commonly-cited examples of incivility include:

* Refusing an opposing counsel's reasonable request for a continuance of a hearing, so that opposing counsel has to prepare and file a written motion and go to court to obtain the continuance.

* Intentionally misconstruing the meaning of a discovery request that a five year old child could understand, and responding with irrelevant information, an objection or a claim of privilege.

* Using rude and intemperate language. For example, in the case of *In re First City Bancorp of Texas Inc* (282 F. 3d 864, 5th Cir. 2002), a lawyer referred on the record to opposing counsel as a "stooge," a "puppet," a "deadhead" and an "underling who graduated from a 29th tier law school."

* Using delaying tactics so as to maximize the inconvenience and cost of litigation. For example, the case of *GMAC v. HTFC Corp.* (248 F.R.D. 182, 2008) quotes a deponent's deposition response in which the deponent (on the advice of the depo-

nent's lawyer) provided a lengthy and meandering answer and then in response to the deposing attorney's protest stated on the record that "I'm going to keep going. I'll have you flying in and out of New York City every single month and this will go on for years. And by the way, along the way GMAC will be bankrupt and I will laugh at you."

To curtail lamentable behavior such as this, numerous lawyer associations have developed civility guidelines. A leading example are the "Principles of Civility, Integrity and Professionalism" adopted by ABOTA (the American Board of Trial Advocacy, a national group of experienced trial lawyers). ABOTA's principles are "intended to discourage conduct that demeans, hampers or obstructs our system of justice." For example, Principle 19 states that attorneys should "never take depositions for the purpose of harassment or to burden an opponent with increased litigation expenses."

Many states have also supplemented formal ethical rules with civility guidelines. The enforceability of civility guidelines varies among jurisdictions. However, their drafters hope that even hortatory provisions can increase civility, especially when lawyers discuss them at bar association meetings and in law school classrooms.

Utah's "Standards of Professionalism and Civility" are representative of states' efforts to improve civility among litigators. The Standards' Preamble states that "A lawyer's conduct should be characterized at all times by personal courtesy and professional integrity." Moreover, "Conduct that may be characterized as uncivil, abrasive, abusive, hostile or obstructive impedes the fundamental goal of resolving disputes rationally, peacefully and efficiently."

The specific content of many guidelines suggests that litigators routinely engage in rude and discourteous behavior that first grade teachers would deplore. For example, Utah's Standard 6 provides that "Lawyers shall adhere to their express promises and agreements, oral or written." And Utah's Standard 13 states that "Lawyers shall not file or serve motions, pleadings or other papers at a time calculated to unfairly limit other counsel's opportunity to respond, or to take other unfair advantage of an opponent, or in a manner intended to take advantage of another lawyer's unavailability."

California's "Attorney Guidelines of Civility and Professionalism" also suggest the embarrassing depths to which many litigators' behavior has sunk. For instance, civility guidelines pertaining to the taking of depositions forbid the use of foul and hostile language, the practice of scheduling depositions without prior contact for convenient times and locations, and rude-toned and intimidating questioning. And one of the civility provisions relating to pretrial requests for documents instructs lawyers not to take a "needle in a haystack" approach by providing documents in a disorganized or unintelligible format.

Perhaps surprisingly, you can contribute to the betterment of our system of justice simply by behaving decently and observing the Golden Rule principle of treating others as you would want to be treated.

PART 1

STRATEGIES FOR DEVELOPING ARGUMENT-CENTERED NARRATIVES

————

CHAPTER 2

PERSUASIVE LEGAL NARRATIVES

Chapter 1 introduced the concept of *argument-centered narratives.* Argument-centered narratives aid persuasion by combining the familiarity of stories with the centrality of inference in decision-making. Argument-centered narratives emphasize the evidence that (1) supports the accuracy of your stories, especially your version of important disputed events, and (2) promotes the inferences you seek to establish (or prevent your adversary from establishing). This chapter explains the importance of stories and the typical attributes of persuasive courtroom narratives.

A. WHY STORIES ARE EFFECTIVE

Stories are inter-connected events that typically unfold chronologically. Consider first why effective trial advocacy relies on story-telling.

One reason that stories tend to portray historical events convincingly is simply that stories are a basic form of human communication. We humans may be "hard-wired" to understand events through the lenses of stories. Consider these common examples:

1. Shortly before retiring for the day, Joanna realizes that a credit card is missing from her wallet. Trying to remember where the card may have gone

missing, Joanna mentally reviews the day's events chronologically.

2. On his way to law school one morning, Al overhears a passerby on a mobile phone say that "and then the truck ran right into a plate glass window." Al reflexively turns the brief excerpt into an imagined scenario that encompasses such details as the truck's speed, the building's appearance, how much of the truck went through the window and whether people had to dive out of the truck's path.

Likewise, when people relate happenings to each other, they almost always do so by telling stories. Thus, stories tend to be persuasive partly because they are a familiar way of conveying and receiving information. Stories tend to "normalize" events while helping judges and jurors understand parties' versions of dispute-related events.

Conveying information in the form of stories is also effective because chronology and fact-finding are intimately linked. The inferences that you ask judges and jurors to accept typically grow out of the order in which events took place. Consider this example from the classic courtroom film, *Anatomy of a Murder*. In the film, Lt. Manion is charged with murdering Barney Quill in a tavern. Manion admits to killing Quill, but claims that he was temporarily insane after finding out from his wife Laura that Quill had raped her.

In a dramatic moment in the trial, witness Mary Palant supports Manion's rape claim by producing

Laura's torn panties. Palant explains that she worked in Quill's tavern and that they lived in adjoining rooms. The morning after Quill was shot, Palant found the torn panties at the bottom of the laundry chute that was between their rooms. She found the panties when sorting the tavern's laundry as part of her usual job duties.

Prosecutor Claude Dancer angrily accuses Palant of lying, claiming that she is seeking revenge after her lover Quill dumped her in favor of Laura. Dancer's acusation backfires horribly when Palant reveals that Quill was her father. A stunned Dancer has "no more questions."

If Palant's story seems unimpeachable, it may be because the description above, like the film, masks the true chronology. Re-arranging the key events of Palant's story chronologically, her story is as follows:

1. Barney Quill is Mary Palant's father.

2. Barney Quill is brutally gunned down.

3. The next morning, Palant finds the torn panties while sorting the hotel laundry.

The chronology suggests that Palant might be mistaken, at least as to *when* she found the torn panties. It is of course possible that Palant was working as usual in the hotel laundry room a few hours after her father was brutally gunned down. But perhaps it is much more likely that she took at least one day off to mourn and make funeral arrangements. Isn't that the way people often behave when loved ones die, especially suddenly and violently? If so, Manion had plenty of time to support a phony rape story by having torn panties planted where Palant could find them. In any event, the point is that the chronology of events reveals possible inferences that otherwise are invisible.

B. TIMELINES

With chronology so vital to effective trial advocacy and inference-drawing, *timelines* are one of your most important trial preparation tools. A timeline is a chronological list of important happenings that comprise a party's version of events. From the time you begin to gather information, create timelines and continue to refine and expand them as case investigation proceeds. Most litigation support computer software has a "window" for maintaining chronologies. To keep your eye on the key factual disputes between your and your adversaries' cases, also maintain chronologies representing adversaries' versions of important events.

Effective trial preparation typically entails creating two types of timelines. One type constitutes an overall timeline, based on the combined stories of all witnesses and including information emanating from documents and other exhibits. The second type of timeline is a chronology for each individual witness who may testify at trial.

Include Sources of Information in Timelines. As a trial lawyer, the crucial question for you is not "What do I know?" but rather "What can I prove?" Thus, timeline entries should include a reference to the source through which you intend to offer information into evidence. For example, assume that you represent the plaintiff in a personal injury case growing out of an auto accident, and that when you took the defendant's deposition the defendant testified that "At the time of the accident I was 20 minutes late for an important meeting." Your timeline should mention that the source of the information that the defendant was driving while late for a meeting is "Defendant's Depo, p. ___, lines ___."

Developing effective timelines entails making a variety of judgment calls. One common decision point involves "bookend" events, those that mark the beginning and end of a story. You may not be able to identify the beginning of a timeline simply by asking a client a question such as, "When did the dispute begin?" Clients may not know how to answer such questions, especially if substantive rules create the need for evidence concerning events about which a client lacks personal knowledge. A timeline's beginning and ending are essentially strategic judgments that you have to make in the light of your arguments.

A second common timeline judgment call concerns the level of detail. If timelines are to help you with such tasks as planning witness examinations, identifying inferences and focusing on important conflicts between your stories and those of your adversaries, timelines must necessarily consist of substantially less than all the evidence you will present. How much less is a strategic judgment for you to make according to your arguments. For example, assume that an important timeline event is that "a house was inspected on March 12." The inspection would have involved a variety of activities, changes of location and conversations. How much of this subsidiary information to break out as separate timeline events is a judgment call for you to make according to such factors as the importance of the inspection to your arguments.

A Timeline Example

Assume that your client, Beth, is the plaintiff in a personal injury lawsuit. Beth's paranoia and accompanying mental and emotional difficulties resulted in her being taken to a hospital emergency room for observation. While in a hospital bed, Beth was placed in soft restraints for her own safety. However, Beth freed herself from the restraints and had begun to walk out of the emergency room when a nurse spotted her and with the help of others, returned Beth to her bed. Shortly thereafter, Beth again managed to remove the restraints, left the emergency room and suffered injuries when she was struck by a car while crossing a street. The lawsuit seeks special damages for medical expenses and lost future income as well as general damages for pain and suffering.

The extent of a timeline will necessarily vary depending on such factors as how far along you are in case investigation and what events are most important to your arguments. In Beth's case, the beginning of a timeline that you might make when you are still in the early stages of investigation could look something like this:

1. 8:12 AM—Witness Jones calls 911 and reports that Beth is in her front yard screaming meaningless insults at passing cars and pedestrians.

2. 8:25—Paramedics transport Beth to the hospital.

3. 8:55—Beth in soft restraints in a bed in a communal emergency room, curtains open but the bed is only partially visible from the nurses' station.

4. 9:25—Emergency Room Nurses' Supervisor Johnson begins a meeting for the on-duty emergency room nurses.

5. 9:40—Nurse Slaton observes Beth near an emergency room exit door.

6. Etc.

Timelines do not necessarily dictate the organization of trial presentations. Timelines help you evaluate stories' strength and credibility as well as the important conflicts between your stories and those of your adversaries. But you need not slavishly adhere to chronology during trial.

For example, you may deviate from chronology during a witness' direct examination in order to marshal the evidence supporting an inference you want a judge or jury to accept.

C. ATTRIBUTES OF ARGUMENT–CENTERED NARRATIVES

Standing alone, the advice to "develop narratives" is of limited utility because the story concept is vague and elastic. For example, a story of World War II might consist of "German Chancellor Hitler started the war in 1939 by invading Poland, and Germany surrendered to the Allies in 1945," or the story might run to encyclopedic length. As a result, you cannot make decisions about stories' contents in the abstract. Instead, stories are *inference-driven.* That is, stories' contents depend on the inferences you want judges and jurors to accept (or not accept).

The idea that professionals who seek to provide truth *construct* rather than *find* stories lies behind the book written by historians James Davidson and Mark Lytle, *After the Fact: The Art of Historical Detection.* In the chapter "The Strange Death of Silas Deane," the authors point out that Deane was "a distinctly second-rate diplomat" for the United States during the American Revolution. Suspected by American leaders of profiteering and spying, Deane remained in Europe after the war. He was dependent on his former secretary Edward Bancroft for subsistence, and quite depressed. Deane eventually decided to return to the states in 1789. He took sick on board ship and died.

This summary story suggests that Deane may have committed suicide while sailing back to America. But an inference-driven historian could construct a very different story. Deane's former secretary Bancroft made all the arrangements for Deane to sail home. Bancroft had been a double agent who spied for Britain during the war, and he was an expert on poisons. Perhaps Bancroft gave Deane a slow-acting poison that would kill him while he was at sea, thereby preventing Deane from spilling the beans on Bancroft once Deane returned home. Whether Bancroft was a murderer may never be known for sure. Historians (like litigators) have to deal with probabilities. The point is that you do not *find* stories, you *construct* them. And the stories you construct depend on the conclusions you want judges and jurors to accept.

The subsections below flesh out the advice to "develop argument-centered narratives." They describe common (and sometimes legally required) attributes of persuasive courtroom stories. Chapters 3-5 provide strategies for developing stories that have these attributes.

1. SUBSTANTIVELY CRITICAL EVENTS

If you have the burden of proving a legal claim, your story must encompass *substantively critical* events. Substantively critical events are necessary to have happened if you are to satisfy a legal element. For example:

- The plaintiff's story in a breach of contract case has to include the substantively critical event (or events) of the contract's formation as well as the substantively critical event (or events) of the defendant's alleged violation.

- The employee plaintiff's story in one type of "workplace sexual harassment" case has to include the substantively critical event (or events) constituting workplace sexual intimidation.

2. INFERENTIAL EVIDENCE

As the story concept implies, effective courtroom narratives do not limit evidence to what took place at substantively critical moments in time. Rather, they incorporate circumstantial evidence that gives rise to *inferential arguments*. That is, they provide judges and jurors with a factual basis for inferring that your version of substantively critical events is accurate by embedding those events in larger chronologies. The larger chronologies typically encompass events that take place both *before* and *after* the substantively critical ones.

For example, assume that a substantively critical event in a "whistleblower" case is that "On September 22, Local Water Agency illegally fired the plaintiff in retaliation for plaintiff's revealing that the agency had improperly carried out environmental testing of its water sources." Evidence of *before* events that might add credence to the claim of retaliatory firing is that the plaintiff's supervisors had for years given the plaintiff excellent job performance evaluations. Evidence of an *after* event might consist of evidence that the Agency pressured other employees into signing affidavits stating falsely that the plaintiff's work had been sub-standard. Each of these events would add strength to an inference that the plaintiff's firing was retaliatory.

3. CREDIBILITY EVIDENCE

A persuasive story often includes circumstantial evidence that supports its accuracy and undermines the accuracy of an adversary's story. In this way, courtroom stories tend to be unlike the stories that people commonly relate to each other during social interactions. Most of us generally assume that acquaintances will accept what we tell them, and in any event no one may be around who's in a position to contest our accounts. As a result, we often do not take special pains to include information supporting a story's accuracy.

The situation at trial is of course poles apart. Judges and jurors are total strangers and your adversaries are usually intent on attacking your versions of events and establishing their own stories. Thus, especially to the extent that events are contested, effective stories typically include credibility evidence supporting their accuracy and undermining the accuracy of adversaries' stories. For example, you might include in your story of how an auto accident occurred the information that your key witness is unaffiliated with either party and had an excellent opportunity to observe what happened. Similarly, you might attack the credibility of an adverse witness' story by showing that the witness is unable to recall important details.

The general federal relevance statute, Federal Rule of Evidence 401, does not explicitly refer to credibility evidence. However, evidence bearing on credibility is relevant under the general definition because it makes a fact of consequence more or less probable. Moreover, credibility evidence is explicitly admissible under many comparable state statutes, such as California Evidence Code section 210 ("Relevant evidence means evidence, including evidence relevant to credibility. . ."), which the Advisory Committee's Note to Federal Rule 401 explicitly cites with approval.

4. EXPLANATORY EVIDENCE

People in Western cultures tend to believe in cause-and-effect; that is, that *things happen for a reason.* For example, reports of daily stock market gyrations virtually always include explanations for stocks' rise or fall: "Stocks rose sharply today on a report in a scientific journal that night and day are more closely related than had been previously thought." Explanatory evidence, a sub-set of credibility evidence, thus tends to assist persuasiveness by satisfying a judge or jury that reasonable explanations exist for why events took place as you claim.

For example, if an important dispute concerns exactly what was said during a business meeting, you can bolster your witness' account of what was said by including in the narrative the information that the witness paid especially careful attention to the conversation because the witness' job duties required the witness to carry out any agreements that were reached. Similarly, you can support the credibility of a medical malpractice expert's testimony by asking the expert to comment on any circumstances that led the defendant doctor to provide substandard care.

5. CONTEXTUAL DETAILS

Verbal accounts of past events (even when you support them with documents, "real" evidence and other visual aids) do not have the same reality as events themselves. (The artist Rene Magritte underscored the distinction with his famous painting of a pipe accompanied by the words, "This is not a pipe.") Thus, you can promote a belief that a story is accurate by incorporating contextual details whose primary purpose is to show that the important events your witnesses are describing really did take place.

Contextual details are typically admissible under the general relevance rule of Federal Rule of Evidence 401. The Advisory Committee's Note to the rule states in part that "Evidence which is essentially background in nature can scarcely be said to involve disputed matter, yet it is universally offered and admitted as an aid to understanding." Events typically include words as well as actions, and the hearsay rule (Federal Rule of Evidence 801) does not exclude statements offered to provide context and meaning.

For example, assume that the substantively critical event that you want to show took place at a business meeting was your adversary's agreeing to purchase 300 computers. If you were to call a witness simply to testify to that agreement, a judge or jury may not accept your account simply because your story does not portray the meeting realistically. Details such as where and when the meeting took place, who was present, and what small talk took place may lack substantive importance, but they help to establish the sense of reality that strengthens your desired inferences.

A primary reason for the importance of contextual details is that they encourage to judges and jurors to develop visual images of your clients' versions of events. Most of us are primarily "visual learners," meaning that we understand and remember best what we see. In fact, researchers estimate that most people have accumulated 85% of their learning by seeing information (as opposed to hearing or smelling it, for example). Perhaps you realized the centrality of visual learning earlier in this chapter, when you might have formed an image of a truck crashing through a plate glass window. Of course, you may not be content to rely on judges and jurors converting oral information to visual images on their own. Instead, like teachers and other information-providers, you should look for opportunities to strengthen stories with visual aids. For information on evidence rules governing the use of visual aids and strategies for using them effectively, see Chapters 9 and 10.

Visual Blocks. An exercise based on a children's blocks game can demonstrate the superiority of visual to oral learning. The exercise begins with two players each receiving identical sets of blocks of varied shapes and colors. In the first phase of the game, Player #1 sits behind a small barricade and begins to form the blocks into a structure. Player #2 (who cannot see the structure) tries to copy it based on Player #1's verbal description of what s/he is building. After a few minutes this phase of the exercise concludes and Phase two begins. This time, no barricade separates the players. Instead, as Player #1 begins to form blocks into a new structure, Player #2 copies the structure by looking at it. After a few minutes, the game concludes. The game demonstrates the superiority of visual learning. During the second, visual phase, the copier (who in essence is a judge or juror) keeps pace with the builder and the structures are almost always identical. The pace is much slower during the first, verbal phase, as the builder has to provide numerous details concerning the shape, color and position of each and every block. Even so, errors are almost always evident in the copier's structure when teaching is oral. (The game can be made to more closely resemble a trial if in the first phase, Player # 1 provides information only in response to questions that Player # 2 asks. The pace is likely to be even slower and errors are more likely to occur.)

As your own experience as a consumer of others' stories probably suggests, details are not an unalloyed blessing. Cascades of marginally relevant details are likely to produce tedium and lead judges and jurors to resent your wasting their time. Moreover, a factfinder may well not believe a witness who claims to recall a plethora of minor details, unless you can offer explanatory evidence demonstrating the witness' uncanny knack for recalling them. Thus, as with most story elements, recognizing the point at which details stop fostering persuasiveness and instead induce tedium and disbelief is a matter for your sound judgment.

6. EMOTIONAL EVIDENCE

While all evidence must be logically relevant to be admissible, you might include information in a story primarily because of its emotional impact. Judges and jurors usually want to make decisions that are both legally and morally correct, and emotional evidence tends to further the moral value of stories.

For example, assume that you represent the plaintiff in a traffic accident case. Your story might include the information that at the time of the accident, the plaintiff was on his way to a PTA meeting. This information seemingly has nothing to do with the issue of how the accident happened. Yet it is a contextual detail of the sort that is likely to be admissible, and it tends to portray the plaintiff as a morally good, socially involved citizen. Similarly, you can promote a sense that a verdict in the plaintiff's favor is just by offering evidence of the steps the plaintiff took to get the defendant out of danger.

Again, and as with other story elements, you must exercise judgment with respect to emotional evidence. An overabundance of marginally relevant emotional evidence may spur a judge or jury to infer that your case is devoid of legal merit. Equally damaging in a jury trial is a judge's repeated sustaining of an adversary's objections that evidence you've offered primarily for its emotive value is irrelevant, or that its relevance is outweighed by the danger of unfair prejudice under Federal Rule of Evidence 403.

7. VISUAL AIDS

In the largely oral world of trials, you can often add to stories' persuasive impact by introducing tangible objects ("exhibits") into evidence. Some exhibits constitute "real" evidence. Real evidence is intrinsic to the events giving rise to litigation. For example, the gun used in an armed robbery and the contract at the center of a breach of contract case are items of real evidence. Real evidence typically adds to stories' "shelf life," as judges usually allow jurors to examine real evidence while they deliberate.

Many exhibits constitute "representative" rather than real evidence. Representative exhibits generally illustrate testimony and are created specifically for use at trial. A representative exhibit can be simple and straightforward, such as a hand-drawn diagram of an intersection where a traffic accident occurred, a post-accident photograph of a car or a blowup of a key provision of a written contract. Depending on the issues, the amount in dispute and clients' pocketbooks, sophisticated computer re-enactments of events may also be admissible and helpful.

To offer exhibits into evidence, you will usually have to offer foundational evidence through the testimony of "sponsoring witnesses." For information on how to elicit foundational testimony for many common types of tangible exhibits, see Chapter 10.

8. DEFENSE STORIES

Defendants (and plaintiffs contesting affirmative defenses) may not have the burden of proof, but may nevertheless seek to establish their own versions of events at trial. The circumstances of a case may be such that a judge or jury can reasonably expect a defendant who claims that the plaintiff's account of events is inaccurate to be able to show "what really happened." By offering an alternative version of reality, defendants may provide a judge or juror with a rational basis for disbelieving the plaintiff's version without taking on the burden of proving the alternative version.

Thus, no different from lawyers who represent plaintiffs (and defendants seeking to establish affirmative defenses), lawyers who represent defendants also often support their claims with argument-centered narratives. The factors above serve equally as guides to the contents of both plaintiffs' and defendants' stories.

For example, assume that you represent an employer that has been sued by a former employee for wrongful discharge. In all likelihood, you will attempt not only to undermine the former employee's account of events, but also you will seek to prove that the employer had ample good and legally just cause for the dismissal.

Case Example: The *Hillmon* case. In the famous *Hillmon* case decided in 1892 by the US Supreme Court, an alleged widow sued the life insurance companies that had refused her claims to the proceeds of policies on the life of her allegedly deceased husband, John Hillmon. The companies offered evidence that a corpse found by a campsite was not that of Hillmon, and also offered evidence that the corpse was the body of Frederick Walters.

In one respect, defense attorneys typically have a narrower focus than plaintiffs even when defendants seek to establish inferences of their own. The effect of the burden of proof is that to avoid a non-suit or a dismissal, plaintiffs have to include substantively critical events for every element of a legal claim. Defendants by contrast, can limit stories to the elements they contest. For example, criminal cases in which the defendant relies on an alibi defense are likely to result in a defense story limited to the element of "identity of the perpetrator." Negligence lawsuits in which the defendant admits careless behavior but denies that the behavior caused harm to the plaintiff also will likewise result in a limited defense narrative.

D. CONCLUSION

This chapter has stressed the importance of chronology to persuasion, and has described attributes tending to promote the accuracy and inferential strength of stories. The next 3 chapters explore methods for developing stories that display these attributes.

CHAPTER 3

INFERENTIAL ARGUMENTS

This chapter explains and illustrates strategies for developing inferential arguments. Inferential arguments begin with circumstantial evidence that supports your clients' substantive legal claims or undermines adversaries' claims. They are one of your primary tools for developing argument-centered narratives that help to persuade judges and jurors that your clients' legal contentions are accurate.

A. DEFINITION OF INFERENTIAL ARGUMENTS

Inferential arguments typically link items of circumstantial evidence to discrete elements of legal rules. The items of evidence may either support one of your legal contentions or undermine an adversary's contentions. For example, in the international spectacle that was the O.J. Simpson double murder trial of the mid-1990's, one of the prosecution's inferential arguments was that traces of blood on a glove that the police found at the murder scene (circumstantial evidence) linked Simpson to the gruesome murders (legal element: identity of the killer). A defense inferential argument relied on evidence that one of the officers who arrived at the scene was a racist (circumstantial evidence) as the basis of a contention that Simpson's blood was planted on the glove (legal element: lack of identity).

B. FACTUAL PROPOSITIONS

The legal elements that are the targets of inferential arguments almost always consist of abstract concepts. For example, consider such elements as "breach of the duty of care," "material breach of contract," and "malice aforethought." Each term is an abstract label that does not identify the events of any case-specific story. Thus, an effective way to develop persuasive inferential arguments is to begin by converting abstract elements to case-specific factual propositions.

Converting abstract elements to factual propositions helps you to develop persuasive inferential arguments because each proposition identifies the concrete circumstances that arguably satisfy or undermine an element of a legal rule. Moreover, marshalling evidence according to factual propositions rather than abstract rules increases the likelihood that your arguments incorporate all of the evidence that relates to a legal rule.

Factual propositions are simply case-specific counterparts of abstract legal elements. Consider these examples:

- In a breach of contract action, a factual proposition satisfying the element "not of merchantable quality" would be, "The bicycles' derailleurs failed to meet industry standards."

- In a tort action, a factual proposition satisfying the legal element "breach of duty of care" would be, "The building contractor used termite-infested roofing materials."

- In a murder prosecution, a factual proposition satisfying the legal element of "malice aforethought" would be, "Johnson intended to kill the victim."

Each of the factual propositions above reflects a plaintiff's or a prosecutor's perspective. But when defense attorneys rely on inferential arguments, they too may develop factual propositions that reflect their clients' legal contentions. Consider possible defense counterparts of the propositions above:

- For the element of merchantable quality: "The derailleurs met all industry standards."

- For the element breach of duty of care: "The building contractor used standard roofing materials."

- For the element of malice aforethought: "Johnson lacked an intent to kill."

The short example below illustrates how you can use the events in a story to convert elements to factual propositions. Assume that you represent plaintiff Simone Brett, whose story is as follows:

Simone wanted to buy a collection of baseball cards as a graduation present for her daughter Andrea. On

August 26, Simone attended the annual Mammoth Baseball Card and Chili Cookoff Show at the downtown Sheraday Hilton Hotel. One of the merchants at the show was Lefty O'Righty, a retired baseball player. Simone told Lefty that she wanted a valuable set of cards to give as a graduation present to her daughter, a lifelong baseball fan. Lefty told Simone that he had unusual collections of rare first edition baseball cards, including a set of "Left–Handed All–Star Shortstops" and a set of "Catchers Who Became Nuclear Physicists." Lefty assured Simone that all the cards were original and authentic, and Simone paid $12,000.00 for both sets of cards. Simone later took the sets to be appraised, and learned that the cards were all reproductions, worth at most a few hundred dollars. Simone contacted Lefty to get her money back, but Lefty denied any wrongdoing and refused to refund the purchase price.

At trial, you seek to prove that Lefty defrauded Simone. The standard elements of a fraud claim include (1) making a representation; (2) falsity of the representation; (3) scienter; (4) reasonable reliance; and (5) damages. You may convert each of these abstract legal elements to factual propositions as follows:

Element 1: Making of a Representation. *Factual Proposition:* On August 26, Lefty O'Righty told Simone that all of the baseball cards that Lefty sold to her were original and authentic.

Element 2: Falsity of Representation. *Factual Proposition:* The baseball cards that Lefty sold to Simone were reproductions.

Element 3:. Scienter. *Factual Proposition:* Lefty knew when he told Simone that the cards were original and authentic that they were reproductions.

Element 4: Reasonable reliance. *Factual Proposition*: Simone reasonably believed what Lefty told her because Simone had never previously bought sets of baseball cards, and Lefty was a retired baseball player who made the statements at a baseball card show.

Element 5: Damages. Factual Proposition: Simone paid $12,000 for baseball cards worth at most a few hundred dollars.

You can sometimes satisfy a legal element in two or more ways. In those situations, you may develop a separate factual proposition for each one. For example, assume that Simone's story indicates that Lefty O'Righty made at least one other false representation to Simone that itself supports relief. In this situation you might develop a factual proposition for each false representation:

Element 1: Making of a Representation. *Factual Proposition 1:* On August 26, Lefty O'Righty told Simone that all of the baseball cards that Lefty sold to her were original and authentic. *Factual*

Proposition 2: On August 26, Lefty O'Righty told Simone that no other dealer carried the baseball cards that Lefty was selling.

As a plaintiff or prosecutor, you of course have to establish each element of a claim to the required level of certainty. In most cases however, you may be content to develop factual propositions only for disputed legal elements. For example, if the only dispute in a breach of contract action concerns the materiality of a conceded breach, you may prepare a factual proposition and develop inferential arguments only for the element of "materiality."

C. MARSHAL EVIDENCE AROUND FACTUAL PROPOSITIONS

With factual propositions in hand, begin to develop inferential arguments by identifying what you consider an item of circumstantial evidence that most strongly supports each proposition. For example, in the baseball card scenario above, assume that the dispute centers on Simone's claim that Lefty O'Righty knew that the cards were reproductions. To develop an inferential argument supporting Simone's contention, identify what you think is the strongest item of circumstantial evidence leading to an inference that Lefty knew that his assertion was false.

Linking an item of evidence to a factual proposition creates an *embryonic* inferential argument. To strengthen an embryonic argument, identify additional items of evidence that support the same inference. To identify such evidence, think to yourself, *"My embryonic argument is especially likely to be accurate when..."* The additional items of evidence, which you may think of as "especially whens," strengthen the argument for your desired inference.

For example, assume that in a personal injury case the disputed factual proposition that you want a jury to accept is that the defendant breached the duty of car by speeding. You developed an embryonic argument based on the evidence that the defendant was 20 minutes late for a meeting at the time of the accident. To strengthen this argument, think to yourself, "A person who is 20 minutes late for a meeting is likely to be speeding, especially when...", and identify additional evidence supporting the inference that the defendant was speeding.   For example, the stronger argument you might develop might go as follows: *"The evidence that at the time of the accident the defendant was 20 minutes late for a meeting, that the meeting was an important one, that the defendant had no chance to tell the other attendees that he was running late, and that the defendant was to lead the meeting combine to prove that the defendant was speeding at the time of the accident."*   Marshalling the evidence around the factual proposition creates a portion of your argument-centered trial narrative.

Case Example: "Especially Whens." If you have completed a course in Evidence, you may be familiar with the famous case of *Mutual Life Insurance Co. of New York v. Hillmon,* 145 U.S. 285

(1892). In that case, Sallie Hillmon sued the three life insurance companies who had insured her husband John's life for a total of $25,000. Sallie alleged that she was entitled to the money because John had been accidentally shot and killed at a campsite near Crooked Creek, Kansas. The insurance companies had refused to pay, claiming that they were the victims of fraud. The insurance companies claimed that the body found at the campsite was that of Frederick Walters, who had been duped by Hillmon and a companion named John Brown into accompanying them into a remote part of Kansas so they could kill him, pass him off as Hillmon and collect the life insurance proceeds.

The case went to trial six different times. The first two trials resulted in hung juries, and the third resulted in a verdict for Sallie. The U.S. Supreme Court overturned that verdict in the case reported at 145 U.S. 285 (1892). History then repeated itself: the fourth and fifth trials also resulted in hung juries, and the sixth resulted in a verdict for Sallie. The U.S. Supreme reversed that verdict as well. *Connecticut Mutual Life Insurance Co. v. Hillmon*, 188 U.S. 208 (1902). Over the course of the trials and appeals, Sallie eventually settled with each of the insurance companies.

Consider this excerpt from the argument of insurance defense attorney Charles S. Gleed in Trial #2:

"What was Hillmon's motive in going, in the dead of what he himself has described [in his diary, found on the corpse] as an unusually cold winter, into the empty spaces of western Kansas? He says he went to look for a stock ranch. Have you any such belief? Would you do the same thing? Would you drive day after day over the bleak prairies of western Kansas next January looking for a stock ranch, having no money to buy with if you found one? If you were looking for a stock ranch, would you travel miles and miles along the Santa Fe road? I ask you can you ascribe any motive for this unusual proceeding other than the motive of fraud?"

Here, Gleed's embryonic argument is that Hillmon would not have gone looking to buy a ranch in the dead of winter. He strengthens the argument with two "especially whens:" (1) his path followed the Santa Fe trail, a bleak, uninhabited area, and (2) he had no money to buy a ranch. (You can read more of Gleed's argument, as well as excerpts from the arguments of other counsel, in J.H. Wigmore, *The Principles of Judicial Proof*, pp. 856–896 (1913; Legal Classics Library edition, 1991)).

D. UNDERMINE ADVERSARIES' INFERENTIAL ARGUMENTS

Trial narratives typically focus on disputed factual propositions. Thus, your inferential arguments should also marshal items of evidence tending to undermine an adversary's desired inferences. To do so, identify a factual proposition that your adversary relies on, and think to yourself: *"The adversary's factual proposition may be accurate, except when..."* The "except whens" that you identify undermine the adversary's argument.

For example, assume that you are a prosecutor in a murder case. In support of its factual proposition that the defendant was not the killer, the defense relies on an argument that "The evidence that the bloody glove that the police found at the crime scene was too small for the defendant's hand shows that the defendant was not the murderer." Any "except when" items of circumstantial evidence that you can identify undermine the defendant's desired inference. For example, the evidence that the bloody glove that the police found at the crime scene was too small for the defendant's hand could show that the defendant was not the murderer, *except when a year has elapsed between the time of the murder and the time the defendant tried on the glove and the glove shows signs of shrinkage; blood from both the defendant and the victim is on the glove; and a search of the defendant's residence turned up numerous gloves of varying sizes.*

E. NORMATIVE INFERENTIAL ARGUMENTS

Many factual propositions are *historical*. That is, they make assertions about what took place in the past, and a judge or juror has only to decide whether as a matter of historical fact the proposition is accurate. For example, to decide the accuracy of factual propositions such as "The building contractor used substandard roofing materials" and "Johnson fired the murder weapon," a judge or juror need only decide whether the asserted fact is accurate.

However, many elements of substantive rules call on judges and jurors to make *normative* as well as historical judgments. Normative judgments rest on values and beliefs about acceptable behavior. When they evaluate stories in the light of normative elements, judges and jurors act as the "conscience of the community" and their decisions represent applications of community norms.

Far from constituting "exceptions," normative elements are pervasive. For instance, the central dispute in a breach of contract action may be whether a breach was "material." A civil negligence trial may focus on whether the defendant acted "unreasonably." A wrongful termination trial may center on the whether an employer had "just cause for termination." In such cases, judges and jurors not only have to decide what took place, but also they have to interpret and evaluate what they believe took place according to community values and beliefs.

For example, assume that a prosecutor in a police battery case argues that a police officer used "excessive force" when making an arrest. A juror could not evaluate the argument simply by determining what the police officer did to effectuate the arrest. The juror would also have to evaluate the police officer's behavior according to community expectations about how much force police officers *ought* to be able to use in a situation such as the one that gave rise to the charge. The juror in effect acts as a stand-in for the community when making this decision.

Similarly, assume that an employer contends that it had "just cause" to terminate an employee. As a matter of historical fact, a judge may conclude that the fired employee came to work late on two occasions in a three week time span and misplaced a purchase order. Nevertheless, the judge would still have to decide whether such defalcations constitute "just cause" for termination, and the decision represents the community's value judgment about appropriate behavior by employers and employees.

To develop factual propositions relating to normative elements, refer to *the reasons that a normative standard has or has not been satisfied.* For example, you may formulate normative factual propositions by completing assertions such as the following:

- The breach of the contract was material, in that. . ..

- The police officer's force was excessive, because. . .

- The employee's behavior created just cause for the firing because. . ..

After identifying pertinent items of circumstantial evidence, you may develop normative factual propositions such as, "The employee's misplacement of the purchase order created just cause for termination because it caused the employer to lose its second largest customer." This proposition rests on the value that it's fair to terminate employees whose errors have large negative consequences.

Naturally, the content of normative factual propositions depends on the factual disputes in specific cases. However, considering the following questions may help you identify reasons for asserting that normative elements have or have not been satisfied:

1. *Why was a party's conduct fair and reasonable (or unfair and unreasonable)?* For example, what was unreasonable about the behavior of the police officer charged with using excessive force when making an arrest?

2. *What positive or negative consequences (or potential consequences) flowed from a party's conduct?* For example, what happened as the result of the defendant breaching the contract? What injuries if any did the arrestee suffer as a result of being struck by the officer charged with using excessive force?

3. *Were any less restrictive alternatives available?* For example, did the employer have a reasonable alternative to firing the employee who misplaced the purchase order? Did the officer charged with using excessive force when making an arrest have an alternative to hitting the arrestee with a baton?

4. *Did conduct conform to the customs and practices of a particular trade, industry or profession?* For example, if police officers are taught to immediately handcuff arrestees, did the police officer charged with using excessive force follow this practice? If the employer has a practice of "progressive discipline" of employees, did the employer follow the practice in this case?

These questions will often help you to identify reasons that you can include in normative factual propositions. You'll include the evidence that supports these propositions in argument-centered narratives at trial.

CHAPTER 4
CREDIBILITY ARGUMENTS

Along with inferential arguments (see Chapter 3), *credibility arguments* are a second important component of argument-centered narratives. As the label suggests, the process of developing credibility arguments allows you to identify and emphasize at trial the evidence advancing the credibility of your stories and undermining the credibility of adversaries' stories.

A. IMPORTANCE OF CREDIBILITY ARGUMENTS

Credibility arguments are often vital to success at trial because a major reason that cases go to trial in the first place is that the adversaries have competing versions of how dispute-related events took place. As a result, judges' and jurors' verdicts often grow out of their beliefs about what really happened. Judges and juries do not necessarily choose between conflicting stories. They may formulate their own accounts that match neither party's version. Whatever story a judge or juror ultimately chooses to accept, however, the frequency with which parties offer conflicting versions of past events means that a primary trial task is to advance credibility arguments to bolster belief in the accuracy of your narratives and undermine belief in adversaries' narratives.

B. FOCUS ON IMPORTANT DISPUTES

Effective credibility arguments generally focus on important factual disputes. To present a persuasive story without trying a judge's or juror's patience, develop credibility arguments only for factual disputes that you think a judge or jury will consider important.

Of course you'll have to exercise judgment and common sense in the context of the factual propositions in each specific case to decide whether to develop a credibility argument for a factual dispute. Remember that at the end of the day decisions turn not on your attitude about what's important, but on what a judge or jury is likely to consider important.

To understand how each case's unique factual propositions can influence your thinking about whether a factual dispute is important, assume that a criminal defendant is charged with bank robbery. The bank manager claims that the defendant had been in the bank for about 30 minutes without transacting any business only two days before the robbery. The bank manager's evidence leads to a possible inference that the defendant was "casing" the bank in preparation for the robbery. The defendant disputes the bank manager's account, in part. The defendant admits having been in the bank two days before the robbery, but claims to have been in the bank only for a few minutes, just long enough to use the restroom and then leave.

Is a judge or jury likely to focus on this factual discrepancy? Perhaps the conflict is important if the defense is an alibi, because the defendant's longer stay in the bank bolsters a "casing" conclusion. On the other hand, the dispute may not be seen as important if the defendant admits holding up the bank but relies on a "duress" defense. A judge or jury may not believe that resolving the conflict promotes a decision as to whether the defendant acted under duress.

C. A CREDIBILITY MODEL

The *Credibility Model* set out and explained below facilitates your development of credibility arguments by identifying common factors affecting credibility. Evidence that you identify with the help of the model becomes the evidence you emphasize in argument-centered trial narratives.

Like the elements of substantive rules, the factors in the Credibility Model are abstract. But while elements of substantive rules are created by legislators and judges, the factors in the Credibility Model are grounded in human nature and everyday experience (at least in the Western culture). These factors are such a routine way of evaluating the credibility of information across factual contexts that the Federal Rules of Evidence lack provisions establishing their relevance. Instead, the relevance of credibility evidence is governed by the general relevance statute, Rule 401. That is why many years ago, famed Evidence scholar Dean Wigmore pointed out that the same credibility issues arise in any type of case (civil or criminal), and no matter what its subject matter (e.g., antitrust or medical malpractice).

Factors Affecting Credibility

1. *Credibility of Story*

   Consistency with Common Experience

   Internal Consistency

   Consistency with Established Facts

2. *Credibility of Witnesses ("Source Credibility")*

   Expertise

   Motive or Bias

   Reason to Recall

   Demeanor

   Character for Honesty

Before examining how to use these factors to develop credibility arguments, consider three important caveats. First, the factors in the model work both ways. That is, you consider the same factors whether you try to bolster the credibility of helpful evidence or undermine the credibility of harmful evidence.

Second, the credibility factors generally apply independently of each other. For example, that a story is consistent or inconsistent with everyday experience is likely to be unrelated to the demeanor of the witness who testifies to the story. Thus, you should typically consider each factor separately when trying to identify credibility evidence.

Third, I thought of recommending the mnemonic "CICEMRDC" to help you remember the credibility factors, but decided not to after spraining my tongue in three places trying to pronounce it.

D. "STORY" CREDIBILITY FACTORS

This section considers credibility factors that relate to the content of stories.

1. CONSISTENCY WITH EVERYDAY EXPERIENCE

Rich testifies that he knows his son-in-law J.M. by his initials only; Rich does not know what J. M. stands for. Jenni testifies that while stopped at an intersection waiting for the light to change, she noticed and can recall the license plate number of a car that made a left turn and proceeded through the intersection without incident. Eileen testifies to what took place during an important meeting, but cannot remember where or when the meeting took place.

Without knowing anything about these individuals, or the stories to which these pieces of information pertain, you are likely to conclude that all of the stories lack credibility. Based on years of behaving and interacting with others, you've developed beliefs and understandings about "how the world works" (the world in which you've lived, at least). Common sense is a familiar label for the body of knowledge you acquire through everyday living that allows you to make judgments about people, objects, animals and the like. Your common sense is likely to tell you that people generally know what close relatives' initials stand for, and know where important meetings that they participated in took place. Moreover, common sense tells you that most drivers do not pay rapt attention to every car that passes their line of sight while they wait for a light to change color.

Judges and jurors also rely on common sense and experience when evaluating testimony. Like you, they tend to believe stories that comport with everyday experience and disbelieve stories that conflict with their beliefs about how events typically unfold. The use of experience as a factor in evaluating credibility underscores the importance of the constitutional guarantee of a "jury of one's peers." Parties should be able to address arguments to judges and jurors whose experiences provide them with an adequate experiential foundation to evaluate the arguments.

When developing credibility arguments to *bolster* the believability of helpful evidence, you can take advantage of the influence of common experience in two ways. First, identify admissible evidence leading to an inference that your client's version of events is consistent with everyday experience. For example, you might bolster an eyewitness' account of how an auto accident unfolded with evidence that depicts the ordinary series of events that led to the eyewitness' being in that spot and noticing what took place.

Second, if you recognize that an important portion of your story conflicts with common experience, try to identify *explanatory evidence,* evidence that explains why events unfolded in a seemingly unusual way. For example, assume that your witness is the eyewitness to the auto accident. The accident occurred at 10:30 a.m., and the witness' story is that "I happened to see what happened because I was on my lunch break and I was walking to a café a few blocks away from where I work." Without explanatory evidence, a judge or juror may be suspicious of the story's accuracy because most office workers do not go to lunch at 10:30 a.m. Aware of the potential problem, try to identify evidence that explains away the potential implausibility. The argument-centered narrative that you produce may go in part as follows:

Q: How did you happen to see the events leading up to the collision?

A: I was on my lunch break, and was on that street on my way to a café a few blocks away.

Q: Do you normally go to lunch at 10:30 a.m?

A: No.

Q: Then can you please explain to the jury why you were going to lunch at 10:30 a.m. on that particular day?

A: Sure. That day, the unit that I'm part of had to finish a big report in time for a meeting that was held at 10 a.m. I usually start work at 8:30 a.m., but that morning I was in the office by 6 a.m. to make sure that I finished my part of the report on time. I finished it just in time for the meeting, so after I took care of a few phone calls I went to lunch at 10:30 because I planned to go home by 3:00.

This testimony bolsters the story's credibility by explaining away a potentially implausible aspect of the witness' story.

Similarly, you can *attack* an adversary's version of events by identifying admissible evidence suggesting that it conflicts with everyday experience. The courtroom comedy film *My Cousin Vinny* provides an excellent illustration of how to demonstrate that a story is inconsistent with everyday experience. Vinny is a defense lawyer whose clients have been wrongly charged with robbing and killing a convenience store clerk. A prosecution witness identifies the defendants as the pair he saw enter the convenience store and leave five minutes later, during which time he heard gunshots. Vinny's cross examination reveals that the witness saw the defendants enter the store just as he began to cook his breakfast, and leave the store just as he was about to eat. Vinny's questions also produce the information that the witness had grits for breakfast. Vinny uses this information to destroy the witness' time estimate of five minutes. All the events take place in a small Alabama town, and the jurors know from their own experience that grits need to be cooked for 20 minutes before they are ready to eat. Therefore the interval during which the witness saw two people enter and two people leave the store must have been at least 20 minutes, meaning that there was ample time for Vinny's clients to leave the store before the robbery/murder took place.

"Objection," you might say in response to the point that judges and jurors evaluate stories according to their experiences. "Judges and jurors may never have personally experienced the situations they hear described in courtroom stories. How can I ask them to use their experience to evaluate events that are often unusual and unique?"

"Objection overruled!" Analogy is as powerful a reasoning tool in courtroom decision-making as it is in traditional appellate case legal analysis. Judges and jurors routinely evaluate the believability of testimony about unusual events by analogizing them to familiar ones. For example, perhaps a juror has never known a close relative by initials only. But the juror has probably known relatives and friends by nicknames, or has talked to people who have known others by nicknames. The juror is likely to evaluate the believability of the testimony, "I don't know what my son-in-law's initials stand for" with reference to their and others' analogous experiences with nicknames.

Judges and especially jurors may use everyday experience even when evaluating expert testimony on unfamiliar subjects. For example, an expert may testify that a physically abused child's failure to complain or run away was an example of "Child Abuse Accommodation Syndrome." However, when evaluating the believability of this testimony, a juror may reason, "It doesn't make sense. I've known of a couple of children who were overly disciplined, and they sure let others know about it right away." Or, the juror may disbelieve the expert because of the expert's poor demeanor while testifying. In either case, the juror resorts to everyday experience to evaluate the content of the expert's testimony.

As with all the factors in the Credibility Model, when assessing the plausibility of a story you must be careful not to become a prisoner of your own experiences. Experiences are not uniform, certainly across sub-cultures and even within any single sub-culture. Therefore, a judge's or juror's reaction to disputed evidence may not comport with yours. One way to overcome "experience blinders" is to ask for a friend's or a colleague's opinion about the plausibility of a story. You should also try to learn something about the backgrounds of likely judges and jurors, and to the extent possible select judges and jurors whose experiences are compatible with your arguments.

For all of its ubiquitousness, the use of everyday experience can lead to injustice. Though a judge's or juror's beliefs about "how things usually happen" may be accurate, in any specific situation the un-common may be true. Car alarms occasionally function properly; you may every so often stand in the supermarket line that moves the fastest. The judge or juror whose everyday experience leads to unquestioning disbelief of the uncommon may arrive at a verdict that fails to reflect what actually happened.

2. INTERNAL CONSISTENCY

When judges and jurors evaluate credibility according to everyday experience, they rely on beliefs about the functioning of the "external world." The "internal world" of stories themselves is a second common approach for evaluating credibility. Most people believe that credible stories are internally consistent and remain so from one telling to the next. Judges and jurors are likely to conclude that a witness who speaks with a forked tongue is mistaken, a liar, or a reptile. Thus, you can bolster your version of a disputed story with evidence emphasizing its internal consistency and, insofar as Federal Rule of Evidence 801(d)(1)(B) allows, its constancy from one telling to the next. And you can attack an adverse witness' story by emphasizing internal inconsistencies and changes from one telling to the next.

A primary purpose of pre-trial discovery, especially depositions, is to lock adverse witnesses into their stories. If adverse witnesses change their stories at trial, under Federal Rule of Evidence 801(d)(1)(A) you can offer into evidence inconsistent statements made under oath to attack their credibility. (Under the federal rule, prior inconsistent statements made under oath are also admissible for the truth of their contents.)

Descriptions of events are likely to vary somewhat from one telling to another. Indeed, witnesses who use exactly the same words every time they tell a story are likely to be distrusted for that reason. Thus, when considering whether a judge or juror will regard a story as internally inconsistent, you have to decide whether an alteration in the telling is significant or commonplace.

Case Example: Too much internal consistency. The prosecution growing out of the infamous 1911 labor event known as the Triangle Shirtwaist Fire resulted in a classic example of how to destroy the credibility of an adverse witness who repeated a story in the same words. In a criminal trial of the company's owners, prosecution witness Kate Altermann, a garment worker, testified that when a fire broke out in a garment factory, employees burned to death because the owners illegally kept the building's exit doors locked. Eschewing the usual advice not to let witnesses repeat on cross the stories they have told on direct, defense counsel Max Steuer asked Altermann to "tell us again what happened after the fire broke out." Altermann told her story again using the same words, some of which seemed planted by the prosecution because they were not words that (in common experience) a person like Altermann would be likely to use on her own. When Altermann finished, Steuer asked her to repeat her story a third time. Again, Altermann used the same words. The jury apparently concluded that Altermann had memorized a story created by the prosecution, because the owners were acquitted. You can read about the case in detail in a biography of Steuer written by his son Aron, called *Max D. Steuer, Trial Lawyer.*

While not all variations in the telling of stories give rise to effective credibility arguments, recognize that statements need not be directly contradictory to serve as the basis of internal inconsistency arguments. If the only way you are willing to attack testimony, "The light was red," is with testimony that "The light was green," you will make internal inconsistency arguments about as often as a New York cabbie drives five blocks without honking. Statements may detract from credibility even if they are only somewhat contradictory. For example, assume that an adverse witness has asserted, "The first bowl of porridge was too hot." You might base an inconsistency argument on either of these statements:

- "There was one bowl of porridge on the table."

- "I was so busy I didn't have time to eat."

Of course, you should always be aware of important internal inconsistencies in your witness' stories and prepare to counter an adversary's credibility argument by seeking out possible explanations. For example, assume that at a deposition taken in a civil suit for workplace sexual harassment, your client (the complainant) testifies that she was always alone with her supervisor when the acts constituting harassment occurred. Preparing the client to testify at trial, you realize that the client's current story is that an employee named Billy Bigelow was sometimes present and witnessed the supervisor's unlawful behavior. Since the change of story provides the employer with a chance to attack your client's credibility, you should call the client's attention to the change and ask whether the client can explain the reason for it. Perhaps the client can provide a reasonable explanation (e.g., "Bigelow had threatened to retaliate against me if I mentioned his name in connection with the harassment. But Bigelow left the company a few months ago, so that's not a problem anymore.") If so, you can offer the explanation at trial if your adversary impeaches the client with the inconsistent deposition testimony.

As an officer of the court, your obligation at trial is to elicit testimony that witnesses believe accurate as of the time they testify. Thus, when helpful witnesses change their stories, elicit the truth as they believe it to be at trial along with explanations for the changes. Do not try to hide inconsistencies by advising witnesses to stick to stories they no longer believe accurate. Moreover, any explanations for changes in stories should be a product of witnesses' recollections rather than counsel's suggestions. See ABA Model Rule of Professional Responsibility 3.4: "A lawyer shall not ... counsel or assist a witness to testify falsely."

3. CONSISTENCY WITH ESTABLISHED FACTS

Most people find it easier to choose a restaurant if they first decide what kind of food they want to eat or what neighborhood they want to visit. Similarly, judges and jurors often use what they regard as "established facts" as a touchstone to help them evaluate the credibility of disputed portions of stories. Thus, you can bolster the credibility of helpful stories by including evidence that is consistent with established facts, and attack the credibility of harmful stories by showing that they conflict with established facts.

Obviously, the first step in developing this type of credibility argument is to identify facts that judges and jurors are highly likely to regard as established. Of course, facts may be established because both sides testify or stipulate to them. Judges may also establish facts as true by taking judicial notice pursuant to Federal Rule of Evidence 201. Facts may also be established by evidentiary sources that seem impeccable. For example, a neutral medical expert's testimony may provide established facts concerning the nature of a patient's injury, and a document may provide established facts as to the terms of a contract offer.

To understand how to develop stories that take advantage of the "established facts" factor, assume that you are the prosecutor in a sexual assault case. One of your witnesses is the emergency room physician who treated the complainant shortly after the assault. You are confident that the jurors will accept the physician's description of the complainant's physical injuries as established facts. As a result, you can enhance the complainant's credibility by focusing during direct examination and argument on the details of the attack that are consistent with the physician's description of the injuries. Similarly, you may attack the credibility of the defendant's story by emphasizing that the story fails to account for the injuries that the physician's examination revealed.

E. SOURCE CREDIBILITY FACTORS

This section considers credibility factors that relate to the sources of stories. Witnesses are the most typical source whose credibility may be in issue. But you may also develop source-based credibility arguments for documents, demonstrative evidence and tangible exhibits of all kinds.

1. IN GENERAL

Everyday experience teaches that our belief in information is in part influenced by what we know about its source. For example, your belief in the accuracy of statistics may be influenced by whether they are provided by a politician or a statistician. Social science research generally validates the effect of messengers' personal attributes on the credibility of messages. In one classic series of research projects, groups of listeners heard a speech on issues of the day. Some groups were told that the speaker was affiliated with unpopular groups such as the American Nazi Party. Other groups were told that the speaker was from a mainstream, popular group such as the League of Women Voters. Though all groups heard the same message, listeners' beliefs in its accuracy varied dramatically depending on the speaker's affiliation.

In trial, your ability to control your witnesses is limited. Of three potential witnesses, one a religious leader, one a famous humanitarian and the last a passerby known as Jimmy the Weasel, you know the one who is most likely to be a percipient witness who claims to have information helpful to your case. Also, evidence rules constrain your ability to offer significant evidence of a client's or a witness' good character. Perhaps only as part of selecting an expert witness can you consciously pick and choose based on personal background factors. Thus, you will often need to develop credibility arguments based on the factors set forth below.

2. SPECIFIC VS. GENERAL CREDIBILITY EVIDENCE

A "source" credibility argument may pertain to a witness' entire testimony. For example, you may argue that an adverse witness' bias undermines the believability of the witness' entire story. Or, a source credibility argument may concern only specific evidence. For instance, apart from a witness' overall credibility, you may argue that the witness was driving an open convertible and therefore could not be certain about the words that were exchanged between two passengers in the back seat.

Classifying credibility evidence as either specific or general, while loads of fun in its own right, often affects the timing of when you elicit credibility evidence. That is, you can often emphasize the probative value of "specific" credibility evidence by eliciting it in the context of the portion of the story to which it relates. Eliciting specific credibility evidence in the context of the portion of the story to which it relates can increase the likelihood that a judge will rule that it is relevant.

For example, assume that your witness Sarah will provide helpful evidence about an auto accident. As is typical, you begin Sarah's direct examination with a few background questions. After Sarah testifies to where she lives, you ask her, "How long have you lived at that address?" and expect her to answer "About 28 years." If your adversary objects that the question is an improper effort to elicit evidence of Sarah's good character (see Federal Rule of Evidence 608(a)), the judge may sustain the objection because no other purpose for the question is apparent. However, the relevance of the testimony to support the witness' ability to observe and recall what happened may be apparent if you elicit the same information while asking Sarah about the accident, which took place in the street directly in front of her house.

3. LYING OR MISTAKEN?

The "bottom line" of an inferential argument is always an inference about a substantive legal rule. By contrast, when attacking an adverse witness' credibility, you may have to make a judgment regarding a credibility argument's "bottom line." Will you argue that the witness is mistaken, or that the witness is lying? For example, assume that you offer evidence that an adverse witness was not in a good enough position to observe what the witness claims to have observed. Do you ask the jurors to conclude that the witness has made an honest mistake, or that the witness has committed perjury? Perhaps judges and jurors are more likely to accept a "mistake" than a "lie" argument, but the decision is one that you may have to make frequently.

Case Example: Liar Liar! In 1995's hugely-watched murder trial of O.J. Simpson, the defense team headed by Johnnie Cochran attacked the credibility of police officer Mark Fuhrman. Fuhrman had testified that he found gloves at the murder scene that were stained with blood that turned out to be Simpson's and the victim's. The defense claimed that Fuhrman planted the gloves at the murder scene. To bolster this claim, the defense offered evidence that Fuhrman had frequently used the term "nigger" when referring to blacks, thus suggesting that he had a bias towards Simpson (who was black). The defense also offered evidence that Fuhrman's testimony denying that he had ever used "the 'N' word" was false. The ferocity of this attack meant that the defense's credibility argument could have but one possible "bottom line:" Fuhrman lied when he testified that he found the bloody gloves at the murder scene. The jurors evidently accepted the defense argument, because Simpson was acquitted of murder.

4. EXPERTISE

The source credibility factor of "expertise" is an umbrella term that incorporates all the reasons affecting ability to know whereof one speaks. For some readers, the term "expertise" may bring up an image of people wearing white jackets with stethoscopes in their pockets. Other readers may think of doctors. However, a more accurate scope of expertise is conveyed by humorist Will Rogers' quote, "All of us are dumb, except in different areas." In other words, expertise is not a factor that applies only to witnesses who qualify as experts under Federal Rule of Evidence 702. Rather, expertise includes any information from which a judge or juror might infer that a witness' personal background adds to or detracts from the probative value of the witness' testimony. For example, the following arguments pertain to a lay witness' expertise:

- A bartender testifies that a patron was under the influence of alcohol. The witness' employment arguably provides the witness with expertise that adds to the credibility of the opinion.

- A newly-licensed teen-age driver testifies that a car that shortly afterwards was involved in a traffic accident was going about 65 m.p.h. when the driver saw it. The witness' limited experience as a driver arguably detracts from the witness' ability to judge the speed of cars and thus may reduce the credibility of the opinion.

- A witness testifies that the man seated near him in a restaurant threatened another restaurant patron. The witness' proximity to the alleged threatener, the witness' hearing acuity and the amount of background noise are factors that affect the witness' expertise and therefore the credibility of the witness' testimony.

5. MOTIVE OR BIAS

The motivations that are common factors in credibility arguments are familiar to anyone conversant with Aristotle, Shakespeare, or TV reality programs. Parties' biases are readily apparent. And we all recognize that a witness' testimony may be colored by such considerations as money, love, friendship, money, group loyalty, jealousy, prejudice and money. Perhaps on rare occasions you have even detected your own inclination (always unexercised, of course), to fudge a bit in your own self-interest. On the other hand, as a litigator you may cherish a "neutral" witness with the same rapture with which a botanist cherishes a prize rose.

Though attorneys routinely base credibility arguments on evidence of motive or neutrality, recognize that almost every witness is potentially open to a charge of bias or other improper motive. For example:

- Many witnesses are open to the charge of having a personal or professional interest in a case's outcome, since most of us spend the bulk of our time with people with whom we have a personal or professional relationship.

- Experts are open to bias charges because they are paid for their time, and future employment may hinge on an expert's willingness to give a favorable opinion.

- Even when an employee seeking compensation for a work-related injury must look to the employee's state workers' compensation fund rather than his or her employer, the employer may be susceptible to a charge of bias because future insurance premiums may rise if the employee is successful.

- Witnesses with no prior connection to either party may yet be open to a charge that they are so psychologically committed to their initial story that they obstinately stick to the story in the face of contradictory information.

With so many witnesses potentially open to charges of bias, you will often have opportunities to use this factor to develop arguments attacking an adverse witness' credibility. Of course, your adversaries will have the same opportunities. Thus, you should regularly dust your own witnesses' backgrounds for bias problems and be prepared to address them. With a garden-variety bias charge that would apply equally to all similarly-situated witnesses, you can often reply to an attack with a few dismissive words during final summation: "Of course my client's main witnesses were his mother and father. In whose company would you expect a two-year-old to be?"

Another common tactic is to confront a bias attack head-on during direct examination of your own witness. Attorneys commonly refer to this tactic as "taking the sting out of cross examination." You defuse the adversary's likely attack by referring to it first and in a way that downplays its significance. For example, here you take the sting out of an expected bias attack based on your witness' financial stake in a case's outcome:

Q: Turning your attention to the meeting at which Julie, the general partner, disclosed the liens on the Orange property, please describe what happened.

A: Well, she began by distributing an analysis prepared by her attorney. She said the limited partners would have to come up with another $200,000 if they wanted to hold onto the property. She said she was fully extended, and had no obligation to contribute further financial resources.

Q: Were you a limited partner in the Orange property deal?

A: No.

Q: How did you happen to be at that meeting?

A: Well, I was in a related limited partnership, the Lemon property. Julie was also the general on that one, and I knew that whatever happened with the Orange partnership would affect me.

Q: Are you presently in litigation with Julie on the Lemon property?

A: Yes.

Q: Is your testimony at all affected by the fact that what happens to Julie in this case may affect the outcome of the Lemon property litigation?

A: No. Of course I don't want to lose my money, but I realized going in that the investment was pretty speculative, so I didn't really invest that much. Also, this is a business dispute, and Julie and I are still friends.

Q: O.K. Let's return for a moment to that meeting. After Julie distributed her attorney's analysis. . .

Bringing out the potential financial motive yourself suggests that the evidence is of little probative value. Moreover, on direct unlike on cross, the witness can explain the situation in response to open questions. Eliciting information about the meeting before going into the potential bias may also be helpful. Social science research suggests that you may lessen the effect of motive by eliciting the relevant evidence before delving into the motivation.

6. REASON TO OBSERVE OR RECALL

As previously mentioned, most people in the Western culture believe in cause-and-effect; events happen for a reason. Applying this attitude to witness testimony, belief about the accuracy of testimony is often affected by a witness' having a reason to observe or recall an event. You can bolster credibility with evidence showing that a witness has a particular reason to observe or recall a past event, and attack credibility with evidence that no such reason exists. For example:

- In a breach of contract action, you offer evidence from a waiter that during a May 1 lunch meeting, the waiter heard Binder agree to sell golf equipment to Moore. The waiter offers a reason for recalling the conversation: "They were giving me golf tips all through lunch so I was around their table during most of the lunch hour." You might argue based on this explanation that the waiter had a reason to hear the conversation and that the waiter's version of events is therefore credible.

- In a medical malpractice action, your adversary offers evidence from Andrea that when she was in a hospital emergency room waiting for an MRI, Andrea overheard another patient tell the admitting nurse that "It's been longer than an hour since I had dinner." You might attack the credibility of Andrea's story on the ground that Andrea has no reason to recall or recollect what an unrelated patient said to the nurse.

7. DEMEANOR

Demeanor includes all the ways that witnesses look and carry themselves when they testify. For example, how witnesses are dressed, whether they are attractive, and whether they look at their attorney before answering cross examination questions are factors that can affect credibility.

To some extent, demeanor is beyond your ability to control. Your role as a lawyer doesn't extend to attempting personality makeovers or offering face lifts. But you can take various steps to try to improve a witness' demeanor. For example:

- Suggest that a nervous witness watch a portion of a case in the same courtroom in which your trial will take place, so that (hopefully!) the surroundings seem less intimidating. (If you accompany the witness, be careful not to heighten anxiety by disclosing your own insecurity: "Who is that person sitting higher than everyone else and wearing a black robe?")

- Rehearse testimony, both your direct and an adversary's anticipated cross. (Experienced and successful attorneys have been heard to say things like "In big cases I rehearse every witness' testimony at least 20 times.") Ask questions the same way in your office as you will in court. For instance, don't ask narrow, specific questions during rehearsal and then expect witnesses to elaborate in response to open questions at trial.

- Look for a chance to have a nervous witness hold onto and testify about a tangible exhibit. Many people feel more confident and comfortable when they refer to diagrams or talk about objects they are holding.

- Offer suggestions that make witnesses feel comfortable about how to dress for court. Fancy dress attire is generally a no-no. Instead, and depending partly on a witness' personal and professional lifestyle, you may be content with a general recommendation ("just dress in a way that shows respect for the court") or you may be more specific ("business casual is fine").

Hoping to positively affect demeanor, attorneys sometimes issue a flurry of eve-of-trial instructions to novice witnesses. For example, an attorney may tell a witness to "answer the other side's questions honestly, but don't volunteer information; occasionally look directly at the jurors when answering questions; pause briefly before answering cross examination questions to give me a chance to object if necessary; if you don't understand a question, don't guess at what it means, just say you don't understand."

As sensible as such advice might be, the tactic can backfire because if a witness is nervous to begin with, a raft of instructions may increase anxiety. Also, inexperienced witnesses may apply general advice in a way that you didn't anticipate. For example, a reminder to "look at the jurors occasionally while testifying" may result in the witness' constantly staring at jurors, making them uncomfortable. Thus, you may have to balance the possible gains in demeanor against the risk of harming demeanor by giving witnesses information overload.

Remember too that demeanor is the sum total of a person's traits and appearance. Change a single element, and you may detract from credibility. For example, a witness whose manner of dress is untailored and whose language tends to be colloquial may lose credibility when constrained by "professional" attire and the rules of grammar.

Finally, if despite your efforts a witness' demeanor remains problematic, you might address it during final summation by pointing out that it's unfair and irrational to evaluate a witness according to demeanor. Consider this example:

"Opposing counsel will no doubt try to convince you that Joe is not credible because he seemed nervous and had trouble answering some questions. Does that strike you as a fair way to decide my client's future? Someone who's not a professional witness, who has never testified at a trial before, who answers a subpoena, is understandably nervous and opposing counsel wants you to disregard everything he says? Wouldn't you expect a person in Joe's position to be a bit nervous? Let's not get sidetracked, let's look at what Joe had to say . . ."

Here, you not only ask the jurors to reject what you characterize as an unfair argument, but also you cast the nasty adversary as its proponent.

8. CHARACTER FOR HONESTY

Character for honesty is the final source factor you may consider when developing credibility arguments. Because of the potential of character evidence to turn trials into lengthy morality contests, evidence rules limit the admissibility of character evidence in general and "character-for-credibility" evidence in particular. The primary limitations on using character evidence to bolster or attack credibility are set forth in Federal Rules of Evidence 608 and 609 and are as follows:

- Character evidence supporting a witness' truthfulness is admissible only after the witness' truthfulness has been attacked.

- Truthfulness and untruthfulness are the only traits of character that are admissible on the issue of credibility. In other words, you can't bolster a witness' credibility by offering evidence that the witness has a reputation for peacefulness.

- When evidence of a witness' character for truthfulness or untruthfulness is admissible, the permissible forms of character evidence are (a) evidence of a witness' good or bad reputation for truth-telling; (b) evidence in the form of an opinion about a witness' good or bad character for truth-telling; and (c) evidence that a witness has been convicted of a crime. If the conviction was for a crime involving dishonesty or false statement, the conviction is automatically admissible whether the crime was a misdemeanor or a felony. If the conviction was NOT for a crime involving dishonesty or false statement, the conviction is admissible only if it was for a felony, and then subject to the judge's discretion.

- Subject to judicial discretion, witnesses can be cross examined about specific instances of conduct that didn't result in a conviction if the conduct bears on truthfulness. The cross examiner must be able to demonstrate a good faith belief that the conduct occurred. The cross examiner also must "take the witness' answer," meaning that extrinsic evidence is not admissible to contradict a witness' denial that the conduct occurred.

The upshot of the plethora of limitations is that evidence of "character to prove credibility" may have about the same chance of being admitted as wild salmon have of overcoming five dams to reach their spawning grounds. But if you do include admissible evidence of an adverse witness' bad character in a credibility argument, typically your argument's "bottom line" will be that the witness is lying. "Bad character for truth-telling" and "innocent mistake" don't play well together!

F. CASE EXAMPLE: THE *HILLMON* CASE

Chapter 3 briefly described the *Hillmon* case. In that case, alleged widow Sallie Hillmon sued three life insurance companies to collect the proceeds of policies on the life of her husband John, who she claimed had been accidentally shot to death. The insurance companies refused to pay, denying that the corpse was that of John Hillmon. Chapter 3 provided an example of an inferential argument from one of the closing arguments in the second of the six trials that *Hillmon* spawned. Below are credibility argument excerpts from that same trial, each tied to a factor of the Credibility Model.

CREDIBILITY OF STORY

Consistency with Common Experience

Plaintiff's attorney: "As for the tooth testimony [that unlike the corpse, which had perfect teeth, Hillmon's teeth were in poor condition], it was not possible for two or three dozen witnesses, after from six to ten years, to remember that he [Hillmon] had a tooth out. It was contrary to common sense."

Plaintiff's attorney, ridiculing the defense argument that Hillmon and his companion Brown concealed Walters in their wagon until they could kill him and pass his body off as Hillmon: "Hillmon must have been a marvelous man. One of a party of three, traveling through a settled country, camping out, and stopping at houses, he succeeded in concealing one of the party through the entire journey from Wichita to Medicine Lodge. Not only that, but he vaccinated him, made it work, kept the protesting Brown at bay, and succeeds in his conspiracy. It was a marvelous transaction."

Defense attorney: "[The body] was brought to Lawrence. The alleged widow did not go to see it for three days."

Internal Consistency

Plaintiff's attorney, supporting Brown's credibility: "Brown's whole conduct bore out the theory of innocence. He stayed with the body at Medicine Lodge, and afterwards went with it to Lawrence."

Defense attorney, attacking Mrs. Hillmon's credibility: "Mrs. Hillmon saw the dead body, and stoutly asserted it was her husband. Six months afterwards she acknowledged that it was not, by surrendering her policies. Had she known that to have been the body of her husband, would she not have scorned the proposition of Buchan [a lawyer paid by the insurance companies] that she release the companies?"

Plaintiff's attorney, attacking the credibility of a defense witness who testified that Hillmon had bad teeth: "Colonel Walker was too swift a witness. He could remember about Hillmon's tooth, but he could not tell which leg B.J. Horton had lost, though he had known him and seen him almost every day for many years."

Consistency with Established Facts

Plaintiff's attorney, supporting the contention that the corpse was that of Hillmon and not Walters: "A strong point, and one that destroys the Walters theory with evidence in which there can be no mistake, is the fact that Walters' temples were absolutely bare, while those of Hillmon had hair on them corresponding with the temples of the body, as shown in the photograph and testified to by Lamon, the photographer."

Defense attorney, supporting the contention that the corpse was that of Walters and not Hillmon: "There was a mole on Walters' back, and so there was on the back of the [corpse]. The scars on Hillmon's hands and nose must have been plainly visible. . . and yet the doctors with their magnifying glasses could not find them on the body."

CREDIBILITY OF WITNESSES

Expertise

Plaintiff's attorney: "The plaintiff proved by John H. Brown [who allegedly accidentally shot and killed Hillmon], the person best qualified; by Mrs. Hillmon, the widow, the next best qualified person, that the body was that of her husband."

Defense lawyer, supporting the contention that though the corpse was 5' 11" tall, Hillmon was only 5' 9": "Dr. Miller of Lawrence, who testifies that Hillmon was five feet nine inches, that he measured him, and made a record which is produced in court, is a disinterested and thoroughly reliable witness."

Motive or Bias

Plaintiff's attorney: "Five witnesses at Medicine Lodge, who knew Hillmon and saw the body, testify it was his. They are disinterested witnesses."

Defense attorney: "What interest had the Walters sisters in giving their testimony as they did [that the corpse was that of their brother Frederick]? They had nothing at stake except identification of their brother; they are not after $25,000 insurance."

Defense attorney: "A man's acts must be construed by the light of his motives. . .No test will more surely crush the body of any friend than this test of motive."

Defense attorney, justifying the insurance companies' refusal to pay: "The only motive which the companies can have in prosecuting this case is that of discouraging the sort of crime of which this is a sample, and which today is one of the most prevalent of all forms of fraud."

Reason to Recall

Defense attorney, supporting the contention that Hillmon's teeth were unlike the perfect teeth of the corpse: "Colonel Walker saw the body at Medicine Lodge. He knew Hillmon had a tooth missing. He saw that the teeth of the body were perfect, and he put his finger in the mouth to see if there was a false tooth. It was not there."

Demeanor

Defense attorney: "What were the motives which induced the parents, brother, and sisters of Frederick Adolph Walters to solemnly swear to their brother's death... You saw them on the stand. Did you ever hear the truth more clearly spoken? Did you ever see sincerity more clearly stamped on people's faces?"

Character for Honesty

Defense attorney, supporting the character of various defense witnesses in an era when character evidence rules were looser: "These men are above reproach in their private characters; they are leading churchmen, leaders in society, honorable soldiers, and good men by whatever test they are examined. Dare you, by giving a verdict for the plaintiff, brand these men as perjurers and conspirators?"

CHAPTER 5
SILENT ARGUMENTS

The argument-centered narratives that Chapters 3 and 4 described appeal to the rational processes of inferential reasoning. That is, when you develop stories and respond to those of your adversaries in a way that emphasizes favorable inferences and credibility factors, your arguments are explicit and consistent with evidence rules and the truth-seeking function of trials.

This chapter focuses on *silent* arguments. Arguments are silent when attorneys cannot explicitly identify desired inferences because those inferences are not rationally related to evidence or are otherwise legally improper. When judges and jurors nevertheless draw the desired inferences, silent arguments become part of effective argument-centered narratives.

For example, you put forward a silent argument when you advise a client to dress in a way that you think will impress a group of jurors. Like other inferential arguments, this silent argument links information presented to the jurors (the client's courtroom attire) to a desired inference (the client's credibility). An explicit argument to this effect is improper because the client's attire is not itself an item of evidence. Nevertheless, the client's manner of dress may be a factor that leads a factfinder to infer that the client is credible.

Similarly, a prosecutor's office relies on a silent argument when it assigns to a case a trial deputy who is of the same ethnicity or gender as a defendant. Implicit in the deputy's presence is the silent argument, "I wouldn't be prosecuting this case if the defendant weren't really guilty."

So long as evidence is relevant, you may proffer it at trial even if its primary value is to serve as the basis of a silent argument.   For example, if you represent a plaintiff in a personal injury case growing out of an auto accident, you may elicit testimony from the plaintiff that "I was on my way to a PTA meeting when the defendant's car ran into mine." The plaintiff's destination is properly part of the story, but your underlying goal may be to promote a silent argument that the plaintiff is a deserving litigant.

While you may seek to offer evidence at trial that you hope will be the basis of helpful silent arguments, you also must be aware of the potential to be victimized by silent arguments.   For example, depending on the locale of a trial and the "tenor of the times," clients such as insurance companies, banks, debt collection agencies, tenants, landlords, teenagers and the like may be the targets of adverse silent arguments.   Indeed, in a multi-ethnic, multi-racial society, all people and institutions have the peace of mind of knowing that they may be victimized by stereotypes and prejudice because they belong to groups that are distrusted by members of other groups.

If you cannot completely eliminate the role of adverse silent arguments in decision-making, you may in a variety of ways seek to diminish their influence. One strategy is to explicitly address adverse silent arguments during jury voir dire. For example, you might ask, "Will each of you promise not to give less than full weight to Ms. Beilen's testimony simply because her accent might make her a little difficult to understand?" Few jurors would refuse to give such a promise. By making the promise explicit, however, you make it less likely that jurors will subconsciously be influenced by the witness' accent.

Another tactic is to make a motion *in limine* (pretrial motion) to exclude evidence that might give rise to a silent argument. Obviously, you can't exclude evidence of a witness' accent or a party's ethnicity. But assume that a witness was a member some years earlier of an unpopular social group. If membership in the group has only scant relevance, consider making a motion to exclude the evidence. Under a rule such as Federal Rule of Evidence 403, you'd ask the judge to exclude the evidence of group membership because the danger of unfair prejudice outweighs its probative value.

You may also prepare a jury instruction that tells jurors to decide a case according to the evidence, the arguments of counsel and their experience and common sense, and tells them not to consider, e.g., the defendant's wealth or the plaintiff's country of origin (assuming that such factors are not rationally related to the dispute).

You may also try to counter adverse stereotypes and prejudices by offering *individualizing evidence.* That is, if you can identify a common factual assumption underlying a stereotype or prejudice, you may be able to offer evidence suggesting that the assumption doesn't apply to your particular client. By avoiding a direct attack on the stereotype and instead suggesting that it is inapplicable in a specific case, you may reduce the stereotype's influence on a verdict. (Your personal preference may be to attack harmful and improper stereotypes head-on. However, your duty to a client may require that you adopt a more pragmatic approach. A head-on attack on jurors' racial prejudices didn't help Atticus Finch in *To Kill a Mockingbird* and it may not work for your clients either.) Here are a couple of examples of how you might offer "individualizing evidence:"

- You represent a low-income tenant, and fear that the trial judge harbors a view that low income tenants are irresponsible. In response to this silent argument, your argument-centered narrative may emphasize evidence of the tenant's responsible behavior, such as the tenant's repeatedly seeking out the landlord to resolve a building problem.

- You represent a hospital in a medical malpractice case. Most of the nurses who will testify on the hospital's behalf are foreign-born and were trained in other countries, and you fear that some jurors will think that the nurses made mistakes because they were inadequately trained. In response to this silent argument, you may emphasize evidence of the nurses' training, qualifications and experience.

- **Case Example: A dirty cop.** In the sensational mid–1990's murder trial of O J Simpson, who was black, many police officers were involved in the investigation and testified on behalf of the prosecution. The defense attorneys argued that one of the officers was an overt racist who had often used racial epithets in the past, and that the racist officer planted incriminating phony evidence. The successful tactic was an example of the use of "individualizing evidence." Jurors who believed that police officers as a whole are fair and professional could hold on to their beliefs while attributing the bulk of the problems to a single "rotten apple."

Of course, any evidence that you offer to counter a silent argument must be independently relevant and admissible. For example, the nurses' backgrounds would constitute credibility evidence relevant to their expertise.

You may also respond to silent arguments explicitly during final summation. For example, if you represent a bank you might say something along these lines:

"When we began the case, you all promised that you would not be influenced by the fact that I represent a bank that is suing an individual owner of a small business. Over the last few days I've seen how carefully you've considered what I and my witnesses had to say and I know you will act on that promise and base your decision on the law and the evidence, not on who the parties to the case happen to be."

- **Case Example 1: A powerful corporate defendant.** The *Hillmon* case (see Chapters 3 and 4 for additional discussion of the case), pitted an alleged widow against three large out-of-state insurance companies that had refused the widow's claims to the proceeds of three life insurance policies. An attorney for one of the insurance companies concluded his final argument by asking the jury to "do justice as between corporations and a woman," and not to allow their sympathy to be played out "at the expense of equal and exact justice."

- **Case Example 2: An unpopular political affiliation.** In 1951, Ethel and Julius Rosenberg were tried on espionage charges for passing secret information about the atomic bomb to agents of the Soviet Union. To try to prevent possible anti-Communist beliefs among the jurors from tainting their evaluation of the Rosenbergs' credibility, defense attorney Emanuel Bloch included these remarks in his final summation: "If you want to convict these defendants because you think that they are Communists, and you don't like communism and you don't like any member of the Communist Party, then I can sit down now and there is absolutely no use in my talking. There was no use in going through this whole rigamarole of a three weeks' trial. That is not the crime. . . Ethel and Julius Rosenberg come to you as American citizens charged with a specific crime, and I ask you to judge them the way you would want to be judged if you were sitting over there before twelve other jurors."

Most people consider themselves fair and unbiased; it's always the other slobs who cause the problems. Thus, when you raise the possibility that a silent argument might influence a judge or juror and argue its unfairness and irrationality, you may cause the judge or juror to consciously disavow it. Though conscious intent may not forever eliminate subconscious prejudice, it may for a brief moment counteract it.

PART 2

COURTROOM PRESENTATION STRATEGIES

CHAPTER 6
OPENING STATEMENTS

This chapter describes strategies for presenting effective opening statements. Judges and lawyers regularly remind jurors that "what is said in opening statement is not evidence." As this familiar mantra suggests, you can't offer evidence into the record by referring to it during an opening statement. However, opening statements can be significant because of the other goals you can achieve. For example, an opening statement is your chance to incline a judge or juror to an attitude that justice is on your client's side, to provide a framework that gives meaning to your argument-centered narratives, and to establish trust and rapport. While it's too much of an exaggeration to say that "cases are frequently won or lost during opening statements," the favorable impressions that you create during an opening statement can establish a positive tone for the remainder of a case.

A. CONTENTS OF EFFECTIVE OPENING STATEMENTS

Descriptions of opening statements typically refer to them as "roadmaps" and "overviews." As these terms suggest, your opening statement should provide a preview of your story so that a judge or jury can understand what happened as well as the legal significance of the evidence you later produce. While your opening statement should help a judge or jury *understand* your case, you may not *argue the merits* of your case. For that, you must wait until final argument. Thus, the key to effective opening statements is to convey the justness and legal merits of your claims while remaining on the proper side of the uncertain divide between roadmap and argument.

1. A ROADMAP TO ROADMAPS

Serving a similar function in this chapter to that of opening statements in trials, this subsection provides an overview of the common elements of effective opening statements.

Your Story. Your client's story is an essential portion of every opening statement. While judges vary in their attitudes towards what attorneys may appropriately say during opening statements, virtually all judges permit attorneys to talk about the evidence that they will present as the trial unfolds.

Story-telling furthers your rhetorical goals because stories are a familiar and accepted means of conveying information. The stories you tell should help judges and jurors understand the significance of the evidence that is to come. For example, if you tell jurors in an opening statement in a fraud case that a building contractor tricked your client into paying for costly and unneeded repairs, the jurors will understand the significance of the client's testimony about what the contractor said and did before the client agreed to have the work done.

The timelines and inferential and credibility arguments you prepare prior to trial (see Part 1) promote persuasive opening statements because they enable you to present chronologies that emphasize the credibility of the important evidence supporting your desired inferences.

Theme. An effective theme is a succinct assertion that captures the legal merit of your story. A theme serves somewhat the same function as an advertising slogan. Your theme should serve as a shortcut into a judge's or juror's mind, acting as a reminder that beneath what may seem like complex stories and procedures is a simple truth that merits a favorable verdict. If after a case concludes a judge or juror were asked, *"What was that case all about?"* you'd want them to reply in words that very much resemble your theme.

Substantive rules. Many judges permit lawyers to briefly discuss substantive rules during opening statements (at least in jury trials). Those judges who do generally reason that if jurors are to understand the evidence, an attorney should be able to talk about not only the evidence but also about the legal rules that make it significant. Other judges regard discussion of substantive rules during opening statements as improper argument, reasoning that opening statements should be generally limited to evidence. Judges who hold this attitude may however "pre-instruct" jurors as to applicable substantive rules.

A Bottom Line. You take cases to trial for a patent-ly instrumental reason: you want a judge or jury to take action favorable to your clients. Thus, you also provide understanding by telling a judge or jury, with as much specificity as the case allows, just what action you want taken.

The subsections below elaborate on these opening statement features.

2. ARGUMENT–CENTERED STORIES

Opening statement is generally your first chance to tell your story to a judge or jury, and the story you tell should be argument-centered. As Part 1 de-scribes, an argument-centered narrative consists of a chronology of events that emphasizes the inferential significance and credibility of important helpful evi-dence. Argument-centered narratives mesh well with the purposes of opening statements. The chronology, the summary of the evidence you will present, enables judges and jurors to understand the signific-ance of the testimony you will produce during the remainder of the trial. And by emphasizing evidence that supports your arguments, you connect the story to your legal contentions without violating the rule forbidding argument in opening statement.

For example, consider a portion of the chronology you might present in a case involving an employee's claim for damages for wrongful termination by a bank. The employee, Ms. Ferguson, claims that her supervisor, Al Jones, created a pretext for firing Fer-

guson by so overworking her that she could not possibly fulfill her job assignments. A portion of your
opening remarks might go as follows:

"Starting in August of that year, Al Jones became the supervisor of the loan investigation department in which Ms. Ferguson worked. As you'll
hear, Mr. Jones had no experience in commercial
loans and he was appointed to supervise that department about a month after he became engaged
to Margaret Ward, the bank's President. Ms. Ferguson will explain to you that Mr. Jones began pil-
ing extra investigations on her almost as soon as
he took over as supervisor.

"You'll hear evidence that for years, the company's policy had been for loan investigators such as
Ms. Ferguson to have no more than eight open files
at any one time. Ms. Ferguson was in fact in
charge of ten investigations when Mr. Jones became her supervisor. Yet no other loan investigator
had as many as eight open investigations. Within a
week, Mr. Jones had assigned three additional investigations to Ms. Ferguson. They were the Hart,
Schaffner and Marx loans. Ms. Ferguson had to
carry out due diligence investigations into the advisability of the bank's making these loans within
a month, by mid-September. Ms. Ferguson will testify, and her co-worker Sharon Pinkney will confirm, that Ms. Ferguson told Mr. Jones that the only way she had a chance to carry out due diligence
within the required time was if he assigned two

other employees to help her. Mr. Jones refused, and instead ordered Ms. Ferguson to complete her work before the deadlines for making the loans.

By the mid-September deadline, Ms. Ferguson understandably had not completed her due diligence and the bank was unable to go forward with loans to Hart, Schaffner and Marx. After those potential loan customers went elsewhere, Mr. Jones summoned Ms. Ferguson to a meeting in his office. Also present at that meeting. . ."

This opening statement excerpt is generally chronological. This portion of the chronology begins when Al Jones became your client's supervisor, continues through her work assignments, and concludes with a meeting that took place after she was unable to complete those assignments.

At the same time, the statement marshals evidence around your arguments. For example, to support your desired inference that the reason that Ms. Ferguson did not complete her assignments on time is that she was overworked, you point out that she was already carrying a heavier load than her colleagues when she was assigned additional work. You also support the credibility of your client's story by mentioning that another employee, Ms. Pinkney, will confirm it (relying on the credibility factor, "consistency with established facts").

Though this portion of the statement is argument-centered, at no point does it bleed over into improper argument. For instance, you refer to Ms. Pinkney's testimony so as to suggest that it makes your client's story credible. Yet that suggestion is a result of the way you marshal the evidence, not of an explicit (and probably improper) statement that Ms. Pinkney's evidence establishes the credibility of your client's story.

Defendants' Stories. Because plaintiffs have to offer at least enough evidence to sustain the burden of proof, the narrative aspect of opening statements may seem more aligned with their outlook than with that of defendants. However, defendants too typically have stories to tell and opening statement is a useful time for defendants to tell them. (Defendants often have a choice as to *when* they make opening statements; see below.)

Whether or not they have the burden of proof as to any claim, defendants often present evidence to support defense stories. For instance, a defendant whose negligence allegedly caused an auto accident may offer evidence tending to prove that it was the plaintiff who was negligent, and a criminal defendant charged with bank robbery may offer alibi evidence. In such situations, opening statement considerations apply to defendants the same as they do to plaintiffs.

Perhaps less obviously, even defendants who rely entirely on the burden of proof and will not offer evidence often have stories to tell. For example, assume that a defendant charged with armed robbery will attack the prosecution eyewitnesses' identifications, but will neither testify nor call an alibi or character witness. Nevertheless the defense attorney's opening statement may tell a story about the weaknesses in the identifications that the attorney plans to explore during cross examination.

3. THEMES

A theme is primarily a mnemonic device, a shorthand summary that captures the essence of your story and its legal merit. The succinctness of themes makes them memorable, and their potential power rests in their ability to affect jurors' attitudes towards evidence as it unfolds. You promote the persuasiveness of your arguments when favorable evidence causes a theme to echo in a judge's or juror's mind. You may emphasize a theme by repeating it, perhaps near the outset and at the end of an opening statement, and later during closing argument.

A good strategy for developing a theme is to reduce a story to a key sentence or two and provide a reason for events happening in the way you claim they did. Examine these possible themes:

- A prosecutor in a criminal case: "In an effort to scare a family of bears into thinking that their house was haunted and selling it cheap, the defendant broke into the house, destroyed chairs, ate food and rumpled beds."

- A defendant in a criminal case: "This is a case in which coercive police tactics caused two highly suggestible witnesses to mis-identify a completely innocent person." (Note that this theme does not depend on the defense offering its own version of events. Even a defense attorney who intends to rely entirely on poking holes in the prosecution's evidence could articulate this theme.)

- A plaintiff in a civil wrongful discharge case: "You'll hear evidence about an outstanding employee of the bank who was fired by a supervisor who tried to shift blame for a series of bad loans to her."

- The defendant in the same civil wrongful discharge case: "You'll hear a story about a bank that protected thousands of depositors and employees by discharging a greedy employee who wanted to be a branch manager so badly that she prepared phony reports to make it look like she was doing a great job."

Each theme briefly describes what happened, and suggests why events took place as you claim. Each thus constitutes a shorthand mnemonic that may encourage judges or jurors to evaluate the evidence they hear in a way that favors your arguments. Of course, your evidence should be consistent with your theme. For example, it does little good to say during a plaintiff's opening statement that a supervisor fired an employee in an effort to shift blame for bad loans, and then introduce evidence showing that the supervisor's actual motivation was a romance gone sour.

4. BOTTOM LINES

You don't want to conclude an opening statement with a juror thinking something like, "That's a strong and sad story, but what am I supposed to do about it?" By explicitly revealing to jurors the decision you want and expect them to make when the case is turned over to them (or at least the framework of a decision), you help jurors understand the significance of evidence and evaluate it fairly.

For example, as the prosecutor in a drug case, you may tell the jurors that "At the conclusion of the case I'll ask you to find the defendant guilty of possession of illegal drugs for purposes of sale." The bottom line may make the jurors particularly alert to prosecution evidence as to the quantity of drugs that the defendant possessed as well as to how it was packaged and stored.

By identifying a desired bottom line early on, you also give jurors a chance to "live with it" and thereby may enhance its acceptability. For example, assume that you represent a criminal defendant. The jurors may adopt a negative attitude towards your evidence and arguments if throughout the trial they assume that you will ultimately argue in support of a not guilty verdict. However, they may keep a more open mind if they understand from the outset that your bottom line is a lesser-included offense. (That said, some criminal defense attorneys insist that their bottom line is always "not guilty.")

You cannot necessarily predict at the outset of a case what your desired bottom line will be at its conclusion. Nevertheless, you usually can at least identify the framework of an anticipated outcome. For example, assume that you represent the plaintiff in a personal injury case. The complaint asks for "damages according to proof," and at the time of opening statement you are uncertain about how much to mention by way of damages. You may also not want to constrain the jurors by mentioning a specific sum during your final summation. Even so, you can provide something of a bottom line during opening statement: "At the conclusion of the case, I'll ask you to award damages to Ms. Miller in the amount that, after you hear all the evidence, you think fair and just to compensate her for her medical expenses, lost wages and pain and suffering."

Representing a defendant in a criminal case, you may ultimately want to press for a not guilty verdict even if you realistically expect that your client will probably be convicted of *something*. In that circumstance, your opening statement bottom line may go along these lines: "The evidence will support only one conclusion, that Mr. Houston acted in self-defense. Mr. Houston is not guilty of any crime whatsoever, and certainly is not guilty of assault with a deadly weapon." This bottom line paves the way for a not guilty argument while leaving room for a verdict of simple assault.

5. SUBSTANTIVE RULES

Judges have loads of discretion with respect to the discussion of legal principles during opening statements. Their attitudes can vary widely, even among different judges in the same courthouse. If you're not already aware of the attitude of the judge who will preside over your case, you should raise the issue during a pre-trial conference.

Some judges resolve the issue by themselves pre-instructing jurors as to relevant substantive rules and basic decision-making principles such as burdens of proof. Judges who follow this practice may permit you only a brief reference at most to legal principles.

Other judges leave it to counsel to review legal principles during opening statement. They generally do so in the belief that it's up to attorneys to help jurors understand the legal significance of evidence and to do so the attorneys should be permitted to talk about both the evidence and the rules that create its significance. However, even judges who permit you to discuss legal rules probably will not permit *argument* as to the rules.

For example, a judge may allow you to say something like, "You'll hear evidence that the defendant fraudulently induced Mr. Edwards to agree to have costly and unnecessary repairs done to his house. Now as the judge will tell you in more detail at the end of the case, fraud consists of deceptive conduct that is intended to and does cause harm to another person." However, you cannot argue that "You'll hear evidence that the defendant never even bothered to inspect the master bathroom before recommending a host of expensive repairs, and you can conclude from that evidence that the defendant knew that the recommendations were without foundation."

B. EFFECTIVE PRESENTATION STRATEGIES

As you've no doubt heard throughout life, "It's not just what you say that matters, but how you say it." The subsections below discuss strategies for enhancing the content and delivery of opening statements.

1. LEVEL OF DETAIL

A recurrent strategic decision involves how much detail to include in the story you tell on opening statement. By varying the level of abstraction, you may reduce virtually any event to a single sentence, or expand it to encyclopedic length. So long as you conform to any time limits set by the presiding judge, you have to determine how much detail is helpful.

For example, one of the sample opening statement excerpts above mentions that Ms. Ferguson, suing for wrongful termination, had to carry out "due diligence" when investigating the advisability of the bank that had employed her making loans to potential customers. In an actual opening statement, you'd have to decide how much detail to go into with respect to the term "due diligence." You might say nothing more, leaving it to Ms. Ferguson or even an expert witness to explain what due diligence in the loan investigation context consists of. Or, you might provide an explanation of greater or lesser length.

Similarly, another excerpt concerned a claim that a builder contractor defrauded a homeowner named Mr. Edwards. At a high level of abstraction, you may cover a series of contacts between the contractor and Mr. Edwards with a single sentence, such as, "Mr. Edwards will describe a series of meetings during which the defendant repeatedly told him that his house was in imminent danger of collapse and needed immediate structural repairs." At a lower level of abstraction, you may describe any single conversation in great detail. For instance, you may mention where and when it took place and, consistent with the expected testimony and rules of evidence, what each participant said.

From a positive perspective, details can add authenticity to stories by suggesting that the events you're describing really did take place. Details also may help stories "come alive" by making events and people vivid and memorable.

Yet excessive detail can make an opening statement tedious to listen to, and if (as is often true) a judge imposes a time limit, too much time devoted to the details of some events may force you to ignore others.

Moreover, just as an overly detailed movie preview can destroy any interest you might have in seeing a film, so may excessive details in an opening statement cause a judge or jury to have less interest in your witnesses' testimony. A juror may think, "No need to pay much attention to the witness, the attorney already covered this stuff." (For example, if you've described the meaning of "due diligence" at length, jurors' minds may wander when you ask your client Ms. Ferguson to explain the concept during her testimony.)

Too, if witnesses simply rehash what you've already said during opening statement, you may create an impression that they are adhering to a rehearsed script.

Finally, the more details you include in an opening statement, the greater the chance of creating conflicts between what you say the testimony will be and what it actually is.

As a result, you have to be cognizant of the trade-offs with respect to details and exercise professional judgment as best you can. The arguments you've developed before trial can serve as a useful basis for decision-making. For instance, you might generally provide more details with respect to evidence marshaled around important arguments, and less detail about events that serve primarily to move the chronology along.

2. SEPARATE CHRONOLOGIES

Stories may be too complex for you to communicate through a single chronology. For example, in a products liability case, activities concerning research, marketing and patent protection of the product might have been occurring more or less simultaneously. If all of these activities are important to your legal claims and you expect a judge or juror to understand your story, you might consider breaking the story into three separate chronologies, one for each activity.

3. DON'T TALK LIKE A LAWYER (OR LIKE HOW YOU THINK LAWYERS TALK)

Too many novice lawyers seem to think that sounding lawyerly requires substituting complex for everyday terminology. "Cars" become "vehicles," abstract legal concepts like "malice aforethought" substitute for the concrete evidence that might satisfy the concepts, and words like "grantor" and "aforesaid" creep into their discourse. If you talk like this during opening statements, you'll rapidly erode rapport and lose the attention of your audience.

Although courtroom dialogues are filled with formalities and are governed by customs and evidence rules, generally the way you talk inside courtrooms should be very much the way you talk with friends. Use familiar, vivid words and explain unfamiliar concepts (or forgo them entirely in favor of everyday equivalents). For example, compare the plaintiff's opening statement excerpts below in a trial concerning a bicyclist who was injured when the quick-release mechanism on the front wheel of the bike allegedly malfunctioned and caused the bike to collapse.

Example 1: "Though I remind you that what I say is not evidence, I expect the evidence to show that the bicycle was ridden reasonably during that journey at what constitutes a normal speed and in a normal manner. The evidence will further show that an uneven surface in the vicinity of railroad tracks so jarred the bicycle that the quick-release mechanism on the front wheel was loosened, causing the wheel assembly to give way and my client to fall off the bicycle and strike the ground."

Example 2: "Joy was out for a bike ride on a typical late summer day. School was approaching, but she and her two friends had a few more days to relax and enjoy summer vacation. They decided to see a movie, and headed down 17th Street towards Montana Ave. They were pedaling at a normal rate of speed, as they had plenty of time to get to the movie. Michael rode across the tracks, and then MaryAnn. Of course they bumped up and down a bit, but they had no problem at all. Then Joy pedaled across. Suddenly her bicycle began to shake and bounce. Just as Joy got across the tracks, the quick-release mechanism on the front tire came loose and the front wheel collapsed. Joy was thrown to the ground."

Example 1 is unlikely to impress listeners. The language is repetitively legalistic (e.g., "the evidence will show. . ."), it's cast in the third person ("the quick-release mechanism on the front wheel was loosened"), and the injured rider is abstractly referred to as a "client." Overall, the description is flat and awkward, making it difficult for a listener to develop a mental image of what actually happened. Example 2 by contrast tells a concrete story that encourages listeners to picture events in their minds. The story personalizes the client ("Joy") and its language is conversational, vivid and evocative. Both opening statements conform to the rules, but No. 2 is far more likely to create an attitude that justice is on the plaintiff's side.

4. EFFECTIVE PERFORMANCE TECHNIQUES

If you've made it into or out of law school, you've spent a lot of time in lecture halls and no doubt are familiar with effective verbal communication techniques. Litigators occasionally take acting classes to enhance their verbal and physical skills. However, you needn't be a polished actor to present yourself in the courtroom in a way that captures jurors' attention and bolsters their trust and confidence in you. You can "be yourself" while adding to your repertoire other speakers' presentation techniques that have impressed you.

Perhaps the single most effective strategy you can employ is to talk directly to jurors when making an opening statement. Make eye contact with individual jurors. No matter how impressive a statement seems on paper, it loses much of its impact if you bury your face in papers or a computer screen and read it. Moreover, what you write down will inevitably be more formalistic than what you say extemporaneously. Write out an opening statement if you must, but have at most an outline or refresher notes with you when you speak.

For all of their ritualistic formality, trials are simply a setting in which human communication takes place. Judges and jurors may not be your friends, but neither do they shed their personalities when they enter a courtroom. Vary your tone of voice, use facial expressions that are appropriate to your words and smile when the situation calls for it. Try to eliminate or reduce "verbal tics," such as repeatedly punctuating statements with "you know" and "uh." Apologize sincerely for misstatements or remarks that come out wrong. Realize that you need not be perfect to succeed at trial, just be yourself.

Another simple strategy for enhancing a verbal presentation is to speak somewhat slower than you ordinarily do. Whenever you speak across a public space, as you do when talking to jurors in a courtroom, you can help listeners absorb what you say by slowing down your delivery. Moreover, if you use a slower pace you'll probably be less anxious if you momentarily pause to collect your thoughts.

Finally, your body language should convey your belief in the legal merit of your case. Stand confidently, and if you must remain at a podium try at least to stand to its side so that the podium doesn't act as a barrier to effective communication. Even if a judge permits you to move around a courtroom, do not repeatedly pace back and forth. Gesture with your hands as you ordinarily might, and do not leave them in your pockets or use them to click a pen or tap on the podium when you are speaking.

Consider visually recording yourself giving a mock presentation, perhaps in the privacy of your home or office. Talk about any subject you like. If you watch the recording, alone or with a few empathic friends, you are sure to find opportunities to improve your presentation skills.

5. VISUAL AIDS

Unless you can verbally achieve the charisma of Marc Antony addressing the citizens of Rome while standing over the body of the recently-deceased Julius Caesar, consider incorporating visual aids into your opening statements. Visual aids help capture listeners' attention and add persuasive impact to an opening statement. Most people are visual learners, and they are accustomed to receiving information from visual sources such as computers and TV screens. Judicious use of tangible exhibits adds variety to your presentation, and your own confidence and energy level may increase when you can hold and refer to a tangible object while talking.

You may incorporate two types of visual aids into an opening statement. One type consists of exhibits that you intend to offer into evidence. Just as you may refer to the testimony that you expect witnesses to give, you can refer to and display tangible exhibits that are admissible in evidence. For example, if you plan to offer a gun that was allegedly the murder weapon into evidence, you can display the weapon to the jurors during opening statement (barrel down). Similarly, you can display and discuss tangible admissible items such as photographs, contracts and other documents. To add punch and enable all the jurors to see an exhibit at once, you may display it electronically via a Power Point slide or similar source.

So long as visual aids fairly conform to expected evidence, you can also illustrate your opening remarks with visual aids even if you will not offer them into evidence. For example, assume that you represent Megacorp and that you plan to call as witnesses a number of employees who work in different departments of Megacorp. Solely for the purpose of helping jurors understand your opening statement, with the judge's permission you may prepare and refer to a chart illustrating the relationships of the employees to each other and to Megacorp.

6. "THE EVIDENCE WILL SHOW . . ."

No better way exists to deaden an opening statement than to precede virtually every sentence with the mantra, "The evidence will show." It won't be long until the jurors begin counting how often you repeat the phrase instead of listening to what you have to say. The phrase itself doesn't guard against an "improper argument" objection, because an assertion such as "All the adversary's witnesses are lying fools" is no less argumentative if you precede it with, "The evidence will show that . . ." If you've believed ever since you were in the second grade that an opening statement is incomplete unless it contains the words "The evidence will show," use it once around the time you start talking and then scrap it.

7. OPENING STATEMENT BOILERPLATE

Like contracts and other documents that create legal rights and obligations, opening statements tend to include boilerplate that attorneys mention partly because attorneys have traditionally mentioned it. For example, you may open with "May it please the court;" introduce yourself, your client and other witnesses who may be present in the courtroom; thank the jurors for their participation and expected attention to the evidence; tell the jurors what an opening statement is; and explain how your case will proceed.

While introductory remarks can help "break the ice" and help ease you and the jurors into the task at hand, excessive introductions can waste a valuable resource: jurors' attention. The *primacy principle* suggests that jurors are more attentive at the beginning of an opening statement than they are as you continue to speak. So make a few introductory remarks if you think them helpful but keep them to a minimum. Observing other attorneys' opening statements can help you decide what to say that best suits your style, personality and the arguments you rely on.

C. FOLLOW THE RULES

The Federal Rules of Evidence do not include a specific provision governing opening statements. Rule 611 does allocate to judges "reasonable control over the mode of interrogating witnesses and presenting evidence." This provision recognizes that except as modified by rules, judges should continue to follow the general processes of trial that developed under common law principles. Thus, the rules explained in this section are general guides to the scope of opening statements. Judges have wide discretion in their interpretation.

1. ARGUMENT

"Don't argue" is undoubtedly the most widely agreed-upon rule governing opening statements. (Don't argue with this assertion!) Nevertheless, you may present an argument-centered narrative on opening statement. That is, you may marshal evidence so as to emphasize the credibility and inferential significance of evidence without crossing over into argument. However, you may not argue that your story is credible, compare the credibility of your story to that of an adversary, or assert that circumstantial evidence satisfies a substantive legal rule. If an opinion would be improper for a witness to give under Federal Rules of Evidence 701 (lay witnesses) and 702 and 704(b) (expert witnesses), your stating the opinion constitutes improper argument. A good rule of thumb here is, "If a witness will not testify to it, you probably cannot refer to it during opening statement." Compare these examples:

1. "Little Jimmy was standing ten feet away from where the collision occurred, and he had an unobstructed view of what happened."

2. "Little Jimmy, standing but ten feet away from where the collision occurred, had the best opportunity of all the witnesses to observe what happened, and therefore his testimony is particularly credible."

Example No. 1 presumably refers to testimony that Jimmy will give, and though it impliedly bolsters Jimmy's credibility it constitutes proper opening statement. No. 2 by contrast is improperly argumentative. No witness will testify that Jimmy had "the best opportunity . . . to observe," or that he is especially credible. The assertions improperly refer to the inference that you want the judge or jurors to draw.

The line between proper opening statement and improper argument can be hard to discern and often is in the eye of the beholding judge. By analogy, consider the philosophy of great sculptors like Michael Angelo and Rodin, who thought of themselves as "liberating" the objects they created from the large blocks of marble in which they'd been concealed.

Think of final summation as a large block of marble, and opening statement as what you create by chipping away the portions that constitute improper argument.

Because you may not be certain about where a judge will draw the line against improper argument, many attorneys reason that when in doubt, err on the side of argumentativeness. If an adversary objects, and if the judge sustains the objection, you can apply the chisel to the remainder of an opening statement.

Definitional niceties aside, be aware that proper opening statement is sometimes in the ear as well as the eye of the beholder. An argumentative tone of voice increases the likelihood that a judge will sustain an "improper argument" objection.

2. INADMISSIBLE OR UNAVAILABLE EVIDENCE

Since opening statement is a preview of or a roadmap to the evidence that will be forthcoming at trial, it follows that you cannot refer to evidence that you know is inadmissible or unavailable. For example, a prosecutor should never refer to a defendant's prior misconduct (perhaps as evidence of motive) unless the judge has ruled that it is admissible.

If you refer to evidence that you do not produce, the consequences can be severe if the judge concludes that it's likely to influence jurors despite an admonishment to disregard it. For an egregious misstep, a judge may declare a mistrial, sanction you and your client, and perhaps even cite you for an ethical violation. (ABA Model Rule of Professional Conduct 3.4(e) provides that "A lawyer shall not...in trial, allude to any matter that the lawyer does not reasonably believe is relevant or that will not be supported by admissible evidence.") At the very least, failing to produce evidence that you mention during opening statement provides an adversary with ample ammunition to attack your case during final argument: "Opposing counsel presented a great case during opening statement. Too bad that it's not the case that you heard from her witnesses."

At the time of opening statement, you may be uncertain about the admissibility or availability of evidence. For example, you may seek to offer evidence of an assertion that constitutes hearsay but that may be admissible under a hearsay exception. Or, you may be uncertain as to whether a witness who is beyond the court's subpoena power will voluntarily appear and testify. Or, a witness may be a "waffler," showing a willingness to testify to information on some occasions but not others.

If you want to refer to evidence but are uncertain of its admissibility, consider making a *motion in limine* seeking a ruling that the evidence is admissible. If the judge grants your motion, you may then refer to the evidence in opening statement. If the judge denies the motion, or postpones a ruling until you actually offer the evidence later in the case, play it safe and do not refer to the evidence in opening statement. Similarly, if you are unsure of whether a witness will voluntarily appear, or what a witness who will appear will testify to, better practice is not to refer to the information during opening statement.

Case Example: Unfulfilled promises. Refer again to the widely-watched 1995 televised trial of former football star O.J. Simpson for murdering his ex-wife Nicole Brown Simpson and her companion Ron Goldman. During opening statement, defense attorney Johnny Cochran told the jurors that the defense would offer evidence from a nationally known expert in spousal abuse that Simpson did not have traits associated with abusive husbands. Cochran also promised to offer evidence as to the actual murder's identity. Despite making these promises to the jury, the defense offered none of this evidence. The prosecution however failed to capitalize on these omissions, and Simpson was acquitted of the murder charges.

3. EVIDENCE SOLELY WITHIN AN ADVERSARY'S CONTROL

The rule against referring to inadmissible or unavailable evidence during opening statement extends to the situation in which your adversary will decide whether to offer evidence. Based on depositions, pre-trial discussions and the like, you may reasonably expect an adversary to call a certain witness or offer particular evidence. But unless you are prepared to call that witness or offer that evidence yourself, you should not refer to the evidence during opening statement.

For example, assume that you are a prosecutor in a criminal case in which the defense is an alibi. Defense counsel has indicated that the defendant plans to testify to an alibi, and pursuant to your jurisdiction's pretrial disclosure rules the defense has also identified an alibi witness. Nevertheless, on opening statement you should not refer to the defendant's or the alibi witness' expected testimony or to the evidence that you intend to offer to undermine their credibility. If the defense opts to rest without calling a witness, you will have improperly referred to evidence that you did not produce.

In civil cases, Federal Rule of Evidence 611(c) recognizes parties' power to call their adversaries or witnesses aligned with their adversaries as hostile witnesses. If you are prepared to call a hostile witness under Rule 611(c), you may refer during opening statement to the evidence you reasonably expect to elicit from that witness.

4. VOUCHING

The long-standing "voucher" rule prevents you from asking a judge or juror to factor your character, experience or your personal belief in the merits of your cause into the decision-making process. See ABA Model Rule of Professional Conduct 3.4(e): "A lawyer shall not... in trial, assert personal knowledge of facts in issue... or state a personal opinion as to the justice of a cause, the credibility of a witness, the culpability of a civil litigant or the guilt or inocense of an accused."

One reason for the rule is that as a matter of fairness to parties, lawyers' reputations or past experience should not enter into verdicts. More narrowly, lawyers' characters, experiences and personal beliefs do not constitute evidence, making reference to them improper. During opening statement (or at any other time), remarks such as these are improper:

- "I only take cases that I am confident are legally just."

- "Never before in my experience as a practicing lawyer have I represented a client whose case was as meritorious as this one."

- "I know from my many dealings with my client that she is a person who tells the truth."

Lawyers' in-court behavior may constitute a kind of "circumstantial evidence" of personal belief that avoids the voucher rule. (You may also view the behavior as a "silent argument" that a client's cause is legally just.) For example, when you speak to jurors in a way that connotes your confident belief in your client's cause, or when you confer with your client in view of jurors, you provide circumstantial evidence of your personal belief in your cause.

So long as it is apparent that your remarks relate to evidence, during opening statement you can generally refer to what you think or believe the evidence will be without running afoul of the voucher rule. For example, you may conclude an opening statement by saying something like, "When you've heard all the evidence, I think you will conclude that Ms. Rodriquez told the truth and that the defendant's car ran the red light."

5. PRIMA FACIE CASES

Before embarking on an opening statement on behalf of a plaintiff, find out whether you are in a jurisdiction that sets a "prima facie" trap for unwary plaintiffs' counsel. In some jurisdictions, if you have the burden of proof but do not include enough potential evidence in your opening statement to satisfy the burden, defense counsel may ask for and the court may grant a non-suit. Regardless of whether you will in fact offer sufficient evidence to make out a prima facie case, you may have to refer to that evidence if you present an opening statement.

D. COMMON JUDGMENT CALLS

The subsections below briefly examine judgment calls that may commonly confront you when you prepare to make an opening statement.

1. VOLUNTEERING WEAKNESSES

Should you refer during opening statement to weaknesses in your evidence that your adversary is almost certain to bring out at trial? An advantage to doing so is to "take the sting out" of an adversary's argument by showing that "I have nothing to hide." Besides, ignoring apparent weaknesses makes you susceptible to an adversary's charge during final argument that you were less than candid during opening statement. Yet trotting out weaknesses gives them substance, and may conflict with your later argument that a supposed weakness is unworthy of serious consideration.

For an example of how you might exercise your judgment, assume that you are the prosecutor in the courtroom comedy film, *My Cousin Vinny.* The case involves a trial of two defendants who allegedly robbed a convenience store and killed the clerk. You intend to call three eyewitnesses who will testify that they saw the defendants either enter or later leave the store or both, right around the time of the robbery/murder. If you refer to their testimony during opening statement, should you mention that none of them were in the store at the time of the crime and that none of them actually saw the crime? If one of the eyewitnesses was under the influence of alcohol at the time he says that saw the defendants run out of the store, should you mention this to the jury? If a second eyewitness can be impeached with a prior conviction, should you mention that during opening statement?

One way to evaluate such questions is to view evidentiary weaknesses as information whose introduction is within an adversary's control. That perspective suggests that you not refer to the evidence. Yet failure to acknowledge an obvious weakness may convey an impression that you are trying to sell a sow's ear as a silk purse.

Perhaps a sound decision depends on how integral a weakness is to your overall story. For example, as the prosecutor in *My Cousin Vinny* you might choose to mention that none of the eyewitnesses actually observed the crime because their locations are central to their stories about what happened. Mentioning the influence of alcohol and the prior conviction are more problematic, because they are external to their stories about what took place at the time of the crime.

2. DEFENSE OPENING STATEMENTS

Defense attorneys typically have a choice between immediately following plaintiffs' opening statements with their own, or delaying their openings until after plaintiffs rest, just prior to the defense case-in-chief. A traditional advantage of "delay" is that if plaintiffs don't know what the defense story will be, then plaintiffs are unable to respond to the story during their case-in-chief. This advantage is less significant in an era of settlement discussions, wide-open discovery and pre-trial conferences. Usually, adversaries are well aware of each other's stories and contentions prior to trial.

Another potential advantage of a "delay" strategy is that sitting through the plaintiff's case gives defense counsel a chance to target opening statement according to the evidence that actually emerged during the plaintiff s case-in-chief, and the jurors' reactions to that evidence.

Perhaps more significant are the factors that weigh in favor of defendants immediately following plaintiffs' openings with their own. Immediate defense responses keep the defense's "foot in the door," reminding the jurors as the plaintiff's case takes center stage to keep an open mind. Also, an immediate defense response can help the jurors understand the significance of testimony that the defense elicits on cross examination.

A *mock opening statement* provides a defense attorney with some of the advantages of an argument-centered opening statement without locking the defense into a specific line of defense. Consider this example:

"I will make my remarks very brief, you'll hear the evidence later. As you listen to the plaintiffs' witnesses, remember that when Mr. Jones gets a chance to offer evidence you will hear a very different version of events. The rules allow plaintiffs to present evidence first. Listen to that evidence carefully, but keep an open mind so that you can listen to Mr. Jones' evidence just as carefully. I am confident that when you weigh all the evidence you will conclude that the plaintiff has not met the burden of proof and render a judgment for Mr. Jones."

Though largely conclusory and lacking reference to any actual testimony, the statement's brevity may cause a judge to allow it. However, if you are allowed to conduct voir dire questioning, you can cover much of the same ground at that time. In general, opening statement is too important a persuasive opportunity to waste with a mock opening.

3. BENCH TRIALS

The extent to which the techniques in this chapter apply to bench trials depends in part on whether an "all-purpose judge" hears a case. A judge assigned to preside over a judge trial on the day of trial is often as factually in the dark as jurors would be, and you might present much the same opening statement to the judge that you would to jurors. All-purpose judges generally handle cases from initial filing onward, and thus are likely to be familiar with the relevant factual issues. All-purpose judges may even urge you and an adversary to forgo opening statements altogether. However, you should be reluctant to waive opening altogether. A modified argument limited to your crucial arguments is a good fall back position.

E. OPENING STATEMENT EXAMPLE 1

Below are excerpts from an opening statement in a case in which a group of physicians sued the trustees of a medical malpractice insurance group to which they belonged for damages caused by the trustees' alleged negligence. The group, an "inter-indemnity exchange," was formed for the purpose of allowing member physicians to lower their medical malpractice premiums, and the plaintiff physicians claimed that the trustees' negligence caused them to lose the benefits of group membership. Below are excerpts from the plaintiffs' lawyer's opening statement, with occasional annotations by the author.

"His Honor touched on it, but what I am here to do is to make it easier for you to see what the evidence is going to be when you actually see and hear it. I am going to provide you with a road map or a bird's-eye view of what we expect the evidence to show that will be presented to you for your consideration.

"I am also going to show you or tell you, rather, the questions we are going to ask you to answer when you are doing your job in the jury room; and let me repeat what His Honor said, that everything I say here is just lawyers talk. It's not evidence. The only evidence will come from the witness chair and through stipulations."

Comment: This is the sort of "boilerplate" that attorneys often include at the outset of opening statements. As you see, the parties had agreed ahead of time to submit specific questions to the jurors at the end of the case, and the lawyer advised the jurors at the outset what their task would ultimately be.

"You see on the desks two little cards, one says "DIT Members" and one says "DIT Trustees." DIT stands for Doctors Inter-indemnity Trust. The evidence is going to show that DIT was a trust that was formed as a result of legislation that... provided for the formation of something called an inter-indemnity agreement, and I will explain what the evidence will show that is in a minute.

"This agreement was intended to allow doctors to pool their resources and their funds together to contribute it into a trust fund which they would use to cover medical malpractice claims that were raised against them. The concept was that the doctors would be able to more efficiently conduct the defense of the claims of medical malpractice against them because one of the earmarks of the inter-indemnity arrangement that this law provided was that the organization would be run by the doctors for the doctors...The inter-indemnity arrangement... required all the doctors to contribute an initial contribution .. and the amounts of the contributions varied from the type of practice the doctors had...Each of the doctors each year while they were a member had to pay moneys in. They were like fees or dues and they would be paid quarterly. If at the end of the year they had spent more money than they had available, they had to pay that as well by virtue of assessments."

Comment: Because the concept and purpose of an inter-indemnity trust is so unfamiliar, the attorney explains its operations in detail. By mentioning that the trust was set up pursuant to state law, the attorney also assures the jurors that its aims and operations were desirable and legitimate. The attorney is not here telling a story, but providing the background for the story that he will later tell.

"The evidence is going to show that some of the other reasons these doctors joined was not only costs, but this was a company run by doctors for doctors and they liked that thought. All of the board of trustees had to be doctors. . .And the law which covered this specifically said that the trustees are fiduciaries; and by fiduciaries, that means they hold certain kinds of duties which His Honor will explain to you at the conclusion of the case. . .Some of the doctors joined because they were told when they were joining that they were going to be very selective on who they let in, so that they wouldn't let in people who were prone to having claims against them, so there would be fewer claims and their expenses would be lower."

Comment: The lawyer repeats that the trust was run by doctors for doctors, suggesting that his clients acted sensibly and reasonably in joining. By mentioning the group's selectivity, the lawyer implies that his clients are top-quality doctors. This information might constitute improper character evidence if offered to support the credibility of testifying plaintiffs, but in the context of "background information on the trust" the information escapes censure. The lawyer refers to the governing law by briefly defining the term "fiduciaries," but leaves a fuller explanation to the judge.

"In (month, year), there was a membership meeting of DIT. . .We believe we are going to prove that the disclosure materials that the trustees provided to the members at that time were not sufficient to satisfy their fiduciary duties to the members . . . what the trustees did was they did not do the hands-on management every single day of everything that went on in this inter-indemnity arrangement. They entered into an arrangement with a company that. . . decided how much assessments would have to be made and would give their recommendation to the board of trustees. The evidence is going to show that the board of trustees did everything [the management company] told them, and did not make any independent investigation of their own, even when they were surprised when [the management company] told the board of trustees, 'We are in trouble. We do not have enough money to pay the claims. . .We are going to have to assess the members about $8 million in this last quarter just in order to keep current while we are going.' The trustees, you will hear from their examination, were surprised by this. They had no idea what was being done to that trust."

Comment: The lawyer here begins to tell the story, starting with the point in time when the trustees learned from the management company that the trust was in financial difficulty. The lawyer emphasizes the trustees' fiduciary duty to the members, because the lawyer will ultimately ask the jurors to infer that the trustees breached this duty. The lawyer refers to expected testimony by the defendant trustees, but as the lawyer's comments are presumably based on their deposition testimony, the lawyer refers to evidence that he can produce.

"Now, the trustees were surprised when [the management company] told them that this was a dire, dire situation because the feeling was that when the members found out, they would leave. They had a right to withdraw from their membership so long as they were in good standing. But then in an even more surprising event, [the management company] said, "We have been negotiating for the last few months with [an insurance company], it's a regular medical malpractice insurance company that is well known in this state. If you can get 75% of the members to go ahead with this deal, we can solve our problem. And the deal was that [the insurance company] would take over the insurance needs of the members .. So what did they do? The trustees met and said, "That's a great idea." We are going to adopt it. . . So what did the board of trustees do? Instead of telling the members right away, they delayed. . . they didn't say a word to the members to whom they owed this fiduciary duty about anything that was going on. . . until the chairman of the board of trustees. . . sent a letter with a whole bunch of documents, which we will be sharing with you, in which they explain this. . . And in the letter they said, "By the way, you have to respond by Oct. 16 (less than three weeks later) whether you are going to go with [the insurance company] and whether you are going to approve this plan of winding up and termination of the trust which goes hand in hand with it."

Comment: The lawyer continues telling the story, re-emphasizing the defendants' fiduciary duty (which now seems to constitute a theme) and their concealment of the trust's financial problems. The lawyer might have added a visual component to the opening statement by showing some of the important documents to the jurors, or projecting at least some of the key phrases in the documents onto a screen.

"I have to check my time. I am trying to talk slow enough so that I can be understood, but keep track of my time because I only have an hour. What happened to these doctors was that. . .all the money was spent. It was spent paying claims, as far as I know. I have no reason to know otherwise, but it was spent by [the management company]. . .The money was all gone. They still had claims out there that had to be paid. . . And so what happened? The following month [a receiver] was appointed. And what did the receiver discover? He discovered from his expert accountant that DIT had been what we call in the insurance industry 'upside down' for three or four years at a minimum. . .He discovered irregularities in the operation of the trust as well, and he will be here to discuss these with you. And there's more. . ."

Comment: Still proceeding chronologically, the lawyer describes how the trustees' failure to manage the trust properly caused it to become bankrupt. The attorney also discloses a possible weakness: that he has no evidence that either the trustees or the management company pocketed any of the trust's assets or diverted them to their own uses. The story will center on bad management, not (as the jurors might anticipate) fraud and theft. Though it is seemingly a minor matter, some jurors may be confused by the lawyer's phrase, "what *we* call in the insurance industry upside down." Why is the lawyer in the insurance industry, some may think. Jurors are often attentive to tiny details, and unless explained this phrase may cause some to speculate about whether the lawyer represents a group of doctors or an insurance company, and if the latter what impact if any that should have on the outcome.

"What happened is that [the receiver] got a judgment against my clients, and we are going to ask you to have the trustees pay the amount of those judgments back to my clients because we are claiming that that judgment would not have been entered into if the trustees had done their job, exercised their due diligence, some independent investigation, and actually knew what was going on financially in that trust so that they could have planned for it rather than just abdicating their responsibilities... Now when all is said and done here, we believe the evidence is going to show that the trustees failed to exercise the diligence that His Honor is going to tell you that a fiduciary has to exercise, and that in many, many ways, more than just what I am telling you here because I don't want to just say everything otherwise we will be going on for two days rather than an hour; and that our clients, the DIT members, have been harmed terribly by this and substantially."

Comment: The lawyer here articulates the rationale for the damages he will ask the jury to award, re-emphasizes the trustees' fiduciary duty, and portrays the plaintiffs as victims. He also tries to keep the jurors' "heads in the game" by telling them that they will hear so far undisclosed evidence as the trial proceeds.

"We believe that when the case is all over, when you have heard all the evidence and you have heard all the law, you will be satisfied that the DIT trustees did breach their fiduciary duties. This is lawyers talk. It is not evidence. It is not argument. I hope it showed you a little bit more what you are going to be hearing while you are here. It is really not a complicated case. I know there are a lot of big words that I have been throwing around, and entities, inter-indemnity arrangements, things like that, but what it all comes down to is trust, one word, t-r-u-s-t. We all know what trust is, and I don't mean the kind of trust like the DIT where you hold moneys in trust. The evidence is going to show that the DIT members trusted and relied upon the DIT trustees not to do anything that would cause harm to the DIT members. They couldn't conceive of it because the DIT trustees were also members. My clients couldn't conceive that the DIT trustees would do anything that would harm themselves, much less our members; but we believe that the evidence is going to show that by their inaction. . . my clients are suffering as a result of that, and we are going to ask you to award them money damages as a result. Thank you very much, ladies and gentlemen."

Comment: The lawyer concludes by stressing that unfamiliar terms and financial complexities to the side, the case for damages is a simple one. This is a frequent plaintiff stratagem, because it suggests that the story at bottom is a familiar one, well within the jurors' competence to decide. The references to "trust" are suggestive of a theme, but the attorney fails to make the theme explicit.

F. OPENING STATEMENT EXAMPLE 2

The opening statements below are from the film *Philadelphia* (1993). The film centers on a civil employment discrimination lawsuit. Plaintiff Andrew Beckett sues the law firm in which he was employed as an associate attorney for firing him illegally when the partners realized that he had AIDS (at the time of the film an incurable and always-fatal disease). An analysis of the legal propriety of the openings and of the lawyers' strategies follows the opening statements.

Plaintiff's Opening Statement

Ladies and gentlemen of the jury. Forget everything you've seen on television and in the movies. There's not going to be any last-minute surprise witnesses, nobody's going to break down on the stand with a tearful confession. You're going to be presented with a simple fact. Andrew Beckett was fired. You'll hear two explanations for why he was fired, ours and theirs. It is up to you to sift through layer and layer of truth until you determine for yourselves which version sounds the most true. There are certain points I must prove to you. Point number one. Andrew Beckett was—is—a brilliant lawyer, great lawyer. Point

number two.   Andrew Beckett, afflicted with a
debilitating disease, made the understandable,
the personal, the legal choice to keep the fact of
his illness to himself.   Point number three.   His
employers discovered his illness.   Ladies and gentlemen, the illness I'm referring to is AIDS.   Point
number four.   They panicked.   And in their panic,
they did what most of us would like to do with
AIDS, which is to get it and everyone who has it
as far away from the rest of us as possible.   Now
the behavior of Andrew Beckett's employers may
seem reasonable to you.   It does to me.   After all,
AIDS is a deadly, incurable disease.   But no matter how you come to judge Charles Wheeler and
his partners in moral and human terms, the fact
of the matter is when they fired Andrew Beckett
because he had AIDS, they broke the law.

Defendant's Opening Statement

Fact. Andrew Beckett's performance on the job
varied from competent, good to often times medio-
cre to sometimes flagrantly incompetent.   Fact.
He claims he's the victim of lies and deceit.   Fact.
It was Andrew Beckett who lied, going to great
lengths to conceal his disease from his employers.
Fact.   He was successful in his duplicity.   The
partners at Wyant Wheeler did not know that
Andrew Beckett had AIDS when they fired him.
Fact.   Andrew Beckett is dying.   Fact.   Andrew
Beckett is angry because his lifestyle, his reckless
behavior has cut short his life.   And in his anger,

his rage, he is lashing out and he wants someone to pay.

Analysis

1. The assertion in the plaintiff's opening statement that Beckett was a "brilliant" and "great" lawyer may be a strategic error. Beckett can succeed by showing that the law firm fired him because he had AIDS; he need not in addition prove his legal brilliance.

2. The plaintiff's opening statement tells the jurors that it's up to them to determine which version of events sounds the most true (sic). The assertion does not accurately reflect juror decision-making, as jury studies tend to show that jurors create their own versions rather than choose between competing versions. More problematically, the assertion may misstate the law as it disregards the plaintiff's burden of proof.

3. The opening statements suggest possible themes: the plaintiff's statement refers to the law firm panicking, while the defense statement refers to Beckett's anger. Both attorneys could have increased the rhetorical strength of their statements with more explicit thematic appeals.

4. The defense lawyer's final two assertions constitute improper argument.

5. The plaintiff takes a calculated risk by telling the jurors that like he does, they might judge the defendants to have acted reasonably and morally. The plaintiff emphasizes the jurors' obligation to decide the case according to law, not according to that era's widespread fear of AIDS. At the same time, the jurors may be reluctant to "punish" people who even the plaintiff concedes acted reasonably and morally.

6. Both opening statements have a "bullet point" quality. Neither statement provides a story or a roadmap to evidence.

7. Tip: To enhance your opening statement skills, you might develop an argument-centered opening statement for each party based on the admittedly limited information provided above (or watch the film for more information).

CHAPTER 7

DIRECT EXAMINATION

Success at trial typically depends on effective direct examinations.

This pronouncement may seem heretical if your trial images come from movies and television. In popular culture, direct examinations tend to take a back seat to intense cross examinations that wring murder confessions out of nervous witnesses or powerful final summations that win over previously hostile judges and jurors.

In reality, you'll usually elicit the most important evidence supporting your arguments on direct rather than cross examination. Moreover, studies tend to suggest that judges and jurors infrequently change their minds based on what attorneys say during final argument. As a result, direct examinations that effectively communicate argument-centered narratives are typically your best opportunity to produce a favorable verdict.

A. OVERVIEW

Direct examination is a form of stylized story-telling in which evidence emerges through a series of questions and answers. The ritualized format responds to a number of concerns. From your perspective as a direct examiner, questions are your chance to shape witnesses' stories so as to most effectively communicate your arguments. For example, you can employ open questions to encourage witnesses to describe events in their own words, and narrow questions to target specific details so that you can marshal together and emphasize items of evidence supporting the same argument. From your perspective as an adversary, your opponent's direct examination questions provide you with notice of the information that the questioner seeks, giving you a chance to object if appropriate. From a judge's perspective, direct examination questions provide some assurance that testimony is elicited efficiently and in a way that conforms to evidence rules.

Typically, each witness' direct examination testimony unfolds over a number of phases, which later sections of this chapter examine in more detail. The usual phases are these:

- *Background questions.* Background questions break the ice and help you convey the idea that your witnesses are real and credible people who observed or participated in actual events. While background questioning is typically brief, it can be extensive if you need to establish that a witness is qualified as an expert under Federal Rule of Evidence 702.

- *Scene-setting questions.* Scene-setting questions give you a chance to establish lay witness' personal knowledge (see Federal Rule of Evidence 602). You can also use scene-setting questions to help judges and jurors visualize the scenes of events. As stories progress from one event and locale to another, you may set scenes multiple times as stories unfold.

- *Story questions.* Direct examinations consist primarily of argument-centered narratives. Within overall chronologies you typically organize testimony so as to emphasize your legal contentions.

- *Conclusion.* Conclude direct examinations on a high note rather than have them fade off into the sunset by ending on an unimportant detail (or even worse, with an adversary's sustained objection).

B. FOLLOW THE RULES

The subsections below explain the most important evidentiary rules affecting direct examination questioning. (Section C below examines separately the rules and strategies that relate to forms of questions, including the use of leading questions.) The guiding principle is set forth in Federal Rule of Evidence 611, which authorizes judges to "exercise reasonable control over the mode and order of questioning witnesses and presenting evidence." This vague language effectively continues questioning policies and customs as they developed at common law, while providing judges with discretion to control the scope and duration of testimony according to such factors as its importance and a witness' responsiveness to questions. Rule 611 also provides leeway for judges to establish idiosyncratic ground rules, such as whether you must stand at a lectern when questioning witnesses. Always check with judges, their clerks or other courtroom personnel to ascertain what if any such ground rules a trial judge expects you to follow.

1. WITNESS COMPETENCY

Early common law competency rules barred many potential witnesses from testifying. If a case was based on a barroom brawl, and the only potential witnesses were the interested participants, their spouses, the village idiot and an agnostic, probably nobody could testify! (Intentionally or not, competency rules may have prevented trial backlogs!)

Federal Rule of Evidence 601 abolishes the common law restrictions by making virtually everyone competent to testify. (Echoes of some of the common law competency restrictions may be heard in attacks on credibility. For example, a witness' mental disabilities may affect the witness' credibility, but not affect competency.) Because the effect of Rule 601 is to presume competence, you generally need not do anything to establish a witness' competence. However, if a witness is a young child or is obviously and seriously infirm, a judge may ask you to elicit foundational *voir dire* testimony demonstrating that a witness understands the duty to tell the truth and has at least a modicum of physical and mental ability to observe, recollect and communicate.   Under Federal Rule of Evidence 104(a), the burden is on the party proferring a witness to convince a judge of the witness' competence by a preponderance of the evidence.

For example, assume that you are prosecuting a father for physically abusing his 6 year old son, Johnny. Your witness is Johnny's little sister Emily, who is 4 years old. *Voir dire* questions demonstrating Emily's competence may go as follows:

Q: Emily, do you know why you are here today?

A: Yes, it's because of my daddy and Johnny.

Q: Who is Johnny?

A: My brother.

Q: Where do you live, Emily?

A: I live with my mommy and daddy and Johnny in an apartment. We live on Elm Drive.

Q: Can you tell us what the apartment looks like?

A: It's pretty. I have my own room, and Johnny and my mommy and daddy too. There's a kitchen, and a big room with a TV in it. I like to play in the backyard.

Q: Do you go to school yet, Emily?

A: Yes. My teacher is Mrs. Hawkins, she's really nice.

Q: What kinds of things do you do in school?

A: I know my letters and Mrs. Hawkins is teaching us how to read. I like to paint pictures and play soccer, too.

Q: Emily, do you know what it means to tell the truth?

A: Say what happened. Don't tell a lie.

Q: If I were to tell you that I'm wearing a big red rubber nose right now, would that be the truth or a lie?

A: That's silly. That's a lie.

Q: And if I were to tell you that Santa Claus is a capitalist economy's marketing tool. . . I'm sorry Emily, I didn't mean to make you cry. I withdraw the question and I'll ask this one instead. Emily, what happens if you tell a lie?

A: My mommy gets mad at me and sends me to my room.

Q: So is it bad to tell a lie?

A: Yes.

Q: Will you tell us the truth today?

A: Yes.

Q: Nothing further as to competence, Your Honor.

Judge: Objection? Hearing none, I rule that that the witness is competent to testify. Please continue.

Foundational questioning of the type illustrated above demonstrates that the child witness understands the duty to tell the truth and is capable of observing, recalling and communicating.

2. PERSONAL KNOWLEDGE

Federal Rule of Evidence 602 requires that lay (non-expert) witnesses testify based upon personal knowledge. Should a dispute about a witness' personal knowledge arise, the proferring party's burden is to offer evidence that is "sufficient to support a finding" that a witness has personal knowledge, the lower foundational threshold of Federal Rule of Evidence 104(b). Typically, you establish witnesses' personal knowledge through their own direct examination testimony, as in this brief example:

1. Q: What did you see when you arrived at the scene?

2. A: I saw the wolf laughing, and piles of straw laying all over the place.

3. Q: Did you hear the wolf say anything?

4. A: Yes. The wolf said, "I huffed and I puffed and I blew the house down."

As is typical, the witness' own testimony above establishes that the witness personally observed the scene where the events took place and heard the wolf's statement.

By contrast, assume that the questioning had gone as follows:

1. Q: Do you know about an incident in which a house collapsed?

2. A: Yes, I know about that incident.

3. Q: What happened?

4. A: A laughing wolf claimed to have huffed and puffed and blown a straw house down. Piles of straw were lying all over the place.

This second set of questions and answers does *not* demonstrate the witness' personal knowledge. The witness may "know about that incident" from reading about it online, from hearing friends describe the incident, or from watching a television news story about the incident. As a result, potential valid objections to Question No. 3 include "lack of foundation," "speculation," "lack of personal knowledge" and "hearsay." To allow the above witness to demonstrate personal knowledge, you might have phrased Question No. 3 as follows: "How do you know about that incident?"

3. DO NOT TESTIFY

Your role as a direct examiner is to ask questions, not to rehash or comment on evidence already in the record or to provide new information to judges and jurors. This same principle means that you cannot ask questions whose effect is to assert that information is accurate. Consider these questions:

- Q: Mr. Johnson testified earlier that the alarm went off at 11 a.m. What is your recollection?

- Q: If as Mr. Johnson testified earlier the alarm went off at 11 a.m., why were you still in bed at 11:30?

Even if Johnson in fact testified as your questions suggest, they are improper because they assert what the testimony was. Judges commonly sustain a *Counsel is testifying* objection to such questions.

For a variant of this impropriety, assume that there's been no testimony as to an alarm going off. Nevertheless, the questioner asks:

Q: If an alarm went off at 11 a.m., why were you still in bed at 11:30?

Again, the questioner inserts information into the record in the guise of asking a question. Judges commonly sustain an objection that *The question assumes facts not in evidence* to such questions.

4. HOUSEKEEPING RULES

The rituals of trial extend to a variety of courtroom customs that enhance orderliness. This section explores customs that primarily arise in connection with direct examination. Many of these customs are subject to the whims of individual judges and even to courtroom architecture, so always check on these matters with the judge or court clerk before trial starts.

a. The Well

The Well constitutes the unmarked area between counsel tables and the judge's bench. To enhance judges' personal security, this area has traditionally been off-limits to lawyers and witnesses. Unless a judge invites you to enter The Well, behave as though that part of the floor consisted of quicksand. Otherwise the bailiff may suddenly yank you out of The Well by your collar, which can be embarrassing in mid-trial.

b. Sitting and Standing

Unlike at weddings and theaters, ushers are not available in courtrooms. To find your place in an unfamiliar courtroom, look for the jury box or the witness box. Plaintiff's counsel table is usually the one closer to that box.

Show respect to the court by standing whenever you address a judge directly, whether to make an argument or interpose an evidentiary objection.

If you want to respond to opposing counsel's objection, ask permission from the judge to do so. If you want to respond to an objection but the judge rules before you have a chance to do so, you may ask for permission to respond: "May I be heard on that ruling, Your Honor?"

Many judges, especially if you are in federal court, will require you to stand at a lectern when examining witnesses (or addressing a jury).

No matter where in the courtroom you are during direct examination, seek and obtain a judge's permission before approaching the bench or a witness. For example, if you want to make an evidentiary objection out of the hearing of a witness and jury, say something like, "May I approach the bench Your Honor?" If the reason isn't obvious and the judge asks, you might say something like, "For the purpose of demonstrating the relevance of this line of questioning." Similarly, if you want a witness to testify about a specific portion of a document, you may ask for "permission to approach the witness to point out the paragraph I want her to explain." Return to your "mark" when the reason you approached a witness no longer exists; don't continue to stand in front of the witness and ask questions.

c. Converse in the Triangular

A custom of trial that may take some getting used to requires you to address all comments to the judge, even though opposing counsel, the real target of your remarks, is standing right next to you. For example, assume that you want to advise a judge that opposing counsel is unfairly attempting to back out of a stipulation. Do not talk to counsel directly: "Why are you trying to get out of the stipulation we agreed to three days ago?" Instead, address the remark to the judge: "Your Honor, Ms. Boland agreed to this stipulation three days ago and now, after the witness has been excused, is suddenly attempting to withdraw it." (Fortunately, the custom is not pursued to its logical conclusion. The judge will not pretend that neither counsel can hear what the other one said and repeat everyone's remarks!)

d. Client Involvement

As their legal representative, you speak for clients inside the courtroom except when they testify. A judge may impose sanctions on a client whose remarks or behavior disrupt a trial, and you may feel like imposing sanctions if a client tugs at your sleeve and makes suggestions while you question witnesses or speak to a judge. Thus, make sure that clients understand that they speak through you inside the courtroom. And you might arm clients with an electronic device (or an old-fashioned notepad and pen), advise them to record their thoughts and possible questions, and promise to review them promptly. This strategy satisfies many clients' understandable desire for involvement in their own cases, while your reviewing a client's notes and conferring with them in open court may constitute a silent argument that a client is intelligent, responsible and trustworthy.

C. FORMS OF QUESTIONS

Forms of questions range from extremely broad ("Please tell us what you know about this case") to extremely leading ("You are the killer, right?") During most direct examinations you'll undoubtedly pose questions of varying breadth somewhere between these extremes. This section examines the rules relating to forms of questions as well as their common strategic advantages and disadvantages.

1. OPEN QUESTIONS

Open questions are the basic direct examination "coin of the realm." Open questions call attention to topics but allow witnesses to answer in their own words. Thus, open questions further the direct examination policy that evidence should come from witnesses and not questioners. Examples of open questions include:

- "Please describe what happened after Mr. Dumpty reached the top of the wall." This question calls the witness' attention to an event (Dumpty on the wall) and a particular period of time within that event (after Dumpty is on the top of the wall). The form of the question is open because "what happened" is up to the witness to say.

- "Please tell us what was said in that conversation." This question calls the witness' attention to a topic (a conversation) and its form is open because it allows the witness to determine the content of the answer.

- "Describe the appearance of your left palm two months after the surgery." This question is open because it calls the witness' attention to a specific topic (a palm's appearance) and time period (two months after surgery) but relies on the witness for the description.

- "After you fell down in front of the steamroller, what happened next?" Again, the question is open because it refers to an event and a time period but calls on the witness to provide the evidence.

Open questions have advantages in addition to complying with direct examination questioning rules. Because they are *witness-centered,* open questions focus judges' and jurors' attention on your witnesses rather than on you (unless you inadvertently ask questions while wearing a bright red rubber nose.) Open questions also tend to promote witnesses' credibility. Rather than appearing to give memorized, programmed responses, witnesses choose their own words.

Nevertheless, open questions are subject to two major limitations. First, despite your best pretrial preparation efforts, some witnesses will not answer open questions credibly. Their answers may obscure your arguments (by omitting important information, for example) and draw objections (by referring to improper or extraneous information). Consider these examples:

The Detailer. Witnesses may provide so many details in response to open questions that the responses sound canned and memorized. Consider this example:

Q: What happened after you arrived at the wall?

A: This odd-shaped person was sitting on top of the wall. The wall was at least 15 feet high. How long he had been sitting there, I couldn't say. He looked odd to me because his body was oval-shaped, and he was very pale. But he looked like a good egg. He kept yelling, "I'm going to jump" in a very high-pitched voice. He must have said this at least 10 times in the minute that I watched before he jumped. . .

Such an answer is unlikely to be credible. The witness provides so many details that the answer sounds artificial and rehearsed.

The Partisan. Witnesses may use the flexibility that open questions provide to vilify an adversary or unleash social commentary. Again, credibility suffers:

Q: What happened after you got to the wall?

A: Well, that wall has been a deathtrap for years. Dumpty is the fifth person I can remember who has gotten stuck on it in the last year. Will the king ever do anything except send his men out on horses each time a tragedy occurs? Anyway, there he was. . .

This witness' partisanship suggests that the witness is more likely to fit events into the witness' preconceived ideas than to describe accurately what actually happened.

The Digresser. Witnesses may lack the law's sense of logical relevance, and get side-tracked:

Q: OK, you're at the wall. Then what happened?

A: Getting to the wall wasn't easy, I'll tell you. There were horses everywhere; all the king's horses must have been out on the streets. When I saw Mr. Dumpty up there, I got really frightened. It reminded me of the time my brother. . .

Such answers quickly exhaust a judge's or juror's patience.

In situations such as these, you may have to exercise more control over the scope of answers by asking narrower, *attorney-centered* questions. For example, instead of asking an open question like, "What happened after you got to the wall?" you might ask, "When you got to the wall, what was the very first thing you saw?" And instead of asking a witness, "Please tell us what was said in that conversation", you might ask, "What if anything did you hear Jones say about the computer contract during the meeting?"

A second limitation of open questions is at the same time one of their benefits: they typically elicit less-than-comprehensive answers. The answers to open questions typically allow you to probe for omitted details, thereby allowing you to follow up with *closed questions* that probe for details according to their importance to your arguments.

Finally, you may tend to rely more on closed than open questions during background and scene-setting questioning. Usually you neither want nor will you be allowed by a judge to engage witnesses in an extensive review of their lives, and scene-setting questioning is ordinarily preparatory to the more significant testimony to come. Of course, exceptions exist. When qualifying witnesses as experts, for example, you may rely on open questions. Open questions such as, "Please describe your experience in the field of animal psychology" invite experts to do exactly what you pay them to do—impress judges and jurors with the experts' specialized knowledge.

2. CLOSED QUESTIONS

Closed questions focus on specific items of evidence. While closed questions do not suggest a desired answer, neither do they invite witnesses to describe events in their own words. Examples of closed questions include:

- "What color was the car?"

- "How long did this conversation last?"

- "What reason if any did the chicken give for crossing the road?"

- "You mentioned the word yute. What's a yute?"

- "When the tree fell, did you hear a noise?"

Closed questions are *attorney-centered* in that they allow you to direct witnesses to those aspects of events that support your arguments. Closed questions are important direct examination tools because (as mentioned above) witnesses do not ordinarily supply all your desired information in response to open questions (nor would you want them to!). Closed questions are natural follow-ups to open ones, allowing you to emphasize arguments by controlling the timing, scope and content of answers without leading.

For example, consider this open question and response:

Q: After you arrived at the wall, what happened?

A: Well, this odd-shaped person kept saying things like, "I'm going to jump. I'm going to jump." After a few minutes he pitched forward and fell all the way to the ground. By that time the king's men had arrived on their king's horses, but it was too late.

As is typical, the response to the open question is sufficiently rich to move the story forward credibly, yet conclusory enough to allow you to pursue additional details with closed questions. For example, assuming the details were important to your arguments, you might ask questions such as:

Q: You say the person was odd-shaped. What was his shape?

Q: What was his tone of voice when he yelled, "I'm going to jump?"

Q: Can you estimate how many king's horses were there?

Closed questions are also an effective way of steering witnesses around topics you want to omit from stories. (Despite the wording of the oath, witnesses are not capable of telling and rarely do you want them to tell the *whole* truth.) For example, assume that a witness has personal knowledge of case-related events that took place on the 1st, the 10th and the 20th of a month. The conversation of the 10th is unimportant to your arguments, so you'd like to move the testimony directly from the conversation of the 1st to that of the 20th. An open question might be ineffective. If you ask, "What happened next?" after concluding testimony about the conversation of the 1st, you're likely to hear about the conversation on the 10th. A closed question is probably a better choice: "Do you recall another conversation that took place on the 20th?"

3. NARRATIVE QUESTIONS

Narrative questions (or more precisely, "questions that call for a narrative response") are broad forms of open questions. Judges tend to regard open questions as calling for a narrative response when questions invite witnesses to describe a series of events that unfolded over time. Consider these examples:

"Please describe the events culminating in the contract."

"Tell us everything you can remember about the robbery."

"How did the final design of the spacecraft come about?"

If you are the direct examiner, you may value such questions because they are maximally witness-centered and invite witnesses to describe large portions of stories in their own words. However, those same qualities often lead judges to sustain objections to narrative questions. Beyond the basic fear of listening to lengthy answers from people who have not attended law school, judges also protect opposing counsel's right to know what information is sought, in case all or part of the information is objectionable. Yet no fixed line separates proper open questions from improper narrative ones. Federal Rule of Evidence 611 gives judges discretion when ruling on *calls for a narrative response* objections.

Judges are most likely to allow narrative responses by "professional" witnesses, such as forensic experts and police officers. Judges tend to trust such witnesses to answer succinctly and in accord with evidence rules. If you want to ask narrative questions of an ordinary lay witness, a judge might grant you similar latitude if you first show that the witness is similarly precise. Consider this example:

Q: Now, Ms. Ihori, where were you at about 6 P.M. on the afternoon of June 1?

A: I had just arrived at the Star and Garters Tavern, and was getting ready to work the evening shift.

Q: Please tell us what happened after you arrived.

Opp: Objection, the question calls for a narrative response.

Judge: Sustained.

Q: Were there any customers in the tavern when you arrived?

A: Two or three, as I recall. It was pretty quiet.

Q: Did you notice Ms. Ray, the lady seated over there?

A: As I recall, she entered the tavern shortly after I arrived.

Q: Did you see where she went after she entered the tavern?

A: She sat down in a booth near the jukebox.

Q: Did you approach her?

A: Yes, I went over to get her order.

Q: And then what happened?

Opp: Objection, question calls for a narrative response.

Judge: I'll allow it.

A: One of the customers. . .

The second "what happened" question is no less narrative in form than the first. But perhaps because the witness has demonstrated in response to narrow questions that she can be trusted to answer succinctly, the judge allows the critical information to emerge through a narrative response.

Judges may also permit *pseudo-narratives*. Pseudo-narratives ask witnesses to describe events in their own words, but contain subtle limiting features. Consider these questions:

- "Did anything *unusual* happen?"

- "What *next* occurred?"

- "*Then* what happened?"

The italicized words impose subtle limits. The first limits a witness to whatever was "unusual." (Of course, the question may puzzle the convenience store clerk who is testifying in the 57th robbery in which the clerk has been victimized.) The others suggest a temporal limit: the questions do not invite the witnesses to relate entire series of events. The subtle limits that pseudo-narratives impose can provide a useful way to elicit testimony in witnesses' own words while remaining within the rules.

Whether or not a question calls for one, your (or an adversary's) witness may launch into a narrative response. For example, a witness asked to estimate the speed of a car may begin to describe the entire accident and its aftermath. If you're conducting the direct examination, you may worry that the response will draw an objection and suggest that the witness is partisan and untrustworthy. Therefore you may interrupt the witness at an early convenient point. When the witness has stopped talking, ask another question and perhaps preface it with a remark such as "Please listen carefully to my questions and confine your answers to the questions." (Judges often permit attorneys to give such instructions to problem witnesses.) If your adversary's witness launches into an improper narrative response to a non-narrative question, again your first task is to get the witness to stop talking. The judge and especially the court reporter will appreciate your not trying to talk over witnesses. Perhaps you can stand up, say "excuse me" and hold up your palm in a "Stop" gesture. Then you may object that *The witness is narrating*, or that *There is no question pending*.

4. LEADING QUESTIONS

The basic principle of direct examination is that information is provided by witnesses' answers rather than lawyers' questions. Federal Rule of Evidence 611(c), the only federal rule of evidence specifically directed at forms of questions, advances this principle by maintaining the common law rule that generally forbids the use of leading questions on direct examination. Leading questions would frustrate the purpose of direct examination by allowing direct examiners to put words into the mouths of willing friendly witnesses. Although not clear from the text of the rule, its general prohibition of leading questions extends to re-direct examination.

Rule 611(c) allows leading questions when "necessary to develop the witness' testimony," and illustrations and analyses below help you to understand the vague language of this exception.

a. Leading Questions Defined

Questions are clearly leading when they constitute little more than assertions in question form. Consider these examples:

- "The car was red?" (asked in a questioning tone of voice)

- "Isn't it true that you never saw the document?"

- "A tree falling in a deserted forest still makes a sound, doesn't it?"

Questions need not be so obviously leading to qualify as improper during direct examination. *No matter what the form of a question, a judge may regard it as leading if it incorporates important evidence. Again, witnesses' answers and not your questions should provide important information.* For example, assume that an important issue in a car accident case concerns the color of the traffic signal at the time the defendant's car entered the intersection. You ask a witness:

"Had the light turned red before the defendant's car entered the intersection?"

For a second example, assume that you are the prosecutor in a robbery case in which the primary issue is the robber's identity. You ask an eyewitness:

"Is the defendant seated over there the person who grabbed the purse at gunpoint?"

Neither of these questions is leading in form, as neither asserts the questioner's desired answer. Nevertheless, as the light's color and the robber's identity are central to the outcomes of the cases, the questions are leading. Here are proper versions of the above questions:

- "To your personal knowledge, what was the color of the light when the defendant's car entered the intersection?"

- "Do you see the person who grabbed the purse at gunpoint in the courtroom?"

b. Legitimate Uses of Leading Questions

Given that substantive rules have developed exceptions to many of the Ten Commandments, the existence of exceptions to the "no leading questions on direct" rule should not surprise you.

Frederal Rule of Evidence 611(c) itself identifies an important exception: you may use leading questions when you conduct a direct examination of adverse parties, witnesses identified with adverse parties, or witnesses whose behavior (usually while testifying or during depositions) demonstrates that they are "hostile" to your client's claims. For example, suppose that you depose a person who happened to observe a traffic collision in which your client was involved. The witness has no formal ties to either party, but at deposition the witness' clipped answers, delays in answering, refusals to answer and snide retorts to questions demonstrated hostility to your client. If you nonetheless call the witness on direct examination (perhaps the witness can provide a key item of evidence supporting your arguments), you may ask the judge for permission to treat the witness as hostile for the purpose of asking leading questions.

Encompassed by the "except as necessary to develop the witness's testimony" language of Rule 611(c) are a variety of other legitimate uses of leading questions on direct examination. One circumstance in which judges typically allow the use of leading questions arises when witnesses have *testimonial infirmities* that make it difficult for them to testify in their own words. For example, young children may be too frightened by the courtroom atmosphere to choose their own words, and witnesses who are elderly or ill may not have the strength or attention span to do so. A judge may permit you to lead when it is evident that responding to leading questions is the only efficient or possible way for an otherwise-competent witness to testify.

Judges typically also allow you to use leading questions when you elicit *preliminary (undisputed) evidence.* In this situation, efficiency concerns outweigh an interest in rigid adherence to formal rules. For example, a judge may allow you to use leading questions during background questioning or scene-setting phases of a direct examination.

Example: Background Questioning

Q: Mr. Attila, you are a barbarian?

A: Yes.

Q: And you've been a barbarian for eight years?

A: That's right. Well, nine if you include my senior sacking and pillaging internship.

Example: Scene–Setting Questions

Assume that a dispute involves what took place during a certain meeting. The parties agree that the meeting took place and the general purpose for the meeting.

Q: You attended a meeting on the 26th of August, correct?

Q: The meeting took place in your office, right?

Q: Frick and Frack also were at that meeting?

Q: The purpose of the meeting was to discuss the buyout proposal?

Q: Now, please tell us what took place. . .

Another common practice allows the use of leading questions to *refresh witnesses' recollections.* Forgetfulness can have the durability of plastic bottles dumped into landfills; it can survive even the most ardent preparation sessions. If a judge can conclude from a witness' answers that the witness has first-hand knowledge but has forgotten an item of evidence or two, the judge will probably allow you to secure the evidence with a leading question. For example, assume that a witness has begun to describe the events leading up to an auto accident, and you expect the witness to testify that the defendant was talking on a mobile telephone at the time of the collision. You silently curse your fate as the witness has an unexpected failure of recollection, but use a leading question to get the information you are after:

Q: What else did you notice about the defendant's car?

A: I think that's about it, I'm not sure.

Q: I apologize if my question wasn't clear. I'm asking you about the driver of the blue car, and want you to tell us what else if anything you noticed about that driver.

A: Nothing that I can think of now.

Q: Well, did you see an object in the driver's hand?

A: I know there was something, I just don't remember.

Q: Could the driver of the blue car have been talking on a mobile phone?

A: Oh, that's right, the driver was talking on a mobile. Sorry, I just drew a blank for a second there.

Notice in this example that you don't jump to the ultimate leading question at the first indication of forgetfulness. Instead, you approach cautiously, like a cat circling an unknown object. The preliminary questions may stimulate recollection, obviating the need for a leading question. When necessary, however, you can often resort to a leading question.

You may also use leading questions to *lay evidentiary foundations*. This use is generally authorized by Federal Rule of Evidence 104(a), which provides in part that when determining the admissibility of evidence, a judge "is not bound by evidence rules, except those on privilege." For an example of this use of leading questions, assume that you want to offer a hearsay statement into evidence as an "excited utterance" under Federal Rule of Evidence 803(2). Questioning may go as follows:

1. Q: And what happened immediately after the collision took place?

2. A: I ran over to the pedestrian to check on whether she was badly hurt.

3. Q: Seeing a pedestrian struck by a car must have been frightening?

4. A: It really was.

5. Q: You were physically affected by what you saw?

6. A: Yes, I could feel my heart start racing. I was nervous and really stressed out.

7. Q: Did you say anything to the pedestrian while you were under this sense of stress?

8. A: Yes.

9. Q: Please tell us what you said to the pedestrian.

10. A: . . .

Questions No. 3 and 5 above are leading, but almost all judges would consider them proper because they establish the foundation for the admissibility of a hearsay assertion. Of course, if foundational evidence pertaining to important evidence is in dispute, a judge has discretion to insist that you follow the usual direct examination rules.

Another commonly-recognized use of leading questions is to *repeat testimony*, often for the purpose of getting everyone in the courtroom back "on track" with a story following an extended delay, perhaps for a recess or extended legal argument. You may proceed as in this example:

Q: Sorry, Ms. Resnik. I realize that, sitting in the witness chair for the last three weeks listening to legal argument, you've become something of an expert on the business records hearsay exception. Before the interruption, you testified that you designed the firm's accounts receivable computer program, correct?

A: Ah yes, I remember it well.

Q: And that you prepared the manual which is Defendant's Exhibit B?

A: Yes, that's right.

Q: And you explained how you trained Mr. Houston to use the program?

A: Yes.

Q: All right. Now let me ask you. . .

Finally, judges may allow you to *conclude* a direct examination with a leading question or two concerning a witness' most crucial testimony:

Q: To conclude, Mr. Tobias, you inspected the condensers immediately upon their arrival in the plant?

A: Yes.

Q: And you found none that were defective?

A: Correct.

Q: I have nothing further at this time.

The last two commonly-allowed uses of leading questions do not really conflict with the purpose of the rule that generally forbids the use of leading questions on direct examination. Since the questions refer to evidence that is already in the record, you are not inserting new evidence into the record in the guise of asking questions.

c. Leading Questions and Credibility

Ultimately, whatever their propriety, leading questions can be a poor choice because they tend to detract from witnesses' credibility. Consider this brief example:

Q: Mr. Wall, you live on Walnut St. in Walla Walla?

A: Yes.

Q: You were in the U–Serve U–Pay gas station on the afternoon of May 4?

A: Yes.

Q: A robbery took place at that time and place?

A: Yes.

Q: You were standing near the cashier when someone rushed in with a gun and demanded all the money in the register?

A: Yes, that's right.

Q: Did the person then take the money and run?

A: Yes.

Q: And the person you saw robbing the gas station is the person seated over there? (pointing to defendant)

A: Yes.

Evidence rules to the side, this examination offers a judge or juror no basis for believing the witness. The examination creates the impression that any utterance by the witness longer than one word might destroy the questioner's case. Imagine, for example, the stirring closing argument the prosecutor might make based on the testimony above:

"You remember the testimony of the eyewitness, Mr. Wall. He testified without hesitation, and I quote, 'Yes.' "

From this perspective, the worst direct may not be one filled with leading questions that repeatedly draw objections, but rather one filled with leading questions that do not.

D. GETTING STARTED

The subsections below explain, illustrate and analyze effective strategies for the opening stages of argument-centered narratives.

1. BACKGROUND QUESTIONS

Most direct examinations begin with information about a witness' personal background. Background questioning can bolster a witness' demeanor and confidence because people are generally less apt to display nervousness when they talk about themselves. Background questioning can also enhance a witness' credibility because the information portrays the witness as a real human being, not just an impersonal source of evidence. Admittedly, evidence pertaining to a witness' background is not strictly relevant under the definition of Federal Rule of Evidence 401. However, as the Advisory Committee's Note to the rule acknowledges, "Evidence which is essentially background in nature can scarcely be said to involve disputed matter, yet it is universally offered and admitted as an aid to understanding."

Personal background questioning is usually quite short. A judge is likely to permit questioning about where a witness lives, whether the witness is employed, and if so what the witness' job duties generally entail. You may also be able to elicit testimony about a witness' marital status, and whether the witness has children. Whether background questioning is more extensive (assuming you want it to be) is subject to a good dose of judicial discretion. At some point extensive background questioning shades over into "good character" evidence, which is generally inadmissible under Federal Rules of Evidence 404 and 608. For example, a judge may construe questions delving into a witness' charitable good works as an improper attempt to offer evidence of the witness' good character.

Background questioning is generally more than perfunctory in two common situations:

- You seek to qualify a witness as an expert under Federal Rule of Evidence 702. (See Chapter 11.)

- A lay witness' background is relevant to testimony. For example, assume that a lay witness will testify that a driver who was involved in an auto accident was going too fast to make a left turn safely. (Opinions such as these from lay witnesses are often admissible under Federal Rule of Evidence 701.) If the witness happens to be a race car driver, or for other reasons is experienced in judging car speeds and road conditions, more extensive background questioning is appropriate and likely to be admissible. For example, examine this potential background testimony:

1. Q: Ms. Gillig, how are you employed?

2. A: I work in the local British consulate offices.

3. Q: What are your general duties there?

4. A: I arrange visas, coordinate official visits, and often give talks to community groups about life in the UK.

5. Q: Where do you reside?

6. A: On Eastbourne Avenue, in the Larchmont section of the city.

7. Q: And how long have you resided there?

8. Opp: Objection. Irrelevant.

9. Judge: Counsel, any response to the objection?

10. Q: Yes, Your Honor. This matter involves an incident that occurred one block away from Ms. Gillig's residence. The length of time she has lived in the neighborhood bears on her familiarity with the scene of the accident and thus relates to her ability to observe and recall the events.

11. Judge: I'll allow it, but do move on.

12. Q: Ms. Gillig, do you remember the question?

13. A: Yes, I've lived there. . .

In the absence of a relationship between Question No. 7 and an issue in dispute, the objection may well have been sustained.

When information relating to a witness' background is relevant to a disputed issue, you might add to its impact by eliciting it along with the event to which it is relevant, rather than during the introductory phase of direct examination. In the example above, for instance, you might have delayed asking Gillig how long she lived in the neighborhood until you elicited testimony about the incident.

2. SCENE–SETTING QUESTIONS

Scene-setting questions typically mark the transition from background to story questioning. An ancient aphorism counsels that "All beginnings are hard," and this advice can apply to direct examinations. To understand the potential problems, consider this dialogue that might follow background questioning:

Q: Ms. Franklin, turning your attention to the afternoon of March 12, can you please describe what happened after you entered the jewelry store?

Opp: Objection. Vague; calls for a narrative response.

Judge: Sustained.

Q: Ms. Franklin, did you see the defendant commit a robbery on the afternoon of March 12?

Opp: Objection, leading.

Judge: Sustained.

Seemingly, you are caught between the Scylla of overly broad questions and the Charybdis of leading ones. Scene-setting questions can help you steer a steady course between these questioning pitfalls. The idea is to embark on the substance of testimony by asking about an *undisputed contextual aspect* of an event. Because the undisputed context is "preliminary matter," you can ask a leading question. A question or two about the context sets the scene, and direct is underway. Generally, at least one of the following details is likely to be undisputed:

* the event itself;

* the presence of a person who participated in that event; or

* the location of the event.

Thus, you can usually begin a direct examination by starting with a leading question referring to one of these contextual features. For example, return to the testimony of Ms. Franklin above. If the defense is mistaken identity, the defendant is unlikely to contest the fact that a robbery took place. Thus, you may set the scene for Franklin's testimony by calling her attention to the event itself:

Q: Ms. Franklin, I want to call your attention to a robbery that took place on March 12. Do you recall it?

A: I sure do.

Q: Where were you when that robbery took place?

A: I was in Spencer's Jewelry, on the corner of Market and Chestnut.

Q: With reference to the diagram that has previously been marked People's No. 3 for identification, can you please show us where you were in the store when you first became aware that a robbery was in progress?

A: Sure. . .

By incorporating an undisputed event in a leading question, you have seamlessly launched the story. Of course, if Ms. Franklin has been a lightning rod for robberies, your "event" question may have to be more specific:

Q: Ms. Franklin, I want to call your attention to a robbery you witnessed in which the robber was dressed as the Easter Bunny. Do you recall it?

If a party's presence at the scene of an event is undisputed, you may set the scene by calling a witness' attention to that party. For example, assume that the defendant admits to having been in Spencer's Jewelry Store on the afternoon it was robbed, but claims that he left the store before the robbery took place. In this circumstance, you may set the scene as follows:

Q: Ms. Franklin, I want to call your attention to the defendant, seated over here. Do you see him?

A: I do.

Q: Did you see him on the afternoon of March 12?

A: I did.

Q: Was that in Spencer's Jewelry Store?

A: Yes.

Q: Where were you when you first noticed the defendant?

A: I was. . .

If the "event" and "identity" are both in dispute, an alternative way to set a scene is to ask a witness about the location where the story begins:

Q: Ms. Franklin, I know this constant starting over is hard on you, but it's not easy being an example in Trial Advocacy in a Nutshell. Do you recall being in Spencer's Jewelry Store in early March of this year?

A: I do.

Q: Do you recall the date when you were in the store?

A: Yes, it was March 12.

Q: Did anything unusual happen while you were in the store on March 12?

A: Yes, I was in the store when it was robbed.

Q: With reference to the diagram that has previously been marked People's No. 3 for identification. . .

Once you've set a scene, one way to develop a story further is to use *scene-change* questions. Scene-change questions take you into the *action phase* of a story by asking witnesses to describe how the scene they have already testified to changed. Because the witness and not you testifies to the change, you avoid any issue of leading. You may proceed as follows:

1. Q: Ms. Franklin, did the clerk in the jewelry store continue to show watches to you?

2. A: No.

3. Q: Why not?

4. A: Because all of a sudden someone came up to her and said "This is a robbery. Keep quiet and do exactly what I say and no one will get hurt."

Question No. 1 is a scene-change question because you ask the witness to describe how if at all the scene that she initially set changed. In non-leading fashion, the scene-change question takes the story into its action phase. A witness' typically negative reply (No. 2) may also promote jurors' attention.

Remember that the scene-setting technique is one you can use throughout a direct examination. As a chronology proceeds and locales change, you may choose to precede action with foundational evidence that helps judges and jurors visualize the scenes where activities took place.

E. ARGUMENT-CENTERED STORIES

Despite the ritualized question/answer format of testimony and your need to conform testimony to rules of evidence, direct examinations are stories and many of the same principles that make for good stories make for good direct examinations. For example, as Chapter 2 explains, in direct examinations as in other types of stories, events generally emerge chronologically; details tend to make stories credible, understandable, vivid and memorable; and the stories appeal to listeners' hearts as well as their minds.

Yet the need to persuade judges and juries that stories prove (or prevent an adversary from proving) legal claims means that effective direct examinations are also *argument-centered*. That is, direct examinations stress substantively-critical events, marshal evidence according to the inferences you want judges and jurors to draw, and explain why events took place.

1. IMPORTANCE OF ARGUMENT-CENTERED DIRECT EXAMINATIONS

Judges routinely admonish jurors not to form opinions about cases until after they have heard all the evidence and arguments. If jurors (or judges, for that matter) routinely listened to evidence without evaluating the evidence or the witnesses who provide it, the utility of emphasizing and marshaling helpful evidence during direct examination would not be as great. You might then be satisfied with getting evidence into the record and then organizing it persuasively around legal claims during closing argument.

However, research by cognitive scientists indicates that all of us, including judges and jurors, evaluate information continuously as we take it in. Jurors generally make judgments about witnesses' credibility as they testify, organize evidence into stories as it emerges, and at least preliminarily evaluate those stories' legal merits. Argument-centered direct examinations respond to the simultaneous intake and evaluation of information by marshaling evidence so as to emphasize its credibility and inferential significance.

Argument-centered direct examinations also capitalize on the *mind set* phenomenon. The mind set phenomenon suggests that the impressions that judges and jurors begin to form as evidence emerges may be difficult to alter. For example, if a juror forms an initial impression that a witness lacks credibility, persuading that juror to believe the witness is an uphill battle. Test the mind set phenomenon yourself by comparing the impressions you get of the people described by the following sets of adjectives:

1. Generous, trustworthy, humorless, self-centered, obnoxious.

2. Obnoxious, self-centered, humorless, trustworthy, generous.

Both word sets contain the identical adjectives. Yet you may have formed a more favorable impression of No. 1 than No. 2, and if so the mind set phenomenon is the likely reason. No. 1 frontloads qualities that are likely to generate a positive mind set, and that initial mind set may have endured even as the negative qualities emerged.

Continuous evaluation of information combined with the mind set phenomenon support the desirability of argument-centered direct examinations. If you wait until closing argument to demonstrate the credibility and inferential significance of helpful evidence, your persuasive efforts may be too late.

2. ATYPICAL CHRONOLOGIES

Human minds are not like computers, and pristine chronologies are not always possible. You may nevertheless seek to elicit effective direct examination testimony by providing as much of a sense of order as is reasonably possible. For example, witnesses may not remember precise dates when case-related events span a long period of time. In such situations, even an approximate date can help a judge or juror understand a story:

"I'm not certain about when we first contacted Fledgling to talk about developing a spacecraft, but it was sometime in the early summer of two years ago."

Another way to provide a sense of chronology when witnesses are uncertain about dates is to clarify the relative order of events:

"I'm not sure when it happened, but I am certain that the chicken came before the egg."

"I can't remember exactly when he started parking in front of my house all the time, but I know it was before I started working for the child services agency."

When stories consist of separate strands of events that occur over roughly the same time period, you might organize stories according to *mini-chronologies*. That is, develop a separate chronology for each strand. For example, assume that the distribution of an allegedly defectively manufactured product is preceded by economic feasibility studies, design and manufacture of prototypes, consumer surveys, patent applications, and manufacture of the product. All of these pre-distribution events probably occurred simultaneously, not sequentially. A single chronology of all of them would probably be more confusing than helpful. Instead you might elicit mini-chronologies, asking witnesses who will testify to more than one type of pre-distribution activity to discuss each separately.

Finally, recognize that in a variety of circumstances, chronology is either impossible or unnecessary. For example, when events consist of numerous activities that transpire rapidly in a short span of time, you cannot feasibly ask witnesses to provide chronologies. For example, consider this question:

"In this clash between thousands of Ostrogoths and Visigoths, when the archer you've referred to as Leon exited his horse, was that before or after the 23rd cannon from the right was fired?"

Even testimony about topics discussed by the parties to a single conversation may not readily be ordered chronologically. In such situations, you can often help witnesses testify more effectively by treating an entire episode as a single event and eliciting details without regard to chronology. For example, when eliciting information about what was said by the parties to a conversation, you might proceed topically instead of chronologically. That is, ask topical questions (e.g., "What else did you talk about during this conversation?") rather than time-ordered ones (e.g., "What was the next topic you discussed?").

F. EMPHASIS TECHNIQUES

The subsections below explain and illustrate strategies that allow you to adhere to direct examination rules while emphasizing the portions of stories that support your legal contentions.

1. FRONT LOAD IMPORTANT EVENTS

While direct examination stories generally emerge chronologically, one way you can emphasize an important portion of a story is to *front load* it. That is, elicit an important portion of a story out of chronological order, typically early in a direct examination. Chronology is such a familiar pattern that a departure may itself capture a judge's or juror's attention. Moreover, by taking advantage of the *primacy principle,* an early departure from chronology allows you to elicit information at a time when a judge or juror may be paying particular attention to what a witness has to say.

For example, assume that you represent Derian, a defendant charged with murder. Derian contends that a gun went off accidentally while Derian and the alleged victim were playing a game. On direct examination, you want Derian to describe his relationship with the alleged victim, as the relationship helps to explain how and why the accident happened. However, your most important argument grows out of Derian's version of the accident itself. If you elicit events chronologically, the jury will not hear about the accident until after Derian describes the relationship. In this situation, you may choose to front load the accident by beginning Derian's direct examination with his account of the accident. You can then trace the relationship and the events leading up to the accident chronologically.

A variation of the front loading technique is to begin a direct with a summary reference to the evidence supporting your principle argument, and then proceed chronologically. You give a juror a "preview" of your version of a key event, which may heighten the juror's attention when you later cover the event in detail.

For example, assume that you represent the defendant in a libel action. Your client is a gossip columnist for a tabloid paper. The columnist allegedly damaged a celebrity's career by writing falsely that the celebrity had had a normal upbringing and had always been a faithful spouse and caring parent. Your client's defense is that the allegedly libelous language was not in the column when your client submitted it to the publisher for the final time. To emphasize the key portion of your client's story while deviating only momentarily from chronology, you might begin the direct examination as follows:

(Preliminaries have concluded)

Q: Let me begin by handing you Plaintiff's Exhibit No. 1, the article. Do you recognize it?

A: Yes, this appears to be the article in its published form.

Q: Do you see the underlined language, "Attila Jr. had a normal upbringing, and has always been a faithful spouse and caring parent."

A: I do.

Q: Did you write those words?

A: I did not.

Q: Were they in the column as you finally submitted it to your publisher?

A: They were not.

Q: OK. Let's go back now to when you first started to work on the story. . .

This sequence of testimony elevates your client's denial to the beginning of direct examination, but saves detailed testimony about this portion of your client's story for its proper sequence in the chronology.

2. LAYERED QUESTIONING

Layered questioning is an approach of emphasizing important events by pursuing them through a combination of open and closed questions. A typical pattern of layered questioning may proceed as follows:

- Begin to focus on an event with a closed question.

- Use one or more open questions to reveal information about the event in a witness' own words.

- Return to closed questions to emphasize additional event-related details.

By shifting back and forth between closed and open questions you reveal the layers of important events that witnesses can recall without using leading questions or asking questions that have been "asked and answered."

For example, assume that you represent the plaintiff in a negligence suit growing out of a traffic accident. You conduct the direct examination of a passerby. A portion of the direct may go as follows:

1. Q: And what is the next thing that you saw?

2. A: The defendant was talking on a mobile phone.

3. Q: Were you able to see the defendant's hands?

4. A: Yes.

5. Q: Please describe for us what you saw.

6. A: Well, only the defendant's left hand was on the steering wheel. He had a phone in his right hand and he was holding it up to his ear. He moved the phone away from his ear a couple of times when he looked down.

7. Q: What do you mean by "he looked down?"

8. A: As he was driving in my direction, I saw him glance down towards his lap. At the same time, I saw the hand holding the phone also move down in the direction of his lap. I couldn't see his lap, of course.

9. Q: How many times did you see him glance down towards his lap?

10. A: Two times for sure.

11. Q: How is it you paid close enough attention to notice how the defendant was driving?

12. A: I was just starting to cross the street. When I saw the defendant was talking on a mobile phone, I kept my eyes on him because I didn't want to cross until we made eye contact.

13. Q: With reference to the first time you saw the defendant glance down towards his lap, please describe as best you can what you saw.

14. A: OK. . .

In this excerpt, you intersperse open and closed questions to ferret out information about a defendant's driving in the moments just prior to an accident. You follow up a closed question (No. 3) with an open one (No. 5) asking the witness to elaborate on the previous answer (No. 4) in the witness' own words. No. 7 is also an open question that asks the witness to elaborate further on a previous answer. No. 9 is a closed question, and you follow it up with an open question (No. 13). While probing for these important details, you also bolster the witness' credibility by demonstrating that the witness had a reason to observe the defendant's driving. (Nos. 11–12). By using closed questions to focus the witness on specific details and open questions to elicit additional information about those details in the witness' own words, you peel away the layers of the event in a way that allows you to bolster credibility and emphasize the evidence supporting your desired inferences.

3. "NO, NO, NO" TECHNIQUE

An effective strategy for emphasizing what *did* happen is to ask a series of closed questions about what did *not* happen. For example, assume that you represent a patient who claims that Doctor Rex botched a knee replacement operation and failed to

disclose the surgical risks. A portion of your questioning of the patient may go as follows:

Q: And what happened during the consultation?

A: We looked at the X rays of my knee and Dr. Rex
said that because the entire miniscus in both of my
knees was gone, arthroscopic procedures wouldn't
help and that I needed total knee replacements.

Q: Did Dr. Rex say anything to you during this
consultation about the risks of knee replacement surgery?

A: He just said that I was a great candidate for the
surgery, and that I'd be able to resume normal activity within a few weeks after the surgery.

Q: Did Dr. Rex advise you of any risks connected to
the surgery?

A: He just said there was a very slight chance of infection, as with any surgery.

Q: Did Dr. Rex say anything more about the risk of
infection?

A: No.

Q: Did Dr. Rex mention anything about the risks of
replacing both knees at the same time?

A: No.

Q: Did Dr. Rex say anything during this consultation about the effect of replacing both knees at the same time on the recovery time?

A: No.

Q: Other than the risk of infection, did Dr. Rex say anything to you at all about the risks of doing two knee replacements at once?

A: No.

Here, the series of "No's" in response to questions about the risks that the doctor should have but neglected to mention emphasize the patient's account of what did happen.

4. POINTS OF REFERENCE ("LOOPS")

Point of reference questions allow you to emphasize already-given testimony by incorporating the testimony in a subsequent question. Use the strategy judiciously, lest a judge conclude that you are testifying in the guise of asking questions, or unfairly gilding the lily. This technique is sometimes called "looping," as the point of reference in a question loops back to a previous answer.

For example, consider this direct examination excerpt:

1. Q: What happened next?

2. A: The other guy ran behind a truck. He reappeared a few moments later with brass knuckles on his right hand.

3. Q: After he reappeared with the brass knuckles, what happened?

In No. 3, you ask the witness to move ahead with the chronology. The point of reference or "loop" ("after he reappeared with the brass knuckles") serves to clarify the chronology while emphasizing that portion of the story.

Instead of moving a witness forward in a chronology, you can also use the point of reference strategy to elicit additional details about existing events. For example:

1. Q: What happened next?

2. A: The other guy ran behind a truck. He reappeared a few moments later with brass knuckles on his right hand.

3. Q: Can you describe these brass knuckles that you say he reappeared with?

You can also use the point of reference technique to clarify ambiguous testimony. For example, a witness describing the converging paths of six cars into an intersection may testify, "That car was going 35 m.p.h." Or, describing a dispute between two women, a witness may testify, "She called her a no-good endomorph." Such ambiguities are likely to confuse everyone in the courtroom, including you. Points of reference questions can clear up ambiguities like these:

Q: You testified that a car was traveling at a speed of 35 m.p.h. To which car were you referring?

Q: Which woman called the other a no-good endomorph?

Finally, you might use a point of reference to emphasize precisely where your and your adversaries' stories differ. Examine this excerpt:

Q: If Mr. Shakespeare testified earlier that the soup contained eye of newt and toe of frog, wool of bat and tongue of dog, would you agree with him?

A: No, definitely not. The actual contents were . . .

The point of reference allows you to juxtapose your client's version of events with that of your adversary. By referring to Shakespeare's testimony in the form of a question, you avoid improperly making an assertion in the guise of asking a question.

5. BASES OF CONCLUSIONS AND OPINIONS

Much of what passes for factual information in everyday life tends to be vague and conclusory in the courtroom, when judges and jurors scrutinize testimony in the light of conflicting stories. For example:

- In a personal injury case, a plaintiff testifies that "my back has hurt me ever since the accident."

- In a will contest case based on a testator's incompetence, a friend may testify that the testator "was very forgetful during the last two years of her life."

- In a landlord-tenant breach of warranty of habitability case, a tenant may testify that "the ceiling leaked whenever it rained."

- In a wrongful discharge case, an employee testifies that the plaintiff "was really surprised when she got the promotion."

Each of the above excerpts constitutes *second level testimony*. That is, each is an opinion or a conclusion based on underlying data. While the opinion or conclusion might be admissible under Federal Rule of Evidence 701, you can present a more persuasive story by eliciting the underlying observations as well. For instance:

- Ask the plaintiff with the bad back for illustrative examples of when the pain was noticeably bad.

- Ask the testator's friend for illustrative examples of the testator's forgetfulness.

- Ask the tenant to describe the leaky ceiling and its consequences on specific rainy days.

- Ask the employee to testify to the behavior that led the employee to conclude that the wrongful discharge plaintiff was surprised by the promotion and how the plaintiff manifested surprise.

Eliciting data underlying conclusions and opinions about important topics is an effective way of developing argument-centered narratives.

6. EXHIBITS

Illustrating stories with tangible exhibits is an effective and increasingly almost necessary strategy for bolstering witnesses' credibility and supporting your desired inferences. Many exhibits constitute *real evidence*, such as the weapon used in a crime or the contract that was allegedly breached. Other exhibits are *demonstrative,* meaning that they are illustrative of testimony and created for the purposes of trial. Examples include a hand-drawn diagram of the intersection where a traffic accident occurred, and (more expensively) a computerized depiction of the process resulting in the manufacture and sale of an allegedly defective product. For further discussion of exhibits, see Chapter 10.

The "C*SI* Effect." Many prosecutors claim the existence of a "*CSI* Effect." *CSI (Crime Scene Investigations)* is at the time of writing a popular dramatic television series in which the stories focus on the role of forensic scientists in solving crimes. Prosecutors often complain that jurors who watch shows like *CSI* are reluctant to convict unless the prosecutors offer evidence from forensic experts, even though such evidence is non-existent, unnecessary or prohibitively expensive. Whether a *"CSI* Effect" is real or imagined is unknown.

7. VERBALIZING GESTURES

Witnesses may respond to questions with gestures that are meaningful only to someone watching the testimony. To clarify the record (e.g., for the benefit of the court reporter and appellate court judges) and to emphasize testimony, convert gestures to verbal evidence. Consider this frequent situation:

Q: Did the defendant respond to your comment?

A: (The witness responds by shaking her head up and down.)

In this situation, you might follow up simply by asking the witness to answer verbally:

Q: Can you please answer the question "yes" or "no" so the record is clear?

Alternatively, when a gesture is unambiguous a judge may allow you to clarify a non-verbal response yourself: "For the record, the witness shook her head up and down to indicate that the answer is 'yes.' "

A common variation of this situation is as follows:

Q: Did the defendant respond to your comment?

A: Uh huh.

Responses such as "uh huh" and "uh uh" are inherently ambiguous. To provide clarity and emphasis, follow up as if the witness had responded with a non-verbal head shake.

The situation can become more complex when witnesses testify to distances by referring to the courtroom, or explain events with gestures. For example, consider the following bit of testimony:

Q: How far from Mr. Dumpty were you when he fell?

A: About from me to you.

The answer is only intelligible to those inside the courtroom. Again, you might provide clarity and emphasis by asking the witness to restate the distance verbally:

Q: Can you tell us in feet approximately what the distance was?

Realize, however, that witnesses can be notoriously bad at estimating distances. Asked to estimate the distance verbally, the witness above may say something like "I'd guess about 20 yards." If that's way off, the strategy creates a conflict between the two responses. A useful strategy for avoiding such conflicts is for you to put your own estimate in the form of a question. Thus, the dialogue above may have gone as follows:

Q: How far from Mr. Dumpty were you when he fell?

A: About from me to you.

Q: Would you say that's a distance of about 10 feet?

Alternatively, you might respond to the answer, "About from me to you," by saying, "Let the record reflect that the witness indicated a distance of about 10 feet." A statement like this neither leads the witness nor constitutes attorney testimony, because you merely clarify the testimony.

Many courtrooms have a chart indicating the distance from the witness box to various points in the courtroom. In this situation, you might follow an answer such as, "About from me to you," by asking the judge to consult the chart and indicate for the record the distance referred to by the witness.

The problem of translating witnesses' gestures to words becomes stickier when gestures pertain to a "dynamic" activity. For example, assume that while physically describing a fight, a witness testifies that, "She went like this, and he did this, then she put her arm up under here, and his head snapped back like this." Even the best play-by-play sports announcer couldn't paint a complete verbal picture of the fight. In such situations, consider a "freeze frame" approach. As the witness physically simulates a dynamic event, stop the action at key points and verbally describe the witness' position at each point: "You're indicating now that the woman was standing almost directly behind the man; her right arm was around his neck, forcing his face upward at an angle of about 45 degrees, and her left hand was around the man's left wrist, and she was holding his left arm behind him bent at the elbow, in what you might call a half-nelson hold. Is that about right? Were you playing Twister?"

8. SILENT ARGUMENTS

As you know from Chapter 5, silent arguments are tacit inferential conclusions that jurors may arrive at based on preconceptions and stereotypes.   If you think it likely that your client or witness will be victimized by a silent argument, direct examination gives you an opportunity to address it. You'll need to identify the source of the preconception or stereotype, and if possible offer testimony that may counter it.

For instance, assume that your client Joan is a debt collector. You worry that some jurors will distrust Joan because of a preconception that debt collectors use devious collection practices to extract more money than they deserve. While you may not eliminate these jurors' general bias, you might elicit evidence from Joan that might cause them not to tar her with the bias. For example, examine this bit of testimony:

Q: What happened next?

A: I sent the debtor a letter explaining that our only remaining option was to attach the bank account.

Q: Why did you send this letter?

A: My business practice is to advise consumers of the steps I can take in an effort to work out a payment schedule whenever possible.

Such testimony may incline jurors to view your client as an exception to the general rule about debt collectors' behavior and to evaluate the evidence fairly without regard to the preconception.

G. CONCLUDING DIRECT EXAMINATIONS

The *recency* principle suggests that judges and jurors may be particularly attentive to the final few questions and answers of a direct examination. To take advantage of possibly heightened attentiveness, (a) clue jurors in to the fact that the end is 'nigh, and (b) conclude directs on important points.

An effective strategy for accomplishing these goals is to return to one or two key pieces of evidence that a witness has already provided. So long as it is clear that you are concluding a direct examination, judges often allow the questions over an objection that the questions have been asked and answered. This is often a situation in which the formalism of evidence rules gives way to rhetorical function of trials. For an example of how you might conclude direct examination, consider this brief excerpt:

Q: Just a couple of more questions, Ms. Woods. Again, how many weeks of work did you miss?

A: Sixteen.

Q: And what was your family's income during those sixteen weeks?

A: Nothing.

Q: No further questions at this time.

When you promise a "couple of questions," be sure to abide by your promise!

H. REDIRECT EXAMINATION

Under Federal Rule of Evidence 611, judges have discretion with regard to allowing re-direct examination and its extent. The purpose of redirect is not for you to rehash witnesses' entire stories, but rather to allow you to delve into topics that arose for the first time on cross examination or to clarify events that cross examination may have muddied. Because redirect examination typically targets specific topics, opportunities for story-telling on redirect are limited. However, if a cross examiner skips back and forth in time in an effort to confuse a witness, a judge may allow you to clarify the chronology by taking the witness back through the sequence of events.

A frequent use of redirect examination is to elicit explanations for inconsistencies that emerge during cross. For example, assume that you are the prosecutor in a robbery case, and that during direct examination your eyewitness identified the defendant as the robber. The cross examiner elicits evidence that shortly after the robbery, the eyewitness told the police, "I probably couldn't identify the robber—I didn't get a very good look." If the witness has an explanation, and you didn't surface the inconsistency and explanation during direct examination, redirect is your opportunity to allow the witness to explain:

Q: Why did you tell the police that you probably couldn't identify the robber?

A: It was right after the robbery, I was really scared and my first reaction was not to get involved.

Q: Was that statement you made to the police accurate?

A: No. As I testified earlier, I got a full face view of the defendant for a couple of seconds.

Q: And why are you willing to identify the defendant here in court today?

A: I've thought about it, and I want to do what's right.

Q: Is there any doubt in your mind about the defendant's being the person who robbed the store?

A: None whatsoever.

As mentioned above, the general policy that redirect examination is limited to topics that arose during cross generally prevents you from exploring topics that you overlooked during direct and that did not arise during cross. If you want to explore new topics on redirect, consider asking the judge for "permission to re-open the direct examination." If the information you neglected to elicit is sufficiently important, a judge has the power under Federal Rule of Evidence 611 to grant the request. Naturally, if your request is granted, opposing counsel can conduct re-cross examination with respect to the new evidence.

I. SAMPLE DIRECT EXAMINATIONS

This section provides analyses of three different direct examinations. While in actual cases testimony will be more extensive, the same principles apply.

SAMPLE DIRECT EXAMINATION NO. 1

Assume that you are the prosecutor in a murder case in which the defense is mistaken identity. Your witness Marcus Nieman is to testify that he saw the defendant at the crime scene. After background questioning concludes, the testimony proceeds as follows:

1. Q: Mr. Nieman, calling your attention to the date of March 31 of last year, at around 6:00 P.M., where were you at that time?

2. A: I was taking my dog Cinders for the regular evening constitutional, and I was on the block next to where I live.

3. Q: Do you recall the name of the street?

4. A: Yes, Nutmeg Street.

5. Q: Can you please briefly describe that part of Nutmeg Street?

6. A: OK. It's all residential, mostly older apartment buildings two or three stories high. The street was quiet that afternoon. Just an occasional car went by and the only person I saw was her. (pointing to the defendant)

7. Q: What side of Nutmeg were you on at that time?

8. A: Well, it's a north-south street, I was walking north along the east side of the street.

9. Q: Were you on a sidewalk?

10. A: Yes.

11. Q: Does anything separate the sidewalk from the roadway?

12. A: Yes, a strip of grass. I think it's called a parkway. It's not too wide, about 10 feet wide I'd say.

13. Q: Did you finish the walk as you regularly do?

14. A: No. I saw that lady over there (pointing to the defendant) run out of a car and into one of the apartment buildings.

15. Q: How far from the defendant were you when you saw her run out of the car?

16. A: No more than 20 feet, I'd estimate. About the same distance as from me to you.

17. Q: What was the lighting like?

18. A: It was twilight, not yet dark. I had no trouble seeing her.

19. Q: Did anything obstruct your view of the defendant?

20. A: No. She stopped the car on the side of the street I was walking on, so there was nothing between me and her when she ran out of the car.

21. Q: Are there any trees along the parkway?

22. A: Yes, all along the block. But there weren't any of them between me and her.

23. Q: Can you describe the car that you say the defendant ran out of?

24. A: It was dark, a sedan type, I can't tell you more than that.

25. Q: When did you first notice the defendant?

26. A: When she stopped the car next to the curb. I noticed her because she stopped really abruptly just a

few feet in front of me off to the left of where I was walking.

27. Q: Could you see the defendant's face before she got out of the car?

28. A: No. I was behind her car and I couldn't see much inside it.

29. Q: Please describe exactly what you saw after the defendant ran out of the sedan.

30. A: She ran out the driver's side of the car and she had a gun in her left hand. That really shook me up. I remembered I'd just walked past a tree, so I ran over to it and hid behind it. From there I watched her run into one of the apartment houses on the east side of the street, the side I was walking on.

31. Q: If you hid behind a tree, how is it you were able to see the defendant?

32. A: I poked my head out from behind the tree.

33. Q: OK, before you ran to the tree, did you see the defendant's face?

34. A: Yes. She ran towards the houses in front of her car, and I could clearly her face from the side. Her face wasn't blocked by the car or anything.

35. Q: How long did you look at her before you ran to the tree?

36. A: A couple of seconds, I'd say.

37. Q: Did you see her again after you hid behind the tree?

38. A: Yes. When I poked my head out to see what was going on, I could still see a little of her face from the side and back. After that I just saw her running from behind.

39. Q: How was she dressed?

40. A: I remember she was wearing what looked like tennis shoes, jeans and a short dark jacket.

41. Q: Did she have a hat on?

42. A: No.

43. Q: Can you tell us which building she ran into?

44. A: At the time I just noticed that it was a three story brick building. I went back later to check the address, it's 11358 Nutmeg.

45. Q: Can you tell us anything more about the gun?

46. A: I can tell you that it was a semi-automatic pistol.

47. Q: And how could you tell that?

48. A: I've owned semi-automatics in the past, and I often go to shooting ranges and fire different kinds of weapons.

49. Q: What happened after the defendant ran into the building?

50. A: I had forgotten to take along my cell phone, so I had to run back to my place to call the police. The dog wasn't too happy about finishing the walk early. By the time I went back a couple of hours later, the police were there and the building had been sealed off.

51. Q: Mr. Nieman, please look at the defendant and tell us whether she is the person you saw run out of the car with a gun and go into 11358 Nutmeg.

52. A: She is.

53. Q: No further questions at this time.

Analysis

1. The major events in Nieman's story emerge chronologically. He is walking a dog when he sees the defendant pull her car over to the curb, run out of the car and enter a building. After the defendant goes into the building, Nieman goes home to call the police. Yet deviations from chronology explain the story and add to its credibility. Nieman explains his background with guns in the context of his identification of the type of gun the defendant carried (Nos. 45–48). And, Nieman doesn't mention that he forgot his cell

phone until he explains why he went home to call the police (No. 50).

2. Scene-setting questions (Nos. 1–12) provide a backdrop of the events. In an actual case, of course, you might seek to add greater visual impact to the story with a diagram, a photo blowup or other form of visual aid. No. 13 is a scene-change question.

3. The examination is argument-centered in that it marshals and thereby emphasizes Nieman's credibility and the evidence supporting your desired inference that the defendant was the armed person who ran into the apartment house where a murder took place. With respect to credibility, the testimony refers to several factors suggesting that Nieman had a good opportunity to observe the defendant (Nos. 16–22). Moreover you suggest Nieman's fairness and honesty by eliciting his inability to see the defendant before she got out of the car (Nos. 27–28). With respect to your desired inference, the bulk of the testimony (Nos. 29–42) bolsters your argument that the defendant is the person who Nieman saw.

4. The direct examination incorporates explanatory evidence. Nieman explains why he happened to notice the defendant in the first place (No. 26), and why he recognized the weapon she carried as a semi-automatic (Nos. 45–48).

5. You conclude the examination on a strong note by asking the witness to repeat the identification (Nos. 51–52).

SAMPLE DIRECT EXAMINATION NO. 2

This second direct examination example grows out of a civil case in which the plaintiff Don Evans has sued defendant Joanne Jones for fraudulent concealment. Evans alleges that Jones intentionally neglected to disclose that the roof of the house that Jones sold to Evans leaked and needed to be replaced. Jones claims that she did tell Evans that the roof leaked even after she'd repaired it. You represent the defendant Jones, and a portion of her direct examination goes as follows:

1. Q: Now Ms. Jones, I'd like to direct your attention to the second time the plaintiff came by to look at the house, on June 3. Do you recall that event?

2. A: I do.

3. Q: How did that visit come about?

4. A: Mr. Evans had called the day before and told me that he liked the house when he'd seen it a few days earlier. He said he liked the idea that neither of us had a broker, we could both save some money that way. He wanted to know if he could stop by to see it again after work. I said that would be fine, and it was sometime between 5:30 and 6:00 when he came by.

5. Q: Can you briefly describe what took place when the plaintiff came to the house on June 3?

6. A: He walked through the house by himself for a few minutes. He said he wanted to make sure that

his memory of what it looked like was accurate. Then we walked through it together. He had some questions about the neighborhood, what it was like, where I shopped, that sort of thing. We ended up in the kitchen, and that's when we agreed on the sale terms.

7. Q: Did you talk to the plaintiff about the condition of the roof on June 3?

8. A: Definitely. I told him that the roof had leaked during some heavy rains in January, and that I'd hired a roofing company to patch it. I also told him that after it was repaired I had a small leak in the same area during a particularly heavy storm in February, but that on the other days it had rained I hadn't had any problems.

9. Q: Ms. Jones, let me ask you a few questions about the condition of the roof before you sold the house to the plaintiff. When did you first have a problem with it?

10. A: It would have been in January, about six months before I sold it to Mr. Evans. It started leaking during a heavy rain storm.

11. Q: When you say it leaked, what do you mean?

12. A: A steady drip in the corner of the ceiling in the second bedroom.

13. Q: What did you do when you noticed the leak?

14. A: Well, of course I put a bucket under it and tried to keep things as dry as I could. And I called a roofing company that a neighbor recommended, Lopez Roofing Company.

15. Q: What happened next with respect to the leak?

16. A: It took a couple of days before someone from the roofing company came out, because they had to wait until it stopped raining. But they repaired the roof a couple of days later. (Jones testifies that she paid for the work, and you offer the receipt for the roof repair into evidence. It was signed by "Johnson" on behalf of the company.)

17. Q: Did Mr. Johnson say anything about your needing a new roof?

18. A: No. He actually said the roof generally seemed in good condition and to call again if I had any more problems.

19. Q: Was that it so far as problems with the roof are concerned?

20. A: Actually, no. There were a few days of pretty heavy rain in early February, and one of those days I came home to find that I still had a very small leak in the same bedroom. I called Lopez Roofing again, but got a recorded message that the phone had been disconnected and there was no new number.

21. Q: Did you contact a different roofing company?

22. A: No. I was going to, but the leak stopped. It rained on quite a few days later in February and during March, but the ceiling never leaked again. I figured that whatever the problem was, it had fixed itself.

23. Q: When did you decide to sell the house?

24. A: I'd thought about selling it for over a year. I'd been notified that I'd been left a pretty large inheritance from a relative and I thought it would be fun to live in a larger house that was closer to the city center. But I didn't list it for sale until May, after I'd actually gotten the money.

25. Q: Did you use a real estate broker?

26. A: No.

27. Q: Why not?

28. A: I really wasn't in a huge hurry to sell. I wanted to take my time looking at other neighborhoods, so I thought I'd just put it on the market myself and see what happened. I have a friend who's a broker, and she said I could check with her if I ran into any snags.

29. Q: After you put it on the market, what happened?

30. A: Quite a few people came by. Most were the usual looky-loos, but I had a few people other than Mr. Evans who were seriously interested.

31. Q: Can you remember any of their names?

32. A: There was an Edgar Allen and a James Fenimore. One or two others, but I remember I had serious discussions about the price with them.

33. Q: When did you first meet the plaintiff?

34. A: Mr. Evans came by on May 27. When I had an open house I had a signup sheet for visitors to sign, so I know that's the date.

35. Q: What can you recall about meeting him for the first time?

36. A: I showed him through the house. He asked some questions about the house, like how old it was, how old the water heater was, whether it had copper pipes, those kinds of questions. But mostly he seemed interested in the general layout. Square footage, how many bedrooms, the size of the yard, whether he'd be able to add on another bedroom, that sort of thing.

37. Q: Do you recall any discussion about the roof on May 27?

38. A: No. I don't think it came up, and at that point I didn't know if he was a serious purchaser. He stayed for about 10–15 minutes, and he said he'd think about it and contact me again if he was really interested.

39. Q: And did you meet with the plaintiff again?

40. A: Yes, on June 3. That's the meeting I mentioned before, when we talked about the roof.

41. Q: Please tell us what happened during this meeting.

42. A: We walked through the house again. Mr. Evans said he'd seen quite a few houses and liked mine a lot. He made an offer that was pretty close to what I was prepared to accept, so we didn't have to haggle very much about that.

43. Q: After you had agreed on a price, what happened?

44. A: He said that he would have his inspector go through the house, and that the sale was contingent on whether everything checked out OK.

45. Q: How did you respond?

46. A: I said that was fine with me, I'd never buy a house without having an inspector go through it. I told him to have the inspector contact me so we could make a definite appointment.

47. Q: Did you and the plaintiff talk about anything else on June 3?

48. A: Yes. He asked me if I'd had any problems in particular with the house. I told him that it had generally been a great house, not a lot of problems at all. I told him that I'd had a leak in the second bedroom

in January, but that I'd had the roof patched and that so far as I could tell the roof was fine.

49. Q: Did you tell the plaintiff anything else about the roof?

50. A: Yes, I mentioned that a small leak had re-appeared in February, after the roof had been patched, but then it hadn't leaked any more after that even though there'd had been a lot more rainy days.

51. Q: How did the plaintiff respond to what you told him about the roof?

52. A: He said that it didn't sound like a major problem, and he was glad I'd said something because he'd make sure his inspector checked out the roof carefully.

53. Q: Ms. Jones, if you thought the roof problem had been taken care of, why did you mention it to the plaintiff?

54. A: I wanted to be honest, because I wasn't 100% sure that the roof was OK. And I figured the inspector would notice that the roof had been recently patched, so I didn't want Mr. Evans to think I was trying to hide anything. And if I had to knock a bit off the sale price for roof repair, I could live with that.

55. Q: Is there any reason in particular that you can remember talking to the plaintiff about the roof on June 3?

56. A: Yes. I remember we talked about the roof when we were in the spare bedroom, and I pointed out where the leak had been.

57. Q: Earlier you mentioned that Edgar Allen and James Fenimore were serious potential buyers. Do you remember whether you mentioned the roof problem to them?

58. A: I did. I told them about the leaks and the repair, just as I did with Mr. Evans.

59. Q: Do you recall having your deposition taken by counsel for plaintiff?

60. A: Yes, of course.

61. Q: Do you remember that plaintiff's counsel asked you at that time whether you had mentioned the roof problem to other potential purchasers?

62. A: Yes. I testified then that I couldn't remember the names of other potential purchasers.

63. Q: So how is it that you are now able to testify that you mentioned the roof problem to Edgar Allen and James Fenimore?

64. A: I had put their names in a computer file that I stopped updating and deleted months before the deposition. So at the deposition I just couldn't remember the names of other potential purchasers. At your request I found out how to access the deleted file, and that's why now I can remember their names.

65. Q: Now, at some point did a house inspector contact you?

66. A: Yes. . .

Analysis

1. Ms. Jones' story of the sale is generally chronological. However, you "frontload" her testimony that she discussed the leaky roof with Evans (Nos. 7–8) and then return to this topic in more detail at its proper point in the chronology (Nos. 48–58). Thus, you retain the benefits of chronology while taking advantage of the *primacy principle.* The primacy principle suggests that listeners are likely to be especially attentive to and have greater recall of information they hear at the beginning of a presentation. The organization emphasizes your key argument that Mr. Evans was aware of the problems with the roof.

2. The testimony is argument-centered in that it: (a) emphasizes the event in which your client disclosed the problems she'd had with the roof (Nos. 5–8; 40–56); (b) supports the credibility of your client's story by explaining that she didn't have a motive to conceal the roof problem and that she expected the inspection to reveal the problem (No. 54); and providing a reason for remembering the discussion (Nos. 55–56); and (c) bolsters the inference that your client revealed the problem to Evans by emphasizing that she is honest (No. 54) and had mentioned the roof problem to other prospective purchasers (Nos. 57–58).

3. Nos. 59-64 illustrate the "take the sting out of cross" technique. Anticipating that opposing counsel will cross examine your client about inconsistent deposition testimony, you elicit the inconsistency yourself and ask your client to explain why it occurred.

SAMPLE DIRECT EXAMINATION NO. 3

This illustrative direct examination consists of Atticus Finch's direct examination of Tom Robinson in the film *To Kill a Mockingbird* (1962). In this classic tragic story, poor black sharecropper Tom Robinson is charged with raping Mayella Ewell, a white woman, in a small southern town in the 1930's. In front of a hostile all-white jury, Finch takes on the hopeless task of defending Robinson. Finch's direct examination of Robinson is set forth below.

1. Q: Now Tom, were you acquainted with Mayella Violet Ewell?

2. A: Yes sir. I had to pass her place going to it from the field every day.

3. Q: Is there any other way to go?

4. A: No sir, none's I know of.

5. Q: And did she ever speak to you?

6. A: Why yes, sir. I tipped my hat when I go by. Then one day she asked me to come in and bust up a shifarobe for her. She gave me the hatchet and I

broke it up. And then she said I reckon I'll have to give you a nickel, won't I?

7. Q: I said, "No ma'am, there ain't no charge."

8. A: Then I went home. Mr. Finch, that was way last spring, way over a year ago.

9. Q: And did you ever go on the place again?

10. A: Yes sir.

11. Q: When?

12. A: Well, I, I went lots of times. It seemed like every time I passed by yonder, she'd have some little something for me to do, chopping kindling and toting water for her.

13. Q: Tom, what happened to you on the evening of August 21st, last year?

14. A: Mr. Finch, I was going home as usual that evening, when I passed the Ewell place, with Mayella on the porch, like she said she was. And she said for me to come there and help her a minute. Well, I went inside the fence and I looked around for some kindling to work on, but I didn't see none. And then she said to come in the house, she has a door needs fixing, so I follows her inside and I looked at the door, and it looked all right. Then she shut the door. All the time, I was wondering why it was so quietlike. Then it come to me. There was not a child on the place. And I said, Miss Mayella, where are the

children. She said, they all gone to get ice cream. She said it took her a slap year to save seven nickels, but she done it, and they all gone to town.

15. Q: What did you say then?

16. A: Uh, I said something like, uh, "Why Miss Mayella, that's right nice of you to treat 'em." She said, "You think so?" "Well," I said, "I best be going." I couldn't do nothing for her and she said Oh yes I could, and I asked her what. And she said to just step on the chair yonder and get that box down from on top of the shifarobe. So I done like she told me and I was reaching, when the next thing I know she grabbed me around the legs. She scared me so bad I hopped down and turned the chair over. That was the only thing, the only furniture disturbed in the room, Mr. Finch, I swear, when I left it.

17. Q: And what happened after you turned the chair over? Tom? You've sworn to tell the whole truth. Will you do it? What happened after that?

18. A: Mr. Finch. I got down off the chair and I turned around. And she sort of jumped on me and hugged me around the waist. She reached up and kissed me on the face. She said she'd never kissed a grown man before and she might as well kiss me. She asked for me to kiss her back. I said, "Miss Mayella let me out of here." And I tried to run. Mr. Ewell cussed at her from the window, said he's gonna kill her.

19. Q: And what happened after that?

20. A: I was running so fast, I don't know what happened.

21. Q: Tom, did you rape Mayella Ewell?

22. A: I did not, sir.

23. Q: Did you harm her in any way?

24. A: I did not.

Analysis

1. Finch's direct examination illustrates a variety of effective direct examination techniques. Robinson's story unfolds chronologically, starting with brief testimony about an interaction that took place over a year before the alleged rape. (No. 8) The "before" interactions are relevant circumstantial evidence to suggest that Mayella might have initiated the sexual contact on the day of the alleged rape.

2. Question No. 3 elicits testimony that rebuts a potential silent argument that Robinson passed by the Ewell's home in order to develop a relationship with her.

3. Finch uses three open questions (Nos. 13, 15 and 17) that allow Robinson to explain what happened in his own words. While No. 13 may be an objectionable narrative question, Nos. 15 and 17 are

proper because they have temporal limits that narrow their scope.

4. Finch concludes the chronology with two questions (Nos. 21 and 23) that allow Robinson to deny explicitly that he attacked Mayella Ewell.   For greater emphasis, Finch might have both begun and concluded Robinson's testimony with these denials.

5. Robinson testifies to statements made by him, Mayella and Bob Ewell.   Neither Robinson's nor Mayella's statements would be barred by the hearsay rule because they are relevant without regard to their accuracy.   For example, Robinson testifies that Mayella told him that she has a door that needs fixing (No. 14).   The statement is relevant to demonstrate that Robinson had a legitimate reason to enter the house, and that Mayella wanted to be alone inside the house with Robinson.   Similarly, Robinson's statement that it was "right nice" for Mayella to treat her siblings to ice cream (No. 16) is relevant to provide context and meaning and to show that Robinson was not acting aggressively.   Finally, Robinson testifies that Bob Ewell looked through the window threatened to kill Mayella (No. 18).   Ewell's threat would probably qualify for admission as an excited utterance under Federal Rule of Evidence 803(2), as Ewell has personal knowledge of an interaction that would be shocking in a small southern community of the early 1930's.   The threat is relevant to show that Ewell believed that Mayella rather than Robinson initiated the sexual encounter.

While this is an opinion, a judge would be likely to admit it under Federal Rule of Evidence 701.

6. Despite its strengths, the testimony lacks information that an actual as opposed to a fictional Finch would be likely to include in Robinson's direct examination. Most importantly, an actual Finch might ask Robinson to explain events in a way that would allow the jurors to acquit him of rape while holding on to their prejudices. For example, Finch might signal to the jurors that Robinson "knows his place" by having him testify that he knew it was wrong to go into Mayella's house, and did so only because he was obligated to comply with a white woman's request. (You may have to set aside your political beliefs in order to represent an unpopular client effectively.)

7. Moreover, the direct examination lacks details that would allow listeners to visualize the scene and understand what actually happened. For example, Finch might ask Robinson to refer to a diagram of the room and the location of the window where Bob Ewell stood. Robinson might also get off the witness chair and demonstrate physically key moments of Mayella's aggressiveness, perhaps using Finch as a stand-in to illustrate how she grabbed him around the waist and how he broke free to run out of the room. Finch might also have emphasized Mayella's aggressiveness by using the "no,no,no" technique to elicit Robinson's denials that he had physical contact with Mayella when they were on the porch,

when he went inside the house, when he looked at the door and when he stepped on the chair.

8. The contemporary jurors would no doubt have known what a "shifarobe" was. If not, Finch might have added an element of expertise to Robinson's testimony by asking him to describe the appearance of this piece of furniture.

J. COMMON JUDGMENT POINTS

The sections below explore issues that commonly arise in connection with direct examination, and suggest factors to consider when you address them.

1. Should You "Remove the Sting" (of Harmful Evidence)?

Almost all stories are vulnerable to some sort of criticism. Perhaps a witness has been previously convicted of a felony, or stands to gain if a trial's outcome is successful for your client. Perhaps a witness has said something in the past that conflicts with trial testimony, or was absent when an important part of an event occurred. Because few witnesses are "perfect," a frequent judgment call is whether to reveal the weakness during direct examination or leave it for your adversary to develop on cross.

The primary reason to surface weaknesses during direct examination is to *take the sting out of cross.* Even if the adversary goes into the matter again on cross, by doing so yourself first on direct examination you may prevent the adversary from unnerving a witness and making an impact on the jury. Moreover, you may impress a jury with the fairness of your presentation, implying that "My client has nothing to hide." Finally, when you surface weaknesses during direct, you can provide witnesses with an immediate chance to offer an explanation that reduces their impact. By contrast, when harmful evidence comes out on cross, an explanation (if any) may not come out until redirect, by which time distrust of a witness may already have gotten a firm foothold in jurors' minds.

Yet routine surfacing of weaknesses on direct can be disadvantageous. One risk is that you may surface weaknesses of which your adversary is unaware. Just as we may be conscious of a physical blemish that others don't notice, so may you wrongly credit adversaries with omniscience they don't possess.

Second, even an adversary who is aware of a weakness may not try to exploit it during cross examination, fearing that the witness will have an explanation that vitiates a seeming inconsistency.

When deciding whether to try to take the sting out of cross, important factors to consider include the following:

- A witness' importance. Generally the more important a witness, the better to "lay all your cards on the table."

- The centrality of the weakness to the overall story. If a weakness is central to a story (e.g., an eyewitness' view of events was partly obstructed), the better to surface it during direct.

- Whether a witness has a reasonable explanation for an inconsistency or implausibility. The more persuasive the explanation, the more the reason to surface a weakness and the explanation during direct.

- An adversary's knowledge of a weakness, to the extent you know.

2. What Do You Do When Multiple Witnesses Can Tell the Same Story?

Another common judgment point is what to do when two or more witnesses can provide the same story. For example, your clients may be the spouses or the business partners who participated nearly equally in the transactions resulting in a lawsuit. Or, perhaps you can present numerous potential witnesses who attended a raucous political demonstration and are prepared to testify that your client did not throw rocks at the police. The judgment you have to make is which and how many witnesses to call. (Under Standard 4–5.2 (b), ABA Standards for Criminal Justice, you generally have an ethical obligation to consult with a client before making this decision.).

One risk of calling multiple witnesses is that you may lead a judge or juror to think that you "must not think that 1 should believe the first witness, otherwise why are you calling all these other ones?" Also, the more witnesses you call, the more likely are inconsistencies and weaknesses to appear. Jurors prone to "a chain is only as strong as its weakest link" reasoning may evaluate your case by focusing on the credibility of your weakest witness.

Finally, just as a word repeated over and over may lose meaning, so may evidence that is repeated lose its meaning, or at least its emotional impact.

Other factors militate in favor of calling multiple witnesses. A juror may infer that witnesses who you might have called but did not would have given harmful testimony. (A commonly-given jury instruction advises jurors of the permissibility of such an inference.) And if a witness you do not want to call is a client, you may severely strain the attorney-client relationship.

Here are a few options to consider when multiple witnesses are available. One strategy is to elicit a complete story from only one of the witnesses, and elicit *partial stories* from others. For example, you might ask one business partner to describe the events resulting in a contract, and limit the other partner's story to what took place during a key meeting.

Another strategy is to ask opposing counsel to *stipulate* to the testimony of witnesses who you might but choose not to call. The wording of such a stipulation would be along the lines of, "If they were called and sworn as witnesses, A, B and C would testify as follows: ..." This form of stipulation permits opposing counsel to stipulate to testimony, without in any way conceding the accuracy or the credibility of the stipulated testimony.

3. In What Order Will Witnesses Testify?

When you plan to call two or more witnesses, the small size of witness boxes demands that only one of them testify at a time. Hence, you must decide in what order they will testify. Almost always, order of witnesses is purely a tactical decision; few rules mandate a particular order.

Again relevant to a decision are the principles of primacy and recency, which suggest that we may remember best what we see or hear first and last. The application of these principles to trials is by no means clear, because the experiments from which they were derived tend to consist of people staring at rows of letter combinations, and then trying to recall as many combinations as possible. To the extent that the results of such experiments apply in trial settings, you might think of beginning and ending with your "strongest" witnesses. Witnesses whose testimony is less significant, or whose manner of testifying is less than stellar, might be grouped in between.

You may choose among a variety of factors when deciding which witnesses are "strongest." Ideally, both your first and last witnesses will be the founders and heads of charitable and religious organizations, and will have available visual recordings of the opposing party declaring, "It was all my fault, and they should get at least 10 times what they've asked for." Unfortunately, all too often witnesses are unassailable on cross but of secondary significance, or impeachable on several grounds but of vital legal significance. If you find yourself in this situation, which witnesses are stronger is a matter for your judgment.

You may also measure strength according to the tone you are attempting to set for your overall story. For example, if the primary appeal of a case is to jurors' emotions, a strong witness might be one who will describe events that create empathy for your client. If the primary appeal is rational or scientific, your strongest witness might be an expert. In a civil case, your strongest witness might be the adverse party, examined as a hostile witness. (See Federal Rule of Evidence 611(c)). On the other hand, you'd probably never consider a witness who was eliminated by the first question on a television quiz show to be your strongest witness.

A strong witness may also be one who can provide a chronological overview of important events. Just as during Opening Statement, a chronology can help jurors understand the relationship of individual items of evidence to your arguments. For example, assume a civil suit for damages growing out of a typical urban traffic nightmare that resulted in cars littering the road for hundreds of feet. Representing the plaintiff, you've developed an argument based on Arlene's testimony that shortly before the accident the defendant said, "I've got to hurry, I'm late for the meeting." Arlene's credibility is unassailable, but her story is limited to the statement. A second witness, Jeff, was a passenger in the plaintiff's car. Jeff can describe the accident from beginning to end. However, the defendant can attack Jeff's credibility based on Jeff's friendship with Arlene and the fact that Jeff had drunk a couple of beers shortly before the accident. Who is the "stronger" and therefore lead witness, Arlene or Jeff? Perhaps the latter, because he can provide an overall chronology of events.

At the recency end of a case-in-chief, you may prefer to call a client as your last witness. Judges typically grant motions to exclude witnesses from the courtroom until after their testimony. Excluded witnesses cannot listen to or discuss the testimony of other witnesses. Parties, however, cannot be excluded. A client who testifies last, therefore, has the benefit of hearing the direct and cross of all the other witnesses before testifying.

The order of witnesses is not always within your control. For example, the medical expert who was to be your leadoff witness may be called in to emergency surgery and be unavailable until the second day of trial. Judges often refuse to grant continuances for such reasons, insisting that you have backup witnesses available. A judge's need to keep up with a calendar is likely to outweigh your desire to fashion the order of witnesses.

Another situation is when the testimony of Jenni, a witness you want to call first, will refer to an exhibit whose foundation can only be laid by Josh. You might have to call Josh first. Alternatively, you might make an *offer of proof* demonstrating that you can lay a sufficient foundation through the testimony of Josh. Then ask the judge to permit Jenni to testify concerning the exhibit, on the condition that if the proper foundation is not subsequently laid, Jenni's testimony will be stricken. Also, you might ask opposing counsel to stipulate to the exhibit's admissibility. Finally, if neither of these options is available, you might call Josh first for the limited purpose of laying a foundation for the exhibit. Ask the judge for permission to delay the remainder of Josh's testimony until later in your case-in-chief. Opposing counsel may object under Federal Rule of Evidence 403 that calling and recalling witnesses will produce undue delay, but the judge has discretion under Rule 611 to grant the request.

K. WITNESS PREPARATION STRATEGIES

Unlike British barristers, you not only don't have to wear white wigs to court, but also you can meet with clients and witnesses prior to trial to prepare their testimony. Despite the cynical "woodshedding" label often attached to pre-trial preparation, effective preparation is ethical and it facilitates the search for justice by helping witnesses testify accurately and efficiently. Of course, you must comply with Rule 3.4 of the ABA Model Rules, which provides in part that a lawyer shall not "falsify evidence, counsel or assist a witness to testify falsely."

Typically, the major witness preparation activity is a mock direct examination. Use the same vocabulary and manner in your office that you plan to use in the courtroom. Both you and a witness should feel comfortable with a story, yet not so structured that questions and answers sound scripted. As some experienced litigators put it, you want to "rehearse testimony over and over until it sounds spontaneous." (In one trial advocacy panel discussion in which the author participated, a well-known and quite successful litigator indicated that he usually rehearses stories at least 20 times!)

The following strategies can increase the effectiveness of mock direct examinations:

Annotate a mock direct examination by pausing to provide feedback in the context of specific responses. For example, you may suggest that a witness elaborate further in response to an open question, or remind a witness not to elaborate when narrow questions call for either a yes or no or a similarly short response. In general, feedback on specific responses is more likely to be effective than abstract suggestions that might trouble a Broadway stage veteran, such as "Make them like you."

- If a witness' response conflicts with a prior statement, ask for an explanation and consider incorporating the explanation in the direct examination.

- If you plan to offer exhibits during a witness' testimony, or ask a witness to mark a diagram, include that process in the mock examination.

- Ask witnesses not to guess at the meaning of questions or at answers. Assure them that if they can't understand a question they should say so and you will rephrase it. Moreover, if they momentarily forget information, you can refresh their recollection if necessary. Putting witnesses at ease about potential "blind spots" often prevents them from occurring.

- Target feedback at problematic areas of testimony, but remember to praise helpful and appropriate responses. For example, you may say something like, "You're doing fine. Just talk to the judge and jury like you're talking to me and you have nothing to worry about." Witnesses who believe in themselves often testify with more confidence and enhance their credibility.

Pretrial preparation meetings should be *witness-centered.* Invite witnesses to ask questions if they are uncertain about their testimony or the trial process. Perhaps based on what they've seen in a film or television show, or perhaps heard about from a friend who appeared in court as a witness or juror, witnesses may surprise you with the idiosyncratic nature of concerns that you cannot anticipate.

Assure non-client witnesses that pretrial preparation is a perfectly legitimate activity. If a witness thinks that preparation is improper and is asked by a cross examiner as to whether a meeting took place, the witness may nervously try to deny it and undermine their credibility.

Another strategy for bolstering witnesses' confidence and hence their credibility is to help them understand how their testimony fits in with your overall story.

Also, explain the courtroom process. Will witnesses be "on call," meaning they can go about their daily activities normally so long as they can be in the courtroom within two hours after you summon them? Will they be in the courtroom while other witnesses testify, or will they have to wait in a hallway? Can they discuss their testimony with other witnesses? Procedural issues such as these tend to be quite mysterious to non-lawyers, and you can put witnesses at ease by telling them what to expect. If you think it helpful, you or a colleague may accompany a witness to watch a portion of a trial in the courtroom in which your trial will be held.

L. FINAL TIPS

Here are a few final tips for presenting effective direct examinations. When you examine witnesses, do so *from the trier of fact's perspective, asking the questions they'd like to ask if only they had a chance.* (Judges increasingly allow jurors to submit questions they want the judge to put to witnesses. Judges confer with attorneys before asking such questions.)

Just as when you address judges and jurors directly, use normal language and not "legalese" when you examine witnesses. If you want to know whether Jones got out of a car, don't ask whether "an individual then exited the vehicle." If you want to know whether Jones went to the bank, don't ask whether Jones "had an occasion to proceed to the bank."

When witnesses use unfamiliar terms, ask for explanations of their meaning. This is true whether a witness is an expensive expert who uses a Latin scientific term, or a percipient day laborer who uses work-related jargon. You might also ask witnesses to explain unfamiliar terms with *examples.* The excellent courtroom comedy film *My Cousin Vinny* has a great example of this technique. Expert witness Mona Lisa Vito (who is defense lawyer Vinny's fiancée-it is a comedy film, after all) testifies that she can tell from skid marks that the car that made the marks had Positraction. Vinny asks Mona Lisa to explain what Positraction does, and her answer provides an example that is familiar to all the jurors: If your car is stuck in the mud and it doesn't have Positraction, the tires will spin uselessly.

Watch witnesses as they testify. Not that they are likely to sneak out of court when you are not looking, but jurors may take cues from your behavior. If you look at notes or otherwise fail to pay attention to witnesses while they answer questions, jurors may infer that what they have to say isn't very important or has been thoroughly memorized. Also, even a well-prepared witness can give a surprise answer. If you are not paying attention, you may ask a follow-up question to the wrong testimony:

Q: What did you see next?

A: I don't remember anything else.

Q: What color was it?

Finally, eliminate or at least reduce a variety of *verbal tics* such as *echoing* witnesses' answers, prefacing questions with phrases like *I See* and *uh huh,* and thanking witnesses for testimony. Whether out of nervousness or simply a desire to buy time to think, questioners sometimes preface questions with verbal tics like these. A transcript might look like this:

Q: What happened next?

A: He huffed and he puffed.

Q: I see. And then what?

A: After a few minutes he blew the house down.

Q: Blew the house down. Uh huh. Can you describe. . .

Verbal tics are annoying, and judges may even regard them as inappropriate lawyer comments on testimony. If you are prone to verbal tics, awareness is a major step in eliminating them. Unlike radio personalities, you need not fill the courtroom air with constant verbiage. Silence is perfectly acceptable while you consider your next question.

CHAPTER 8
CROSS EXAMINATION

Direct examinations are typically *witness-centered*. Open questions and other direct examination strategies described in Chapter 7 focus judges' and jurors' attention on witnesses and help them tell stories in their own words. Cross examination, by contrast, is typically *attorney-centered*. On cross examination you rely on leading questions to tell stories in *your* words. The cross examination stories are typically far from "the whole truth." Rather, the truth that you elicit on cross examination is primarily limited to the aspects of truth that advance your arguments.

A. THE MYSTIQUE OF CROSS EXAMINATION

Cross examination carries a mystique that makes it resemble a boxer who possesses both a tremendous knockout punch and a glass jaw. The mystique suggests that there's a "right question" that if asked will produce triumph. However, always lurking is a "wrong question," that if asked will produce shattering defeat.

Popular culture is undoubtedly partially responsible for the mystique. In scores of films and television shows such as the classic series *Perry Mason*, cross examiners routinely save their clients' lives by wrenching dramatic last-minute confessions to murder from witnesses, spectators or even jurors. But an equally common image in popular culture is the thunderingly aggressive cross examiner who slinks back silently to counsel table after a witness gives an unexpected answer that sinks the cross examiner's entire case. (For a classic example, watch icy prosecutor Claude Dancer's final cross examination come to a disastrous end in *Anatomy of a Murder* (1959).

Also contributing to the mystique of cross are true life stories about Great Trial Lawyers, which inevitably focus on their cross examination skills. Consider again the oft-told tale of defense attorney Max Steuer in the "Triangle Shirtwaist Fire" trial of 1911. As you may recall, this watershed moment in American labor history involved a fire that broke out in a Manhattan sweatshop called the Triangle Shirtwaist Company. The owners were charged with criminal negligence after a fire broke out and killed numerous employees. The prosecution's main witness was Kate Altermann, who testified that she saw a garment worker burn to death while trying to escape through a locked exit door. Trampling on the Received Wisdom against letting a witness retell a story on cross examination, defense attorney Steuer repeatedly asked Altermann to "Please tell us again what happened." Each time, Altermann told the story using identical words, and words that a person of her background would be unlikely to use. The cross examination convinced the jurors that Altermann had memorized a story supplied by the prosecutor, and the defendants were acquitted.

Academics too have contributed to the mystique of cross. The great evidence scholar John Henry Wigmore (who of course never cross examined a witness in court in his life) wrote that cross examination was "the greatest legal engine for the discovery of truth ever invented." And during his celebrated "Sermon on the Mount" evidence lectures, the late Professor and Judge Irving Younger threatened to haunt any trial lawyer who asked a non-leading cross examination question before trying 25 cases. Finally, trial advocacy treatises often describe the disastrous details lurking in the minds of adverse witnesses, just waiting for the wrong questions to elicit them.

For example, the "nose story" illustrates the doom awaiting the cross examiner who asks "one question too many." The story involves a defendant who allegedly bit off his victim's nose. A prosecution eyewitness testified that the defendant did the dastardly deed. Up steps the cross examiner, and the cross proceeds in essence as follows:

Q: Where did the fight take place?

A: In the middle of the field.

Q: Where were you?

A: On the edge of the field, about 50 yards away.

Q: What were you doing there?

A: Just looking at the trees.

Q: You had your back to the fight?

A: Yes.

Q: The first you knew there was a fight was when you heard the alleged victim scream, right?

A: That's true.

Q: You didn't turn around until after the alleged victim screamed, correct?

A: Correct.

Q: How can you say, then, that my client bit off the person's nose?

A: Because I saw him spit it out.

The last question, of course, is the dreaded "one too many." Until that point, the cross had severely undermined the eyewitness' claim to have seen the crime. However, the question could not have been that damaging. Had the cross examiner not asked it, surely the prosecutor would have elicited the information on redirect examination. The point is that cross examination, let alone a single question, is rarely as crucial to trial outcomes as popular culture, attorney war stories and legal treatises tend to suggest.

For example, consider this embarrassing situation that arose early (very early) in the author's career. Representing on appeal a client who had been convicted of setting seven grass fires, the author filed a motion seeking an order from the trial judge releasing the client on bail pending appeal. At the hearing on the motion, three witnesses testified in support of the bail request. (Strange but true, in the rural area where the fires were set all three witnesses were members of the jury that had voted to convict!) The prosecutor responded with a surprise witness: the county Fire Marshal. The Marshal testified that in the weeks prior to the client's arrest, 40 fires had been set in various parts of the community; and that none had been set since the client had been in jail. The author wasted no time asking a cross examination question to which he did not know the answer:

"Did you have any information connecting my client to these 33 other fires?"

Of course, the answer was a disastrous "yes," just as the Received Wisdom suggested that it would be. Nevertheless, the mistake was not fatal. The judge granted the motion.

This section is not an invitation to reckless cross examination. By all means, do not encourage adverse witnesses to describe events in their own words, or ask questions whose answers you cannot anticipate. The point is that a single cross examination question is unlikely to make or break a case. Typically, an ineffective cross simply rehashes a witness' direct testimony, whereas an effective cross develops additional evidentiary support for an argument you already planned to make.

Nevertheless, the mystique of cross examination has the potential to undermine your efforts. A belief that you're supposed to win every case on cross examination may goad you into fierce but pointless combat with every adverse witness. Or, a fear that one question will prove fatal may cause you to forsake judgment and inspiration. Freed of the responsibility to provide a clear chronology and able to limit your questioning to evidence supporting your arguments, you may often find cross examinations easier to conduct than direct examinations.

B. FOLLOW THE RULES

The subsections below explain common *evidentiary* rules that affect cross examination.

1. STAY WITHIN THE SCOPE OF THE DIRECT

The so-called American Rule (as opposed to the English Rule) is that the scope of direct examination determines the scope of cross. That is, you can explore a topic on cross examination only if your adversary opened it up on direct. The American Rule's general purpose is to give parties control over their presentations.

If you hope to delve into new topics with adverse witnesses, you'll have to follow one of two routes. You can ask a judge for permission to go into the new topics during cross examination. A judge has discretion to grant the request, and may want to in order to avoid the inefficiency and delay that often occurs when a witness has to be excused and later recalled for additional testimony. If a judge does allow you to explore new topics on cross, you probably won't be able to ask leading questions with respect to the new topics.

If the judge refuses permission, perhaps in response to your adversary's opposition, you'll have to recall the witness for additional testimony during your case-in-chief, or when you next have a chance to call witnesses.

Judges tend to interpret the scope of direct broadly, because of the convenience of eliciting everything a witness has to say at once. Moreover, since the scope of direct includes witnesses' credibility, any evidence pertaining to credibility is within the scope of direct.

2. AVOID ARGUMENTATIVE QUESTIONS

"Cross" is not the same as "angry" examination. You are not allowed to vilify adverse witnesses or put argumentative questions to them. Judges have discretion to decide where to draw what can be a fine line between improperly hostile or argumentative questions and proper leading ones. In general, a question is improperly argumentative if it asks a witness to respond to your legal contentions, to comment on another witness' testimony, or if it belittles or tends to humiliate a witness. Consider these examples:

- "Do you expect the jury to belives the testimony of a twice-convicted felon?"

- "If you were already half an hour behind schedule for that important meeting, you would have been speeding in an effort to get there as soon as possible, isn't that right?"

- "Is it possible that the two youths entered the store, picked 22 specific items off of the shelves, had the clerk take money, then leave, then two different men drive up in a similar looking car, go in, shoot the clerk, rob him, and then leave?" (This complex question was put to a prosecution eyewitness by the defense attorney in the courtroom comedy film, *My Cousin Vinny*.)

- "Are you calling my client a liar?"

- "Doctor Wu is in a better position than you to decide how your daughter got injured, wouldn't you agree?"

- "You wouldn't recognize the truth if it were written on stone tablets that were carried down a mountainside, would you?"

These questions are improper. Rather than simply challenging an adverse witness' account of events, they are excessively hostile and seek to compel a witness to respond to the questioner's argument.

3. BASE QUESTIONS ON A "GOOD–FAITH BELIEF"

You should have a "good faith belief" in the accuracy of information embedded in cross examination questions. This is especially true for questions suggesting that an adverse witness has engaged in immoral or illegal conduct. For example, you should not ask questions such as, "Have you ever been convicted of a felony?" or "Had you been downing martinis for hours just before you observed the collision?" unless you have a legitimate factual basis for asking them. If you lack a factual basis, judges will not take kindly if you respond to an adversary's objection by saying something like, "I just thought I'd ask. The witness can answer no if it's not true."

What constitutes a good-faith belief is within a judge's discretion to determine. If information is of a type for which a documentary record almost surely exists, such as the record of a felony conviction, you'll probably need to produce the document in order to ask a question. By the same token, information left on your answering machine by an anonymous midnight caller probably never constitutes the basis of a good-faith belief.

If you doubt the adequacy of your information, seek a ruling before you ask a question. Otherwise, you may appear to a jury to be an unfair bully if a judge sustains an adversary's objection and explains to a jury that you had no basis for asking an embarrassing question. For an extreme or repeated violation, a judge may sanction you and declare a mistrial.

4. COMPLY WITH THE "COLLATERAL EVIDENCE RULE"

The collateral evidence rule prevents parties from offering extrinsic evidence to impeach adverse witnesses on unimportant points. The term does not appear in the Federal Rules of Evidence, but the policy is subsumed in Rule 403. As a result, if you seek to discredit a witness on a point that a judge deems unimportant (collateral), you have to confront the witness during cross examination or forgo the impeachment. Another way to say this is that you may be allowed to ask the question during cross, but if a point is collateral you have to take the answer.

For example, assume that you are the defense attorney in a bank robbery case. After a prosecution eyewitness testifies to entering the bank and observing a robbery in progress, a portion of your cross examination goes as follows:

Q: You entered the bank after parking in the rear car park?

A: That's correct.

Q: You parked in a disabled parking space?

A: Right, I have a disabled placard.

Q: You are a regular customer of the bank?

A: Yes.

Q: At the time of the robbery there were four disabled parking spaces in the rear car park, correct?

A: I think there were only three disabled spots. Still are only three for that matter.

Assume that the rear car park in fact has at all relevant times had four disabled parking spaces. For purposes of the collateral evidence rule, the issue is whether you could later offer extrinsic evidence of this fact. If you cannot link the number of spaces to the witness' ability to observe and remember what took place during the robbery, the number of spaces relates to a collateral issue and extrinsic evidence would be inadmissible. You are limited to asking the question during cross examination, and must take the witness' answer.

5. QUOTE TESTIMONY ACCURATELY

During cross examination you may refer to testimony that a witness gave on direct. When you do so, restate the testimony fairly and accurately. If rhetorical zeal leads you to alter a witness' testimony, your adversary can object that you are "misquoting the witness" or "mischaracterizing the evidence." If the judge sustains the objection, jurors may perceive you as trying for an unfair advantage.

For example, suppose that you represent the defendant in a civil assault and battery case. On direct examination, the plaintiff testifies that your client shouted and cursed in a loud voice just before beginning the attack. On cross examination, you ask, "You testified on direct that my client was upset, right?" The question does not fairly capture the witness' testimony and is improper.

C. ESSENTIAL QUESTIONING STRATEGIES

In the general culture, informal "rules" regulate such matters as dating, dressing and double-dipping chips into dips at parties. Equally embedded in trials are the *legal culture's* informal rules for effective cross examinations. The subsections below explain and illustrate effective cross examination questioning strategies.

1. RELY ON LEADING QUESTIONS

Leading questions are almost always the backbone of effective cross examinations. Leading questions are essentially assertions in question form. For example, "The light was red, wasn't it?" and "The light was red?" are both leading questions; in the latter example your tone of voice should convey the expectation that you have asked a question that the witness is to answer.

Leading questions are the coin of the cross examination realm because they allow you to control both the *subject matter* and the *scope* of answers. A basic rule of trial is that answers have to be responsive to questions. Thus, in response to a leading question such as "The light was red?" the witness' response has to concern the color of the light, and can consist only of "yes" or "no."

Of course, leading questions are not so powerful that you can use them to bend adverse witnesses to your will. For example, fanciful exchanges such as the following are unlikely to occur:

Q: On direct, you testified that the light was green, correct?

A: Yes, I said that.

Q: And during your marriage vows, you stated that the light was green, did you not?

A: Yes, that's right.

Q: You swore to the world's religious leaders that the light was green?

A: I did.

Q: Now, the light was actually red, wasn't it?

A: Yes, the light was red, I admit it. Wow, leading questions are really powerful.

If leading questions cannot coerce adverse witnesses into changing the content of answers, they can help you elicit those aspects of the truth that support your arguments. Many of us are prone to dichotomous thinking, so that information is either true or false. A better approach to cross examination is to think of truth as multi-dimensional, and your task as using leading questions to elicit aspects of truth that support your contentions.

For example, assume that a piece of information that supports one of your arguments is that after Jack fell down and broke his crown, "Jill came tumbling after." You might ask:

- An open question: "What happened after Jack broke his crown?"

- A leading question: "After Jack broke his crown, Jill came tumbling after, correct?"

The witness can respond to the open question by describing various aspects of the event, all of which might be true. For instance, the witness might testify to Jack's crying, to Jack's physical appearance, or to what the witness said after seeing Jack's crown break. If the witness does mention Jill, the witness may instead of using your preferred words testify that "Jill slipped on the hill a bit later." The leading question, by contrast, allows you to target the aspect of the truth that supports your argument.

2. ASK SINGLE–ITEM QUESTIONS

To maximize the effectiveness of a leading question, limit it to one assertion. Single-item questions tend to increase judges' and jurors' comprehension, lend persuasiveness to your cross, and discourage lengthy responses and explanations. Compare the sequence of single-item questions below with the complex question that follows it:

Q: "You walked into your supervisor's office, correct?"

Q: "You told her that you didn't care what she wanted you to do?"

Q: "Then you called her a sorry excuse for a manager?"

Q: "And you walked out of the office?"

Q: "You slammed the door?"

Q: "When you walked into your supervisor's office, you told her that you didn't care what she wanted you to do, called her a sorry excuse for a manager, walked out of the office and slammed the door, isn't that right?"

The second question covers the entire event with a single question. Compared to the first series of questions, the latter is harder for a listener to follow, and is more likely to produce a lengthy, explanation-filled answer. The complex question is also more likely to draw an "argumentative" or "compound question" objection, further diluting the impact of cross.

Single-item questions also allow you to provide emphasis by stringing together a series of favorable responses. For example, a series of "yes" answers to the sequence of questions above is likely to make a greater impact than the single "yes" response to the second question.

Tone of Voice: To further promote short responses, your demeanor and firm tone of voice should convey an expectation that the witness is to answer only "yes" or "no." (The oft-depicted cine-lawyer technique of yelling questions from two inches away is firm, but improper.)

3. DON'T ASK "WHY"

A corollary of the cross examination "rule" that you should rely primarily on leading questions is that you should generally not ask "why" an event took place. Because questions starting with "why" are necessarily open, they allow and indeed promote lengthy answers. Moreover, "why" questions put the content of answers beyond your control. Any reason a witness chooses to give is relevant and responsive to the question, even if the reason would have been inadmissible but for your question.

For example, in *People v. Harris,* 87 Cal.App.2d 818 (1948), Harris was charged with armed robbery of a jewelry store. At trial, the jewelry store owner identified the defendant as the robber. On cross examination, the defense attorney attacked the owner's credibility with a prior inconsistent statement: at an earlier preliminary hearing, the owner had testified that he was not certain that the defendant was the culprit. The defense attorney then asked the witness "why" at trial he was able to identify the defendant when he was unable to do so weeks earlier. The ill-advised question allowed the owner to provide an explanation that suggested that the defendant had a propensity for violence. The night before the preliminary hearing, the owner testified, he'd gotten a phone call from a man who identified himself as the defendant's brother, and the brother said that if the owner identified the defendant as the robber, he and the defendant would make sure that the owner was a dead man. The owner was willing to identify the defendant at trial because as the defendant and the brother were by then both in jail, the owner no longer feared telling the truth. Thus, the defense attorney's "why" question surfaced an explanation that negated the inconsistency. But for the "why" question, the prosecutor may not have been allowed to offer evidence of the brother's threat and imprisonment.

A second "don't ask why" example comes from the toxic torts case described in the book and film, *A Civil Action* (1998). The case involved a group of parents in Woburn, Mass., who sued Beatrice Foods and W.R. Grace for illegally dumping chemicals into the town's water supply, causing many children to become sick or die. At one point, the owner of Beatrice Foods testified that he never would have allowed chemical dumping to occur. Plaintiffs' attorney Jan Schlichtmann asked him "why" he could be so sure that no dumping took place. The "why" question produced a lengthy narrative in which the owner described the generations of his family who had owned and cared for the land, as well as his own love of the land. By the time he was done answering the question, the owner sounded like a more dedicated environmentalist than Schlichtmann.

Even if "why" questions do not produce such unfavorable answers, they certainly encourage adverse witnesses to determine the content and length of answers. As a general rule, therefore, avoid asking them.

4. AVOID THE "ONE QUESTION TOO MANY"

The problem of asking "one question too many" generally arises when a cross examiner has elicited circumstantial evidence tending to undermine an adversary's desired inference. The cross examiner then asks one question too many in an effort to attack the desired inference directly. The hallmark of a "one question too many" is that it does not seek additional evidence, but rather asks a witness to agree to a cross examiner's conclusion.

In classical illustrations of the danger of "one question too many" the question elicits devastating new information. For example, recall the classic "bit off the nose" example set forth above. After the eyewitness testified that the defendant bit off the victim's nose, the cross examiner elicited circumstantial evidence undermining the eyewitness' credibility: the eyewitness' back was to the fight until after the victim screamed. The "one question too many" directly attacked the eyewitness' conclusion, suggesting that the eyewitness couldn't possibly know whether the attacker bit off the nose. By going beyond the circumstantial evidence relating to credibility and attacking the ultimate conclusion, the cross examiner goaded the eyewitness into revealing new and harmful information. (Witnesses are unlikely to admit that everything they've said is wrong!)

This next example of the danger of asking one question too many is taken from the notorious 1951 espionage prosecution of Ethel and Julius Rosenberg, the "atomic spies." (For a compelling analysis of the case and the attorneys' trial strategies, see Louis Nizer, *The Implosion Conspiracy* (1973)) David Greenglass was an admitted co-conspirator of the Rosenbergs and at the time of the trial had already pleaded guilty. Greenglass testified in part that he had reproduced sketches of the atom bomb that Rosenberg had passed along to the Soviet Union. Cross examining Greenglass, defense attorney Emanuel Bloch tried to show that Greenglass lacked the ability to make the sketches:

Q: When you went to high school and Brooklyn Polytech, did you fail in your subjects?

A: I was quite young at the time, about eighteen, and I liked to play around more than I liked to go to school, so I cut classes almost the whole term.

Q: How many of the eight courses that you took did you fail?

A: I failed them all.

Q: You never got a science degree?

A: No.

Q: Did you ever study calculus, or thermodynamics, nuclear physics or atomic physics?

A: I did not.

Q: Do you know what an isotope is?

A: I do.

Q: What is it?

A: An isotope is an element having the same atomic structure but having a different atomic weight.

Each of the last two questions was one too many. Defense attorney Bloch had effectively undermined Greenglass' testimony by focusing on his school records. The answers to the final two questions suggested that Greenglass may well have had enough knowledge to make sketches of an atomic bomb.

A "one question too many" is also likely to be argumentative. For example, a version of the "nose" cross examiner's last question is "You don't know whether my client bit off the nose, do you?" Even if it produces no new harmful information, a judge would likely uphold an adversary's "argumentative" objection. In either event, the question may undo your gains.

To avoid asking "one question too many," recognize when you are no longer seeking additional evidence, but rather are seeking to coerce a witness into agreeing with your desired inference. This is a situation that is especially likely to produce one question too many.

5. AVOID ASKING QUESTIONS YOU DO NOT KNOW THE ANSWER TO

The Murphy's Law assumption behind the advice not to ask a question you do not know the answer to is that the answer will inevitably be harmful. More importantly, the advice is a reminder to plan cross examination with the same care as direct examination. Typically, pre-trial discovery produces documents, depositions, affidavits and the like and so allow you to anticipate direct examination as well as the answers a witness is likely to give to your cross examination questions. Especially until you have substantial trial experience, ask leading questions targeting anticipated answers supporting your arguments.

Return to prosecutor Claude Dancer's cross examination of surprise defense witness Mary Palant in the film *Anatomy of a Murder* (1959). Dancer is prosecuting Lt. Manion for murdering Barney Quill. After

Palant produces evidence supporting Manion's defense of temporary insanity, Dancer furiously attacks her credibility. The final portion of his cross-examination of Palant goes as follows:

Q: In the grip of what Mr. Biegler (defense counsel) might call irresistible impulse, you rushed in here because you wanted to crucify the character of the dead Barney Quill, isn't that true?

A: No, I thought it was my duty.

Q: Your pride was hurt, wasn't it?

A: I don't know what you mean.

Q: Ms. Palant, when you found the panties, was your first thought that Barney Quill might have raped Mrs. Manion or that he might have been stepping out with Mrs. Manion?

A: (To the judge) What does he mean? I don't know what he means.

Judge: Mr. Dancer, I must ask you to put straight questions to the witness.

Q: Here is a straight question Your Honor. Ms. Palant, were you Barney Quill's mistress?

A: I was not.

Q: Do you know it was common knowledge in Thunder Bay that you were living with Quill.

A: That's not true. Barney Quill was my...

Q: Was what, Ms. Palant? Barney Quill was what, Ms. Palant?

A: Barney Quill was my father.

Q: (in a stunned tone) No further questions.

Unaware of the father-daughter relationship, Dancer undermines his attack on Palant's credibility by asking questions though he was ignorant of the true circumstances. While this sort of devastation undoubtedly happens more regularly in courtroom dramas than in real trials, the scene is a valid cautionary reminder not to ask questions that you do not know the answer to.

D. A CROSS EXAMINATION SAFETY MODEL

Traditionally, much cross examination advice emphasizes the types of questions *not to ask*. By contrast, the following Cross Examination Safety Model serves as a guide to types of questions that you *can ask*. The Safety Model is as follows:

Highly Safe Questions

Witness' Provable Prior Statement

Consistency with Established Facts

Medium Safe Questions

Consistency with Everyday Experience

Assumed Testimony of Unavailable Witness

Unsafe Questions

Fishing

The discussion of the Safety Model below assumes that based on your arguments, you have identified evidence supportive of your arguments that you hope to elicit on cross examination. The Safety Model helps you assess the likelihood that a cross examination question will produce a favorable answer, based either on the likelihood that the witness will provide that answer, or on your ability to contradict an unfavorable answer. Thus, the Model focuses attention on what you can prove, not on the uncertainty surrounding what an adverse witness may say. The Model does not instruct you to "Ask only safe questions." You may decide to ask unsafe questions (to fish), but should understand when you are doing so to increase your chances of a successful catch.

The subsections below explore the features of the Safety Model.

1. HIGHLY SAFE QUESTIONS

Questions in this category are most likely to produce favorable answers.

a. Witness' Provable Prior Statement

A question is highly safe if your desired answer is consistent with a witness' *provable* prior statement.

A prior statement is provable if you can offer the prior statement into evidence as a prior inconsistent statement if the witness fails to give your desired answer. For example, a prior inconsistent statement might be provable because a witness made it during a deposition, or to another person who you can call as a witness. The question is safe because either the witness will confirm the prior statement, or you can impeach a changed story with the prior statement. (Under Federal Rule of Evidence 801(d)(1)(A), the prior statement is admissible as substantive evidence if it was made under oath, as in a deposition. Otherwise, it is admissible only to impeach the inconsistent trial testimony.)

For example, assume that you represent an injured plaintiff in a medical malpractice case. On cross examination of the defendant doctor, an anesthesiologist, you want to offer evidence that the doctor knew that the plaintiff had eaten a meal within one hour of surgery. This evidence supports your argument that the doctor carelessly used the wrong anesthetic. Your question would be something like:

Q: Doctor, at the time you administered anesthetic you were aware that the plaintiff reported that she ate a meal within the preceding hour, correct?

This question is highly safe if:

- At the doctor's deposition, the doctor testified, "I was aware that the patient reported eating a meal within the preceding hour."

or

- The doctor mentioned to a colleague who is available to you as a witness, "I knew that the patient had reported eating a meal within the preceding hour."

or

- A nurse who is available to you as a witness mentioned to the doctor that "The patient reported eating a meal within the preceding hour."

The reason that the question is highly safe is that either the doctor provides your desired answer, or you can later contradict an unfavorable answer by reading from the doctor's deposition or by calling the colleague or nurse as a witness.

Note that your question makes no mention of its source. Your question would have been improper had you asked, "Doctor, according to what you said in your deposition (or told your colleague or were told by your nurse), at the time you administered anesthetic you knew that the plaintiff had eaten a meal within the preceding hour, correct?" Reference to any of the earlier statements would run afoul of the hearsay rule unless and until the statement is admissible to contradict the witness' trial testimony.

Working backwards, realize how your ability to ask highly safe questions at trial often depends on effective deposition questioning. To serve as the basis of a highly safe question, a prior statement must leave a witness without "wiggle room" to explain away a seeming inconsistency. The more vague or imprecise a former statement, the less useful it is as the basis of a highly safe question. Often, of course, you have no control over the content of a prior statement. You are stuck with whatever a witness wrote in a memo, shouted to a neighbor, or said in a banner attached to the back of a blimp. But when you do have control, as during deposition questioning, try to pin witnesses down to the exact statements you want them to repeat in court.

For example, assume that you represent Bud Porter, a consumer who allegedly was defrauded into buying a set of supposedly rare baseball cards in mint condition. Your contention is that the seller intentionally concealed the fact that many of the cards were damaged or readily available on the open market. A portion of the seller's deposition testimony was as follows:

Q: When you first met Mr. Porter, did you show him what he'd be buying?

A: No, I didn't actually show Porter the set of baseball cards.

On cross, this questioning ensues:

Q: You never actually showed the set of baseball cards to Mr. Porter, did you?

A: Yes, I did.

Q: At your deposition, you testified, did you not, "I didn't actually show Porter the set of baseball cards."

A: I did say that. But if you'll notice, your deposition question asked only about my initial meeting with Mr. Porter. Today you asked if I ever showed him the set of baseball cards and I did. We got together the next day, and showed the set to him then.

In this example, your cross examination question is not highly safe because it does not precisely track the deposition testimony.

b. Consistency With Established Facts

A cross examination question is also highly safe if your desired answer is consistent with established facts. Established facts are those that in your judgment a judge or juror is nearly certain to accept as accurate. For example, the source of established facts may consist of information in a document that has been or will be offered into evidence, or of testimony by another witness that you are confident a judge or juror will believe. In such situations, if the witness fails to provide your desired answer, you argue for the accuracy of your version of events based on the established facts.

For example, a judge or juror is likely to regard an almanac as authoritative as to the phases of the moon. Therefore, if supported by an almanac, this question would be highly safe: "The moon had set a good hour before the time you claim to have seen the defendant by moonlight, isn't that right?" Either the witness provides your desired answer, or you offer that portion of the almanac into evidence. (Before he became President, Abraham Lincoln won a case by doing just that. Lincoln's ploy is memorialized in the 1939 film *Young Mr. Lincoln.*)

Similarly, a judge or juror is likely to regard a parish priest as authoritative as to the time that a Mass was celebrated on a given evening. Therefore, based on what a priest has told you, the following question to another witness would be highly safe: "Mass was celebrated at St. Swithens that night at 10:00, correct?"

2. MEDIUM SAFE QUESTIONS

When you base questions on the factors explained in this subsection, a good likelihood exists either that a witness will provide a favorable answer, or that a judge or juror will disbelieve an unfavorable one. However, your ability to contradict an unfavorable answer is based on argument rather than on provable evidence.

a. Consistency With Everyday Experience

Questions are medium safe if your desired answers are consistent with everyday experience. If a witness does not give your desired answer, you argue that a judge or juror should disbelieve the answer because it conflicts with everyday experience (it is implausible). Questions in this category are only medium safe because a judge or juror may evaluate everyday experience differently than do you, and because witnesses may offer explanations that vitiate seeming implausibilities.

For example, assume that you represent the defendant in an auto accident case. Gail Lawton, a witness for the plaintiff, testified on direct that she was stopped at a red light when she saw the defendant make a left turn at an unsafe speed and bear down on the plaintiff, who was in the crosswalk. Lawton did not see the actual impact, however, because moments earlier she had turned away to check on the color of the light. You contend that the plaintiff never was in the crosswalk, and that the accident happened at a point well beyond the intersection, when the plaintiff dashed out suddenly from between two parked cars. A portion of your cross of Lawton goes as follows:

1. Q: You noticed a car making a left turn?

2. A: Yes.

3. Q: And this car was speeding?

4. A: Correct.

5. Q: You also believed that a woman was in the crosswalk, in the path of the car?

6. A: That's right.

7. Q: You must have immediately feared for this woman's safety?

8. A: Yes.

9. Q: You immediately realized that the woman was in danger of being hit by the car?

10. A: Yes.

11. Q: That must have been frightening?

12. A: It was horrible.

13. Q: You realized that the collision was imminent?

14. A: I did.

15. Q: Yet you must have been hoping that somehow the woman would escape injury?

16. A: Yes.

17. Q: You were very concerned about what would happen to her?

18. A: I was.

19. Q: Yet at that moment you turned away to check on the color of the light?

20. A: Well, yes.

Here, everyday experience is the source of questions about how an individual is likely to react when a collision is imminent. Either the witness will agree that, e.g., she was concerned for the woman's safety (No. 17), or you will argue that her denial is implausible. The questions support your argument that the plaintiff was not in the crosswalk, else the witness would not have turned away from the impending tragedy.

Testimony from the widely-publicized first murder trial of Eric and Lyle Menendez in the early 1990's provides another example of cross examination based on consistency with everyday experience. The Menendez brothers were charged with murder after admittedly killing their wealthy Beverly Hills parents. The brothers' defense was a form of self-defense. They contended that they genuinely (though mistakenly) believed that their parents were about to kill them following years of sexual abuse. Their first trial resulted in a hung jury; the second produced two murder convictions.

In the first trial, a key item of defense evidence was Eric's testimony that he was shocked when shortly before the killings, he saw his mother pull off Lyle's toupee. To rebut Eric's testimony that he didn't know until then that Lyle wore a toupee, the prosecution called Lyle's ex-girlfriend, who testified that some months earlier, Eric had told her that Lyle wore a toupee. The defense cross examination of the ex-girlfriend was substantially as follows:

Q: Tell me about the time when you had this conversation with Eric. What day of the week was it?

A: It was a long time ago, I don't remember the exact date.

Q: You don't even remember the month, is that right?

A: I remember approximately the time I was out there.

Q: What's the approximate time?

A: It could have been in the spring, I don't know— January, February, March, April.

Q: What were you doing this day that you say you had this conversation with Eric Menendez?

A: Just talking to Eric.

Q: The whole day?

A: No.

Q: So what did you do the rest of the day?

A: I don't recall, it was a long time ago.

Q: What else did you talk about with Eric?

A: I don't remember.

This cross examination was the basis of an argument attacking the ex-girlfriend's credibility. The defense argument was addressed to what it hoped was the jurors' everyday experience that people who are telling the truth about an event can remember more than a single isolated remark.

Finally, consider this cross-examination excerpt from the classic courtroom drama, *A Few Good Men* (1992). Lt. Kaffee defends two Marines stationed at Guantanamo against a charge of hazing Private Santiago so seriously that Santiago died. The defense is that the Marines were ordered by their commander, Col. Jessup, to carry out a "Code Red" on Santiago. Jessup insists that he gave no such order, and that in fact he had ordered that Santiago be transferred off the base. Seeking to show that Jessup did not order a transfer, Kaffee cross examines Jessup as follows:

Q: Colonel, we have the transfer order that you and Markinson co-signed ordering that Santiago be on a flight leaving Guantanamo at 6:00 the next day. Was that the first flight?

A: The 0600 was the first flight.

Q: You flew up to Washington this morning. Is that right?

A: Yes.

Q: I notice you're wearing your class "A" dress uniform in court today. Did you wear that on the plane?

A: I wore utilities on the plane.

Q: You brought your dress uniform?

A: Yes.

Q: Toothbrush, shaving kit, underwear?

A: I brought a change of clothes and some personal items.

Q: After Dawson and Downey's arrest Santiago's barracks were sealed off and its contents inventoried. "Four pairs camouflage pants, three long-sleeve khaki shirts, three pairs of boots, four pairs green socks, three green T-shirts." I'm wondering why Santiago wasn't packed.

A: (No answer)

Q: I'll tell you what. We'll get back to that one in a minute. This is a record of all phone calls made from your base in the past 24 hours. After being subpoenaed to Washington, you made three calls.

A: I called Colonel Fitzhughes to let him know that I would be in town.

The second call was to arrange a meeting with Congressman Richmond of the House Armed Services Committee. And the third call was to my sister Elizabeth.

Q: These are phone records from Gitmo for September 6, and these are 14 letters that Santiago wrote in nine months requesting-- in fact, begging-- for a transfer. Upon hearing the news that he was finally getting his transfer Santiago was so excited that do you know how many people he called? Zero. Nobody. Not one call to his parents saying he was coming home. Not one call to a friend, saying, "Can you pick me up at the airport?" He was asleep in his bed at midnight, and according to you he was getting on a plane in six hours. Yet everything he owned was hanging neatly in his closet and folded neatly in his footlocker. You were leaving for one day. You packed a bag and made three calls. Santiago was leaving for the rest of his life and he hadn't called a soul and he hadn't packed a thing. Can you explain that? The fact is, there was no transfer order. Santiago wasn't going anywhere. Isn't that right, Colonel?

In this excerpt, Kaffee clearly violates evidence rules by essentially testifying to such matters as the clothes in Santiago's closet and the contents of his letters. Putting such problems to the side, the excerpt is an excellent illustration of cross examination argument based on "inconsistency with everyday experience." Kaffee's questions suggest that if Santiago had been told that he was being transferred and would be leaving the base in a few hours, he surely would have packed his clothes and phoned family members and friends. His failure to carry out these activities is circumstantial evidence that supports an inference that Santiago was never told about a transfer because a transfer order was never given.

b. Assumed Testimony of an Unavailable Witness

Questions can also be medium safe when you have favorable information but lack a source through which you can offer it into evidence. For example, perhaps you cannot locate the person who is the source of the information, or perhaps the source is uncooperative and claims an inability to recall the information. In such situations, if the same information is known to the witness you are cross examining, you may try to elicit it on cross. If your questioning demonstrates that you are aware of the information and the witness' knowledge of it, and if you also imply that you can contradict an undesired answer, the witness may provide the favorable information on cross.

For example, assume that as the prosecutor in a murder case you want to establish that at least five seconds elapsed between a pair of gunshots. Bobbie, an eyewitness to the shooting, gave this information to your investigator but is unavailable to testify. You hope to elicit the information during cross examination of defense witness Asimow, another eyewitness to the shooting. Your cross might go as follows:

Q: You were seated at the bar when the shots were fired, correct?

A: That's right.

Q: Other people were in the bar as well?

A: Sure, a few others.

Q: Do you recollect that a young woman, with dark hair and wearing a blue dress, was also in the bar?

A: I think I remember someone like that. I wasn't paying close attention to other customers.

Q: Well, she was seated about five seats from you, near the tasteful moosehead on the wall?

A: That seems right.

Q: And you spoke to her briefly about the kind of beer she was drinking?

A: Maybe, I don't really recall.

Q: Well, would you know if the woman's name was Bobbie?

A: No. she didn't tell me her name.

Q: But she was sitting about 10 feet from you?

A: About.

Q: And you had no trouble hearing the shots?

A: None at all.

Q: They were loud, like firecrackers?

A: I'd say so.

Q: Then it's safe to assume that Bobbie was near enough to have heard the shots also?

Opp: Objection, Your Honor. Calls for a conclusion.

Judge: It's close, but the author gets to make the rulings. I'll allow it. You may answer.

A: I suppose so.

Q: Now, there was a five second interval between the shots, right?

A: . . .

The questions concerning the circumstances of the shooting and Bobbie's location may convince Asimow that Bobbie can contradict an inaccurate answer, motivating Asimow to provide your desired information. Of course, the technique might fail utterly if an adverse witness realizes that the rebuttal witness is unavailable. Here, for example, you shouldn't refer in a question to "Bobbie, the woman whose current whereabouts are a complete mystery to me."

You can use this same technique when the evidence you hope to elicit is based on the witness' own prior statement. If you cannot independently prove up the prior statement (e.g., the witness to whom the statement was made is unavailable), consider asking questions reminding the witness of the circumstances surrounding the making of the prior statement. For example, assume that in the example above, Bobbie had told you that Asimow had told her that five seconds elapsed between the shots. Bobbie, however, is unavailable to testify. When you ask Asimow about the time that elapsed between the shots, Asimow replies, "I don't recall exactly." The following series of questions might elicit your desired information:

Q: Do you recall speaking to a young woman in the bar?

A: Vaguely. I talked to a lot of people that night.

Q: Yes, but I'm referring to a woman you talked to about a minute after the shots were fired. Do you recall that?

A: It's all pretty hazy.

Q: She was wearing a blue dress, and she asked you if you were OK?

A: I remember something like that.

Q: You said you were fine, and said something about your experience in the army?

A: It's possible.

Q: And didn't you tell this woman that at least five seconds elapsed between the shots?

A: . . .

The questions might well goad Asimow into an accurate answer because they suggest that you are so familiar with the circumstances of the conversation that you can probably contradict an inaccurate response.

3. UNSAFE QUESTIONS ("FISHING")

Generally, unsafe questions are those whose answers you cannot rebut. You hope that a question can uncover favorable evidence, but must "take the answer" if it is unfavorable.

When you cannot ask highly or medium safe questions, "No questions" may be a reasonable alternative to fishing. However, fishing is sometimes necessary. For example, perhaps you represent a criminal defendant who will neither testify nor present evidence, so you have to cross examine if you are to present evidence at all. Or, you may choose to fish based on an intuitive judgment about a witness' vulnerability.

Fishing is the type of cross examination which is most likely to result in a rehash of evidence given on direct examination. The following suggestions for alternatives may help you avoid that result:

* *Ask open rather than leading questions.*

For example, if you want to know whether anything might have impaired a witness' ability to observe an event, consider asking a question such as, "Describe your activities in the hour preceding the event." One reason to ask open questions is a tactical one: witnesses who describe events in their own words sometimes unwittingly provide helpful information. A second reason is legal: evidence and ethical rules generally forbid you from suggesting information in the absence of a good-faith belief that the information is accurate. For example, without a good-faith belief, you could not ask, "Did you ingest cocaine in the hour preceding the event?"

* Use an "if what you say is true, what else would be true" strategy.

Using this approach, you probe surrounding details and avoid frontal assaults on testimony. Witnesses rarely recant on cross what they said on direct. As in this example, witnesses almost always stick to their stories:

Q: On direct, you testified that my client said, "I mean the Peerless ship that is painted red," correct?

A: Right.

Q: Are you sure my client said that?

A: I am.

Q: Really, really sure?

A: Yes, I was right there.

Q: Gee, my client says different. Are you sure you're sure?

A: . . .

Here, you do more than fish. You sit idly in a boat waiting for fish to jump in, and it rarely happens. Instead of hoping that witnesses will suddenly change their testimony, ask about details surrounding important events that a witness should be aware of if the witness' testimony were accurate. If the witness cannot testify to the details, you have a basis for arguing that the important evidence is inaccurate.

To identify the surrounding details about which you might inquire, ask yourself, "If what this witness says is true, what else is also likely to be true?" For example, assume that you are to cross examine a witness whose direct testimony is, "I am a former Olympic high jump champion." If what the witness says is true, you would expect the witness to recall numerous details related to winning the chanpionship medal. If the witness cannot recall important details, you have a basis for arguing that the witness should not be believed. For example:

Q: What year did you win the Olympic championship?

A: I don't remember.

Q: What was your winning height?

A: I'm not sure.

Q: Where did you win the championship?

A: Don't remember that either.

* *Probe for details.*

As the name implies, a "probing for details" cross asks for additional information about events to which a witness has already testified. If the witness is able to recall only scant details, or purports to remember a plethora of seemingly insignificant details, you've probably undermined the witness' credibility.

For example, assume that an important event concerns the contents of lunchtime conversations that had taken place about a decade before the trial. A witness who claims to be able to recall not only the details of what was said, but also the order in which topics arose, in numerous different conversations, is unlikely to be believed.

Probing for details can be especially effective when inquiries concern measurable quantities such as time and distance. People are notoriously poor judges of such matters, and often create conflicts in their testimony. For example, a witness who says he had a "good view" of an event might estimate the distance as "50 yards." Similarly, students in the author's Trial Advocacy class have estimated the length of a 300 foot law school hallway anywhere from 75 to 450 feet!

* *Use a "Hop, Skip and Jump" questioning pattern.*

This strategy does not require you to engage in calisthenics in the middle of trial. Instead, you intentionally probe events non-sequentially. Some witnesses can testify believably only if they stick to a memorized chronology. Non-sequential probing may demonstrate the dearth of their actual recall. A brief example of "hop, skip and jump" questions is as follows:

Q: After the lunch meeting, you and Mr. Even met twice more, first a week later, and then two weeks later?

A: Yes.

Q: At the lunch meeting, you discussed the quality of cotton fiber that was to be shipped on the Peerless?

A: Yes.

Q: And he said it would be Surat cotton, of middling fair quality?

A: Yes.

Q: He mentioned this again during the third meeting?

A: I'm not sure, I think so.

Q: How about during the second meeting?

A: I can't recall now.

Q: In the third meeting, you never asked Mr. Even to clarify what he meant by "middling fair quality, right?"

A: The third meeting? I don't remember.

Q: And during the initial lunch meeting?

A: Maybe, I think so.

Here, the non-sequential questioning may suggest uncertainties that didn't appear on direct examination. However, be aware that a judge may consider rapid topical shifts to be argumentative. Moreover, a judge or juror may empathize with a witness and attribute any confusion to what the judge or juror perceives to be unfair questioning. A final risk is that you may confuse yourself even more than a witness.

* *Be alert to topics that an adversary avoids or that seem problematic for a witness during direct examination.*

Topics that you might reasonably expect an adversary to cover on direct examination, but which are ignored, ore often fruitful subjects to explore on cross. You run a small risk that an adversary is *sandbagging*, omitting a topic intentionally with the expectation that you will barge in and elicit damning evidence yourself. Another risk is that the judge will deem your questions to be beyond the scope of direct and therefore improper. If so, as suggested above, you might ask the judge for permission to extend the scope of the questioning, and if permission is granted you may have to follow direct examination rules with respect to the new topics.

E. ARGUMENT–CENTERED QUESTIONING

The lists of questioning "do's and don'ts" above provide you with a basis for developing cross examination questions that are legally proper and that minimize the risk that an adverse witness will repeat the unfavorable evidence that came out on direct or hit you with new and unanticipated harmful evidence.

This section suggests strategies for developing the *content* of questions. As with the other phases of trial, your cross examinations too should be *argument-centered.* That is, guide your questioning according to the *inferential, credibility* and *silent* arguments you seek to establish.

Often you'll have an easier time communicating arguments during cross examination than during direct examination. On direct, you generally have to, among other things, provide background information about witnesses, set scenes, and encourage witnesses to testify in their own words. Important as those strategies may be, satisfying those needs may make it harder for you to communicate to judges and jurors the connections between evidence and your arguments. On cross examination, by contrast, you are generally freed of these questioning responsibilities and can hone in on the evidence that supports your arguments. Moreover, on cross you have less of a need to pay attention to chronology, and can often elicit evidence according to the argument it supports regardless of its chronological relationship to other evidence.

The following example suggests how you might organize cross examination questioning so as to support an *inferential* argument. Assume that you represent a plaintiff in an automobile personal injury case. One of your factual propositions is that the defendant was driving in excess of the speed limit. Read through the cross examination from a judge's or juror's perspective, and try to identify the argument that underlies the questioning:

Q: At the time of the accident you were 20 minutes late for a business meeting, correct?

A: That's true.

Q: This was a meeting you had personally arranged?

A: Yes.

Q: This was an important meeting, wasn't it?

A: More or less like other business meetings, I'd say.

Q: Well, the meeting was with a representative of a big company that you hoped would become a customer of yours, right?

A: Yes.

Q: This representative had already cancelled two previous meetings?

A: I think so.

Q: Your answer is yes?

A: Yes.

Q: And you had no way to tell the customer that you were running late, did you?

A: No, my cell phone was out of juice.

If the cross examination is effective, you should recognize the argument that the plaintiff seeks to communicate. The argument is that people who are 20 minutes late to a meeting are likely to drive in excess of the speed limit, especially when they've arranged the meeting themselves, the meeting is with a potential new customer, they are unable to inform the potential new customer that they are running late, and the potential new customer has cancelled two previous meetings.

Had the evidence been organized chronologically instead of by argument, the cross might have masked the inferential significance of some of the evidence. For example, the defendant's arranging the meeting would have taken place well before the defendant set off for the meeting on the day of the accident. Had the examination proceeded chronologically, quite likely many other questions would have separated the arranging of the meeting from the accident, obscuring the former's inferential significance.

For a second example, consider the use of cross examination questioning to support a *silent* argument. As you may recall, silent arguments arise when evidence gives rise to possible inferences that cannot be asserted explicitly. The example is drawn from the first trial of brothers Eric and Lyle Menendez for murdering their parents. A prosecution witness testified that Eric had told her months before the killings that Eric knew that his brother Lyle wore a toupee. (This testimony tended to undermine the brothers' "imperfect self-defense" argument.) On cross examination, the defense attorney attacked the witness' ability to recall Eric's remark. The cross then continued substantially as follows:

Q: Why were you talking to Eric on that occasion?

A: I was visiting the house, so I stopped by his room to say hi.

Q: Did you stay in the house?

A: No, I stayed in the guesthouse.

Q: You stayed in the guesthouse with Lyle, correct?

A: Yes.

Q: You didn't always stay in the guesthouse?

A: No, I just stayed with Lyle sometimes.

Q: So you weren't in the house talking to Eric because you were sleeping there?

A: No.

This cross examination suggests that the witness is untrustworthy because she "sleeps around." The defense attorney could not argue this explicitly, so could not offer the evidence as "relevant to a silent argument." However, the evidence comes in (subject to Federal Rule of Evidence 403) as relevant to the defense argument that the conversation never took place at all.

F. IMPEACHMENT WITH PRIOR INCONSISTENT STATEMENTS

A common and intensely rule-regulated form of impeachment is based on witnesses' prior statements that conflict with their courtroom testimony. Cross examiners look for opportunities to use this type of impeachment because judges and jurors tend to distrust witnesses who "blow hot and cold," and because questioning based on provable former statements is highly safe. This section examines strategies for impeaching adverse witnesses with prior inconsistent statements.

1. EVIDENTIARY RULES

Federal Rule of Evidence 801(d)(1)(A) makes witnesses' prior inconsistent statements admissible for the truth of their contents if the prior statements were made under oath. If a prior inconsistent statement was not made under oath (e.g., it was made during a casual conversation between two co-workers), the statement is admissible only to cast doubt on the accuracy of the conflicting courtroom testimony.

For example, assume that on direct a witness testifies, "The light was green." On cross, the witness admits to saying two months before trial that "The light was red." If the earlier statement was made under oath (e.g., during a deposition), the earlier statement constitutes substantive evidence that the light was red. Otherwise, a judge or juror can consider the earlier statement only for its effect on the witness' credibility. (In a few jurisdictions, such as California, the contents of a prior inconsistent statement are admissible as substantive evidence regardless of whether the statement was made under oath.)

2. IMPEACHMENT OPTIONS

When you are prepared to impeach a witness with a prior inconsistent statement, you may either:

- Confront a witness with the prior statement during cross examination; or

- Forgo cross with respect to the prior statement, and instead offer the statement into evidence when it is your turn to present evidence. (In the parlance of trial, you offer *extrinsic* evidence of the prior statement.) You may also offer a prior inconsistent statement into evidence if you confront the witness with the prior statement during cross and the witness denies making the prior statement (or makes only a qualified concession).

Evidence rules impose two limitations on your ability to use the second option above. As mentioned earlier, if the inconsistent statement relates to a collateral matter, your only choice is to confront the witness with the statement during cross, and you must take the answer. Second, if you plan to offer extrinsic evidence of a prior inconsistent statement, you must not excuse a witness from giving further testimony at the conclusion of cross. (Federal Rule of Evidence 613(b)) This affords the proponent of the witness an opportunity to recall the witness to offer an explanation for the inconsistency.

A reason to confront a witness with a prior inconsistent statement during cross examination is to make an immediate impact on a judge or juror. By contrast, the impact is likely to be diminished if hours or even days pass between the time a witness gives testimony and the time you offer a prior inconsistent statement into evidence.

On the other hand, forgoing cross and instead offering extrinsic evidence of a prior statement avoids the risk that the impeached witness will launch into an immediate explanation that undercuts the value of the impeachment. ("I did once say that the light was red. But that's because your client was holding a gun to my head.")

3. "I DON'T REMEMBER" TESTIMONY

An issue that frequently arises is your right to impeach "I don't remember" testimony with a prior statement. The issue arises this way:

Q: The light was red, correct?

A: I don't remember.

Assume that you can offer evidence that on a prior occasion, the witness had said that the light was red. Traditional doctrine does not allow you to offer the prior statement into evidence to impeach the "I don't remember" testimony. The reasoning is that it is not inconsistent for a witness to forget information. However, in these circumstances other options may be open to you:

- If the witness is a party, offer the prior statement as a party statement. (Federal Rule of Evidence 801(d)(2))

- If the prior statement was made under oath, ask the judge to rule that the witness is unavailable with respect to that point and offer the statement as "former testimony." (Federal Rule of Evidence 804)

- Argue that the inability to recall is feigned and an equivalent to a denial. If the judge agrees, you can offer the prior statement into evidence as inconsistent with the witness' implied denial.

4. EFFECTIVE IMPEACHMENT STRATEGIES

To impeach witnesses effectively with prior inconsistent statements, you may follow a three-step process. Assuming that a witness has given testimony on direct that you plan to impeach on cross, begin impeachment by *pinning the witness down* to that testimony. That is, ask the witness to repeat the testimony that the witness gave on direct. By pinning down the direct testimony, you emphasize the inconsistency and prevent the witness from claiming that "I misspoke on direct."

The second step is to *enhance the credibility of the prior statement* by eliciting circumstances suggesting the prior statement's accuracy. This second step is especially important when the prior statement is admissible as substantive evidence that advances your argument.

Third, elicit the contents of the prior statement.

The following example illustrates this three step process for impeaching a witness with a prior inconsistent deposition statement:

1. Q: The light was green when you first saw the car, correct?

2. A: Yes.

3. Q: You had your deposition taken in this case, did you not?

4. A: Yes, I did.

5. Q: And when you testified at your deposition you took an oath to tell the truth, correct?

6. A: Yes.

7. Q: You took the same oath then that you took today?

8. A: Yes.

9. Q: I take it that your memory of events was fresher at the time of your deposition than it is now?

10. A: Maybe, it was almost a year ago.

11. Q: And you were told that you could look over your deposition before signing it, correct?

12. A: Yes, but I didn't. . .

13. Q: Excuse me, I'll repeat the question. You were told that you could look over your deposition before signing it, correct?

14. A: Yes.

15. Q: Your Honor, I'd like to read from Page 64, lines 7–11 of what has been previously identified as the witness' deposition.

16. Judge: You may proceed.

17. Q: Question. What color was the light when you first saw the car? Answer. It was red. Were you asked that question and did you give that answer?

18. A: Yes.

19. Q: Now let's turn. . .

Here, you first pin down the witness' direct examination testimony (No. 1). Alternatively, some attorneys prefer to include the phrase, *"You testified during direct examination that* the light was green when you first saw the car, correct?" Next, you elicit evidence about the circumstances under which the prior statement was made that may enhance its credibility (Nos. 5–14). Many of these questions are taken from the standard deposition "preamble." Finally, you read the inconsistent statement into evidence (No. 17). Alternatively, you might have read the statement into evidence at No. 5, before you enhanced credibility. The direct juxtaposition of the inconsistent statements may magnify the impeachment's effect.

If the prior inconsistent statement had been in a letter or report written by the witness, you'd have to authenticate the exhibit before reading from it:

1. Q: The light was green when you first saw the car, correct?

2. A: Yes.

3. Q: May I approach the witness, Your Honor? I am showing you a document marked Exhibit 22 for identification. Do you recognize it?

4. A: Yes, that's a report I prepared after the accident.

5. Q: That's your signature at the bottom of page 2?

6. A: Yes.

7. Q: And you prepared the report only two days following the accident?

8. A: Let me check. Yes.

9. Q: I take it that you wanted the report to be as accurate as possible?

10. A: Yes.

11. Q: Your Honor, I'd like to read from Page 2, the second paragraph of Exhibit 22. "The light was red when I first saw the car." That's what you wrote in this report, correct?

12. A: Yes.

13. Q: Now let's turn. . .

Again, you repeat the direct testimony (No. 1), enhance the prior statement's credibility (Nos. 7–10), and then offer the statement (No. 11). As before, you might have offered the prior statement into evidence before enhancing its credibility. Note that Question 9 is based on everyday experience, and therefore is "medium safe." However, a witness is unlikely to dispute the point.

In each of the above examples, you MOVE ON after the impeachment is complete. Though you may be justifiably proud of yourself for carrying out impeachment with a prior inconsistent statement successfully, bells won't ring, the judge won't applaud and the adversary won't write out an immediate check. To make up for this lack of drama, you might be tempted to push further with questions such as, "So you lied on direct when you testified that the light was green?" or, "Why have you changed your story?" Restrain yourself. The first question is argumentative; the answer to the second risks eliciting an explanation that adds your name to the author's as unfortunate developers of the "mystique of cross."

Adhering to a number of other practices will enhance the effectiveness and professionalism of impeachment:

- When you pin down a witness' direct examination testimony, parrot it exactly. If you paraphrase, a witness may balk, opposing counsel may object that you are misquoting the witness, and the force of impeachment may be diluted.

- If you plan to impeach two or three items of testimony with prior statements, pin down each one before proceeding with impeachment.

- Remember that you cannot impeach one witness with the statement of a different witness. For example, if adverse witness Jerry testifies, "The light was green," you cannot cross examine him by asking, "Louise says that the light was red, correct?"

5. OMISSIONS IMPEACHMENT

A corollary to impeachment with a prior inconsistent statement arises when you reveal during cross examination that the witness neglected to disclose on an earlier occasion information that the witness testified to on direct. Underlying the impeachment is an argument that the witness' failure to disclose the information earlier casts doubt on the witness' direct examination testimony. The key to this form of impeachment is demonstrating that the information is of a type that the witness could reasonably have been expected to disclose prior to trial.

A typical example of this form of impeachment arises in criminal trials, when a prosecutor's cross examination of a defense alibi witness reveals that the witness had not disclosed the alibi to the police prior to trial. The prosecutor's argument is that if the alibi story were true, the witness would surely have come forward prior to trial (especially if the witness knew that the defendant was languishing in jail, unable to post bail).

For a second example of this type of impeachment, assume that a plaintiff's witness in a breach of contract case testifies that she attended a meeting in which the plaintiff and defendant agreed, among other things, that the duration of a complex import-export agreement would be five years. The defendant claims that no agreement on duration was arrived at during the meeting. The defense attorney's cross examination reveals that the witness had the duty to take notes at the meeting, and the attorney has marked the notes as an exhibit and the witness has authenticated them. The cross examination continues as follows:

Q: You understood that the notes you were taking would be furnished to both parties, correct?

A: Yes.

Q: You wanted those notes to be as accurate as possible?

A: Yes.

Q: And as complete as you could make them?

A: Well, I wasn't supposed to write down everything everyone said.

Q: But if a matter were important to the final agreement, you understood that you were to include that in your notes, right?

A: Yes.

Q: And you agree that the duration of an agreement is an important term of an agreement?

A: Yes.

Q: And you understood that as of the time of the meeting, didn't you?

A: I'm sure I did.

Q: Now I'm handing you Exhibit 4, which you've testified are the notes you took of the meeting, and I ask you if anywhere in those notes you said anything about the duration of the agreement. Please take your time.

A: I don't see it.

This cross examination suggests that the witness had a business duty to include discussion of important contract terms in her notes of the meeting, and that the duration of an agreement is an important contract term. Thus, the absence of any reference to duration in the notes suggests that no agreement was reached as to that term and casts doubt on the witness' conflicting testimony on direct.

G. CHARACTER EVIDENCE IMPEACHMENT

Federal Rules of Evidence 608 and 609 define the circumstances under which parties can use character evidence to attack the credibility of adverse witnesses. To limit mudslinging, the rules provide that truthfulness is the only trait of character that is relevant to credibility. This section explains cross examination strategies for impeaching witnesses with evidence of bad character for truth-telling.

Rule 609 governs the admissibility of prior convictions to attack witnesses' truthfulness. Subject to a few exceptions set forth in the statute, the rules are these:

- If the witness to be impeached has been convicted of a crime involving dishonesty or false statement (e.g., perjury or forgery), evidence of the conviction is admissible without regard to whether the underlying crime was a felony or a misdemeanor, and the judge has no discretion to exclude evidence of the conviction. (The requisite dishonesty or false statement that automatic admission requires must be based on the elements of the crime that gave rise to the conviction, and cannot be based on the manner in which the crime was carried out.)

- If the conviction was for a felony *not* involving dishonesty or false statement (e.g., assault with a deadly weapon or burglary), evidence of the conviction is admissible subject to judicial discretion under Rule 403. (The usual 403 balancing test is reversed if the witness to be impeached is a criminal defendant, so that the "default" position is exclusion.)

- If the conviction was for a misdemeanor *not* involving dishonesty or false statement, evidence of the conviction is inadmissible.

If you seek to impeach a witness with a prior conviction, you have to demonstrate a good-faith belief that the conviction occurred. Judges generally require production of the record of conviction, since documentation is readily available.

Cross examination based on a prior conviction is generally short:

Q: Ms. Smith, you are the Susan Smith who was convicted of a felony two years ago, correct?

A: Yes.

Q: And the conviction was for operating an illegal Ponzi scheme, is that right?

A: Yes.

The cross examiner could not explore the details of the crime or its consequences. At the same time, prior convictions are not collateral. Had Ms. Smith denied that she had been convicted of a felony, the cross examiner could offer the record of the judgment of conviction into evidence.

Rule 608(b) provides that, subject to judicial discretion, parties may cross examine adverse witnesses about specific prior acts of misconduct that did not result in a conviction, so long as the conduct bears on untruthfulness. Again the cross examiner needs to demonstrate a good faith basis that the misconduct occurred, and judges often require documentation. For example, you may use a police report, deposition testimony, or an affidavit to persuade a judge that the specific act that you want to confront a witness with actually occurred. Cross examination based on a "prior bad act" may unfold as follows:

Q: Mr. Ellis Atie, you applied for admission to Knight Law School two years ago, correct?

A: I did.

Q: And as a part of your application, you prepared and submitted a personal statement, is that right?

A: Yes.

Q: And in that personal statement, you said that you were a former Olympic high jump champion, didn't you?

A: I didn't exactly say that.

Q: Well, didn't you say in that statement that you were an Olympic athlete and that you had won a gold medal in the high jump competition?

A: I may have said that.

Q: You did say that, didn't you?

A: Yes, I did.

Q: But isn't it a fact that you never were an Olympic high jump champion?

A: That's true.

Q: You've never won an Olympic medal of any type, have you?

A: No.

Lying on an application is the type of "prior bad act" conduct that a judge has discretion to allow a cross examiner to inquire pursuant to Rule 608(b). And as the example demonstrates, a cross examiner can press a recalcitrant witness to admit that the specific act occurred. But if at the end of the day a witness denies that the bad act occurred, that is the end of it. Extrinsic evidence of the conduct is inadmissible. The evidence is collateral, and the cross examiner must "take the answer." Consider this example:

Q: Ms. Shiner, at one time you were employed as an accountant by Horner Corporation, is that right?

A: Yes, I worked at Horner for a few years.

Q: And when you applied for that job you submitted a written resume to Horner's human relations office?

A: That's true.

Q: Showing you what has been marked Plaintiff's Exhibit No.1 for identification, is this a copy of the resume you submitted to Horner Corporation?

A: It looks like it.

Q: Please examine Exhibit No.1, and tell us whether you state on the resume that you received an MBA from UCLA's Anderson School of Management.

A: It does say that.

Q: The statement on your resume is false, isn't it?

A: I deny that.

Q: Well, you hadn't in fact received an MBA from the Anderson School when you applied for a job with Horner, had you?

A: I'm not sure of the timing of my education and when I wrote this resume.

Q: That's not what I asked you. At the time you submitted this resume to Horner, you falsely claimed that you had received an MBA from the Anderson School, isn't that right?

A: I can't say for sure because I don't recall the timing.

Here, the cross examiner presses a witness to admit making a false statement on a written resume. The witness' responses are evasive, and while the cross examiner does not have to accept the witness' initial denial, the judge has discretion to cut off the questioning. If as here a witness persists in denying the misconduct, the cross examiner ultimately must take the answer.

If you plan to impeach an adverse witness with character evidence (or oppose such impeachment), good practice is to seek an advance judicial ruling as to its propriety. You might do so through a pre-trial *motion in limine,* or during trial before impeachment begins. If you refer to a prior conviction or specific bad act and a judge decides that your questions were improper, your conduct may result in a costly mistrial.

H. IMPEACHMENT—OTHER BASES

Evidence rules closely regulate impeachment based on prior inconsistent statements and character evidence (see Secs. F and G above) more so than they do other forms of impeachment. The subsections below examine other bases of impeachment that commonly arise during cross examinations. Admissibility of impeachment in these situations is governed largely by Rules 401 (relevance) and 403 (balancing probative value against unfair prejudice and other factors).

1. BIAS

Bias evidence suggests that harmful testimony is a product of an adverse witness' emotional or financial stake in the outcome of a case. In the example below, the attorney representing plaintiff Cal Culus cross examines Al Gebra, who has testified on behalf of the defendant in a patent infringement case:

Q: Mr. Gebra, you and Mr. Culus graduated two years ago from the same school of engineering, correct?

A: That's right.

Q: And during your senior year you had to design and build a working model, right?

A: Yes.

Q: And when you had some trouble producing a design you asked Mr. Culus for help, isn't that true?

A: Yes. We all did this.

Q: But Mr. Culus told you that he was under a lot of pressure and didn't have the time to help you with your design, isn't that true?

A: Yes, he wouldn't help me.

Q: And this made you angry, didn't it?

A: I was a little upset.

Q: Weren't you upset enough to tell Mr. Culus that you looked forward to getting even with him some-day?

A: I might have said something like that, but that doesn't mean I'm lying.

Q: But right after the graduation ceremony, didn't you tell Mr. Culus to his face, and I quote, "Just you wait, I'll get even with you for screwing up my senior year?"

A: OK, I said that.

Bias is non-collateral. Had Gebra denied making the statement to Culus, the cross examiner could have called a witness to prove up Gebra's threatening statement.

This second example of cross examination based on an adverse witness' bias is taken from the 1953 trial of the so-called "atomic spies," Ethel and Julius Rosenberg. Alleged co-conspirator David Greenglass and his wife Ruth were relatives of the Rosenbergs and both were alleged participants in the plot to steal atom bomb secrets and pass them to the Soviet Union. Cross examining Greenglass, defense lawyer Emanuel Bloch suggested that Greenglass had a strong motive to testify to whatever the prosecutors wanted him to:

Q: You have known your wife Ruth since childhood days?

A: Yes.

Q: Did you love her when you married her?

A: I did.

Q: Do you love her today?

A: I do.

Q: Do you love her more than you love yourself?

A: I do.

Q: Did you at any time think of your wife while you were down here telling your story to the FBI?

A: Of course I thought of her.

Q: Did you think of your wife with respect to the fact that she may be a defendant in a criminal proceeding?

A: I did.

Q: Now, Mr. Greenglass, your wife has never been arrested, has she?

A: She has not.

Q: And she has never been indicted, has she?

A: She has not.

Q: And your wife is at the present time home, taking care of your children, isn't that right?

A: That's right.

Through this questioning, Bloch hoped to establish that Greenglass lied about the Rosenbergs to protect his wife. With another series of cross examination questions, Bloch also impeached Greenglass' credibility based on his motive to cooperate with the prosecution:

Q: How long ago have you pleaded guilty?

A: A year ago.

Q: Have you been sentenced?

A: No.

Q: Do you believe the court will be easier on you because you are testifying here?

A: I don't believe that in testifying I will help myself to that great an extent.

Q: Will you clarify that?

A: To any great extent.

Q: To any extent.

2. CONTRADICTION

Contradiction is a form of impeachment that attacks the accuracy of an adverse witness's testimony. For example, assume that a plaintiff's witness in an auto accident case testified on direct examination that the witness had just left a bakery and was eating a jelly donut at the time the witness observed the collision. The defense attorney's contradiction-based cross examination might go as follows:

Q: You say that you were eating a jelly donut at the time you observed the accident?

A: That's right.

Q: Isn't it true that you were eating a bran muffin?

A: That's not right. It was a jelly donut.

Q: And you also testified that you had walked out of a bakery just before observing the collision?

A: Yes.

Q: Isn't it true that you had just walked out of the bar where you had just spent the better part of an hour consuming sour apple martinis?

A: No, that's not true.

Here, the cross examiner seeks to contradict two items of evidence provided by an adverse witness. Following the witness' denials, the cross examiner can offer extrinsic evidence on non-collateral (important) matters. Whether the witness was munching on a donut or a muffin at the time of the accident is almost surely collateral. The cross examiner would have to "take the answer" on that point. But evidence that the witness had been drinking martinis in a bar is potentially important, as it pertains to the witness' ability to observe and recollect what happened. That point is non-collateral, and extrinsic evidence to prove up the contradiction would be admissible.

3. TESTIMONIAL IMPAIRMENT

A cross examiner can impeach an adverse witness' testimony with evidence suggesting that external or internal factors cast doubt on the witness' ability to perceive or recollect events accurately.

External factors include a witness' distance from the locale where the events to which the witness testified took place, and poor lighting or physical obstacles that impaired the witness' ability to observe the events to which the witness testified. Internal factors include a witness' impaired hearing or vision, and the witness' having been under the influence of alcohol or drugs at the time events described by the witness took place. The following sample cross examination is based on an adverse witness' internal impairment:

Q: Mr. Wintroub, while sitting at a lunch counter you overheard the details of the contractual arrangements between the plaintiff and the defendant?

A: Right.

Q: Now Mr. Wintroub, you are familiar with the Johnson Hearing Clinic?

A: Yes.

Q: In fact you've been a patient of the director, Dr. Richard Johnson, for over a decade?

A: I've been seeing him, yes.

Q: And you've been treated by Dr. Johnson for hearing loss, isn't that true?

A: Yes.

Q: You've had surgeries on both of your inner ears, correct?

A: Yes.

Q: But those surgeries didn't restore you to normal hearing, did they?

A: No.

Q: Your hearing is at best less than half of normal?

A: I suppose.

Q: So you almost always wear a hearing aid on each ear?

A: Yes.

Q: But on the day you were sitting at the lunch counter you weren't wearing hearing aids, were you?

A: No.

Q: You didn't have on a hearing aid in either ear when the conversation between the defendant and the plaintiff took place?

A: No.

I. EMPHASIS STRATEGIES

In general, emphasis is a natural byproduct of following the cross examination strategies this chapter suggests. If you limit cross examination to evidence supporting your arguments, and marshal that evidence using one-item leading questions, you focus judges and jurors on the strengths of your arguments. The subsections below suggest additional emphasis strategies.

1. "NO, NO, NO"

"No, no, no" is an emphasis strategy that you can use during both cross and direct examination. The strategy consists of eliciting a string of negative responses. For example, you can elicit a series of negative responses to emphasize what *did* occur by suggesting alternatives that did *not* occur. The cross examination below illustrates this strategy:

Q: It was a bear that went over the mountain, wasn't it?

A: Yes.

Q: It was not a person?

A: No.

Q: Or a gorilla?

A: No.

Q: Or a deer?

A: No.

Q: It was a bear?

A: Yes.

2. ULTIMATE CONCLUSION QUESTIONS

No matter how effectively you marshal circumstantial evidence effectively, your desired inference may not be as self-evident to a judge or jurors as it is to you. *Ultimate conclusion questions* increase the likelihood that fact finders understand your desired inference, even when (as is typically true) a witness disagrees with that inference.

The questions in the illustrative cross examination below are based on a defense cross examination in the media-frenzy 1990's rape trial of William Kennedy Smith. Kennedy Smith, a member of the politically powerful Kennedy family, was charged in Florida with raping a young woman by the name of Patricia Bowman. On direct examination, prosecution witness Ann Mercer testified that she was Bowman's good friend, and that on the night of the alleged rape, Bowman called Mercer and asked her to hurry to the Kennedy estate and drive her home. When Mercer got to the estate, a hysterical Bowman told Mercer that she had been raped by Kennedy Smith. A portion of the defense attorney's cross examination of Ann Mercer was substantially as follows:

Q: Ms. Mercer, after receiving the phone call from Ms. Bowman you immediately drove to the Kennedy estate, correct?

A: That's right.

Q: And when you got there she told you that she had been raped?

A: Correct.

Q: But you didn't take her immediately to the hospital, did you?

A: Not immediately, no.

Q: And you didn't immediately call the police, did you?

A: No.

Q: Instead, you walked around the estate with Mr. Smith looking for Ms. Bowman's shoes, right?

A: That's right, she wanted her shoes.

Q: You walked through a dark house with a man you had just been told was a rapist?

A: Yes I did.

Q: And you walked alone with this alleged rapist down to the beach?

A: Yes.

Q: And it was dark where you were walking, correct?

A: Yes.

Q: Ms. Mercer, isn't it true that the reason you were alone with Mr. Smith and didn't call the police right away is that Ms. Bowman never told you that she had been raped?

A: That's not right. She told me exactly what I testified to.

The last question is an ultimate conclusion question. The defense attorney would not of course expect a favorable answer, for that would be tantamount to an admission of perjury. Rather, the defense attorney had marshaled together items of circumstantial evidence from which the jury might infer that Bowman did not tell Mercer that Bowman had been raped. The ultimate conclusion question identifies and emphasizes the desired inference, while allowing the witness to do no more than insist that her testimony was accurate.

J. SELECTIVE USE OF OPEN QUESTIONS

Open questions are generally undesirable during cross examination because they take control of a story from you and hand it to witnesses. However, you can realize a number of benefits through occasional and judicious use of open questions. For example, open questions can break up the sense of "verbal bullying" that a long series of leading questions sometimes produces. Also, occasional open questions connote that you have nothing to fear from the whole truth.

Contextual details often furnish a safe harbor for the use of open questions during cross examination. For example, the defense attorney who cross examined Ann Mercer in the illustration above might have asked Ann Mercer to "please describe the beach" where she and the defendant walked. The beach's appearance is a contextual detail, so the question does not offer the witness a chance to re-tell the entire story and it is unlikely to produce new damaging evidence. Moreover, any description of the beach furthers the defense attorney's argument that Mercer did not rush for assistance and therefore had not been told by Bowman that a rape had occurred. Thus, the open question is safe.

You may also use open questions when you seek a particular answer and are reasonably confident that the witness will provide it. For example, during a deposition an adverse witness may have willingly given testimony that favors your case. At trial, the adversary did not elicit the information on direct examination, and you fully expect that the witness will testify at trial consistently with the deposition testimony. In such a situation, you may choose to seek the information with an open question.

As suggested in the Cross Examination Safety Model, you may also use open questions if you have no choice other than to "fish." In this undesirable situation, the chance that a witness will unexpectedly reveal helpful information is higher if you encourage witnesses to talk with open questions.

K. ORDER OF QUESTIONING

Cross examination questioning typically proceeds topically rather than chronologically. That is, you may often marshal evidence around topics, regardless of the topics' chronological relationship to each other. Thus, a decision you may have to make concerns the order of topics. Assuming that you will pursue evidence for more than one argument, or that you will pursue two or more topics that pertain to the same argument, what principles can help you decide on an order of topics? While ultimately you have to rely on your best judgment in the context of a specific witness and case, the following factors can help you decide where to start.

- When you hope both to elicit new favorable information and to impeach unfavorable testimony that a witness has already given, address the former task first. Once you attack a witness' credibility, the witness may become wary and qualify whatever favorable information you do elicit.

- Begin with a topic that advances your strongest argument.

- Alternatively, begin with a topic that allows you to ask the safest questions. Even if the argument is not your strongest, the early success may detract from the witness' confidence and overall credibility.

- Begin cross with whatever topic direct finishes. Like the bull who makes a dramatic entrance by charging directly at the matador, you leap into the fray by taking up right where direct left off. This tactic takes advantage both of primacy and recency: the direct examiner's final topic is your first one.

L. FORGOING CROSS EXAMINATION

Throwing a witness to a cross examiner is akin to throwing a teenager a set of keys to a new sports car. Typically, neither can resist the temptation to "do something." However, sometimes your best option is to rephrase the common aphorism to state, "Don't just do something, sit there." That is, at the conclusion of an adverse witness' direct examination, you may indicate that you have "*No questions.*" The reason is that if you cross examine and accomplish nothing, you've probably boosted an adversary's case even if you do not elicit additional harmful evidence. Unlike with love, it can be worse to have crossed and lost than not to have crossed at all.

One situation in which forgoing cross may make sense arises when you rely on a normative argument. Your normative argument may take the form of, "My adversary's story, even if accurate, does not support the adversary's desired inference." You may undercut this type of argument if on cross examination you engage an adverse witness on factual quibbles. The risk is that by seeking to yet failing to undermine the witness' factual account, you add force to the adversary's normative position as well.

For example, assume that you represent a parent charged with child abuse for leaving a baby unattended in a car for a short period of time. Your client admits to leaving the child alone, but argues that doing so was justified by a sudden emergency. If you unsuccessfully attack an adverse witness' account of the parent's absence, you might undermine your normative argument.

A second situation in which you might reasonably forgo cross arises when a witness' testimony relates to an issue you don't dispute. For example, if you represent a defendant who is only contesting damages, you might forgo cross of a "liability" witness.

Beyond categories such as these, you will have to rely on professional judgment when deciding whether to forgo cross. For example, if a judge or jury seems impressed by an adverse witness, all your cross may do is extend the witness' time on the stand and the positive impression. Whenever you cross examine, you implicitly promise to elicit favorable information. If you fail to live up to your promise, you may damage a case even if you uncover no new damaging evidence.

M. RESPONDING TO EVASIVE ANSWERS

Though you frame the most leading question using your most assertive demeanor, witnesses may respond evasively or non-responsively. Though such responses may detract from a witnesses' credibility, they may also prevent you from eliciting your desired response. Consider this dialogue:

Q: The bear then went over the mountain, correct?

A: Where else could it have gone?

The answer seems to tacitly concede that the bear went over the mountain. Yet if where the bear went is important to your argument, the answer is evasive because the record does not explicitly reflect your desired response. The strategies described below can help you elicit unambiguous responses while emphasizing an adverse witness' evasiveness.

1. REPEAT THE QUESTION

The simplest strategy for responding to an evasive answer is to simply repeat the question:

Q: The bear then went over the mountain, correct?

A: That bear was always getting loose.

Q: But the bear did go over the mountain, correct?

A: Yes.

Alternatively, you might ask the judge to have the court reporter re-read a question. Do not yourself ask a court reporter to re-read a question; this is the judge's domain, not yours. To save time, however, most judges will prefer that you repeat a question.

2. "I DIDN'T ASK X, I ASKED Y"

A slight variation on the strategy above can more effectively emphasize that a witness' answer was evasive. The strategy goes as follows:

Q: The bear then went over the mountain, correct?

A: That bear was always getting loose.

Q: I didn't ask you whether the bear was always getting loose. I asked you if the bear then went over the mountain.

A: Yes.

3. MOVE TO STRIKE AND REPEAT A QUESTION

A still more aggressive response to an evasive reply is to re-ask a question while moving to strike the non-responsive answer. For example:

Q: The bear then went over the mountain, correct?

A: That bear was always getting loose.

Q: Your Honor, I move to strike the witness' answer as non-responsive.

Judge: Motion granted. I instruct the jurors to disregard the witness' last answer.

Q: All right, I'll ask you again. The bear then went over the mountain, correct?

A: Yes.

4. JUDGE'S INSTRUCTION TO ANSWER

Especially when a witness has been evasive on more than one occasion, you may ask the judge to instruct the witness to answer. In front of a jury, such an instruction may appear to ally the judge with your client. You should simply ask the judge for an instruction, rather than launch into an oral law review article on the harm done by evasive witnesses:

Q: The bear then went over the mountain, correct?

A: That bear was always getting loose.

Q: Your Honor, will the court please instruct the witness to answer the question.

Judge: Witness, please answer counsel's question.

Q: All right, I'll ask you again. The bear then went over the mountain, correct?

A: Yes.

Some judges may allow you personally to instruct a witness to answer. However, unless a judge explicitly authorizes you to do so, make your request through the judge.

5. AVOID ARGUING WITH WITNESSES

No matter what your private opinion of an adverse witness' credibility, your courtroom behavior must show respect to the court and the institution of trial. One aspect of this attitude is to refrain from arguing with witnesses or answering their questions. You can subtly point out that if witnesses want to ask questions, they will first have to go to law school:

Q: You leaped without looking, correct?

A: What would you have done in that situation?

Q: What I would have done is not the issue, and I am not under oath. You did leap without looking, correct?

A: Yes.

In the heat of battle, you may well be tempted to reply: "Glad that you asked. I would have. . ." However, as you are not a witness, save such ripostes for negotiation or closing argument.

6. "MAY" AND "MIGHT"

"May" and "might" are two classic weasel words that can deceive you into thinking that a witness has given your desired response. Consider this exchange:

Q: The chicken reached the other side, correct?

A: It may have.

The answer is neither a denial nor a positive response. Thus, you should press for a further response:

Q: Colonel Campbell, isn't it a fact that the chicken did reach the other side?

A: Yes.

N. RESPONDING TO EXPLANATIONS

When you attack a witness' story on cross examination, you run a risk that a witness will try to repair the damage by volunteering an immediate explanation. For example, a witness may try to explain away a seeming implausibility or an inconsistent statement. You cannot prevent an adversary from eliciting an explanation on redirect examination. However, it is generally in your interest to prevent a witness from offering an explanation during cross. This section examines strategies that may help you do so.

1. REFUSE REQUESTS TO EXPLAIN

Adverse witnesses are sometimes thoughtful enough to ask you for permission to explain an answer. Generally, unless you anticipate the explanation and welcome it, your best response is a polite refusal. Consider this example:

Q: You never saw him holding the gun, right?

A: May I explain?

Q: Please just answer the question. Your attorney will have a chance to question you after I finish. You never saw him holding the gun, right?

A: That's right.

Here, the witness asks for permission to explain, and you sensibly keep control of the testimony by refusing.

2. IGNORE AND REPEAT

Witnesses are more likely to blurt out explanations unexpectedly than to ask for permission in advance. In such a situation, you may respond by ignoring an explanation and emphasizing a witness' evasiveness by repeating your question:

Q: You never saw him holding the gun, right?

A: Correct, but I saw it on the ground less than a foot away from him after I heard the shot.

Q: I'll ask you again. You never saw him holding the gun, correct?

A: That's right.

This technique allows you to emphasize evidence supporting an argument without arguing with a witness.

3. INTERRUPT AN EXPLANATION

Another way to defend against an unexpected explanation is to cut it off in mid-response. Do not shout down or talk over a witness. Stand (if you are sitting), perhaps hold out your hand in a "stop" position, and signal with a phrase like "Excuse me" that you expect the witness to stop testifying. Then ask your next question. The strategy may unfold as follows:

Q: You never saw him holding the gun, right?

A: Correct, but I . . .

Q: Excuse me, but you've answered the question. Now let me ask you again, you didn't see him holding the gun?

A: No I didn't.

4. MOVE TO STRIKE

If you're cross examining the World's Fastest Blurter or the notion that it's not polite to interrupt is too embedded in your consciousness to switch off at the courtroom door, you may be unable to prevent a judge or jury from hearing an explanation. A fall-back position is to object to the explanation, move to strike it and ask the judge to instruct the jury (if one is present) to disregard the answer. The usual ground for objection is that an explanation is "non-responsive," though of course an explanation may also be objectionable as hearsay, irrelevant or violative of some other evidentiary rule. The process may go as follows:

Q: You never saw him holding the gun, right?

A: Correct, but I saw it on the ground less than a foot away from him after I heard the shot.

Q: Your Honor, I move to strike everything after "correct" as non-responsive and ask that you instruct the jury to disregard it.

Judge: Granted. Jurors. . .

Judges will not necessarily sustain such an objection, especially when they believe that an answer would be misleading without the explanation. However, often judges will grant the request and leave it to opposing counsel to elicit the explanation on redirect examination.

5. IMPLAUSIBLE EXPLANATIONS

The above strategies regard explanations as enemies to be prevented or eliminated. However, witnesses impeached with inconsistent statements or implausible actions may offer explanations that only further detract from their credibility. In such situations, an effective response is to ask further questions emphasizing an explanation's implausibility:

Q: Now, you testified on direct that the robber had a scar, is that correct?

A: Yes.

Q: Do you recall talking to Officer Fox, just a short time after the robbery?

A: Yes.

Q: And Officer Fox asked you some questions about the robbery?

A: That's right.

Q: And he asked you for a description of the robber?

A: Yes.

Q: You wanted to be as accurate as possible in your description, correct?

A: Of course.

Q: And your memory of the robbery was fresher when you spoke to Officer Fox than it is now, correct?

A: I guess so.

Q: Didn't you tell Officer Fox that the robber had no distinguishing marks?

A: Yes, but you've got to understand that I was really nervous when I spoke to the Officer.

Q: That's understandable. But your nervousness did not prevent you from telling the Officer that the robber was about 6' tall, did it?

A: No.

Q: And you still stand by that statement, correct?

A: Yes.

Q: And your nervousness didn't prevent you from telling the Officer that the robber weighed about 180 pounds?

A: No.

Q: Your nervousness only prevented you from failing to tell the Officer that the robber had a scar?

A: I guess so.

These questions suggest the implausibility of the witness' "nervousness" explanation. While witnesses will not always cooperate by offering implausible explanations, think twice before moving to strike an explanation.

6. PRE–INSTRUCTING WITNESSES

Aware of a witness' propensity to explain answers, you might consider preceding a question with an instruction such as, "Please just answer this question yes or no." However, some judges consider such comments to be an improper attempt to intimidate a witness. A subtler and more allowable alternative is to phrase an instruction as a question: "If you can fairly answer my next question yes or no, will you do so?"

7. "CLOSING THE DOOR"

The strategy called *closing the door* consists of asking a witness whose testimony you plan to impeach about possible reasonable and credible explanations before you launch into the impeachment. If a witness confirms an explanation, you have an opportunity to forgo the planned impeachment. If the witness does *not* confirm the explanation, you can go forward with the planned impeachment with the assurance that you have already eliminated the most likely and reasonable explanations.

The courtroom film *My Cousin Vinny* (1992) provides an excellent illustration of the use of the close the door strategy. In the film, two people rob a rural southern convenience store, and shoot and kill the clerk. A prosecution eyewitness, Tipton, identifies the defendants as the people he saw enter the store just as he was beginning to cook his breakfast, and leave the store when he was ready to eat his breakfast five minutes later, just after Tipton heard gunshots. Cross examining Tipton, defense attorney Vinny wants to establish that at least 20 minutes elapsed between the time Tipton saw the defendants enter the store and the time that Tipton saw what were two other people, not the defendants, leave the store after shooting the clerk. Vinny's cross examination of Tipton is substantially as follows:

Q: According to your testimony, it took you five minutes to cook breakfast?

A: That's right.

Q: Do you remember what you had?

A: Eggs and grits.

Q: How do you like your grits? Do you cook them regular, creamy or al dente?

A: Just regular, I guess.

Q: Do you use instant grits?

A: No self-respecting southerner uses instant grits. I take pride in my grits.

Q: So Mr. Tipton, how could it take you five minutes to cook your grits, when it takes the entire grit-eating world 20 minutes?

A: I don't know. I'm a fast cook I guess.

Here, Vinny's argument is based on a fact that all the southern jurors would readily accept, that it takes 20 minutes for grits to cook. But before confronting Tipton with the cooking time of grits, Vinny closes the door on two explanations that Tipton might offer as to why he cooked his grits only for 5 minutes on the day of the crime: he cooks his grits "regular," and does not use instant grits.

O. "CROSS" EXAMINATION?

Dramas often offer a quite literal picture of "cross" examination. Cross examiners are routinely portrayed as snarly megalomaniacs to whom Attila the Hun would find it hard to relate. Some clients may prefer such a combative style, concluding that "my attorney was really in there battling for me."

Judges however tend to regard such behavior as improper and unethical, and jurors may perceive you as an unfair bully. If so, jurors may empathize with witnesses regardless of whether the jurors believe their testimony. Even snide remarks can bring judicial opprobrium and juror hostility:

Q: You arrived there about 3 P.M.?

A: I'm not sure.

Q: You're not sure of much, even the time.

Judge: Counsel, I'm striking that remark from the record. Confine yourself to asking questions or you'll have me to deal with.

By all means ask questions firmly and when appropriate insist on answers in a professional manner. But stepping over the line into nastiness usually does more harm than good.

P. "YOUR STORY" CROSS EXAMINATION

A "your story" cross consists of confronting adverse witnesses with the version of events to which your witnesses will testify. For example, assume an assault prosecution in which each party claims that the other "started it." As the defense lawyer, you might conduct "your story" cross as follows:

Q: Mr. Rogers, what really happened is that you started the argument by calling my client a pusillaneous tetrahedron, correct?

A: No I did not.

Q: Didn't you pick up a bottle and walk towards my client with it?

A: That's not what happened.

Q: Etc.

As with "ultimate conclusion" questions, you do not expect a "your story" cross to produce favorable answers. After all, witnesses rarely answer the implied question, "Aren't you an abject liar?" affirmatively. Nevertheless, the benefits of this form of cross include:

- You avoid fishing.

- A judge or juror may perceive you as fair for giving an adverse party a chance to respond to your version of events.

- As a defense attorney, you may offset some of the plaintiff's "mind set" advantage by reminding a jury during the plaintiff's case-in-chief of your version of events.

- In a criminal case in which the defendant will not testify and will call no witnesses, a "your story" cross may be your only opportunity to put a competing version of events before a jury.

- Often, parties to a dispute agree to at least certain events. To the extent that an adverse witness agrees with "your story" questions, the witness accredits your client's version.

Q. PREPARING WITNESSES FOR CROSS EXAMINATION

Unless they are "repeat players" in the trial process, your clients and witnesses are likely to have derived many of their ideas about cross examination from popular culture, primarily films and television shows. If so, they are likely to be anxious at the prospect of cross examination. After all, popular culture frequently depicts cross examiners as being right in witnesses' faces as they hurl nasty, belittling and accusatory questions at their cowed victims. (For a classic portrayal of this type of cross examination, see prosecutor Claude Dancer's cross examination of Mary Palant in the film *Anatomy of a Murder*.)

Thus, one of the best ways to help inexperienced clients and witnesses testify comfortably and confidently is to assure them during a pre-trial meeting that the way cross examination is often depicted in films and television does not represent reality, and that in any event it is your job to protect the witness against any unfair questioning.

You may also talk to witnesses about "cross examination do's and don'ts." Matters that you may want to review with witnesses include the following:

- Witnesses should answer questions in the same manner during cross examination as during direct examination.

- Witnesses should look at the cross examiner when answering, not at you. Witnesses who repeatedly look at their attorneys before answering a cross examiner's questions can appear fearful and uncertain of their testimony.

- Witnesses should tell the truth without worrying about whether it helps or hurts either party. Moreover, if asked on cross examination whether you gave any instructions to the witness, the witness can answer, "Yes. I was instructed to tell the truth."

- Witnesses should not worry about the propriety of questions. Unless you object, they should answer fully and fairly but should not volunteer information.

- Witnesses should not guess. If they don't know how to answer a question or have forgotten information, they should say so.

- Pretrial meetings between lawyers and witnesses are perfectly legitimate, and if asked witnesses should forthrightly say that you met with them to review their expected testimony.

- You or a colleague might also accompany a witness on a pre-trial visit to the courtroom in which the trial will take place. Familiarity with the setting and the process can help relax anxious witnesses. Again, if you do take a witness to court, be careful not to give away your own inexperience with comments such as, "No, I don't know what you call that person in the front of the courtroom who's wearing a black robe."

The potential downside of pre-trial instructions like these is that they may add to witnesses' anxieties. After all, witnesses not only have to remember what happened, they also have to remember your instructions. Thus, perhaps the most effective preparation strategy you can follow is to conduct a mock cross examination. If possible, ask a colleague to cross examine a witness, anticipating as best you can the content of the questions and the cross examiner's style of questioning.

Annotate a mock cross examination by interrupting questioning and providing feedback on a witness' answers and demeanor. Context-specific advice is often more helpful than general instructions such as those above. While you may direct much of your feedback at problematic responses, praise witnesses when they do well. Praise is likely to bolster witnesses' confidence, and in turn the credibility of their testimony. Throughout, remember that no privilege attaches to conversations that you have with non-client witnesses, so the conversations are fair game for cross examination.

R. PROTECTING YOUR WITNESSES

Effective cross examination strategies include protecting your own witnesses from an adversary's improper cross examination questioning. Below are common objections that you may need to employ when adversaries cross examine your witnesses. (For a discussion of other objections and objections procedures, see Chapter 13.)

1. "OBJECTION, ARGUMENTATIVE"

Make this objection when your adversary asks your witness to respond to an argument or comment on another witness' testimony. Examples of argumentative questions include:

- "Which is the lie—your deposition testimony or your direct examination testimony?"

- "Why should the jury believe the word of a convicted felon?"

2. "OBJECTION, COUNSEL IS NOT ALLOWING THE WITNESS TO FINISH ANSWERING"

Dissatisfied with the direction of a witness' answer (and perhaps with his or her own question), a cross examiner may ask a second question before your witness concludes answering the first one. If your adversary believes that an answer is non-responsive or improper on other grounds, your adversary should object and obtain a ruling. Otherwise, your witness is entitled to answer a question.

3. "OBJECTION, COUNSEL IS BADGERING (HARASSING) THE WITNESS"

This favorite objection of cine-lawyers arises when your adversary poses questions at a rapid pace that don't allow you time to object (if appropriate) or your witness to think. Just as hearing *Flight of the Bumblebee* may cause a diner to become flustered and eat too fast, so may rapid-fire questions cause witnesses to make careless mistakes. This tactic is not what the Constitution means by a "speedy trial."

4. "OBJECTION, COUNSEL IS MISSTATING THE EVIDENCE (MISQUOTING THE WITNESS)"

When an adversary confronts your witness with previously-given testimony, be sure that the adversary quotes testimony accurately. For example, assume that on direct examination your witness testifies, "I stared at the defendant through the open window for at least five seconds." On cross, the adversary asks this question:

Q: Now, when you got this pretty good look, did you . . .

This question misquotes the witness. Moreover, whether "staring through an open window for five seconds" constitutes a "pretty good look" is for a judge or juror to determine, not for an adversary to characterize during questioning.

5. "OBJECTION, ASKED AND ANSWERED"

This objection is appropriate when an adversary repetitively questions your witness on the same topic. Just as the Wicked Stepmother in *Snow White* seemed to think that repeated questioning would lead the mirror to provide a better answer as to "who is the fairest of them all," so cross examiners may think that repetitive cross examination inquiries into the same topic will produce more favorable answers. Cross examination can be confrontational, and judges often do permit cross examiners to explore the same topic in more than one context. Limits exist, however, and you may use this objection to seek a ruling that a topic has been sufficiently probed and it's time to move on.

6. "OBJECTION, BEYOND THE SCOPE OF DIRECT"

As mentioned earlier, the so-called American rule of cross examination provides that cross examination is limited to subjects that arose during direct examination (including issues that pertain to credibility). You may interpose this objection if your adversary seeks to delve into new topics. Even if the judge allows the adversary to question with respect to the new topics, your objection may prevent the adversary from using leading questions.

7. "OBJECTION, ASSUMES FACTS NOT IN EVIDENCE"

This objection typically arises when an adversary prefaces a question with a direct or implied statement. For example, your adversary may ask, "Dr. Johnson has found that my client had a concussion, so you struck my client in the head, correct?" If Dr. Johnson hasn't testified, and indeed even if Dr. Johnson HAS testified, the question is improper. In the latter instance, a more correct objection would be, "Counsel is testifying."

CHAPTER 9

SATISFYING FOUNDATIONAL REQUIREMENTS FOR NON-TANGIBLE EVIDENCE

Even the most improvisational jazz artist greats are masters of the musical scales. In the same way, even the most rhetorically gifted trial advocates need to be masters of the foundational rules of evidence. Foundational rules establish requirements for admitting evidence into the record. This chapter explains and illustrates the process of satisfying foundational requirements for common types of non-tangible evidence, or what many judges and lawyers refer to as "laying foundations." (Chapter 10 illustrates how to lay foundations for common forms of tangible evidence, including real and demonstrative evidence.)

Laying a foundation resembles painting a room. In each situation you have an end goal in mind: a freshly-painted room or the admission of an item of evidence. But to reach either goal you have to engage in preliminary activities. When you paint a room, the typical preliminary activities include sanding, scraping and priming. At trial, the preliminary activities comprise "laying a foundation."

A. INTER-PERSONAL COMMUNICATIONS

Witnesses commonly testify to inter-personal communications such as conversations and statements. The communications may be made face-to-face, over a telephone or electronically. To offer the contents of communications such as these into evidence, one type of foundational requirement you may have to satisfy involves content-based rules of evidence such as the hearsay rule (see below for sample hearsay foundational showings). But in addition to laying a foundation satisfying a content-based rule, you typically also need to lay a "who, where and when" foundation for the communication itself. Such a foundation typically consists of testimony describing the parties to the communication and where and when the communication was made.

When witnesses testify to face-to-face conversations with people they know, the foundational showing is usually brief. Consider this sample of testimony:

1. Q: Did you have a second meeting with Andre?

2. A: I did, we had dinner.

3. Q: Please tell us what was said during this meeting.

4. Opp: Objection, lack of foundation.

5. Judge: Sustained.

6. Q: When did this dinner meeting take place?

7. A: Sometime in mid-June, about two weeks after our initial meeting.

8. Q: This mid-June meeting also occurred at Blassie's Bistro?

9. A: Yes.

10. Q: Did anyone other than you and Andre participate in the meeting?

11. A: No, it was just the two of us.

12. Q: OK, now please tell us what was said during this meeting.

13. A: . . .

The questions following the objection lay a foundation for the conversation by eliciting evidence about when it took place, where it took place, and who participated in the conversation. As No. 7 indicates, the "when" element of the foundation can be satisfied even if a witness can provide only a time estimate rather than a precise date. And as No. 8 reminds you, you can if you choose use leading questions to lay a foundation even on direct examination.

The "who" element of a foundation can get more complex with non-face-to-face communications. For example, for telephone conversations you have to authenticate the conversation under Federal Rule of Evidence 901 by eliciting testimony indicating how the witness knows the identity of the other party to the conversation. Under Federal Rule of Evidence 104(b), the proferring party's burden is to offer foundational evidence that is sufficient to support a finding of the other party's identity.

Even in such situations, establishing the requisite foundation is straightforward if your witness can demonstrate personal knowledge of the other participant's identity. The sample foundational testimony below establishes the identity of a participant to a telephone conversation:

Q: Did you ever speak to Andre again?

A: Yes, a week later when I phoned him up.

Q: How did you know it was Andre you talked to?

A: I've known him for years, we've talked often and I know his voice.

You might use the so-called *telephone directory doctrine* provided for by Federal Rule of Evidence 901(b)(6) to establish the identity of a previously-unknown participant in a telephone conversation. For example, assume that your witness seeks to testify to a conversation between the witness and an employee of a national retailer. The foundational testimony might go something like this:

Q: Ms. Jones, did you inform R.E.J. of the problem?

A: I sure did, I phoned the company immediately.

Q: How did you go about contacting the company?

A: I found a contact number for REJ on its website home page. I phoned that number and after working my way through a few voice mail selections I talked to a man who said "R.E.J. customer service-how can I help you?"

Chapter 10 discusses the process of laying foundations for tangible communications such as electronic mail messages.

B. RECOLLECTION REFRESHED

Testifying in front of judges and under oath can be nerve-wracking, and even well-prepared witnesses may suffer temporary lapses of memory. This section briefly explains common options for eliciting testimony to information that witnesses can provide but have momentarily forgotten.

Refreshing recollection scenarios typically arise during direct examinations. The simplest solution is to refer to the forgotten information in a leading question. While leading questions are normally improper on direct examination, a common exception allows you to lead when it is apparent that a witness knows information but has momentarily forgotten it. The interests in efficiency and an accurate record are strong and the risk that the leading question is putting words in the witness' mouth is small. Consider this example:

1. Q: Mr. Smith, who besides yourself attended the meeting?

2. A: Let's see, there was Al, David, Kristin, and... I know the rep from Chicago was there, at the moment I can't remember her name, sorry.

3. Q: Was it Alison?

4. A: Right, Alison. Thanks. That was all of us.

Here, the judge can be confident from the answer in No. 2 that the witness has personal knowledge of the forgotten attendee's name but has momentarily forgotten it. A leading question (No. 3) is therefore appropriate.

As Federal Rule of Evidence 612 recognizes, you may also use documents to refresh witnesses' recollections. Assuming that a document is available, this strategy can be preferable to leading questions when what is forgotten is more than an isolated item of evidence. Rules allow you to refresh recollection with any type of document; the document need not have been prepared by the witness nor be admissible in evidence. However, the rule allows your adversary to examine the document and introduce relevant portions of it into evidence, even if you showed the document to the witness prior to trial. In some jurisdictions, a judge may allow an adversary to examine a document used to refresh recollection prior to trial even if it is otherwise privileged. Therefore you need to exercise caution when refreshing recollection with a document. (And now you know why many cross examiners' first question is, "Did you review any documents in preparation for your testimony?")

The process of refreshing recollection with a document often goes something like this:

1. Q: OK, now please tell us what was said during this meeting.

2. A: We talked about the frustration of trying to define objective reality in a postmodern world. Brette said that social groups wage a continuous battle for the dominance of their view of reality.

3. Q: Did Brette mention any groups in particular?

4. A: I'm sure she did, what those groups were I can't remember at the moment.

5. Q: Might it refresh your recollection if you looked at the book, "Post–Modernity in a Nutshell?"

6. A: It might.

7. Q: Your Honor, I've marked for identification as Plaintiff's Exhibit No. 5 and shown to opposing counsel the book "Post–Modernity in a Nutshell."

(To witness:) Please look at pages 95–96 of Exhibit No. 5 and tell us if it refreshes your recollection as to the social groups that Brette may have mentioned.

8. A: All right.

9. Q: (After removing the book) Is your memory now refreshed?

10. A: Yes, I remember now.

11. Q: Then I ask you again, what social group or groups did Brette mention as waging a continuous battle for the dominance of their version of reality?

12. A: Brette mentioned. . .

This excerpt illustrates a typical procedure for refreshing recollection with a document. After the witness expresses a failure of recall (No. 4), you begin to lay the foundation by asking if looking at a document might enable the witness to recall the forgotten information (No. 5). After opposing counsel and the witness have a chance to examine the document, you remove it and ask if it has in fact refreshed the witness' recollection (No. 9). Removing the document and asking foundational question No. 9 preserve the notion (which may be fictional) that a witness is testifying from present memory and not simply testifying to what a document says. (Its contents may be inadmissible hearsay).

A judge may not allow you to refresh recollection if a witness' response constitutes a denial rather than a failure of recollection. Consider this example:

1. Q: Did another meeting take place?

2. A: No.

3. Q: Permission to refresh the witness' recollection, Your Honor?

4. Judge: Denied. The witness testified that no other meeting took place, not that the witness couldn't remember whether another meeting took place. Proceed with questioning.

If a denial such as that above means that you are unable to refresh recollection, you might have to resort to impeaching your own witness pursuant to Federal Rule of Evidence 607. For example, you might offer into evidence the witness' inconsistent deposition testimony. One way to avoid this awkward process is to incorporate the element of recollection in questions so as that a negative answer seemingly constitutes a failure to recall. For example, assume that Nos. 1 and 2 in the dialogue above went as follows:

1. Q: *Do you recall* whether another meeting took place?

2. A: No.

By incorporating the element of recall, No. 1 provides the judge with a basis for construing the response of "no" as indicating lack of recall, and for allowing you to refresh recollection.

C. LAY WITNESS OPINIONS

1. TWO PRONGS FOR ADMISSIBILITY

Federal Rule of Evidence 701 provides that lay witnesses with personal knowledge can offer opinions that are "helpful to clearly understanding the witness' testimony or to determining a fact in issue." Rule 701 creates a two-pronged foundational requirement. One prong consists of testimony demonstrating a witness' personal knowledge of the information on which an opinion rests. The second prong consists of persuading the judge that the opinion is helpful. Often, opinions are helpful because they add a "you just had to be there" element that a witness' recitation of details alone cannot adequately provide. Judges determine the "helpfulness" of an opinion under Federal Rule of Evidence 104(a), but often evaluate the sufficiency of a witness' personal knowledge to arrive at an opinion pursuant to Rule 104(b)'s lower "sufficient to support a finding" burden of proof.

For example, assume that on behalf of the plaintiff who was struck and injured on a residential street by a car driven by the defendant, you want to offer a passerby's opinion that the defendant was driving dangerously just prior to the accident. Succinctly, the foundational testimony might go as follows:

1. Q: Over what period of time did you observe the defendant's car prior to the accident?

2. A: I'd estimate 5-6 seconds.

3. Q: How long have you been a driver?

4. A: Since I was 16, about 25 years ago.

5. Q: And have you often driven on residential streets such as the one where the plaintiff was struck?

6. A: Sure. Countless times. I live on a very similar street.

7. Q: Based on your experience as a driver, can you estimate how fast the car driven by the defendant was travelling during the 5-6 second period?

8. A: At least 45 mph.

9. Q: What were the weather conditions at the time of the accident?

10. A: There was a steady drizzle. I had my umbrella out and the streets were wet.

11. Q: What else did you observe about the location where the plaintiff was struck by the defendant's car?

12. A: The plaintiff was crossing the street at the corner, and there were a few kids playing in the rain in front of a house near the corner.

13. Q: In your opinion, based on the observations you've testified to, do you have an opinion as to whether the defendant was driving safely before striking the plaintiff?

14. A: I do.

15. Q: And what is that opinion?

16. Def. Attorney: Objection, improper opinion.

17. Judge: Counsel for plaintiff, any response before I rule?

18. Plaintiff's Attorney: Just briefly. The opinion is clearly based on the witness' personal observations. And it's helpful to the jury's accurate understanding of what happened because it provides information that only someone who saw the events leading up to the collision can provide and that the underlying observations by themselves do not.

19. Judge: I'll allow the opinion.

20. Q: Do you recall the question?

21. A: I do. My opinion is that the defendant was driving dangerously fast.

Here, the witness provides two opinions, one as to the car's speed (No. 8) and the other as to the dangerousness of the speed (No. 21). The helpfulness and admissibility of the opinions is supported by the witness' experience as a driver (Nos. 4, 6) and personal knowledge of the circumstances (Nos. 10, 12).

This second example of a lay witness opinion is taken from the film *Let Him Have It* (1991), which is based on a notorious 1953 English trial. Two youths, Derek Bentley and Chris Craig, were charged with murdering a police officer in the course of unsuccessfully attempting to burgle a warehouse. A surviving police officer, Sgt. Fairfax, testified for the prosecution that after Bentley was arrested, Craig pulled out a gun and pointed it at Fairfax. Sgt. Fairfax's testimony continued much as follows:

1. Q: How far from you was Craig when he pointed the gun at you?

2. A: Craig was standing about four feet in front of me.

3. Q: What happened after Craig pointed the gun at you?

4. A: I asked him to hand over the gun to me.

5. Q: Then what happened?

6. A: Bentley was standing just a couple of feet from me, and I heard him shout, "Let him have it, Chris."

7. Q: What did Bentley mean by this?

8. A: He meant that Craig should start firing.

9. Q: What happened next?

10. A: Craig shot me in the shoulder, and a few minutes later Craig shot and killed another police officer.

Sgt. Fairfax's opinion (No. 8) is based on his personal knowledge of the circumstances as they existed on the rooftop at the time of the shooting. But as to one component of the opinion—what Bentley intended to communicate to Craig—Fairfax lacks personal knowledge. As a result, the helpfulness of the opinion is questionable. The judge could have insisted that Fairfax explain his reasons for believing that Bentley intended to tell Craig to shoot, as opposed to telling Craig to hand his gun over to the police officer. If Fairfax can provide those reasons, the jury may be in as good a position as Fairfax to decide what Bentley meant by his statement, so the opinion would not be "helpful."

2. INEBRIATION

Based on everyday experience, lay witnesses commonly provide an opinion as to another person's sobriety or lack of sobriety. The foundation may go briefly as follows:

Q: Ms. Rogers, do you know the defendant Willa Fallon?

A: Yes. We both live in the college sorority house.

Q: Were you with Ms. Fallon on the night at February 14?

A: Yes, our sorority hosted a Valentine's Day party that night.

Q: Did you see Ms. Fallon during the party?

A: Yes. I talked to her a few times and saw her talking to others and dancing.

Q: Over what period of time were you together at the party?

A: For a couple of hours, from about 10 PM to I guess a little after midnight.

Q: Did you notice whether Ms. Fallon drank any alcohol during that time?

A: Yes. Whenever I saw her or talked to her she always was drinking from a glass of beer or wine, and sometimes drank shots of tequila.

Q: When did you last see her that night?

A: Just after midnight I'd say. She came to tell me and some other girls that she was leaving for the weekend.

Q: And what was Ms. Fallon's physical condition at that time?

A: Not good. She slurred her words, she reeked of alcohol, and her eyes were red and really watery. She could hardly stand up, she had to grab onto a chair or table to keep her balance. She left holding onto some guy I didn't know who was at the party.

Q: Do you drink alcohol Ms. Rogers?

A: I used to have a drink now and then, but I stopped drinking alcohol a couple of years ago.

Q: Prior to the night of the Valentine's Day party, had you spent time with people who have been under the influence of alcohol?

A: Sure, lots of times at college parties, bars and lots of other places. I don't drink but I often see people drink and have too much to drink.

Q: Based on your experiences with people drinking and your interactions with Ms. Fallon that night, do you have an opinion as to whether she was under the influence of alcohol when she told you that she was leaving the party?

A: Yes.

Q: And what is that opinion?

A: She was clearly drunk.

The foundational testimony above is sufficient to support a finding that Ms. Rogers has sufficient experience and personal knowledge to form a reliable opinion as to Ms. Fallon's lack of sobriety.

3. CHARACTER FOR TRUTH-TELLING

Federal Rule of Evidence 608(a) allows a lay witness with sufficient personal knowledge of an adverse witness' character to testify to an opinion that the witness is dishonest. Under Rule 608(a)'s "bad before good" provision, the party who proferred the witness can then call a rebuttal witness to testify to an opinion that the witness has a good character for truth-telling. In either event, an opinion witness cannot testify to specific acts of dishonesty or honesty on which an opinion is based, since Rule 608 does not authorize specific acts testimony.

In the example below, assume that Al Capone has testified for the defendant in a criminal case. Pursuant to Rule 608(a), the prosecution calls Clyde Bonny as a character witness to attack the credibility of Capone's testimony. The foundational testimony may briefly unfold as follows:

1. Q: Mr. Bonny, do you know Al Capone?

2. A: The guy who testified for the defendant? Sure, I know him.

3. Q: How do you know him?

4. A: I've known him for over 20 years, since high school. We both work for the same accounting company and we've worked together on lots of projects over the years.

5. Q: Over what period of time have you worked for the same company?

6. A: Over 15 years now.

7. Q: And how often have you worked together on projects with Mr. Capone?

8. A: At least once or twice a month. We do a lot of our work in teams, but I don't always work with Mr. Capone.

9. Q: Do you ever meet with Mr. Capone socially?

10. A: Yes, mostly together with people at the office for lunch or after work. Maybe once every couple of weeks.

11 Q: Based on your interactions with Mr. Capone, do you have an opinion as to his truthfulness?

12. A: Yes. I'm sorry to say that he's not an honest man.

13. Q: Would you be inclined to believe testimony that Mr. Capone gave under oath?

14. A: No.

This foundational testimony demonstrates that Bonny knows Capone well enough to be able to arrive at an opinion as to Capone's honesty (Nos. 4, 6, 8, 10). Consistent with Rule 608(b), Bonny does not testify to specific instances in which Capone has behaved dishonestly. Some judges allow character witnesses such as Bonny to testify as in No. 14, but other judges exclude this type of testimony as a forbidden specific act.

D. HABIT

Habit evidence is a form of circumstantial evidence that is admissible under Federal Rule of Evidence 406 to prove how a person or business behaved on a specific occasional. For example, evidence that Mindy habitually rolls through the stop sign at a particular corner is admissible to prove that she rolled through it on the date that she was involved in a traffic accident. The foundational showing typically focuses on a witness' familiarity with a person's or a business' relevant behavior over a substantial period of time. In the brief example below, the issue is whether a lost written sales agreement contained a liquidated damages clause.

Q: Ms. Anzalone, how are you employed?

A: I've been Arrowhead's manager of sales operations for almost 15 years.

Q: Does your job as the manager of sales operations include entering into sales agreements on behalf of Arrowhead?

A: Yes. I negotiate and approve all of Arrowhead's sales agreements. I've been in charge of all sales agreements since I started working at Arrowhead.

Q: Are you familiar with liquidated damages provisions?

A: Certainly. Their purpose. . .

Q: Do agreements that you enter into on behalf of Arrowhead routinely include a liquidated damages clause?

A: Definitely. Every sales agreement that I have entered into, numbering into the hundreds over the course of nearly 15 years, has contained a liquidated damages clause.

The witness' testimony is relevant to prove that Arrowhead habitually includes a liquidated damages clause in sales agreements, from which the fact finder can infer that the disputed sales agreement included a liquidated damages clause.

E. MERCY RULE EVIDENCE

The so-called "Mercy Rule," Federal Rule of Evidence 404(a)(2)(A), allows criminal defendants to offer evidence that they possess a good trait of character that is inconsistent with their having committed the charged crime. For example if Mahatma is charged with assault with a deadly weapon, Mahatma may offer evidence that he is peace-loving. Rule 404(a)(2)(A) limits the form of proof to opinion and reputation evidence; defendants cannot offer evidence of specific instances when they behaved in accordance with their good character trait.

The foundation for Mercy Rule testimony typically focuses on a character witness' familiarity with a defendant or a defendant's reputation. The foundational testimony for an "opinion" Mercy Rule character witness may unfold as follows:

Q: Mr. Lincoln, are you acquainted with the defendant George Washington?

A: Yes, we've been friends for well over 30 years, since childhood. And we work together in the same accounting office, Plus or Minus Inc.

Q: Do you see Mr. Washington in the courtroom?

A: Sure, that's him over there (pointing to the defendant).

Q: How often do you see each other?

A: Daily. We often discuss business accounts that we're working on. Our families also socialize, we're very close friends.

Q: Do you have an opinion about Mr. Washington's honesty?

A: I do.

Q: And what is that opinion?

A: He is thoroughly honest.

Q: As you know, Mr. Washington is charged with embezzlement from Plus or Minus. Based on what you know of his character, do you think he is the type of person to commit such a crime?

A: Definitely not. That would be totally out of character.

F. NON-CHARACTER USES OF OTHER ACTS

To prevent trials from turning into lengthy morality plays, and subject to exceptions such as the Mercy Rule, evidence rules generally exclude evidence offered to prove parties' traits of character. But as Federal Rule of Evidence 404(b) indicates, evidence of "other acts" may be admitted for non-character purposes in both criminal and civil cases. Typical non-character purposes include a party's motive, identity or knowledge. The foundational evidence typically demonstrates the relevancy of the other act for a non-character inference and includes evidence sufficient to support a finding of a party's involvement in it.

In the example below, Barnes is charged with assaulting Ramirez on September 24. The prosecutor calls Chu to testify to another act by Barnes tending to prove that Barnes had a motive to assault Ramirez:

Q: Mr. Chu, do you know the defendant Mr. Barnes?

A: Yes, he and I work in the county's public works department.

Q: Does Mr. Ramirez also work in that department?

A: Yes he does.

Q: Do you recall an incident involving Mr. Barnes and Mr. Ramirez that took place after the three of you got off work late after working on emergency street repairs?

A: I do.

Q: Do you recall the date of the incident?

A: Yes, the evening of September 22.

Q: And briefly, what happened on the evening of September 22?

A: When we finished cleaning up in the yard, Barnes said that an office door had been left open. He went inside and came out a few minutes later carrying two computers. Ramirez asked him what was going on, and Barnes said that the office was deserted, that he had disconnected the security camera, and that it was his chance to get a couple of free computers.

Q: How did Mr. Ramirez respond?

A: Ramirez told him to put them back, he'd get us all in trouble. Barnes just laughed and used some words I'd rather not repeat, and put the computers in his car.

Q: Then what happened?

A: Ramirez said that he was going to file a theft report with our supervisor. Barnes said that if Ramirez did that, Ramirez would be very sorry.

Q: Did anything else happen?

A: I saw Ramirez file a theft report the next day, and the supervisor calling Barnes into her office.

In this example, the "other act" (theft of two computers) is not admissible to prove that Barnes has a propensity to violate the law and therefore is guilty of assaulting Ramirez. Rather, the prior act is non-character evidence from which the fact finder might infer that Barnes had a motive to assault Ramirez. As non-character evidence is potentially admissible in civil as well as criminal cases, Chu's testimony would also be admissible in a civil battery trial in which Ramirez sought to recover for damages from Barnes.

G. CHARACTER EVIDENCE IN SEXUAL ASSAULT CASES

Federal Rule of Evidence 413 and similar rules in virtually all jurisdictions allow prosecutors to offer circumstantial evidence of a sexual assault defendant's guilt through evidence of the defendant's commission of similar crimes involving sexual assault. Rule 415 extends the rule to civil cases. The foundation should provide sufficient details of the "other sexual assault" to show similarity, and link the defendant to the assaults.

For example, assume that a complainant seeks damages from the attacker who allegedly groped her from behind her seat in a darkened theater on June 1. To prove that the defendant committed the sexual assault, the complainant calls an "other sexual assault" witness who testifies in part as follows:

Q: Ms. Jones, have you ever seen the defendant before?

A: Yes. I saw him on June 5.

Q: Where was this that you saw the defendant?

A: At the Bijou Theater, I was watching a movie.

Q: And briefly, please tell us what happened.

A: As I was sitting in my seat, I felt some arms reach around my shoulders and fondle my chest area. I shoved the arms away, turned around and screamed. It was light enough in the theater for me to recognize the defendant as the person who grabbed me.

Q: Are you certain that the man seated at counsel table is the man who grabbed you on June 5?

A: Yes. He tried to run off, but an usher grabbed and held him. I walked over and identified him from a foot or two away. There's no doubt that the defendant is the guy who attacked me.

H. COURTROOM DEMONSTRATIONS

Witnesses who describe dynamic events such as physical attacks and inability to engage in normal activities may seek to illustrate their testimony with courtroom demonstrations.

A demonstration may involve more than one person, such as where a crime victim grabs a prosecutor's arm to demonstrate how the defendant grabbed the victim's arm.

A frequent foundational issue concerns the relevance of a demonstration. The party asking a judge to allow a demonstration has to convince the judge pursuant to Rule 104(a) that the witness can provide a meaningful demonstration, and that the demonstration provides information that oral testimony alone cannot fully capture. The counterweight is that the probative value not be out-weighed by the danger of Rule 403 factors such as unfair prejudice, confusion of the jury and undue consumption of time.

The film *Criminal Court* (1946) portrays a courtroom demonstration orchestrated by defense attorney Steve Barnes. The demonstration would be unimaginable today, but it closely parallels a demonstration that took place during a Los Angeles murder trial early in the 20th century. The attorney in the actual case was Earl Rogers, famous both for his courtroom theatrics and his legal acumen. (Rogers represented famed attorney Clarence Darrow when Darrow was tried for jury bribery.) As in that case, the prosecutor in the film presents an eyewitness who testified that he was standing on the street just a few steps away from the victim when the defendant walked up and shot the victim. In abbreviated form, Barnes' cross examination in the film proceeds as follows:

Q: You were standing a few steps from the victim when my client rushed up with a revolver and started firing?

A: That's right.

Q: Were there any other people out on the street?

A: Sure, lots of them.

Q: Didn't they run for cover?

A: Yes, but I didn't.

Q: You mean to tell me that a man with murder in his eyes rushed up with a revolver and started firing, but while everyone rushed for cover you stood calmly by and watched what happened?

A: That's right.

Q: (angrily) You're lying, aren't you?

A: You can't talk to me like that.

Q: (increasingly angry) You're lying in order to put my client in jail. This isn't a trial, it's a mockery. But I'm going to see that justice is done. I'm taking the law into my own hands.

With that, an enraged Barnes reaches into his jacket pocket, yanks out a revolver and waves it in the air. The eyewitness, the jurors, the prosecutor, the judge and the spectators behind the bar duck down and take cover. Barnes then walks to the jury box and asks the jurors to get up and observe the eyewitness, who is hiding behind the witness chair. "There, ladies and gentlemen," says Barnes, "is the man who doesn't flinch at the sight of the gun, who claims that he stood calmly by while one man shot another with a revolver." The demonstration convinced the jurors in the film (as in the actual case) that the eyewitness had lied, and the defendant was found not guilty.

Dramatic and effective though Rogers' demonstration was, today its propriety under Rule 403 is questionable. The witness' response to the gun in the courtroom casts some doubt on the accuracy of his testimony. Yet the courtroom setting is sufficiently distinct from the scene of the actual events that a judge might reasonably conclude that the relevance of the witness' response is substantially outweighed by the danger of unfair prejudice or misleading the jury.

I. HEARSAY STATEMENTS

The rule barring hearsay evidence (Federal Rule of Evidence 802) is riddled with exemptions and exceptions. Had John Keats' interests run to law instead of romantic poetry, he might have written Ode on a Hearsay Statement, and begun it with the words, "How can I admit thee into evidence? Let me count the ways." This section illustrates the foundational requirements for typically oral hearsay exemptions and exceptions. (Chapter 10 reviews exceptions for typically document-based hearsay exceptions such as business records.)

Paraphrasing and the Hearsay Rule. A common misconception is that the hearsay rule ceases to apply if witnesses rephrase hearsay statements in their own words. For example, in a misguided effort to avoid a hearsay objection, a direct examiner may ask a question such as, "Without repeating exactly what was said, can you tell us what Anne said about the computers?" or "Please summarize what Anne said." However, if an out-of-court assertion constitutes inadmissible hearsay, it remains inadmissible whether you offer an exact transcript, a paraphrase or a summary.

1. OPPOSING PARTY STATEMENTS

Federal Rule of Evidence 801(d)(2) provides an exemption that allows a party to offer an opposing party's hearsay statement into evidence. When the hearsay declarant is the opposing party personally, the foundation typically requires little more than testimony by a witness with personal knowledge that the opposing party made the statement. In this example, a plaintiff in an auto accident case offers the defendant's hearsay assertion into evidence:

Q: When did you arrive at the scene of the accident?

A: From what I could tell, just a short while after it happened. Both drivers were out of their cars and talking on their mobile phones.

Q: Was the defendant, seated at counsel table to the right, one of the people you saw?

A: Yes. I was only a few feet away from him.

Q: What if anything did you hear the defendant say?

A: He said he blew past the stop sign because he was in a hurry to get to a meeting.

Federal Rule of Evidence 801(d)(2) provides additional exemptions for statements for which an opposing party is vicariously liable. The necessary foundational testimony encompasses the circumstances defined by the exemption. In the brief example below, the prosecutor of a stepfather charged with sexually molesting his stepdaughter Joanne lays a foundation for an argument that the stepfather's silence constitutes an adoption of Joanne's statement. A judge's finding that "adoption by silence" took place enables the prosecutor to offer the statement into evidence under Rule 801(d)(2)(B) as the stepfather's party statement:

Q: Joanne, did you ever confront your stepfather regarding the incident in the basement that you've just described?

A: I did, I think it was four days later.

Q: What happened?

A: My mom and stepfather were alone in the kitchen after I got home from school. I looked at my stepfather and said I wasn't afraid of him anymore, and that I wanted the whole world to know what he had done to me in the basement.

Q: Please continue.

A: I said here's my mom right here. Why don't you tell her how you made me pull down your pants and touch your privates while you touched me under my sweater.

Q: Did he say anything in response?

A: He told me to shut up and then he ran out of the house. My mom started crying.

Joanne's foundational testimony is probably sufficient to convince a judge pursuant to Federal Rule of Evidence 104(a) that the defendant heard and understood her accusation, that he had the chance to but did not deny the accusation, and that a reasonable person in the stepfather's circumstances would have denied the accusation if it weren't true. Joanne's assertions would be admissible as the stepfather's party statement.

Under the exemption provided for by Rule 801(d)(2)(D), statements made by an employee-declarant on a matter within the scope of the declarant's employment may be admitted as an employer's party statement. In the example below, a state has sued Chemically Best Foods for dumping prohibited chemicals into the state's water supply. The state's attorney lays the foundation for an employee party statement:

Q: Ms. Shackleford, how are you employed?

A: I teach high school calculus and chemistry.

Q: Did you accompany a group of students on a field trip to Chemically Best Foods last May 29?

A: I did.

D: Did you and the students meet with any company representatives?

A: Yes. We were given a tour by Dr. Boris Methany, who wore a badge that identified him as Chief Compliance Officer- Environmental Services.

Q: Did the tour include the company's waste operations?

A: Yes. Dr. Methany showed us the pipes through which the company disposes of chemical wastes and explained the waste process.

Q: Were any questions asked of Dr. Methany about the waste process?

A: Yes. A student asked whether all the dangerous chemicals are removed before the waste is disposed of.

Q: Did Dr. Methany reply?

A: Yes, and I was shocked by his reply. He said that they never test the waste, it's way too slow and expensive, so he has no idea whether the chemicals have been removed.

In the hopefully fanciful circumstances above, the foundation is probably sufficient to prove that Dr. Methany was an employee of Chemically Best Foods and that his statement pertained to a matter within the scope of his employment. The state could therefore offer the statement into evidence as Chemically Best Foods' party statement.

2. PRESENT SENSE IMPRESSIONS

Under Federal Rule of Evidence 803(1), a hearsay statement is admissible as a present sense impression if the foundation convinces a judge pursuant to Federal Rule of Evidence 104(a) that the declarant made it while or immediately after perceiving the event or condition that the statement describes. In the foundational excerpt below, a witness called by the plaintiff in an auto accident case testifies to her own hearsay statement:

Q: And where you and your husband that Sunday afternoon?

A: We were in our car on Interstate 44. He was driving slowly, maybe 15-20 m.p.h because it was foggy.

Q: At some point did a car pass you?

A: Yes, a small red car driven by her (pointing to the defendant) sped past us on the passenger side.

Q: You know the defendant was the driver?

A: Yes. I had turned to look out my window when I heard what sounded like a car with a loud engine coming up on our right. So as she passed us I was looking right into the driver's window of the red car.

Q: Did you say anything to your husband about what you saw?

A: Yes. As soon as the red car went by us and pulled in front of our car, I said that the car was going way too fast for road conditions, and that if she didn't slow down she'd get into an accident.

The foundation is sufficient to support a finding that the witness had personal knowledge of the red car's speed and the defendant's identity. The foundation is also sufficient to convince a judge that the statement described the red car's speed, and that the witness spoke immediately after perceiving the red car. The statement therefore qualifies as a present sense impression.

3. EXCITED UTTERANCES

Under Federal Rule of Evidence 803(2), a hearsay statement is admissible as an excited utterance if the foundation is sufficient to support a finding pursuant to Federal Rule of Evidence 104(b) that the declarant perceived a startling event or condition and convinces a judge pursuant to Rule 104(a) that the declarant made a statement relating to the condition or event while under the stress of excitement it caused.

The illustrative foundational excerpt below arises in a case in which a stepfather is charged with physically abusing his four year old stepson Allan. The foundational witness is the police officer who responded to neighbors' complaints of a child crying. The officer testifies to finding the badly-injured Allan alone in an apartment and taking him to a hospital, where he received emergency medical treatment. Allan said nothing during this entire time. The foundational testimony continues:

Q: You remained with Allan this entire time?

A: Yes. After the doctor was finished, I took him to a small private room.

Q: Then what happened?

A: There was a knock on the door, and a man came in. Allan said, "Daddy! Stepdaddy beat me so bad Daddy." Allan started crying and ran over to the man.

Q: How much time went by from the time you found Allan in the apartment to the time the man entered the room?

A: About two hours.

The foundational evidence establishes that Allan experienced the traumatic event to which his statement to his father relates. Although the statement was made at least two hours after the event, the severity of the abuse and Allan's age should convince the judge that at the time Allan spoke to his father, Allan was under the "stress of excitement" that the abuse caused.

4. MEDICAL HEARSAY

Federal Rule of Evidence 803 (4) provides an exception for declarants' statements that are made to physicians (or other medical personnel) for purposes of and are reasonably pertinent to medical diagnosis or treatment. Under Rule 104(a), the proponent of medical hearsay must convince a judge of the foundation's adequacy.

In the illustrative example below, Fred testifies that he sought medical treatment about two weeks after he was involved as a passenger in a fender bender accident. A portion of the foundational testimony goes as follows:

1. Q: What happened after you were called into the office?

2. A: The nurse took my blood pressure and pulse and asked me why I had come in.

3. Q: What did you understand the purpose of the nurse's questions to be?

4. A: I assumed that the nurse would pass along the information I gave him to the doctor so she'd know how to treat me.

5. Q: And what did you tell the nurse?

6. A: I told him that my back and neck were really sore, and that the pain started about two days after the car I was in was involved in a small accident. I

thought the pain would go away by itself with the help of over-the-counter pain killer but it didn't, it only got worse.

7. Q: Did you say anything else to the nurse?

8. A: I mentioned that the car that hit us had gone through a red light and hit us when our car was already in the intersection.

The foundation establishes that Fred described past and present symptoms and their inception (No. 6) for the purpose of obtaining medical treatment (No. 4). However, the information in No. 8 is not admissible as medical hearsay because the fact that the car that hit the car in which Fred was a passenger went through a red light is not reasonably pertinent to medical treatment.

5. UNAVAILABILITY

The hearsay exceptions provided for by Federal Rule of Evidence 804 rest on foundational evidence showing that, among other things, the hearsay declarant is unavailable as a witness. The most common reason for unavailability is that the hearsay proponent has been unable to procure the declarant's attendance "by process or other reasonable means." Rule 804(a)(5). The hearsay proponent must convince a judge of a declarant's unavailability pursuant to Rule 104(a).

Foundational evidence indicating that an absent hearsay declarant is beyond a trial court's subpoena power is one common method of satisfying Subsection 5.   Assume that a defendant in a Connecticut medical malpractice case seeks to offer into evidence hearsay assertions by Nurse Jackie that would be admissible under the former testimony hearsay exception if Nurse Jackie is proved to be unavailable to testify. The foundational testimony may go as follows:

Q: Mr. Kildare, you are the chief administrative officer at Connecticut General Hospital.

A: Yes.

Q: Are you familiar with Nurse Jackie?

A: Yes. She worked at the hospital for 25 years until she retired six months ago.

Q: Do you know where she currently resides?

A: Yes. She and her husband have moved permanently to their retirement home in Cancun, Mexico.

Q: How do you know that?

A: We were quite friendly, and I know that they were excited about moving to Cancun as soon as they retired. She's emailed me lots of photos of their house and their activities since they moved there.

Q: Have you discussed her willingness to testify as a witness in this trial?

A: Yes. We've talked by phone a number of times and I've sent her emails asking her to testify. I told her that the hospital would pay her travel costs. Jackie said nothing doing, she's done with hospital stuff, she is unwilling to come back for the trial.

Q: Do you have any doubt that your communications were with Nurse Jackie?

A: None whatsoever. I know her voice very well, and her email responses were usually accompanied by family photos.

The foundational testimony above should be sufficient to convince the judge that Jackie will not testify voluntarily and that she is beyond the court's subpoena power. Of course her refusal to return to Connecticut is itself a hearsay assertion. But under Rule 104(a), evidence rules other than privilege do not apply to foundational matters. Moreover, Jackie's statements to Dr. Kildare would be independently admissible for their truth under the "state of mind" exception, Rule 803(3).

A foundation for unavailability may also focus on a party's inability to locate and subpoena a hearsay declarant. Especially when it comes to prosecution witnesses whose hearsay statements are nontestimonial and therefore admissible despite the Confrontation Clause, judges often insist that police officers and prosecution investigators search for missing witnesses thoroughly and repeatedly. In an extreme criminal case, a judge may refuse to rule that a witness is unavailable if the prosecution was aware that an important witness was very likely to go into hiding yet neglected to place the witness in custody pending trial.

Laying a foundation for the unavailability of a witness whose whereabouts are unknown can be difficult even in civil cases. In one California civil lawsuit, an ex-husband sought to establish his ex-wife's unavailability so that he could offer her hearsay statement into evidence. The ex-husband offered the following foundational evidence:

* He hadn't seen or spoken to his ex-wife in over three years.

* A letter sent by him two years earlier to his ex-wife's last known address had been returned as undeliverable.

* A creditor of the ex-wife had foreclosed on the house where she had reportedly been living.

* A number of the ex-wife's creditors had contacted the ex-husband's attorney asking for information on her whereabouts.

* He was unable to find a listing for his ex-wife in any phone directory.

* The ex-wife's attorney was unaware of her whereabouts.

The court ruled that the ex-husband's foundation failed to establish that his ex-wife was unavailable as a witness, because he hadn't demonstrated sufficient "persevering and untiring efforts" to secure her attendance.

6. DYING DECLARATIONS

A foundation for admission of a dying declaration under Federal Rule of Evidence 804(b)(2) typically focuses on the declarant's belief that death was imminent. Assume that in a negligence action brought by the representative of a plaintiff who was severely injured when struck by the defendant's red car, the representative seeks to offer into evidence as a dying declaration the plaintiff's hearsay statement, "The red car never even slowed down." The foundational witness is the EMT who provided emergency assistance to the plaintiff.

Q: Where was the plaintiff when you arrived at the scene?

A: He was laying face-down in the intersection.

Q: What did you observe about his condition?

A: He was bleeding profusely from the head and chest areas. He had a number of fractured bones. He was moaning continuously and was obviously in shock.

Q: What happened then?

A: I carefully rolled him over and did my best to stabilize his back and stop the bleeding.

Q: Did the plaintiff continue to moan?

A: Yes.

Q: Did the plaintiff do anything other than moan?

A: At one point I could see that he was trying to talk. I bent down and heard him whisper that he was dying and that the red car never even slowed down. He tried to say something else, but nothing that I understood. Then he lapsed into unconsciousness.

Q: To your knowledge, has he ever regained consciousness?

A: No. We transported him to the hospital, and he has been hospitalized and unconscious ever since.

This abbreviated foundation should be sufficient to convince the judge pursuant to Rule 104(a) that the plaintiff believed that death was imminent at the time he spoke to the EMT. Moreover, the statement refers to the event that the plaintiff believed to be the cause of his imminent death. Assuming that the trial takes place in a jurisdiction that (1) admits dying declarations in civil cases and (2) conditions admissibility on a declarant's unavailability rather than death, the foundation qualifies the plaintiff's statement to the EMT as a dying declaration.

7. FORFEITURE BY WRONGDOING

Under Federal Rule of Evidence 804(b)(5), hearsay statements are admissible against parties who wrongfully cause (or acquiesce in another person's actions that caused) a declarant's unavailability.

In this illustrative example, Jones is charged with domestic violence for physically attacking his former girlfriend Lucy. Lucy described the attack to a police officer, but then disappeared and the prosecutor has been unable to locate her. Seeking to admit Lucy's statements to the police officer into evidence, the prosecutor calls paralegal assistant Ellis Atee to testify to a conversation he had with Lucy the day before she disappeared. Atee's testimony is as follows:

Q: What happened when you met with Lucy at the shelter?

A: She was very frightened and said she didn't feel safe even though she knew that Jones had been arrested and was in jail. She said that Jones had struck her often before the last attack, and told her that if she ever called the cops, he'd really beat her, just as he had other girlfriends before her.

Q: How did you respond?

A: I told her that the guy was a menace, that the best way to protect herself and other women was to testify and lock him away for a long time.

Q: Then what happened?

A: She said that's easy for me to say, but that she got a phone call a couple of days after Jones was arrested from his brother. She recognized his voice immediately. The brother said that he'd talked to Jones in jail, and that Jones wanted her to know that if she testified against him, the brother would see to it that she never walked again. She said she believed him and that she had to disappear where no one would find her.

Q: Did you try to convince her to stay and testify?

A: Yes. I told her that if she could give me just one day, I'd arrange for her to stay in protective custody. She said that she'd think about it, but that she'd gotten one more threatening message on her mobile phone from Jones personally before she changed her number and that she was really scared.

Q: Did you return the next day?

A: I did, and she was gone. We haven't been able to locate her. (Atee testifies to the unsuccessful effort to locate Lucy.)

The foundational testimony should be sufficient to convince a judge pursuant to Rule 104(a) that Jones procured Lucy's unavailability. Thus, the police officer could testify to her description of Jones' attack.

CHAPTER 10

SATISFYING FOUNDATIONAL REQUIREMENTS FOR TANGIBLE EVIDENCE

Tangible objects such as printouts of electronic messages, photographs, diagrams, contracts, reports and contraband such as weapons and drugs are a common form of evidence. Inside courtrooms, tangible objects become *exhibits*. Even if a party is not legally required to introduce an exhibit into evidence, the party might do so anyway because exhibits often have greater rhetorical force than oral testimony. This chapter explains and illustrates the foundational requirements for many common exhibits, and describes strategies for using them effectively.

Judges may insist that you follow idiosyncratic foundational procedures when offering exhibits into evidence. If you are unsure of a trial judge's preferences, check with the court clerk, bailiff or a more experienced attorney so that you are comfortable with the processes that a particular judge expects you to follow.

A. REAL VS. DEMONSTRATIVE EXHIBITS

Exhibits are either *real* or *demonstrative*. Real evidence is typically *gathered*, while demonstrative evidence is *created* for purposes of trial. *Real evidence* denotes tangible objects that figured in the events that gave rise to litigation. Examples of real evidence include:

- In a murder case, the gun from which the fatal shot was allegedly fired.

- In a personal injury case, the brake that allegedly was defective and caused a motorist to crash.

- In a libel action, the online story in which the allegedly defamatory remarks were made.

- In a case involving workplace sexual harassment, an offensive cartoon that the plaintiff found on her desk.

Demonstrative evidence (sometimes called illustrative evidence) is typically created by lawyers in an effort to provide understanding, persuasiveness and visual appeal to a client's version of events. Examples of demonstrative evidence include:

- A diagram of a jewelry store in which an armed robbery took place.

- Two photographs of a car, one showing its condition before and the other after it was involved in a collision.

- A "Day in the Life" visual recording, depicting an injured personal injury plaintiff performing ordinary tasks.

- An electronic "blow up" of a key phrase in a written contract.

Your use of demonstrative exhibits often depends on your imagination and a client's budget. For example, if you represent the defendant driver in an auto accident case, you may limit the defense to verbal accounts of the events leading up to the collision. Or, you may add an inexpensive visual element through a hand-drawn diagram of the intersection where the accident took place, with witnesses referring to and marking up the diagram as they testify. Or, you may add a more costly visual element to your case by retaining an accident reconstruction expert to prepare and testify with respect to a computerized re-enactment of the accident. Thus, while parties' activities typically determine what real evidence is available, you generally have more flexibility with respect to demonstrative exhibits.

Ethical Responsibilities: ABA Model Rule of Professional Conduct 3.4 provides that "A lawyer shall not unlawfully obstruct another party's access to evidence or unlawfully alter, destroy or conceal a document or other material having potential evidentiary value. A lawyer shall not counsel of assist another person to do any such act."

Rule 3.4 impacts lawyers' ethical duties with respect to real evidence. In civil cases, lawyers and their clients have to respond honestly to adversaries' discovery requests. In criminal cases, lawyers may have to turn over evidence such as contraband to the police, or at least advise clients of their obligation to do so. Nor can defense lawyers serve as repositories of contraband or conceal it from the police by moving it from one location to another.

B. BENEFITS OF EXHIBITS

The Original Writing Rule (Federal Rule of Evidence 1000) may require you to offer a document into evidence. More often, however, trial lawyers offer tangible objects into evidence because it is in their rhetorical interest to do so. Most fundamentally, tangible objects tend to be persuasive because most of us are *visual learners*. That is, we learn most effectively from what we *see* as opposed to from what we *hear*, and typically rely on visual media like documents, television and computers for information. In a trial court you are a teacher of judges and jurors, and visual aids can be one of your most effective teaching tools.

Another benefit of offering exhibits into evidence is that they often have greater shelf life than oral testimony. Oral testimony plays a part in jurors' deliberations only if the jurors remember it (or record it in their notes, if a judge allows note-taking). By contrast, jurors can often take exhibits into the jury room and examine them while they deliberate.

You can also often use exhibits to emphasize important testimony by eliciting evidence twice, once verbally and a second time with reference to an exhibit. In the absence of the exhibit, a judge might sustain an objection that the repetition is objectionable as "asked and answered." Consider this example, in a case in which a plaintiff struck by an errant boomerang has sued the defendant, who allegedly threw it, for damages.

Q: And what happened next?

A: The defendant transferred the boomerang to his left hand and threw it in my general direction.

Q: What was the distance between you and the defendant at the moment you saw him throw the boomerang?

A: I'd say right around 20 feet.

Q: Can you describe the throwing motion for us?

A: Well, he was holding the boomerang by one end, with his left arm over his head. The boomerang was vertical, perpendicular to the ground.

Q: Then what happened?

A: I heard the defendant say, "Watch out." I tried to put my arms in front of my face but the boomerang hit me in the nose and cheek.

(After marking the boomerang as Plaintiff's Exhibit No. 1 and showing it to opposing counsel and the witness, you continue the questioning.)

Q: Please look at the boomerang that has been marked Plaintiff's No. 1 and tell us if you've ever seen it before.

A: Yes, this is the boomerang that the defendant was holding and that he threw in my direction.

Q: Can you please hold the boomerang the same way the defendant was holding it, when it was over his head and perpendicular to the ground?

A: Sure. . .

This brief example illustrates how the use of an exhibit can allow you to emphasize testimony by repeating portions of a story, once verbally and once with reference to an exhibit.

Another advantage of exhibits is that they may provide welcome relief from the "talking heads" format of trials. As a result, judges and jurors may be more attentive to what you and your witnesses say when you incorporate exhibits in your presentations.

Finally, you may need to incorporate exhibits in trial presentations in order to satisfy jurors' expectations. Many jurors derive their beliefs about what happens at trial from movies and television. They see movie and television lawyers offering exhibits into evidence by the carload, and may expect that you should be able to do the same if your case is meritorious.

Not All Exhibits Are Offered Into Evidence.
You may use visual aids during opening statements
and closing arguments even if they will not be (or
were not) offered into evidence. So long as the visual
material you use is supported by evidence in the
record, and of course subject to judicial discretion,
you may illustrate your remarks with visual aids
even though you do not formally offer them into evidence. For example, you may write a time line of key
events on a board in front of the jurors as you deliver
a closing argument. The written time line may emphasize your client's version of events, but what you
write will not be part of the evidence and jurors cannot take the board with them into the deliberations.

C. FOLLOW THE RULES

Unless an adversary stipulates to an exhibit's admissibility, you'll usually need at least one *sponsoring witness* in order for a judge to admit an exhibit
into evidence. Sponsoring witnesses provide testimony that *lays a foundation* making exhibits admissible. While the content of foundational testimony varies according to type of exhibit and the purpose for
which you offer it, in general the process of laying a
foundation is similar for all exhibits. The process
normally consists of the following three steps:

- *Mark* an exhibit for identification and show it
  to opposing counsel.

- *Authenticate* the exhibit.

• *Satisfy* foundational requirements.

The subsections below explain this three step process.

1. MARK EXHIBITS

Marking an exhibit for identification consists of tagging it with a number or letter so as to distinguish it from other exhibits. During trial, refer to a marked exhibit by its number or letter. Think of an appellate judge trying to understand testimony when a transcript reads, "Witness, did you ever see this letter? How about this one?" Contrast: "Did you ever see plaintiff's Exhibit No. 1? How about Exhibit No. 2?" Traditionally, plaintiffs' exhibits are numbered and defendants' are lettered. However, some judges prefer to number or letter all exhibits consecutively, regardless of which party offers them.

Until trial lawyers can convince manufacturers of objects likely to become exhibits to engrave little numbers or letters on them, the marking process will remain manual. Many judges prefer for lawyers to mark exhibits for identification when they first show exhibits to witnesses. Other judges want exhibits marked before trial, either during a pretrial conference or by the court clerk. When you mark exihibtis for identification the process may go as follows:

Example 1:

Q: What is the next thing you saw?

A: He pulled out a knife and started waving it around.

Q: Your Honor, I have here a knife and I am putting the number 1 on the white evidence tag attached to the knife. I've shown the knife to defense counsel. May the knife be marked State's No. 1 for identification?

Judge: It may be so marked.

Q: May I show it to the witness?

Judge: You may. Carefully please.

If the court clerk has previously marked an exibit, you may identify it for the record as follows:

Example 2:

Q: And what happened after that?

A: The car ended up in the tree.

Q: Your Honor, I have here a photograph which the clerk has previously marked as Defense B for identification. I've shown it to counsel for plaintiff. May I show it to the witness?

Judge: Yes, you may.

The marking process can be slightly more involved when you have more than one exhibit of the same type. When you have just one gun, it's fine to mark

Exhibit No. 1 as a "gun." But what if you need to mark four letters, three photos, two turtle doves and a partridge in a pear tree? The record can no longer reflect that Exhibit No. 3 is a "letter" or a "photograph." You'll need an additional distinguishing characteristic. For example, you may mark one exhibit as a "letter dated June 28," and another as a "letter dated July 3." You have two letters dated June 28? Follow the same distinguishing characteristic principle: "Your Honor, I have two letters dated June 28. May the one addressed to Smith be marked Plaintiff's No. 4 and the one addressed to Wesson be marked Plaintiff's No. 5?"

When marking an exhibit for identification, identify it by a neutral feature. For example, don't identify an exhibit as "a letter in which the defendant makes a full, callous and unambiguous admission of every element of our claim for relief."

2. AUTHENTICATE EXHIBITS

Authenticating exhibits means eliciting testimony showing that an exhibit is what you claim it is. (Federal Rule of Evidence 901). For example, authenticating an email message that you claim was written by Clemmie Finn requires foundational evidence sufficient to support a finding that Clemmie was the email's author. When authenticating an exhibit, get it quickly into a witness' hands. Do not wave an exhibit in the air from counsel table. Witnesses get very frustrated when lawyers ask them to identify small exhibits from a distance of 30 feet.

Authenticating an exhibit typically includes these two foundational questions:

- *"Can you please tell us what Exhibit X is?"* This question allows the witness to identify an exhibit.

- *"How do you know?"* This question allows you to establish the sponsoring witness' personal knowledge.

For example, after marking a photograph of a car for identification, you might authenticate the photo as follows:

Q: Your Honor, may I approach the witness?

Judge: Yes you may, and you needn't continue to ask for permission.

Q: Handing you Defense "B," do you recognize what the photo depicts?

A: Yes. It shows the car after it landed in the old oak tree. Pardon the pun, but at that point it was an Oakmobile.

Q: How are you able to recognize Defense "B" as a photo of the car?

A: Well, I saw where it landed after the accident. That's what it looked like all right.

On many occasions you will need more of a foundation to establish a witness' personal knowledge. For example, witnesses may have to explain how they can identify mass-produced items. Consider how a witness might demonstrate personal knowledge in response to the question, "How do you know these are the scissors you saw?" The witness might respond:

"I know these are the scissors because I recognize the attached tag saying, 'Hilary's scissors; don't remove from room.' "

or

"I know these are the scissors because when I picked them up, I taped this tag to one of the blades and wrote my initials on it."

or

"I know these are the scissors because its blades are rusted, just like the scissors I saw that day."

3. SATISFY FOUNDATIONAL REQUIREMENTS

After authenticating an exhibit, you may need to satisfy other foundational requirements. For example, after authenticating a document you may need to elicit foundational testimony demonstrating that its contents are admissible under an exception to the hearsay rule, perhaps by offering evidence that the document constitutes a business record (Federal Rule of Evidence 803 (6)) or that a statement in the document qualifies as a declaration against interest (Federal Rule of Evidence 804 (3)). Or, you may need to argue that the exhibit's relevance outweighs the risk of unfair prejudice (Federal Rule of Evidence 403). Sample foundations establishing the admissibility of common tangible exhibits are set forth in the sections below.

Once you've established an exhibit's admissibility, you may move it into evidence. The usual magical words are, "Your Honor, I ask that Exhibit No. __ be received in evidence." After giving opposing counsel a chance to object, the judge may utter the even more magical words, "Exhibit X is in evidence."

4. LEAVE ADMITTED EXHIBITS IN THE COURTROOM

Even if you've lavished tender loving care on a tangible object for years, once it becomes an exhibit and has been admitted into evidence it becomes the court's property. Don't reflexively put admitted exhibits in your briefcase after a day of trial, lest the judge instruct the bailiff to invite you to spend a night in the local jail. If your client needs an original document that's been admitted into evidence, ask the judge for permission to substitute a copy for the original.

5. "PUBLISH" EXHIBITS

Once an exhibit has been admitted into evidence, you may ask a judge for permission to *publish* the exhibit to the jury. If the judge grants the request, jurors have a chance to examine exhibits immediately. Publishing can be important because the contents of some exhibits may not be immediately apparent to jurors, who are bypassed by the typical process through which exhibits go into evidence. Exhibits go from you to the judge, then to the witness, and after admission to the court clerk. If you want jurors to examine the exhibits before they begin deliberations, you may need to ask the judge for permission to publish them.

Judges may not be anxious to publish exhibits, because testimony necessarily grinds to a halt while jurors pass an exhibit back and forth. Three steps that can help you achieve a favorable ruling are:

- Support the request with an argument as to why the jurors need to see the exhibit immediately: "Your Honor, if I might be heard on my request. This witness will be testifying to an incident that took place in several rooms in a house. If the jurors see the photographs of the rooms now, they will be better able to understand the testimony."

- When feasible, minimize the delay by having a separate copy of an exhibit for each juror to examine.

- Display an exhibit to all jurors simultaneously on courtroom computer screens.

In lieu of taking the time to publish a written document, a judge may ask you (or the sponsoring witness) to read a short portion to the jury. Reading from the document does not violate the Original Writing Rule, Federal Rule of Evidence 1002, because the document is already in evidence.

6. HANDLE EXHIBITS EFFECTIVELY

Your effectiveness at handling exhibits sends strong signals to judges and jurors about your professionalism and preparedness. For example, include in your outline of a witness' direct examination reminders about any exhibits that you plan to refer to during the examination, and have those exhibits close at hand when the examination begins. If you intend to offer or ask a witness to read from a portion of a document, such as a deposition excerpt, that portion should be flagged and marked before you come to court. If you include technology in your presentation, whether it constitutes a Power Point slide or an audio recording, rehearse thoroughly and check to be sure that your equipment is compatible with the equipment in the courtroom. When feasible, consider bringing a "techie" along for help should unanticipated problems develop.

D. FOUNDATIONS FOR COMMON TANGIBLE EXHIBITS

The subsections below explain and illustrate foundational requirements for a variety of common types of tangible exhibits.

1. REAL EVIDENCE

Parties and other witnesses who took part in case-related events typically provide the foundation for items of real evidence. Witnesses with personal knowledge demonstrate the relevance of an object by explaining how they recognize the marked-for-identification object presented to them at trial as the one that figured in a story. A foundation often includes testimony that an object is in the same or substantially same condition as it was when case-related events took place.

For example, assume that a civil torts plaintiff is to lay the foundation for the introduction into evidence of a boomerang that the defendant allegedly threw so carelessly that it struck and injured the plaintiff. The foundational testimony may proceed as follows:

Q: And then what happened?

A: I was struck on the side of the face by a boomerang.

Q: Showing you Plaintiff's No. 1 for identification, do you know what this is?

A: Yes, that's the boomerang that hit me.

Q: How do you know that this is the boomerang that struck you?

A: It fell to the ground just a few feet away from where I was standing. I picked it up and it's been in my possession ever since.

Q: Has the condition of the boomerang changed in any way since you picked it up?

A: No.

If a tangible object has any unique characteristics, a witness may refer to those characteristics while laying a foundation. For example, the foundation laid by the torts plaintiff above may include this testimony:

Q: Is there anything else about Plaintiff's No. 1 that helps you recognize the boomerang as the one that struck you?

A: Yes. When I picked up the boomerang I noticed that it had 6 notches carved into one of the edges. You can see the notches right here on the boomerang.

Professional witnesses such as police officers typically prepare for foundational testimony by marking items that they find at crime scenes and other locations. For example, the foundational testimony of a police officer who found a gun at a murder scene may go briefly as follows:

Q: Did you find anything during your investigation?

A: Yes. I found a handgun in the bushes a few feet away from where witnesses reported hearing gunshots.

Q: What did you do with this handgun?

A: I put on rubber gloves, picked it up and tied a small white tag to the handle. I wrote my initials and the date and time that I found the gun on the tag.

Q: Handing you Prosecution No. 4 for identification, do you recognize what this is?

A: Yes. It's the gun that I found in the bushes.

Q: How do you recognize it?

A: I remember its appearance, and I also recognize the attached tag that has my initials and the date and time I recovered the weapon.

Q: Has the condition of Prosecution No. 4 changed in any way since you first saw it in the bushes?

A: No. It appears to be in exactly the same condition.

Facsimiles. If you can't get hold of the genuine item of real evidence, you may seek to offer a facsimile as "illustrative of testimony." For example, if you haven't been able to acquire the boomerang that struck your personal injury client, you may offer into evidence a facsimile based on the client's foundational testimony that "this boomerang is nearly identical to the one that I was hit in the face with." As in this example, the foundational testimony should make it clear that the exhibit is a facsimile, not the genuine article.

2. CHAIN OF CUSTODY QUESTIONS

When an item of real evidence is fungible or subject to decomposition or tampering, you may have to support a witness' personal knowledge with *chain of custody* testimony. To establish a chain of custody is to elicit testimony demonstrating that the exhibit offered into evidence is both genuine and is in a substantially unchanged condition.   When an object passes among several people before it arrives in the courtroom, each person is a potential link in a chain whose handling of the exhibit is part of a foundation. Under Federal Rule of Evidence 104(b), a proferring party need establish only that the chain of custody foundation is sufficient to support a finding that an exhibit and its condition are consistent with the party's claims.

For example, assume that you are the prosecutor in a case in which the defendant Jones is charged with possession of illegal drugs. Exhibit No. 1 consists of the white powder-filled baggie that Police Officer Krupke found in Jones' backpack. Your chain of custody foundation will at a minimum consist of testimony from Officer Krupke and the police laboratory analyst who tested the baggie's contents and determined that they constitute an illegal drug. Pursuant to Rule 104(b), the foundation should be sufficient to support a finding that the baggie's contents were not tampered with. The chain of custody foundation may unfold along these lines:

1. Officer Krupke testifies that Exhibit No. 1 (the baggie and its contents) is the baggie that he found in Jones' backpack. Officer Krupke recognizes it because "Shortly after I seized the baggie I put this little sticker on the baggie and marked it with the date, the defendant's name and my initials." Krupke testifies that he put the baggie in a large manila envelope marked with Jones' name and the case number, and that he placed the manila envelope in the Forensic Testing Basket in the evidence locker room at the police station. Krupke in addition testifies that on a later date he removed the envelope from the Testing Completed basket and put it into a locked storage area, where it remained until he brought it to court. Finally, Krupke testifies that the baggie and its contents are in substantially the same condition as when he removed it from Jones' backpack.

2. After testifying to his qualifications, police lab technician Dusty Snow provides the following evidence in response to your questions:

Q: What happened on the morning of May 5?

A: I went to the evidence locker room and picked up four manila folders from the Forensic Testing Basket.

Q: I hand you Exhibit No. 2, a manila envelope on which are written the name Jones and a case number. Do you recognize Exhibit No. 2?

A: Yes. It was one of the envelopes that I picked up from the basket on May 5.

Q: And how do you know?

A: When I picked it up, I followed my standard practice of putting my initials, the date and the time of day in the upper right hand corner of the envelope. I see this information on Exhibit No. 2.

Q: Then what happened with respect to Exhibit No. 2?

A: I carried it to the crime lab on the 4th floor and conducted an analysis of the contents of a baggie that was inside the envelope.

Q: Showing you the baggie that has been marked Exhibit No. 1, do you recognize it?

A: Yes, that's the baggie that was inside Exhibit No. 2 and whose contents I tested.

Q: And how do you know that?

A: When I pulled the baggie out of the envelope, I put this sticker on it with my initials, the date and time of day.

Q: Then what happened?

A: I removed a small amount of power from the baggie and performed the standard lab tests. After I completed the testing, I sealed the baggie and placed it back into the manila envelope, Exhibit No. 2, along with my report of the lab test results. I returned the envelope to the evidence locker, marking the date and time of day that I did so on the manila envelope. I put the envelope in the Testing Completed basket.

Q: Have you seen exhibits number 1 or 2 since you returned the manila envelope to the evidence locker room?

A: No.

Q: How much time elapsed for the entire testing process, from removal of Exhibit No. 2 from the evidence locker room to its return?

A: No more than two hours.

Q: During this time, did anyone other than you handle either Exhibit No. 1 or 2?

A: No.

3. PHOTOGRAPHS

The typical foundation for a photograph consists of testimony from a witness with personal knowledge that the photo *fairly and accurately depicts* its contents. For example, assume that you want to lay the foundation for a photograph of a car that following an accident landed in an old oak tree. The foundational testimony might go as follows:

Q: Handing you Defense Exhibit B, do you recognize what it depicts?

A: Yes. It shows my car after it landed in the old oak tree.

Q: How is it you recognize Exhibit B?

A: Well, I saw exactly where the car ended up after the accident. That's what it looked like all right.

Q: Does the photo fairly and accurately depict the condition and location of your car immediately following the accident?

A: It does.

Q: Your Honor, I move Defense Exhibit B into evidence.

Judge: Any objection? Hearing none, Exhibit B will be received into evidence.

When a witness has personal knowledge of a photo's contents, the foundation typically need not include evidence as to who took the photo, when it was taken, or the type of camera or electronic device that was used to take it. For example, no matter when the photo of the car in the example above was taken, and no matter who the photographer was, the photo is likely to be admissible in evidence so long as the witness testifies that it fairly and accurately depicts the condition of the car after the accident.

The most common objection to photos is that they are misleading or unfairly prejudicial (Federal Rule of Evidence 403). For example, such an objection may be made if an exhibit consists of:

- A photo of the scene of a crime or an accident, and the scene changed significantly between the time of the events and the taking of the photo.

- A series of gory autopsy photos in a wrongful death case.

- A photo of a movie starlet without makeup.

Section 403 generally favors admissibility, as an objector has the burden of convincing a judge that an exhibit's relevance is *substantially* outweighed by one or more of the factors that Section 403 identifies.

4. DIAGRAMS

A diagram is a schematic drawing, often depicting a story's crucial moments. As an object that jurors can usually have with them during deliberations, diagrams provide the rhetorical advantages of other tangible exhibits. In addition, the process of marking a diagram can enhance a witness' credibility. Many witnesses who nervously answer questions while rooted to a witness chair are able to testify with confidence when they can stand and mark up a diagram.

Too, diagrams may allow you to emphasize important testimony, as you can sometimes elicit evidence once orally, and then again as a witness marks a diagram. Finally, as compared to exotic exhibits such as visually recorded or computer-generated re-creations of traffic accidents, diagrams are usually cheap. A diagram can be yours for the price of paper and pen, and even that you may be able to cadge from the court.

Though courtroom graphics professionals will be delighted to prepare diagrams for you, often you can simply meet with a witness prior to trial and prepare a skeletal diagram. In court, the witness can identify the scene depicted in the skeletal drawing, testify to its general accuracy, and (with the aid of pretrial preparation) fill in people, objects and their movements while testifying.

A diagram generally is not, and need not be, a photographically accurate representation of a locale. Hence, diagrams tend *not* to be effective for depicting environmental conditions, such as the adequacy of lighting. Nor are they helpful for depicting precise details. For example, a diagram could not exactly trace a witness' physical movements during an argument.

The following diagram lends visual context to this verbal discussion of effective use of diagrams. Assume that you and a witness have prepared the following diagram prior to trial:

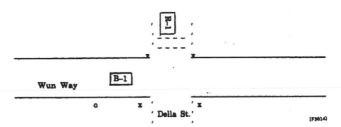

As you see, the diagram can serve only to illustrate a witness' testimony. Without a sponsoring witness, you cannot tell if it pertains to the scene of a crime or a traffic accident, or to an application for a zoning variance. In this case, the foundational testimony may go as follows:

1. Q: Calling your attention to the diagram marked Exhibit A, do you recognize what that is?

2. A: Yes, it's a diagram of the intersection where the accident took place.

3. Q: Do you know how the diagram was prepared?

4. A: Yes. I prepared it the day before yesterday, in your office.

5. Q: What location does the diagram depict?

6. A: It's Wun Way, at the point where Wun intersects Della St. in the Hampstead Garden section of the city. Wun is an east-west street, and Della runs basically north-south at that point. I'm familiar with the intersection and the diagram is accurate though not of course exactly to scale.

7. Q: Did you personally place the markings on the diagram?

8. A: Yes.

9. Q: I notice two rectangles on the diagram. What do they represent?

10. A: The rectangle on Wun is a blue car that was approaching Della, signaling to make a left turn. The other rectangle is the red car that was going south on Della.

11. Q: All right. Please place a "B–1" in the rectangle that represents the blue car, and an "R–1" in the rectangle that represents the red car. Also, perhaps you can place an arrow behind each rectangle to show in what directions the cars were headed when you first noticed them.

12. A: Ok.

13. Q: Looking at the diagram, I also notice four "x" marks and an "o." Please explain what those markings represent.

14. A: OK. The "x" marks are traffic signals on each corner at that intersection. The "o" is where I was standing when I saw the accident.

15. Q: And the pair of dotted lines that crosses Della St., just to the north of the intersection with Wun?

16. A: That's a crosswalk.

17. Q: What were you doing when you were standing at the point marked "o?"

18. A: I was waiting for Aura David to meet me. She's my partner in the interior designer business, and we were going to make a presentation to the law firm of Cooper & Berg, whose offices are there on Wun.

19. Q: Did you continue to watch the cars you've identified as B–1 and R–1?

20. A: Not continuously. I heard a horn, and I thought it might be Aura, so I looked away to my left for a moment or two. I saw it wasn't her, so I glanced toward the intersection again.

21. Q: The intersection of Della and Wun?

22. A: That's right.

23. Q: Did you notice the cars you've labeled B–1 and R–1 after you turned back to look at the intersection?

24. A: Yes.

25. Q: Please place another rectangle on the diagram at the approximate position of the blue car when you saw it for the second time, and label that rectangle "B–2." Do the same for the red car, and label that rectangle "R–2."

26. A: Okay.

27. Q: When the cars were at positions B–2 and R–2, were you still at the position you've marked as point "o"?

28. A: Yes, I was.

29. Q: What is the approximate distance from point "o" to "B–2?"

30. A: I'd say about 40 feet.

31. Q: And the approximate distance between the cars when they were at points "B–2" and "R–2?"

32. A: Pretty close. Maybe about 20 feet.

33. Q: How fast would you say the blue car was going when it was at the point you've marked "B–2?"

34. A: I'd say . . .

Here, you begin by asking the witness to identify the skeletal diagram (Nos. 1–16). As the story emerges, you ask the witness to add to the diagram by showing changes in location (No. 25). Ask witnesses to mark only key changes, lest a diagram begin to resemble an aerial map of the New York City subway system. The markings enable you to clarify a chronology by providing a basis for witness estimates of such matters as distance (No. 30) and speed (No. 34).

To bolster witness credibility and avoid testifying, ask sponsoring witnesses to explain diagram markings. When they do so, you needn't repeat the explanations "for the record." For example, after the witness above testifies that the cars were about 20 feet apart at points "B–2" and "R–2," (Nos. 31–32), you needn't ask the judge to "let the record reflect that at points B–2 and R–2, the cars were about 20 feet apart."

Because diagrams tend to be informal, they are often susceptible to an objection that they are misleading or unfairly prejudicial (Federal Rule of Evidence 403). For example, opposing counsel might argue that a diagram inaccurately shows the location of obstacles that were in a witness' line of vision, or the length of skidmarks. Your general response should be that the diagram is illustrative of testimony, not precisely accurate, and that the adversary can bring out such considerations during cross examination. Under Federal Rules of Evidence 104(b) and 602, a diagram is usually admissible so long as the witness has sufficient personal knowledge to prepare the diagram.

5. THE ORIGINAL WRITING (NEE BEST EVIDENCE) RULE

Federal Rule of Evidence 1002 sets forth a general requirement of an original (or a duplicate) when you seek to prove the contents of a "writing" such as a letter, a recording or a photograph. From a strategic standpoint, the Original Writing Rule coincides with effective advocacy. Even without the rule, lawyers generally seek to offer into evidence writings that support their legal claims.

Thanks to computers and other forms of technology, the rule plays a lesser role in modern litigation compared to common law days. For most of the common law era, generally there was but one original and copies were handwritten and thus not "duplicates." By contrast, any printout of a computer file constitutes an original, and every visual print made from the same negative or computer chip constitutes an original photograph. Photocopied writings constitute duplicates that usually are admissible to the same extent as originals. When you have neither an original nor a duplicate, you may yet be able to offer secondary evidence of a writing's contents by laying a foundation that satisfies an exception to the rule's requirements.

The Original Writing Rule does not establish a "hierarchy" of secondary evidence. If an offeror has available a copy of an original writing whose production is excused, presumably the offeror will offer that copy rather than oral testimony into evidence. However, the rule leaves it up to the offeror to decide whether to offer the copy or oral testimony.

a. Original Writings

The most obvious way to satisfy the Original Writing rule is to offer foundational evidence that a proffered writing is an original. For example, the plaintiff in an auto accident case may testify as follows:

Q: And what happened after you got out of the car following the collision?

A: I took a photo of the passenger side of the car on my mobile phone.

Q: I hand you Exhibit No. 1 for identification, do you recognize what this is?

A: Yes, that's the photo that I took right after the accident?

Q: And how do you recognize it?

A: I saw the side of the car after the collision, and this photo shows exactly what it looked like.

Q: How did you prepare the photo that is Exhibit No. 1?

A: I linked my phone to a printer and printed it out.

b. Duplicates

Mechanically or electronically produced copies of original writings are routinely as admissible as the originals themselves. The foundation for admitting the duplicate of a writing that a plaintiff in a workplace sexual harassment case might proffer may go as follows:

Q: Do you recognize Exhibit No. 1?

A: Yes. This is a copy of the ink drawing that I found on my desk when I returned from lunch.

Q: Do you know how the copy was prepared?

A: Yes, I prepared it myself. I was really shaken when I saw it on my desk, but a few minutes later I went over to the office copy machine and printed out three copies. This is one of them.

Q: Why did you make copies of the drawing?

A: I didn't know if the ink would smear, and anyway the paper that was used was pretty flimsy. I made the copies because I wanted to make sure I had a permanent record of the way I was treated in the office.

c. Original Writing Excused: Contents Not in Issue

If a judge is convinced pursuant to Federal Rule of Evidence 104(a) that a writing's contents are not in issue, the Original Writing Rule is inapplicable. The contents of a writing are commonly not in issue when the probative value of an inscribed tangible object emanates from the object itself rather than from words inscribed on the object. For example, assume that a witness in a personal injury action testifies that "I was walking along the road when I was struck by a falling object that turned out to be a stone tablet containing half of the Ten Commandments." The Original Writing Rule would not require you to produce the tablet, because its communicative aspect is not in issue.

How you phrase a question can determine whether or not the contents of a writing are "in issue."

For example, assume that a police officer took a suspect's oral confession and later had the suspect sign a written confession. If you ask the officer to testify orally to the contents of the written confession, its contents are "in issue" and the Original Writing Rule is applicable. On the other hand, if you ask the officer to testify to the suspect's oral confession, the contents of the written confession are not "in issue" and the Rule does not apply.

The so-called "inscribed chattel" exception to the Original Writing rule can allow you to offer evidence of a tangible object's communicative contents even if you fail to produce the object itself. The exception arises when a judge is convinced pursuant to Rule 104(a) that production of an original is unnecessary. For example, a judge may permit a witness to link a dress shirt to a criminal defendant through oral testimony that the monogram on the shirt front corresponds to the defendant's initials.

d. Original Writing Excused: The Original Is Lost

A foundation that convinces a judge pursuant to Rule 104(a) that an original writing was lost innocently excuses compliance with the Original Writing Rule. The typical foundation for this "oops" exception consists of testimony that a writing at one time existed but can no longer be found despite a diligent search having been made.

For example, assume that Johann has brought a case for libel based on the contents of a letter that he can no longer find. A foundation that would allow Johann to testify orally to the letter's contents may go as follows:

Q: What happened next?

A: Chen sent a letter to me and the three other people on the board, accusing me of stealing the funds.

Q: Johann, do you have any of the letters that you say Mr. Chen allegedly sent to you and the board members?

A: No, I don't.

Q: Can you explain why?

A: I collected all of the letters and put them in a file folder that I mistakenly put into a drawer of a filing cabinet in my office whose contents were scheduled to be put in storage. When I looked for the file folder with the letters in it, about a week later, it was gone.

Q: What did you do then?

A: I immediately contacted Vivian, the office manager, to try to find out where my files had been moved to. Vivian's records indicated that my files could have been moved to two different storage facilities. I went to both of them, and along with storage company employees looked through all the places where the file folder could have been. We couldn't find it.

Q: Did you do anything else to try to find the letters?

A: Yes. I asked other executives and board members to look through the files in their offices, and had the storage companies conduct their own searches. The file folder never turned up.

> **Comment:** This testimony briefly lays a foundation demonstrating that an original writing was innocently lost.

Q: Before putting the letters in the file folder, did you read them?

A: I did. They were all identical.

Q: And are you able to recall the letter's contents?

A: Yes, the letter said. . .

Q: How do you know that Mr. Chen wrote the letter?

A: We've corresponded often, and I am quite familiar with his handwriting.

> **Comment:** As here, the party offering secondary evidence of a writing into evidence must au-

thenticate the original, even if production of the original is unnecessary.

e. Original Writing Excused: The Original Was Innocently Destroyed

Foundational evidence convincing a judge pursuant to Rule 104(a) that an original writing was destroyed innocently (i.e., without fraudulent intent) also allows a party to offer secondary evidence rather than the writing itself. Foundational testimony supporting this exception might go as follows:

Q: Ms. Williston, are you familiar with the terms of the sales agreement that you entered into with Mr. Corbin?

A: Yes.

Q: Please tell us the terms of that agreement.

Opp: Objection based on the Original Writing Rule, the witness cannot testify to the contents of a written document.

Q: I'll lay a further foundation, Your Honor. Ms. Williston, did you and Mr. Corbin enter into a written sales agreement?

A: We did.

Q: Please describe the document on which the agreement was written.

A: Corbin and I discussed the deal over afternoon tea, and at the end of the meal I wrote down the terms we had agreed to on the back of a napkin. We both signed the napkin.

Q: Does that napkin still exist?

A: No. Before I realized what had happened, the waiter had cleared the table and thrown away all the paper items, including the napkin. Corbin and I checked both the bins for recycling items and for garbage, but we couldn't find the napkin.

This testimony establishes that the writing was destroyed without fraudulent intent, allowing the witness to testify to the writing's contents.

6. AUTHENTICATING SIGNED OR HANDWRITTEN DOCUMENTS

To authenticate any tangible object is to produce evidence sufficient to support a finding under Federal Rule of Evidence 104(b) that an object is what you claim that it is. A foundation that is sufficient to support a finding that a claimed person authored a document may be provided by a witness who saw that person prepare or sign the document.

For example, assume that on behalf of a car dealer you seek to offer into evidence a car purchase agreement allegedly entered into by Dee Soto. The foundational testimony may go as follows:

1. Q: Mr. Baker, you are the car dealer's finance manager, correct?

2. A: Yes.

3. Q: Do you recall a transaction involving the defendant Dee Soto?

4. A: I do.

5. Q: This transaction took place on March 31?

6. A: Yes.

7. Q: Can you briefly describe what happened?

8. A: At a salesperson's request, I prepared a purchase agreement for a new car. When the agreement was ready, I called Ms. Soto into my office. After we reviewed the terms of the agreement, she signed it.

9. Q: Who was present during your meeting with Ms. Soto.

10. A: Just the two of us.

11. Q: (Plaintiff's counsel marks a sales agreement as Exhibit No. 1, shows it to defense counsel, and obtains permission to approach the witness.) Mr. Baker, I hand you Exhibit No. 1 and ask if you recognize it?

12. A: I do. This is the agreement that Ms. Soto signed.

13. Q: How do you know this is the agreement that she signed?

14. A: I saw her sign it and recognize her signature. I also recall the terms set forth in the agreement.

15. Q: Your Honor, I offer Exhibit No. 1 into evidence.

The brief example includes "who, what and when" foundational testimony. The witness describes the event (No. 8), testifies to the date it took place (Nos. 5-6) and explains who was present (No. 10). Leading questions, proper during foundational questioning, move the testimony along briskly (Nos. 1 and 5).

Similarly, a witness with personal knowledge of a check's preparation may authenticate a check as follows:

Q: Mr. Ruiz, were you present in Ms. Smith's office on Nov. 16 last?

A: I was.

Q: Was anyone else present at that time?

A: No, just Ms. Smith and me.

Q: And did Ms. Smith write out any checks at that time?

A: Yes. She wrote out a company check to Amalgamated Chemical Co. for $2 million, then we both signed the check.

Q: Showing you Defense D for identification, do you recognize it?

A: Yes, this is the check I just referred to.

Q: And how do you recognize it?

A: I saw Ms. Smith write it out and I recognize the date, the payee and our signatures.

If you lack a witness to a document's preparation or signing, you may authenticate a handwritten document through the opinion testimony of a witness who is familiar with a claimed author's handwriting. For instance, if the car dealer in the first example above is unable to produce a witness who saw Dee Soto sign the purchase agreement, you may call a witness who is familiar with Ms. Soto's handwriting to lay a foundation as follows:

Q: (After marking the purchase agreement as an exhibit, displaying it to defense counsel and obtaining permission to approach the witness) Ms. Packard, I hand you Exhibit No. 1 and ask if you recognize the signature at the bottom of page 2?

A: I do. It's Dee Soto's signature.

Q: How are you able to recognize the signature as Ms. Soto's?

A: I've known her for years. I've seen her sign her name to notes, checks, lots of things over the years.

Q: Can you estimate about how many times you've seen her sign her name to a document?

A: Wow, it's got to be in the hundreds.

Q: And in your opinion, is this Ms. Soto's signature at the bottom of page 2 of Exhibit 1?

A: It is.

7. BUSINESS RECORDS

Federal Rule of Evidence 803(6), the business records exception to the hearsay rule, lays out the foundational requirements for the introduction into evidence of business records. The foundational elements purport to assure the reliability of information in business records by providing that the records be prepared timely and regularly. Often, the foundation is provided by a certificate that complies with Federal Rule of Evidence 902(11) or 902(12). Alternatively, and especially for large organizations that may be "repeat litigation players," the foundational witness is a custodian of records who may know nothing about a particular transaction or series of events but who can testify to an organization's record-preparation and record-keeping procedures.   In such a situation, the foundational testimony may emerge along these lines:

Q: Mr. Abadian, what is your position with Mom and Pop Conglomerate?

A: I am the record-keeping manager for the southeast region.

Q: Do the records include records of merchandise deliveries from Mom and Pop warehouses to retail stores?

A: Yes.

Q: And has Mom and Pop established regular procedures for the keeping of such records?

A: Yes.

Q: Can you please describe those procedures?

A: (The witness describes a process in which drivers enter information into a company database electronically when they load merchandise onto their trucks at warehouses, and again at the time of delivery to retail stores. The information includes drivers' identity, the number of boxes picked up and delivered, and the date and time of pick up and delivery. Each driver has a unique electronic signature, and the company maintains a separate file for each driver's activities.   Drivers produce hundreds of records every month. Mr. Abadian describes how the computer files are maintained and his ability to access those files.)

Q: Mr. Abadian, I show you Exhibit No. 3 and ask if you recognize it?

A: Yes. This is a computer printout of a series of deliveries made by Ed Norton, one of Mom and Pop's drivers, to Kramden Toy Co. in March, April and May of last year.

Q: How are you able to recognize Exhibit No. 3?

A: These are Mom and Pop delivery records; I helped to design the format. I also recognize Ed Norton's electronic signature.

Q: Your Honor, I move Exhibit No. 3 into evidence.

Judge: It will be received in evidence.

8. PUBLIC RECORDS

Federal Rule of Evidence 803(8), the public (official) records exception to the hearsay rule, lays out the foundational requirements for the introduction into evidence of the records of public agencies. Generally, a sponsoring witness is unnecessary; a public official's stamped attestation is the only foundation that you need to produce to convince a judge to admit a public record into evidence. For example, to offer the record of a County Health Inspector's inspection of a restaurant, you would subpoena the desired report from the appropriate county agency. The agency would then submit a copy of the report to the court, with a stamp and attestation indicating that it is a true and accurate copy of the original public report.   Certified public records are self-authenticating under Rule 902.

Rule 803(8)(C) extends the federal public records exception well beyond its common law counterpart by creating an exception for one-shot factual investigations.   The investigator need not even be a public official, so long as an investigation is carried out under the auspices of a public agency. For example, assume that a County Sheriff appoints Anne Attorney to investigate the events leading up to a riot in a county detention facility. Mark Time, a prisoner who was injured during that riot, has sued the county and seeks to offer Attorney's report into evidence. A brief synopsis of the foundation may go as follows:

Q: Ms. Attorney, please briefly describe your professional background.

A: (The witness describes her experience in law enforcement and her criminal law practice experience. This information is relevant to the report's trustworthiness, one of Rule 803(8)'s foundational elements.)

Q: Ms. Attorney, were you retained by the County Sheriff to investigate the events related to a jail disturbance that took place in the Twinned Towers jail facility on March 31 of last year?

A: I was.

Q: Please describe that investigation.

A: (In response to a series of questions, the witness provides a chronology of the investigation and the records that she kept of that investigation.)

Q: Your Honor, I move that Exhibit No. 2, Report of Anne Attorney, be received into evidence.

Judge: It will be received.

Q: Based on your investigation Ms. Attorney, were you able to arrive at an opinion as to whether Deputy Bluto knew that Mr. Time would be alone in his cellblock on the afternoon of the disturbance?

A: I do.

Q: And what is that opinion?

A: Deputy Bluto did know that Mr. Time would be alone in his cellblock.

> **Comment:** This is probably the type of "factual finding" that Rule 803(8)(C) authorizes. However, the witness could not testify to an opinion that Deputy Bluto violated Mark Time's civil rights, as that would constitute a legal judgment rather than a factual finding.

9. COMPUTER RECORDS

Computer-generated evidence is widely accepted by courts without the need for a foundation that establishes the reliability of computers or computer networks. If called on to do so, judges typically judicially notice the reliability of computer technology pursuant to Federal Rule of Evidence 201.

Nevertheless, the need to authenticate a computer record with foundational evidence that is sufficient to support a finding that links the record to a particular individual or entity remains. But with a relative paucity of documents that you can authenticate based on a witness' familiarity with a claimed author's handwriting or signature, you'll need to look to other means of proving that an "item is what the proponent claims it is." Federal Rule of Evidence 901(a).

For example, you may lay a foundation establishing that a computer record constitutes a business or public record. Or, a record containing a trade inscription may be self-authenticating under Federal Rule of Evidence 902(7).

Authentication by content is another long-established method of laying a foundation that you may use for computer records such as electronic mail communications. The foundation consists of evidence demonstrating that the email's contents are sufficient to support a finding of authorship. For example, suppose that you represent the plaintiff in an auto accident case, and you want to offer into evidence an email message that you claim was sent to the plaintiff by the defendant. If the plaintiff testifies to having had an ancient Grecian urn on the front passenger seat at the time of the accident, you can authenticate the message as having been sent by the defendant by demonstrating that the sender includes in the message an ode lamenting the shattering of the urn.

Or, under the *reply doctrine*, you may authenticate a computer record by showing that it was prepared in response to an earlier communication sent to the record's claimed source. For example, in the auto accident scenario, you may offer foundational evidence sufficient to support a finding that the defendant wrote the email by offering evidence that it was sent in response to an earlier message that the plaintiff sent to the defendant.

When a computer record's contents cannot provide authentication and if you have no handwriting for a witness to authenticate, your sponsoring witness might have to be a forensic computer expert who can link a computer record to the person or institution that you claim produced it.

10. FAXED WRITINGS

As is true for computers, courts generally take judicial notice of the reliability of fax (facsimile) machines, which transmit accurate copies of documents electronically from one phone number to another.

The sender of a faxed writing typically seeks to establish that the fax was received by a claimed recipient. Foundational evidence that is sufficient to support a finding of receipt of a fax normally consists of evidence authenticating a fax as the one that the sender properly sent to the recipient's assigned fax number. Most fax machines automatically generate records of sent writings; these records are not hearsay because they are machine-generated information.

The recipient of a faxed writing typically seeks to establish that the fax was sent by a claimed sender. If the sender is a public agency or a commercial enterprise, a fax is likely to bear a self-authenticating heading under Federal Rule of Evidence 902 (7). Otherwise, the traditional rule that the presence of a name on a writing does not by itself authenticate the writing as produced by the named person survives into the digital age. Thus, foundational evidence that is sufficient to support a finding that links a received fax to a claimed sender often includes these features:

* Receipt of the fax by the recipient's fax machine at a particular time and date. Fax machines generally include this information on printouts.

* Information about the recipient's fax machine, including its assigned phone number and its being in working order on a relevant date and time.

* Information that links the fax to the claimed sender. Typically, this can be done through the sending phone number that fax machines automatically imprint on faxes. The content of a fax may also link it to a claimed sender, as may evidence showing that a fax was sent in reply to an earlier communication.

* If a cover sheet accompanies a faxed writing, the cover sheet may also include information linking a fax to a claimed sender.

* Prior fax communications by the recipient with the claimed sender, if any.

As of yet, "receipt of sent fax" presumptions resembling the traditional "receipt of sent mail" statutory presumptions do not exist. Nevertheless, foundational evidence of the sort summarized above typically gives rise to a strong inference concerning the identities of the recipients or senders of faxed writings.

11. TEXTS AND TWEETS

Many current writings that parties offer into evidence are products of digital communication technology, including text messages and tweets. While electronic messages such as these may identify a sender and a receiver, the presence of those names alone (even in the form of an electronic signature) is ordinarily not sufficient to constitute evidence sufficient to sustain a finding under Federal Rule of Evidence 104(b) that the message was sent or received by a named person or entity.

You can often authenticate electronically produced writings by using familiar methods discussed above, such as the "reply doctrine" and "authentication by content." In addition, you may lay an adequate foundation by offering evidence that the person or entity that you claim authored a text or tweet acted in conformity with its contents. For example, assume that a text message states that your client will receive a hard copy in the post, and the client in fact received a hard copy from the entity who you claim sent the text. The action in conformity with the text message authenticates the text as having been sent by the entity that sent the hard copy.

When traditional authentication methods such as these are not available, authentication of electronic writings may require testimony by forensic computer experts who use sophisticated cryptography to link writings to particular computers. The expenses are typically significant and they usually constitute costs that judges award to victorious litigants. As a result, unless the genuineness of electronic documents is a legitimate issue in high stakes cases, you may ask adversaries to stipulate to authenticity, or to admit in response to Requests for Admissions that electronically produced writings are authentic.

12. RECORDED RECOLLECTION

When you are the proponent of a witness who cannot recall information well enough to testify "fully and accurately," you may be able to offer into evidence the contents of a writing that the witness made or adopted pursuant to the hearsay exception for *recorded recollection* under Federal Rule of Evidence 803(5). The foundation you lay must show that the writing was made or adopted at a time when the matter to which it refers was fresh in the witness' memory, and that the writing accurately reflects the witness' personal knowledge.

For example, assume that you are the prosecutor in a bank robbery case. Eyewitness Holmes wrote down the license plate number of the getaway car but on the witness stand cannot recall the number "well enough to testify fully and accurately." Holmes testifies that he saw the getaway car's license plate, but can remember only that it started with the letters "NOM." When you seek to offer evidence of the complete license plate number, the foundational testimony may go as follows:

Q: What if anything did you do after you lost sight of the car?

A: I pulled an envelope out of my pocket and right away I wrote down the entire license plate number.

Q: Do you have the envelope with you today?

A: Yes, here it is. I've kept it in my safe at home, except when I took it out to show to you and the police.

Q: (After marking the envelope as Prosecutor's No. 1 and showing it to the judge and defense counsel) Mr. Holmes, showing you Exhibit No. 1, do you know what it is?

A: Yes. This is the envelope and the license plate number that I wrote down.

Q: How do you know that?

A: I recognize the envelope and my own handwriting.

Q: How much time elapsed between the time you lost sight of the getaway car and you wrote what's on Exhibit No. 1?

A: I don't know exactly, but it couldn't have been more than a few seconds. Five-six seconds at the most.

Q: Was the license plate number fresh in your memory when you wrote down the license plate number?

A: Yes.

Q: Did you accurately write down the license plate number?

A: Definitely. I knew it could be important information for the police.

Q: At this time, Your Honor, I'd ask that the witness be allowed to read aloud the license plate number that he wrote on the envelope.

Judge: Hearing no objection, the request is granted.

> **Comment:** Most jurisdictions, in accord with Rule 803(5), do not allow the writing itself to be received in evidence.

13. LIVE EXHIBITIONS

Live courtroom demonstrations do not constitute tangible exhibits, but they tend to have similar visual vividness. You may with good reason be reluctant to stage a live demonstration, because of the ever-present risk that things will go wrong. For example, assume that after your witness testifies that "I was standing about 5 feet away from the defendant," you ask the witness to walk to a point in the courtroom that is as far from you as the witness was from the defendant. If the witness walks about 15 feet away from you, you've created an embarrassing conflict.

Moreover, live demonstrations may provoke Rule 403 objections from adversaries. On the probative value side of the Rule 403 balance, an adversary may object that a demonstration adds little to oral testimony. At the same time, the adversary may argue that the demonstration will inflame jurors' passions, consume an undue amount of time, or result in confusion.

The risks of live demonstrations were on display in the film *Philadelphia* (1993). Andrew Beckett sued the law firm that had employed him as an associate for illegally firing him because he had AIDS. (At the time of the film, AIDS was incurable, feared by many as easily transferable and virtually always fatal.) Beckett testifies that the law firm partners knew that he had AIDS because one of them recognized the AIDS lesion on his face. To support the law firm partners' contention that they did not know that Beckett had AIDS, defense lawyer Belinda Conine conducts a live demonstration while cross examining Beckett. The demonstration goes substantially as follows:

Q: You've testified that the lesions on your face were visible to the people you worked with, correct?

A: That's right.

Q: And it's your contention that when the partners were made aware of the lesions, they jumped to the conclusion you had AIDS and fired you.

A: Absolutely.

Q: Do you have any lesions on your face at this time?

A: One. Here, in front of my ear (pointing to the side of his face).

Q: (An assistant hands Conine a shaving mirror, which she holds in front of Beckett) Remembering you are under oath, answering truthfully, can you see the lesion on your face, in this mirror, from three feet away? Answering truthfully.

A: (Beckett examines his face in the mirror) When I was fired, there were four lesions on my face, much bigger. . .

Q: Answer the question, please.

A: No. I can't really see it.

Conine's demonstration has minimal probative value, because of the possibility that though an AIDS lesion may not be visible at the time of trial, it may have been visible months earlier, when Beckett was fired. Thus the demonstration is confusing to the jury, and the judge should have excluded it pursuant to Rule 403.

Rule 403 concerns are equally present when Beckett's attorney Joe Miller responds with his own live demonstration on redirect examination. Miller borrows the mirror from Conine, and questions Beckett as follows:

Q: Andrew, do you have any lesions on any part of your body, at this time, that resemble the lesions that were on your face at the time you were fired?

A: Yes. On my torso.

Q: If it please the court, I'd like to ask Mr. Beckett to remove his shirt, so that the jury can have an accurate idea of what we're talking about.

Conine: We object, Your Honor. It would unfairly influence the jury.

Judge: Overruled.

Q: (After Beckett removes his jacket, tie and shirt, and reveals a torso filled with purple lesions.) Can you see the lesions on your chest in this mirror?

A: Yes.

Though Conine's own demonstration was improper, the judge should have sustained her Rule 403 objection to Miller's demonstration. The large number of lesions on his chest could well inflame the jurors' passions against the law firm partners. Moreover, the demonstration confused the issues because the partners could not have noticed lesions on Beckett's chest, nor did Beckett testify that he had so many lesions on his face when he was fired.

While *Philadelphia* is of course "just a movie," the mirror scene reasonably exemplifies the concerns that live exhibitions tends to raise.

14. PROFESSIONALLY–PREPARED EXHIBITS

Technological advances in professional exhibit preparation make informal diagrams seem as old-fashioned as buggy whips. When jury trials involve large sums of money, litigators often retain professionals who prepare forensic exhibits. Among the more common types of professionally-prepared exhibits are these:

- Enlargements of pages from depositions or contracts, with key language "pulled out" and color-coded.

- Drawn-to-scale metallic diagrams, color-coded and magnetized to allow the easy movement of objects.

- Enlargements of locations with overlays, each overlay showing how the location changed over time.

- "Day in the Life" visual recordings, depicting an injured person's daily activities.

- Computer re-enactments of a series of events, including traffic accidents; crimes; and the processes by which products are developed and brought to market.

Like any other exhibits, professionally-prepared exhibits must be marked and authenticated, and meet evidentiary requirements. The most common objection to such illustrative exhibits is that their probative value is outweighed by the dangers of unfair prejudice or misleading the jury (Federal Rule of Evidence 403). For example, an opponent may claim that whatever is depicted in an exhibit is not supported by evidence in the record. Or, an adversary may claim that a "Day in the Life" visual recording distorts an injured person's condition by showing the person trying to perform one activity after another with no rest in between.

Judges consider such objections very carefully. Since professionals may create exhibits that in subtle ways maximize their psychological impact, judges are often wary of the danger that professionally-prepared exhibits will mislead jurors. Whenever you think it possible that a judge will exclude a professional exhibit that you seek to offer into evidence, ask a preparer to create alternative versions of an exhibit, one more "neutral" than the other. Clients are not fond of spending big money for exhibits that never see the light of admissibility.

When hiring a professional to prepare exhibits, think of the professional as an expert witness. Just as you ordinarily rely on an expert to identify significant evidence, so should you look to an exhibit preparation professional to advise you as to what to put in an exhibit and how to make the exhibit effective. For example, simple exhibits usually have more impact than complex ones, and a professional is likely to know better than you how to convey key evidence clearly and vividly.

CHAPTER 11
EXPERT WITNESSES

Experts are increasingly ubiquitous in litigation. Studies suggest that experts appear in approximately 80% of all civil trials, with an average of four to five experts appearing per trial. Experts testify more frequently than ever before in criminal trials as well, partly due to advances in science and technology and partly because lawyers believe that they need to fulfill the expectations of jurors who watch films and television shows glamorizing the role of forensic scientists. Read any magazine aimed at the trial bar or go to any web site devoted to expert witnesses, and you'll find thousands of experts touting their expertise, experience, credibility and availability for hire.

A number of factors have combined to turn forensic expertise into a growth industry. In an era of specialization experts can testify to "more and more about less and less," meaning that multiple experts are often necessary. Litigators have also become more adept at shaping their claims and cases so as to take advantage of available fields of expertise. And changes made to common law rules by the Federal Rules of Evidence, and Rule 702 in particular, have tended to increase the admissibility of expert testimony.

As helpful and even necessary as experts may be, their importance to modern litigation has its downsides. For example, experts tend to drive up the costs of litigation, the adversarial process tends to goad experts into taking more extreme positions inside the courtroom than they might in their offices or laboratories, and lay jurors more or less plucked off the street often have to evaluate complex, technical and conflicting information that they've never been exposed to previously. The role of experts in the trial process is likely to remain a subject of debate, and rules regulating the admissibility of expert testimony are likely to remain the subject of scrutiny by lawyers, academics, judges and legislators.

A. EXPERTS' VARIED ROLES

Though this chapter focuses on strategies for effectively eliciting expert testimony, experts typically play important roles in litigation well before cases go to trial.

For example, prior to filing a lawsuit you may consult with an expert and seek advice as to a claim's potential merits, what if any further investigation you need to carry out, and what if any additional experts you may need to bring on board. Consulting with an expert prior to filing a complaint may be not only a sensible strategy but a legally necessary one. In some jurisdictions, for example, a medical malpractice complaint has to be accompanied by a medical expert's affidavit to the effect that the expert has reviewed the case and believes that it has merit.

Moving forward to the discovery phase of litigation, litigators typically consult with retained experts with respect to what information to seek and from what sources to seek it. For example, an expert can help you decide what witnesses to depose and what to ask them, whether they are lay witnesses or experts retained by an adversary. If you depose an adversary's expert, you typically are responsible for paying the expert's reasonable fees for the time the expert spends at the deposition. If you are the prevailing party, you should be able to recover the adverse expert's fees as an allowable cost of suit. When an adversary notices your expert's deposition, you should prepare the expert to give accurate and convincing testimony, just as though the expert were about to testify at trial.

At trial, most experts' primary function is to deliver opinions and explain their bases. For example, an expert in a medical malpractice case typically gives an opinion as to whether a defendant physician's treatment of a patient fell below the community's standard of care. A linguistics expert may provide an opinion as to whether the recorded voice that left a bomb threat on an answering machine is that of the defendant. And a warning label expert may testify to an opinion as to whether a pharmaceutical warning label provides adequate notice as to the dangers of using a particular drug. Allowing a witness to offer an opinion that "embraces an ultimate issue" (Federal Rule of Evidence 704(a)) is an example of modern evidence statutes welcoming expert testimony to a much greater extent than did the common law.

Experts do not necessarily testify to opinions. *Educational* experts play a more limited role at trial because of limitations inherent in their field of expertise. For example, eyewitness identification experts typically testify to factors that at least in experimental studies tend to produce mistaken identifications. However, eyewitness identification experts do not offer opinions about the accuracy of case-specific eyewitness identifications, because their expertise does not permit them to assess a specific identification with a sufficient degree of certainty. Similarly, rape trauma syndrome experts may educate judges and jurors about common reactions exhibited by women who have been sexually assaulted, but they do not purport to know whether a particular individual who experienced some of those reactions was sexually assaulted.

B. FOLLOW THE RULES

This section briefly explains the principal rules pertaining to testimony by expert witnesses.

1. PERSONAL KNOWLEDGE

The fundamental principle set forth in Federal Rule 602 that witnesses must testify based on personal knowledge does not apply to experts. (See Federal Rule of Evidence 703) Experts may of course base testimony at least partly on personal knowledge, as when a treating or diagnosing medical expert provides an opinion about the severity of a patient's injuries based partly on the expert's physical examination of the patient. More generally, experts testify by evaluating the case-specific information given to them in the light of the generally-applicable principles that constitute the basis of their expertise. For example, the medical expert who testifies to the severity of a patient's injuries may arrive at an opinion by using the expert's specialized knowledge to evaluate the results of tests performed by other medical specialists.

2. OTHERWISE–INADMISSIBLE EVIDENCE

When arriving at opinions, experts often rely partly on information that is not itself admissible in evidence. Opinions based on inadmissible evidence are admissible so long as "experts in the particular field would reasonably rely on those kinds of facts or data in forming an opinion on the subject." Federal Rule of Evidence 703. Rule 703 gives judges discretion to decide whether to permit experts to testify to the otherwise-inadmissible information. To restrain parties from routinely using experts as conduits for inadmissible evidence, Rule 703 further provides that "the proponent of the opinion may disclose [inadmissible facts or data] to the jury *only if their probative value in helping the jury evaluate the opinion substantially outweighs their prejudicial effect.*" (emphasis added)

3. COMPENSATION

Once they are subpoenaed, lay witnesses who have personal knowledge of case-related information have a legal obligation to appear in court and answer questions. Their only compensation in most jurisdictions is a nominal amount that defrays travel costs. Experts' specialized knowledge, by contrast, is an asset for which experts can demand compensation. Privately retained experts generally charge whatever the market will bear, and their fees vary widely according to such factors as experts' reputations and experience. Judges may ask experts to accept court appointments for a standard fee set by a county.

Ethical rules forbid you from paying contingent fees to experts. ABA Model Rule of Professional Conduct, Rule 3.4, Comment 3. Thus, you cannot agree to pay an expert "$10,000 if we win, $3000 if we lose."

4. RELAXED TESTIMONIAL RULES

While testimonial rules generally do not distinguish between lay and expert witnesses, in practice judges tend to allow experts greater narrative freedom than lay witnesses. Judges often consider experts to be "professional witnesses" who deserve greater freedom to explain and amplify on answers. On the other hand, experts and their opinions are subject to impeachment to the same extent as lay witnesses.

5. RELIABILITY OF A FIELD OF EXPERTISE

In federal and many state courts, a line of U.S. Supreme Court cases beginning with *Daubert v. Merrill Dow Pharmaceuticals*, 509 U.S. 579 (1993) and extending through *Kumho Tire v. Carmichael*, 526 U.S. 137 (1999) has set forth basic principles governing the admissibility of expert testimony. Congress subsequently blended these principles into Federal Rule of Evidence 702. Pursuant to these principles, judges are "gatekeepers" who decide whether an area of expertise is sufficiently relevant and reliable to permit expert testimony.

Rule 702 provides that testimony based on specialized knowledge is relevant if it will "help the trier of fact to understand the evidence or to determine a fact in issue." The rule thus implicitly recognizes a role both for educational experts ("understand the evidence") and opinion experts ("to determine a fact in issue"). The rule's "help the trier of fact" language liberalized the traditional common law rule, which generally admitted expert testimony only if a matter was "beyond the ken" of lay jurors.

The reliability determination includes both the legitimacy of the general principles underlying an expert's specialized knowledge, and the reliability of the methods by which an expert applied those principles to case-specific evidence. Pursuant to Federal Rule of Evidence 104(a), a party seeking to offer expert testimony must offer foundational evidence convincing a judge by a preponderance of evidence that the reliability requirements have been met.

If a judge requires you to demonstrate the reliability of a field of expertise, the foundational evidence you might offer necessarily varies according to the field of expertise. Generally, the opinion or educational expert you've retained will also provide the foundational evidence, although you might need other experts as well. *Daubert* provided examples of factors that judges can use when determining reliability, including (1) whether a theory or technique has been tested; (2) whether a theory or technique has been presented in peer-reviewed journals; (3) a theory or technique's error rates; and (4) whether a theory or technique is generally accepted in a relevant scientific community.

When determining reliability, judges ignore or at least do not limit themselves to the factors set forth in *Daubert*. The *Daubert* factors turned out to be often unworkable, especially when in *Kumho Tire* the Supreme Court ruled that *Daubert* applied not just to novel scientific theories, but to all testimony based on specialized knowledge.

Often, reliability hearings are unnecessary because judges take judicial notice that a field of expertise is reliable. However, the potential exists for foundational hearings to cause judges to exclude expert testimony because the reliability that had been assumed to underlie a field of expertise cannot be established. For example, in the case of *United*

States v. Plaza (2002) a federal district court judge sent shock waves through the legal community by ruling that fingerprint evidence was inadmissible because its underlying principles (such as no two people having identical fingerprints) had not been shown to be reliable. However, the judge reversed the ruling and allowed a fingerprint expert to testify after the prosecutor who proffered the expert offered additional foundational evidence of reliability.

Not all states follow *Daubert-Kumho Tire*, even if their evidence rules track the Federal Rules of Evidence. In some states (such as California) the reliability of a novel field of expertise is governed by a test set forth in *Frye v. United States*, 293 F. 1013 (1923). Under the *Frye* test, expert testimony from a properly qualified expert is admissible so long as the principles are generally accepted in a relevant scientific community.

6. EXPERTS' QUALIFICATIONS

An expert's direct examination generally begins with *voir dire* testimony establishing that the witness is "qualified as an expert by knowledge, skill, experience, training, or education." (Federal Rule of Evidence 702) If you are the proponent of an expert, your adversary may offer to stipulate to the expert's qualifications. While you may want to accept the stipulation to save time, recognize that the *voir dire* phase of testimony may also help you to bolster the expert's credibility by parading the expert's qualifications and experience before the jury. Because an expert's background testimony is relevant to both qualifications and credibility, judges generally do not compel attorneys to accept such stipulations.

The most important feature of the bases of specialized knowledge set forth in Rule 702 is that witnesses do not necessarily need advanced university degrees or a string of publications in order to qualify as experts. If an issue in a case is whether rutabaga was harvested properly, a farmer with years of experience as a grower of rutabaga may qualify as an expert.

7. HYPOTHETICAL QUESTIONS

Common law rules in many jurisdictions limited experts to providing opinions based only on data that was supplied to them by attorneys during trial in the form of hypothetical questions. During an expert's direct examination, the proponent would provide the expert with "hypothetical" information that in fact had to mirror the evidence that had been or would be offered at trial, and ask the expert to give an opinion based on the assumed accuracy of the information. This practice led to endless squabbles about the correspondence between evidence in the record and information in a hypothetical question. Federal Rule of Evidence 703 allows but does not require hypothetical questions; an expert may base an opinion on facts or data "that the expert has been made aware of or personally observed." However, some attorneys prefer to use hypothetical questions because they can be a dandy way of recapitulating evidence for a judge or jury before closing argument.

8. ULTIMATE ISSUES

Another way in which modern evidence rules have departed from common law restrictions is that opinions of expert (and lay) witnesses can pertain to "ultimate issues." (Federal Rule of Evidence 704) For example, a medical expert can testify that a physician's treatment of a patient failed to meet the community's standard of care. A highway design expert can testify that a portion of a road was unreasonably dangerous. And a product safety expert can testify that a product's design is reasonable and fit for the purpose for which it was manufactured.

However, an "ultimate issues opinion" is invalid if it does nothing more than provide a judge or jury with a legal judgment. For example, the medical expert can not testify in so many words that "you should decide this case for the plaintiff." Nor are opinions likely to be valid if they incorporate normative legal standards. For example, the medical expert could not opine that "the defendant doctor was negligent." The difference between a legitimate ("fell below the community standard of care") and an improper ("the defendant was negligent") opinion can be subtle. The difference is that the former is a factual assertion that is within the scope of an expert's specialized knowledge, while the latter incorporates a legal judgment that is within the exclusive province of judges and juries. The latter is improper under Federal Rule of Evidence 702 because the expert's legal assessment does not "help the trier of fact."

C. DIRECT EXAMINATION STRATEGIES

This section explains and illustrates strategies for effectively communicating experts' testimony to judges and jurors.

1. BACKGROUND TESTIMONY (ESTABLISHING AN EXPERT'S QUALIFICATIONS)

Experts' direct examinations typically begin with foundational *voir dire* testimony establishing that a witness is qualified as an expert in a field relevant to a disputed issue. Federal Rule of Evidence 702 refers to "knowledge, skill, experience, training, or education," and background testimony often touches on two or more of these factors.

By way of example, assume that you are the defense attorney in a criminal case in which the principal issue is the culprit's identity. You've called Helen O'Reilly as an eyewitness identification expert to educate the jury as to factors that tend to undermine the reliability of identifications. To establish Ms. O'Reilly's qualifications to provide this testimony, your foundational questioning may go somewhat as follows:

Q: Good morning, Dr. O'Reilly. Can you please tell the jury what your profession is?

A: Yes, I am a Professor of Psychology at Indiana State University.

Q: How long have you been a professor?

A: I was hired with a title of Assistant Professor 23 years ago, and have been a full Professor for 17 years.

Q: Dr. O'Reilly, please describe your educational background.

A: Certainly. I have a Bachelor's degree in experimental psychology from Purdue University. I have a Master's degree in experimental psychology from Washington University in St. Louis, and a Ph.D in experimental psychology from UCLA.

Q: Is it OK if I call you Dr. O'Reilly?

A: Sure, that's fine.

Q: Great. Dr. O'Reilly, you've used the term "experimental psychology" a few times. Can you explain what you mean?

A: An experimental psychologist is trained to conduct research, as opposed to clinical psychologists, who are trained in therapeutic principles.

Q: After getting your Ph.D and before joining the Indiana State faculty, did you have any additional training?

A: Yes, for two years I was what is called a post-doc at UCLA. As a post-doc I taught undergraduate psychology courses and conducted research in the field of human memory.

Q: What courses do you teach at Indiana State?

A: I teach a course on Perception and Memory, a course on The Role of the Psychologist in the Legal System, and a course on Research Methods, how to carry out research as a clinical psychologist.

Q: Do you have a particular specialty within the field of experimental psychology?

A: I've always studied human memory, but for the last 15 years or so I've concentrated on a field called eyewitness psychology.

Q: Have you done research in the field of eyewitness identification?

A: I have.

Q: Has that research resulted in any publications?

A: Yes. I've published roughly 100 articles reporting the results of my eyewitness identification experiments. The articles are published both in peer-reviewed psychology journals and police science journals. I've also published two books on the subject of eyewitness identification.

Q: Dr. O'Reilly, can you please explain what you mean by peer-reviewed journals?

A: It means that articles submitted for publication are reviewed by a panel of experts, mostly professors in my field, and the panel decides whether an article gets published.

Q: Have you ever worked with police agencies?

A: I sure have. When I first got into the field of eyewitness identification, I worked with police agencies to provide training with respect to techniques for interviewing crime victims. I continue to work quite closely with various law enforcement agencies, both in Indiana and elsewhere.

Q: How about prosecutors, have you worked with them?

A: Yes. I've worked with national organizations of prosecutors, helping them develop proper guidelines for dealing with eyewitness identification evidence.

Q: Have you ever previously testified as an expert with regard to eyewitness identification?

A: Yes, somewhere between 250 and 300 times, to be frank I've lost track.

Q: Do you belong to any professional organizations?

A: Yes. I am the President–Elect of the International Association of Forensic Psychologists. Most of the members of the association specialize in human perception and memory, and to be a member one has to be formally nominated and elected. I have been a member of the International Association for about 11 years and have served as its President three different times. I am also a member of three or four other professional groups, but those are open to anyone in the field who pays the annual dues.

Q: Dr. O'Reilly, are you being compensated for your work on this case?

A: Yes. I agreed to compensation at the county's general rate for expert testimony in cases such as these, which is. . .

The qualifications phase of an expert's direct examination can be far more extensive than in this example, and a judge may permit you to supplement the testimony by offering the expert's CV into evidence.

As you can see from the excerpt above, qualifying an expert also presents you with an opportunity to bolster the expert's credibility. Here, for example, you employ open questions and demonstrate that the expert is in no way biased in favor of defendants, because the expert often works with groups of police officers and prosecutors. Similarly, while the expert receives compensation, the amount is set by the county.

Generally, you need not conclude the qualifications phase of direct examination by asking a judge for a formal ruling that a witness is qualified as an expert. Rather you continue on with the testimony, leaving it to the adversary to ask for permission to "*voir dire* the witness as to qualifications" if the adversary disputes them.

The brilliant courtroom comedy *My Cousin Vinny* (1992) depicts an expert witness whose qualifications are based on experience rather than formal education and training. Vinny is an inexperienced defense attorney whose clients are charged with murder. The bumbling Vinny manages to negate prosecutor Trotter's three eyewitnesses. However, an FBI expert testifies that the tire marks made outside the Sack of Suds convenience store where the murder took place were made by the defendants' car, a 1964 Buick Skylark. Vinny counters this surprise testimony by calling his fiancee Mona Lisa Vito as a defense expert witness in "general automotive knowledge." Hilariously though unrealistically in response to prosecutor Trotter's rather than Vinny's *voir dire* questions, Mona Lisa testifies to the experience that makes her qualified to offer an opinion on tire marks. An expletive-deleted version of her *voir dire* testimony is as follows:

Q: Ms. Vito, what is your current profession?

A: I'm an out of work hairdresser.

Q: Now, in what way does that qualify you as an expert in automobiles.

A: It doesn't.

Q: In what way are you qualified?

A: Well, my father was a mechanic. His father was a mechanic. My mother's father was a mechanic. My three brothers are mechanics. Four uncles on my father's side are mechanics.

Q: Ms. Vito, your family obviously is qualified. But have you ever worked as a mechanic?

A: Yeah. In my father's garage. Yeah.

Q: What did you do in your father's garage?

A: Tuneups. Oil changes. Brake relining. Engine rebuilds. Rebuild some trannies. Rebuild rear ends.

Q: Ms. Vito, being an expert on general automotive knowledge, can you tell me what would the correct ignition timing be on a 1955 Bel Air Chevrolet with a 327 cubic inch engine and a four barrel carburetor?

A: It's a question that's impossible to answer.

Q: It's impossible because you don't know the answer.

A: Nobody could answer that question.

Judge: Can you answer the question?

A: No. It is a trick question.

Judge: Why is it a trick question?

A: Because Chevy didn't make a 327 in 1955. The 327 didn't come out until 1962. And it wasn't offered with a four barrel carburetor until 1964. But in 1964, the correct ignition timing would be four degrees left of tap dead center.

Q: Well, uh, she's acceptable Your Honor.

2. EXPLAIN THE FIELD

Many of us may have a general familiarity with various fields of expertise yet lack any real understanding of them. For example, we probably all know something about fingerprinting, voice identification, ballistics, real estate appraising and accounting. However, for any of these areas of expertise, we may need the help of an expert to understand the general principles that constitute experts' specialized knowledge or to understand the methodologies that experts follow to arrive at opinions. To help judges and jurors understand an expert's testimony and promote its credibility, you may follow the qualifications portion of testimony by asking experts to describe and explain their field of expertise. This phase of an expert's direct examination might cover topics such as these:

- What are the general principles underlying the testimony that the expert will give? For example, an eyewitness identification expert might explain the principle that "eyewitnesses who are under extreme stress at the time they observe a suspect tend to make erroneous identifications more often than eyewitnesses who are not under extreme stress."

- How were these general principles arrived at? Here, an expert might explain the research, experiments and other bases that led to the development of the general principles. Some of this information may have been developed and produced by a testifying expert, but often a testifying expert explains a knowledge base to which many experts have contributed.

- What methodologies do experts use to apply general principles to case-specific facts?

- How were these methodologies arrived at, and have they been tested?

- What conditions might limit an expert's ability to arrive at a reliable opinion?

During this phase of direct examination, ask experts to explain complex and unfamiliar principles and methodologies so that they are intelligible to lay judges and jurors. Think of an expert as a teacher, and try to include visual aids, analogies and other effective tools of teaching in examinations.

3. ELICITING OPINIONS

The substance of most experts' testimony consists of opinions and their bases. While many fields of expertise are complex, most opinions draw on the same process of inferential reasoning as lay witness testimony. To understand the similarity in the underlying reasoning process, assume that in a murder case, a prosecution witness testifies that a week prior to the killing, the witness heard the defendant tell the victim, "I'm going to get you if it's the last thing I do." The threat constitutes circumstantial evidence linking the defendant to the killing. Based on everyday experience a judge or juror may infer that the threat makes it more likely that the defendant was the killer.

Experts rely on this same inferential reasoning process when they provide opinions. The difference is that they rely on specialized knowledge instead of (or in addition to) everyday experience to (1) recognize what constitutes circumstantial evidence and (2) draw inferences linking that evidence to conclusions. For example, in the same murder case, a prosecution forensic expert may testify to an opinion based on DNA analysis that (1) residue found at the crime scene is human blood and (2) it is extremely likely that the blood is that of the defendant. The expert's specialized knowledge allows the expert to infer from circumstantial evidence (blood residue) that the defendant was at the crime scene (legal element: identity).

You'll probably find that most experts have opinions not only about the substantive issues in a case, but also about how you should elicit their direct testimony. Valuable as their input might be, testimonial decisions are for you to make. For example, you may elicit an opinion before asking an expert to provide its underlying basis, or you may go chronologically through an expert's analysis and conclude with the opinion. Federal Rule of Evidence 705 allows you to forgo asking an expert to testify to an opinion's "underlying facts or data," though attorneys typically do elicit this information during direct examinations.

As the proponent of an expert, one of your principal tasks is to help the expert communicate opinions and their bases effectively. You need not completely eschew technical terms or jargon. After all, one way to demonstrate expertise to judges and jurors is to show that a witness knows lots of words that they don't. However, make sure that an expert explains obscure terms, and illustrates unfamiliar concepts with familiar examples.

Eliciting testimony in the form of chronological narratives can be as effective with expert as with lay witnesses. For example, you might ask experts to provide a chronology of their activities. Starting from when an expert was initially contacted or retained, ask how the expert went about arriving at an opinion. What information was the expert provided with and what were its sources? Did the expert need and obtain additional information? What tests did the expert perform, and why? What if any tests did the expert deem unnecessary, and why? What if any research did the expert engage in? Experts should communicate not only their opinions, but also the processes by which they were arrived at. Demonstrating that the process by which an opinion was arrived at was fair and thorough and that the methodologies were reliable is an important strategy for persuading judges and jurors that opinions are valid.

As mentioned earlier, Federal Rule of Evidence 703 permits experts to testify despite a lack of personal knowledge. However, experts often do have personal knowledge of case-related events and parties, and when they do your questioning should ordinarily emphasize its role in the expert's analysis. For example, you might ask a real estate appraiser whose opinion concerns the fair market value of raw land to explain how personally walking through the property enhanced the reliability of the opinion.

Similarly, if an expert has formed an opinion while lacking first hand information about events and parties, that too should be evident from your questioning. In such a situation, ask an expert to explain why the lack of personal knowledge in no way detracts from the reliability of an opinion. For example, assume that you are defense counsel in a criminal case and that you have called an eyewitness identification expert to educate the jurors about factors tending to interfere with witnesses' ability to make accurate identifications. The expert probably will not have personally interviewed any of the prosecution eyewitnesses whose identifications you seek to undermine. To counter the potential of the lack of first hand information to undermine the credibility of the expert's opinion, ask the expert to explain why interviews are unnecessary. The expert's reply might go something like, "Since I'm not expressing an opinion as to the validity of any specific identification, it was not necessary for me to interview the eyewitnesses."

Whether an expert first testifies to an opinion and then explains its bases, or vice versa, generally you elicit an opinion by asking whether the expert has an opinion, and following up the affirmative answer by asking what that opinion is. The typical format is as follows:

Q: Do you have an opinion as to (the property's fair market value) or (whether Mr. Jones will regain sufficient strength in his legs to perform as a professional ice skater) or (whether the label adequately warned consumers about the risk of taking the medication with jello)?

A: Yes, I do.

Q: And what is that opinion?

A: . . .

Again, the comedy film *My Cousin Vinny* illustrates effective strategies for enhancing the credibility of experts' testimony. Recall that an FBI expert has testified that the tire marks made by a speeding getaway car were made by a 1964 Buick Skylark, the car that the defendants were driving when they were arrested a few minutes after a convenience store clerk was shot to death. Vinny's own expert witness Mona Lisa Vito then qualifies as an expert in "general automotive mechanics." After prosecutor Trotter stipulates that Vinny's photograph depicts the tire marks, Vinny's direct examination of Mona Lisa proceeds substantially as follows:

1. Q: The defense has argued that two sets of guys met up at the Sack of Suds driving identical metallic mint green 1964 Buick Skylark convertibles. Can you look at the photo of the tire marks outside the Sack of Suds and tell me if the defense's case holds water?

2. A: No, the defense is wrong. I'm positive.

3. Q: How can you be so sure?

4. A: Because there is no way that these tire marks were made by a 1964 Buick Skylark. These tire marks were made by a 1963 Pontiac Tempest.

5. Q: I find it hard to believe that this kind of information can be ascertained simply by looking at a picture. I would love for you to explain.

6. A: The car that made these two equal length tire marks had Positraction. You can't make those marks without Positraction, which was not available on the 1964 Buick Skylark.

7. Q: What is Positraction?

8. A: It's a limited slip differential which distributes power equally to both the right and left tires. The 1964 Skylark had a regular differential, which anyone who's been stuck in the mud in Alabama knows that you step on the gas, one tire spins, the other tire does nothing.

9. Q: Is that it?

10. A: No, there's more. The left tire mark goes up on the curb but the right tire mark stays flat and even. The 1964 Skylark had a solid rear axle. If the left tire went up on the curb, the right tire would tilt out and ride along its edge. But that didn't happen here, the right tire mark stayed flat and even. The car that made these marks had an independent rear suspension. In the 1960's there were only two cars that were made in America that had Positraction, an independent rear suspension, and enough power to make these marks. One was the Corvette, which could never be confused with the Buick Skylark. The other had the same body length, height, width, weight, wheel base and wheel track at the 1964 Skylark, and that was the 1963 Pontiac Tempest.

11. Q: And because both cars were made by GM, were both cars available in metallic mint green paint?

12. A: They were.

13. Q: Thank you Ms. Vito. Thank you very very much. You've been a lovely witness.

Judge: Would you like to cross examine the witness Mr. Trotter?

Trotter: No questions.

Brief though this direct examination may be, Vinny employs a variety of effective questioning strategies. He elicits expert Mona Lisa's opinion at the start of the examination (No. 4), before asking her to explain the bases of the opinion. Vinny's strategy takes advantage of "primacy," a principle that listeners' attention tends to be high at the outset of an interaction. By identifying Mona Lisa's "bottom line" at the outset, Vinny increases the likelihood that the jurors will understand the connections between her opinion and the supporting evidence.

Also effective is Vinny's voicing the skepticism that the jurors are likely to feel: "I find it hard to believe that this kind of information can be ascertained simply by looking at a picture." (No. 5) Vinny presents himself as the jurors' spokesperson; he asks the question they would be likely to ask if only they had the opportunity.

Mona Lisa refers to Positraction, a feature that many of the jurors may have heard of but may not fully understand. Vinny asks her to explain what it means (No. 7), and Mona Lisa's testimony takes on even greater credibility when she provides an illustration that is quite familiar to the local jurors. (The film reinforces the effectiveness of the illustration: the jurors smile and nod to each other when Mona Lisa talks about wheels spinning in the mud.) Use of concrete and familiar examples facilitates lay understanding of unfamiliar concepts.

As is usually true when experts provide opinions, Mona Lisa's testimony conforms to the familiar process of inferential reasoning. Mona Lisa's specialized knowledge of "automotive mechanics" enables her to explain how circumstantial evidence (tire marks) produces a conclusion that the tire marks were not made by the defendants' car.

This section's description of experts' testimony as based on the familiar process of inferential reasoning suggests the way in which the testimony of "educational" experts is more limited. Educational experts use their specialized knowledge to testify about general principles, but they do not evaluate case-specific evidence in the light of those principles in order to draw inferences.

For a second example of how to elicit an expert's opinion, consider the controversial 1951 espionage trial of the so-called "atomic spies," Ethel and Julius Rosenberg. The prosecution claimed that in a conspiracy with their relative David Greenglass and others, the Rosenbergs passed secret information on building an atomic bomb to the Soviet Union. Through Greenglass, who had already pleaded guilty and testified against the Rosenbergs, the government had introduced a sketch that Greenglass had made and that the Rosenbergs allegedly passed along to an agent of the Soviet Union. To prove that the information was secret and vital, the prosecution then called Dr. Walter Koski. In the mid–1940's, Dr. Koski was a nuclear chemist working on the atom bomb project at Los Alamos. After establishing Dr. Koski's qualifications, the prosecutor elicited the following evidence:

Q: What did your work involve?

A: My work was associated with implosion research connected with the atomic bomb.

Q: So that we, as laymen, may understand when you say implosion research, does that have something to do with explosives?

A: The distinction between explosion and implosion is in an explosion the shock waves, the detonation wave, the high pressure region is continually going out and dissipating itself. In an implosion the waves are converging and the energy is concentrating itself.

Q: I take it, concentrating itself toward a common center?

A: Toward a common center.

Q: Is implosion one of the physical reactions incident to the overall action in the atomic bomb?

A: It is.

Q: So as I understand it, your precise job was to make experimental studies relating to this phenomenon of implosion?

A: It was.

Q: Dr. Koski, what is a lens as you knew it in connection with your experiments?

A: A high explosive lens is a combination of explosives having different velocities and having the appropriate shape so when detonated at a particular point it will produce a converging detonation wave.

Q: Once again, so that we as laymen might understand, what is the distinction between an ordinary glass lens and the type of lens you were working on?

A: Well, a glass lens essentially focuses light. An explosive lens focuses a detonation wave or a high pressure force coming in.

Q: Had any other nation been conducting similar experiments at that time?

A: To the best of my knowledge and all of my colleagues who were involved in this field, there was no information in textbooks or technical journals on this particular subject.

Q: And up to that point and continuing right up until this trial, has the information relating to the lens and the experimentation continued to be secret information, except as divulged at this trial?

A: Correct.

(The doctor proceeds to describe his research with different kinds of lenses, which were manufactured at the "Theta" machine shop, where Greenglass worked. His work culminated in the development of a "flat type lens" in 1945. The prosecutor shows Greenglass' sketch to Dr. Koski.)

Q: Would you recognize it as a reasonably accurate replica of the one you submitted to the Theta machine shop?

A: Yes.

Q: The important factor from the experimental point of view is the design, is it not?

A: Correct.

Q: Was that original, novel at the time?

A: It was.

Q: Can you tell us, doctor, whether a scientific expert in the field you were engaged in could glean enough information from the sketch [and other exhibits] so as to learn the nature of the object of the experiment that was involved in the sketches in evidence?

A: From these sketches and from Mr. Greenglass' descriptions, this gives one sufficient information, one who is familiar with the field, to indicate what the principle and the idea is here.

Q: Was the design in the sketch rather than the relative dimensions the primary fact of importance?

A: It was.

This direct examination conforms to many of the strategies described above. The prosecutor asks the expert to explain unfamiliar concepts, and proceeds chronologically through his work on lenses. The example concludes with the opinions that the sketches contained vital and secret information.

D. CROSS EXAMINATION STRATEGIES

The obvious difficulty of cross examining an expert is that you are playing on the expert's turf, which by definition is at least somewhat beyond everyday experience. Fishing is therefore even more hazardous than with non-experts. Thus, unless you also have expertise, you will generally need to rely on your own expert witness, or at least a consultant, to develop safe and meaningful questions.

One method of undermining an expert is to elicit evidence of bias, motive or interest. For example, the size of an expert's fee can suggest that an expert's opinion has been influenced by financial concerns (unless your expert is getting paid even more!). Similarly, evidence that an expert always reaches the same opinion can lead to an inference that the expert adjusts evidence to fit the expert's pre-existing conclusions. One widely-publicized example was a former Texas forensic expert who was tagged with the name "Dr. Death," because in virtually every death penalty case in which he appeared he testified on behalf of the prosecution that a defendant convicted of murder was likely to kill again and therefore was fit for execution. To enhance the likelihood that attorneys will hire them, many forensic experts try to "balance their books" by accepting appointments for parties who have conflicting perspectives (not in the same case, of course!).

Second, you can seek to undermine an expert's qualifications, even if the judge has ruled that the expert is qualified as an expert. For example, you may elicit evidence that:

- an expert's professional training is old and stale;

- an expert has academic training but little or no actual experience;

- an expert is a generalist in a field in which many experts specialize;

- the impressive-sounding organizations of which the expert is a member are open to anyone in the field who is willing to pay the fee; or

- an expert is but a "technician" who operates a machine but has no real understanding of how it works (e.g., a police officer who uses a breathalyzer machine to determine blood alcohol levels in drunk driving cases).

Third, you can attack the credibility of the information on which an expert's opinion is based. For example, assume that a prosecution child abuse expert's opinion that a young child was intentionally injured is based in part on the expert having been informed that the parent who had been caring for the child gave conflicting accounts to a social worker of how the injury occurred. You might undermine the opinion with evidence that the information about conflicting explanations for the injury was incorrect. To set the groundwork for this argument, you might ask the prosecution's child abuse expert, "If it turned out that in fact the parent had given consistent explanations for how the child was injured, might that have an impact on your opinion?"

The three methods described above allow you to cross examine an expert without confronting an opinion head-on. When you do directly attack the accuracy of an opinion, one strategy you may adopt is to ask about possible "exceptions" to the accuracy of an opinion. For example, assume that you cross examine an expert who testifies that a ship captain's hoarse voice on a recording is an indication that the captain was under the influence of alcohol at the time the recording was made. In response to your cross examination questions, the expert may concede that a hoarse voice may also be due to stress and to a person's just having awoken. Evidence that these factors were present at the time the ship captain's voice was recorded would undermine the expert's opinion. (In some situations, even the possibility of alternative explanations can undermine an opinion.)

A second approach for attacking an opinion head-on is to ask about tests that the expert might have but did not perform that could have further substantiated an opinion. Even if the expert responds that additional tests would have been "unnecessary" or "economically unjustifiable," realizing that additional tests could have been done may undermine an opinion in the mind of a lay judge or jurors.

Finally, you might attack an opinion head-on by using the "learned treatise" hearsay exception (Federal Rule of Evidence 803(18)). Pursuant to this exception, you can ask an adverse expert whether the expert considers a certain publication to be "authoritative." If the expert answers affirmatively, you can read into the record a passage that conflicts with the expert's testimony.

CHAPTER 12
CLOSING ARGUMENT

In courtroom dramas, closing argument often resembles the final two minutes of a game of professional basketball. In both, all previous activity seems but prelude to the final moments, when an attorney's rhetorical skills decide a trial's outcome. However, a plethora of psychological research suggests that judges and jurors don't store away evidence for later digestion, as squirrels do nuts. Rather, judges and jurors typically evaluate evidence and organize it into stories as they hear it. By the time of final summation, they often have arrived at tentative if not final decisions.

Thus, do not be content to "get the evidence in the record" and wait until closing argument to persuade judges and jurors of "what it all means." Authors of mystery stories can get away with that approach, but after all they have their readers' undivided attention. At trial, facing an adversary who typically vigorously contests your claims, you need to communicate arguments throughout a trial. From this perspective, look on closing argument as an opportunity to underscore arguments that judges and jurors should already be aware of, and to make explicit the accuracy of your version of events and how that version proves your desired inferences (or prevents proof of the adversary's desired inferences).

A. FOLLOW THE RULES

Closing argument is less subject to evidence rules and judicial direction than direct and cross examination. The relaxed evidentiary standards are exemplified by the judge's response that often follows objections to an adversary's closing argument remarks: "Overruled, it's only argument." However, rules do exist and this section examines the most important ones.

1. FACTS OUTSIDE THE RECORD

The most fundamental rule of closing argument is that you cannot argue "facts outside the record." One way to violate the rule is to inadvertently (presumably!) refer to testimony that was not part of the evidence, or was offered but was stricken from the record: "What? You struck out the testimony that the tenant did not confess to being an axe murderer when talking to the landlord about the rent? I missed that ruling, I withdraw the remark."

A second type of violation consists of referring to evidence admitted for a limited purpose for a different purpose. For example, assume that a prior inconsistent statement that was offered into evidence was not made under oath, and therefore was admitted only for its potential impact on the impeached witness' credibility. An argument relying on the accuracy of the prior inconsistent statement would be improper.

A third form of arguing facts outside the record arises when an attorney offers explanations for why events occurred as the attorney claims they did, when those explanations are not supported by evidence in the record. For example, a prosecutor trying a defendant on theft charges could not argue that "the defendant probably stole the money just so she could take some fancy trips (or feed an expensive drug habit)," unless evidence supporting that inference is in the record.

Arguing facts outside the record typically results in an objection and a judge's admonishment to a jury to disregard a remark. If so, you might respond by apologizing to the jurors, assuring them that you are making every effort to be accurate, and reminding them that they are the ultimate authority regarding the evidence. Be aware, however, that a severe misstatement or repeated misstatements can result in a mistrial and sanctions.

If you are uncertain whether an adversary's closing argument comment amounts to a misstatement of the record, especially in a jury trial you should be reluctant to object. If the judge overrules your objection, jurors may take that as a judicial endorsement of the adversary's argument. If you will have a chance to argue after your adversary finishes, the better alternative to objecting is often to point out that while your adversary may have made a splendid argument, it was not based on the evidence:

"Opposing counsel misled you with the argument that Jack accompanied Jill up the hill. A witness testified only that both Jack and Jill went up the hill. No witness testified that they did so simultaneously. Moreover, their friend Hansel testified that Jack left the house at least 20 minutes before Jill, making it likely that they did not climb the hill together. Now, when you look at the evidence that was actually introduced, you'll see . . ."

2. DRAW REASONABLE INFERENCES

While you cannot argue facts outside the record, you can draw reasonable inferences from evidence that is in the record. For example, assume that in a prosecution growing out of an armed robbery of a convenience store, a prosecution eyewitness testified that he concealed himself behind one of the counters while the robbery was in progress. Reasonable inferences from this testimony include (1) the eyewitness was scared; (2) the eyewitness would have tried to keep from being seen by the robber; and (3) the eyewitness' principal goal was to survive the robbery. If you represent the defendant you might properly refer to each of these inferences even if no witness testified to them, because they reasonably flow from evidence that is in the record.

Besides drawing reasonable inferences, you can also rely on everyday experience and common sense as sources of factual assertions that were not the subject of testimony. For example, a prosecutor trying to explain a robbery victim's initial refusal to identify the culprit to the police could argue that "fear of retaliation often makes people afraid to identify their attackers." This statement would be proper because it is based on a generalization of how people may behave that is grounded in everyday experience and common sense. On the other hand, assume that the prosecutor tells the jurors that "I read in a recent study by the National Justice Committee that 25% of crime victims initially refuse to identify their attackers because they are afraid of retaliation." Unless the study is part of the record, the argument is improper.

3. PUFFING

Puffing is a sales technique by which sellers and advertisers make exaggerated claims in an effort to induce customers to do business. The technique is generally acceptable in the marketplace, in part on the theory that few consumers would seriously believe that "wearing our toe plaster makes you feel like you're walking on air."

A trial is not a commercial venture, and puffing may be less effective a seller of inferences than of toe plasters. Nevertheless, puffing is generally acceptable during closing argument. For example, you may state that "Nelson's credibility is above reproach" even if the adversary impeached Nelson six ways from Sunday. Puffing is tolerated because an occasional excess of zeal is inherent in the adversary system, and because the line between proper and improper inferences is often difficult to discern. Moreover, just as in the marketplace, we can reasonably expect judges and jurors to source discount and exercise independent judgment.

Puffing becomes unacceptable if it amounts to a misstatement of evidence or if your appeal is likely to lead a juror to substitute emotion for reason. For example, assume that a prosecutor argues that a defendant acted like "a wild animal, an evil and rotten beast." Such an argument appeals so strongly to a jury's emotions that a judge is likely to deem it improper.

4. VOUCHER RULE

The long-established rule that lawyers should not vouch for their clients represents a policy that trial outcomes should rest on evidence rather than the lawyers' backgrounds or personal qualities. See Rule 3.4(e) of the ABA Model Rules of Professional Conduct: "A lawyer shall not... assert personal knowledge of facts in issue except when testifying as a witness, or state a personal opinion as to the justness of a cause, the credibility of a witness, the culpability of a civil litigant or the guilt or innocence of an accused." The rule prevents lawyers from explicitly injecting their (or their adversaries') experiences and reputations into a case, or from suggesting that undisclosed reasons justify deciding cases in their clients' favor. For example, the rule against vouching forbids assertions such as:

- "Never in my many years of practicing law have I represented a man who so clearly is not guilty."

- "I have never prosecuted a defendant whose crime was so callous and whose guilt is so obvious."

- "The defense story is preposterous. But defense counsel has no scruples against putting forward phony claims."

- "I would not have taken this case to trial if I didn't believe wholeheartedly in Mr. Relph's innocence."

- "If you knew everything I know about the case, you'd also know that what I'm telling you is the truth."

Each of these assertions improperly asks the judge or jury to decide a case based on factors other than the law and the evidence. At the same time, the legal system may reward subtlety. The voucher rule cannot prevent you from implicitly trying to take advantage of your personal credibility in order to make a positive impression on judges and jurors. You'll have to rely on *silent argument* methods, such as displaying professionalism in your questioning of witnesses and handling of exhibits, establishing rapport and wearing nice looking shoes.

Despite the voucher rule, a judge will generally allow you to refer to your personal opinion, so long as it is clear that your opinion pertains to evidence in the record rather than extraneous factors. Consider the following bit of argument:

> "Jack would have you believe that he went up the hill to fetch a pail of water. However, as Jill testified, and as you might expect, the well was located at the bottom of the hill. In my opinion Jack could not have been telling the truth. I think that Jill's version of what happened is accurate, and it shows that Jack went up the hill for another purpose entirely. I think that purpose will become clear if you look at Hansel's testimony . . ."

The argument refers throughout to the attorney's opinion. However, most judges would not regard it as vouching because the statements relate directly to evidence in the record. If you can mentally substitute the phrase, "I submit that the evidence shows . . ." for "I think . . .," an argument is generally proper.

5. "SEND A MESSAGE" ARGUMENTS

Though sometimes made by lawyers, arguments asking judges or jurors to "send a message" to a community through a verdict are generally improper. For example, a prosecutor cannot argue that the jurors should convict a drug dealer because the verdict "will send a message to drug dealers that they are not wanted in our community." The argument's vice is that it deflects the jurors' attention from the evidence, as a guilty verdict would send the prosecutor's desired message regardless of the defendant's guilt or innocence.

6. MISCELLANEOUS FORBIDDEN ARGUMENTS

In criminal cases, juries have the inherent power to ignore (nullify) the law and acquit a defendant. However, criminal defense attorneys cannot make nullification arguments. For instance, an argument such as, "Even though Mr. Mancias may be technically guilty, you have the power to find him not guilty" is improper.

In civil cases, judges generally forbid *golden rule* arguments. Plaintiffs' attorneys make golden rule arguments when they ask jurors to imagine themselves in a plaintiff's position and award the plaintiff the amount of damages that they would want for themselves.

Generally, lawyers cannot argue the *consequences* of verdicts. For example, a government attorney should not argue in a civil damages case that an adverse verdict may lead to an increase in taxes.

B. ARGUMENT STRATEGIES

Closing argument tends to be the most idiosyncratic phase of trial. More so than the direct and cross examinations you conduct, your closing arguments are likely to be reflective of your unique personality and style, and the rhythm and culture of a specific locale and time period. Relaxed evidentiary rules certainly contribute to the variations in presentation that tend to characterize closing arguments. And when you communicate arguments directly to judges and jurors rather than through witness intermediaries, you are freer to display your own persona.

The sections below examine substantive and stylistic options for presenting persuasive closing arguments.

C. EFFECTIVE ORAL PRESENTATION TECHNIQUES

A closing argument is a form of public speaking. You may never have presented a closing argument, and may be inexperienced in public speaking. However, you have certainly been part of the audience for other effective public speakers, such as high school teachers, law professors (maybe that's a bit of a stretch), lecturers, religious leaders and politicians. One way to develop strategies for presenting closing arguments effectively is to think of the qualities exhibited by public speakers who have impressed you as credible and knowledgeable. Those same qualities are likely to be ones you can emulate to present effective closing arguments, and many of them are reflected in this section's suggestions.

One encouraging message you can take from thinking about other speakers is that you needn't re-make your personality to communicate effectively with judges and jurors. Effective communication is not the province of any one type of style or personality. You may adapt the suggestions in this section to your style and preferences. You may also benefit from practice and feedback on your speaking style, whether it comes from colleagues, Toastmaster groups or communication professionals. Many litigators take acting classes to improve their presentation skills. (Wearing a toga while standing over a slain despot in front of a crowd at the Roman Forum is one well-known effective communication strategy, but not one generally available to trial lawyers.)

One *sine qua non* of an effective closing argument is to address judges and jurors directly. Do not read a closing argument. Typical undesirable by-products of reading a closing argument include loss of eye contact, speaking too fast, inability to adapt to an adversary's unanticipated remarks, and an overall stilted tone. In a public forum such as a courtroom, you should if anything speak intentionally slower than you do when you speak with friends in social settings. Certainly you can prepare an argument in advance, and refer from time to time to notes or an outline as you speak. You may even read a jury instruction or a critical section of testimony verbatim to give it added emphasis. In general, however, you cannot project sincerity and belief in your arguments if you read a closing argument.

Again if you think back to speakers who have impressed you, they probably did not speak in a steady monotone. Try to vary the pitch and pacing of an argument. Carry yourself and speak in a tone of voice that communicates your belief in your arguments.

Another effective communication strategy is to use short sentences and ordinary words. For example, people get out of cars, they do not "exit vehicles." Of course you may need to refer to technical terms, especially when one of your experts used them during testimony or in a report that was received into evidence. If so, if you think their meaning remains unclear, be sure to explain them.

Finally, remember that you need not be a "talking head." If you refer to an exhibit that was offered into evidence, you may hold it up, put it on a screen or otherwise incorporate it in your argument. You may also illustrate your comments with visual aids that you prepare for the purpose of illustrating your arguments. So long as a visual aid fairly conforms to evidence (at least to your version of a story), a judge is likely to allow you to display and refer to it during closing argument. (A visual aid that you prepare for purposes of illustrating your closing argument is not formally received in evidence, and therefore jurors cannot have it with them while they deliberate.)

D. CONTENT OF PERSUASIVE CLOSING ARGUMENTS

Whatever your personal style and oral presentation skills, the primary factor in the effectiveness of a closing argument is likely to be its content. This section analyzes and illustrates strategies for developing persuasive closing argument content.

1. INTRODUCTORY REMARKS

Attorneys have traditionally sought to ingratiate themselves with jurors by beginning closing arguments with introductory remarks. In an era when jurors may have short attention spans, introductory remarks should be brief. Having sat though a trial, jurors typically want to hear whether anything you say can help them decide the case. They are likely to have limited patience for fluff, and extended introductory remarks may lead them to tune you out by the time you begin to discuss the evidence in earnest. Should you think a few introductory remarks helpful in a particular case, you may include one or more of the following topics:

- Thank jurors for their attention and willingness to serve as jurors, and stress the importance of their deliberations to both parties. The trial has probably inconvenienced many jurors, so this gesture is both socially polite and a useful way to demonstrate your fairness and belief in the adversary system.

- Remind the jurors that what you say is not evidence, and that they are the final arbiters of the facts.

Remarks that are introductory but more content-related include the following:

- Mention your desired result. Early disclosure of a "bottom line" can help a judge or juror realistically evaluate your arguments. For example, a juror in a criminal case who understands at the outset that your desired defense verdict is conviction of a lesser included offense rather than a not guilty verdict might give your arguments greater credence.

- When the complexity of an argument merits, provide a roadmap to the remainder of your argument. Mentioning from time to time where you are along the road as an argument progresses can be a useful strategy for enhancing clarity and persuasiveness.

- Briefly describe the legal elements and the factual propositions that satisfy those elements. For example, in a fraud case you might say something like, "The judge will shortly instruct you that one issue we have to prove is reliance. As I'll discuss, the evidence clearly shows that Ms. Woods relied on the bank's offer of construction financing when she purchased the land for a miniature golf course."

- Refer to the burden of proof. This may be especially important if you represent a defendant in a criminal case, but even on behalf of a civil plaintiff you may say something like, "The judge will also shortly instruct you that as the plaintiff we have the burden of convincing you by clear and convincing evidence that fraud took place. I'll discuss what that means in a few minutes. I'm confident that you'll find that we've more than met this burden."

- Refer to the adversary's failure to support its opening statement representations as to the evidence it would introduce.

2. ORGANIZATION

You typically perform a number of tasks in the course of presenting a closing argument. For example, you may put forward a number of arguments, particularly if you have the burden of proving multiple factual propositions. Also, you may argue on behalf of your contentions and attack an adversary's contentions. The following considerations may help you think through the order in which you may carry out such tasks.

In civil cases, normally you should discuss liability issues before damages.

Put your affirmative foot forward with respect to any factual proposition you seek to establish. That is, discuss the accuracy of your factual proposition and the merit of your legal claim before attacking the adversary's position.

Frontload arguments that pertain to the issues that a judge or jury is likely to see as the most important. Base your judgment on such factors as which issues dominated questioning, what questions a judge asked, and jurors' physical reactions to testimony. (e.g., Did jurors seem more intent whenever a particular issue arose?)

When two or more arguments pertain to the same factual proposition, make the argument you consider stronger first. Don't fall into the "last, and most importantly," syndrome. First, studies suggest that the order of arguments affects their persuasiveness, and that unlike dessert, your best arguments should come first. Second, and most importantly . . .

3. CONSIDER AN "EVIDENCE REVIEW"

You naturally discuss evidence in the context of particular factual propositions. For example, you may begin an argument that a driver was careless by summarizing the pertinent evidence relating to carelessness. Should you also, perhaps near the outset of your argument and without regard to a concrete argument, recapitulate the evidence that was introduced during the trial? You may recapitulate your client's version of events alone, or both sides' versions where they vary. The benefits of an evidence review include helping a judge or juror:

- understand complex or technical evidence. While you may do little more than describe evidence already in the record, the additional review and your organization of the evidence may further a judge's or juror's understanding.

- remember the evidence in an extended trial (e.g., two days of testimony extended over eight trial days because of annual "Vasco de Gama Days" holiday celebrations). In such situations, consider a witness-by-witness review of evidence: "Let me briefly review the testimony of the witnesses who testified on the plaintiff's behalf. They were Sonny Boulevard, Max Avenue V, Della Street and Rocky Road, all of whose names are synonymous with many of the byways of our community. Sonny testified... Max attended that same meeting, and he stated ... Della met with the defendant the next day. She described that meeting by telling us ... Finally, Rocky, the wholesaler who is the defendant's main supplier, told us. . ."

- recognize the overall chronology. Blending witnesses' individual stories into a single overall story may be especially important when order has become scrambled during the testimony.

Despite these potential benefits, recapitulating evidence independently of the factual propositions to which the evidence pertains has a variety of potential downsides. Independent recapitulations can be tedious. A judge or juror may tune out when you refer to testimony during an evidence review and then again in the context of a specific argument. Moreover, adding an evidence review layer to arguments may de-emphasize the arguments. Finally, if you fail to mention unfavorable evidence, the adversary may argue that your summary was misleading.

4. PRESENTING INFERENTIAL ARGUMENTS

An inferential argument typically marshals discrete items of evidence and explains why they support your desired inference (or refute an adversary's
desired inference). For example, assume that you
represent Rodrigo Sanchez, a plaintiff in an auto accident case. You've sued a building contractor, Don
Nguyen, for negligence, alleging that because Nguyen
was inattentive to the road while driving, he struck
Sanchez, a pedestrian. An argument marshalling
together items of evidence in the record supporting
your contention that Nguyen was negligent may go
as follows:

"The evidence clearly establishes that the defendant was not paying attention to the road at
the time he ran into Mr. Sanchez. It is undisputed that the defendant was talking on a cell
phone at the time of the accident. It was not a
pleasant social call. Rather, one of the defendant's employees called to tell the defendant
about a major problem that had occurred on one
of his remodeling jobs. Isn't it likely that a building contractor who is hearing bad news about a
big problem on one of his jobs is going to be distracted by the news as he drives? That's especially likely to be true when, as in this case, the
contractor is in the vicinity of the job site when
the call comes through and the problem requires
the contractor's immediate attention. We know
that the problem required the defendant's immediate attention because, as the defendant

admitted when I asked him about it on cross examination, the problem had to be dealt with before the project could continue and the defendant immediately changed course to head for the job site. Moreover, as the president of the company, it was the defendant who had the most to lose if work was delayed. So the defendant had lots of reasons to be thinking about the problem, and as a result was not paying attention to the road when he struck Mr. Sanchez."

This inferential argument begins with an established fact (the defendant was talking on a cell phone at the time of the accident) and explicitly identifies the desired conclusion (the defendant was distracted). The lawyer strengthens the argument with "especially whens," such as that it was a "bad news" call.

5. PRESENTING CREDIBILITY ARGUMENTS

Using the factors set forth in the Credibility Model (see Chapter 4), you may support the credibility of your witnesses and stories and attack the adversary's witnesses and stories. Consider two concerns that potentially arise whenever you attack the credibility of an adversary's version of events.

a. Lying or Mistaken?

When attacking credibility, your desired inference may be either that an adverse witness is lying, or that the witness is mistaken. As a general rule, judges and jurors are more willing to conclude that a witness is mistaken than that a witness is lying. Thus, "mistake" should be your desired inference whenever it is a reasonable one. Such credibility arguments proceed generally along these lines:

> "You can place no faith in Mr. Whittington's testimony. His inability to remember anything that happened prior to their turning onto Manchester, and his conflicting statements to the police officer, render his testimony plainly unreliable. As to his claim that the light in the defendant's direction was green, you must remember that as her husband, he is naturally biased. When a loved one is involved, we often unintentionally remember things the way we wish they were, not the way they actually occurred. You'll see this when you compare Mr. Whittington's testimony with that of Ms. Stockport . . ."

This argument's "bottom line" is that Whittington is mistaken, and therefore his testimony is unreliable. Such an argument is likely to be more persuasive than one which requires a judge or juror to conclude that Whittington lied.

On occasion, the only inference you can reasonably ask a judge or juror to accept is that an adverse witness lied. For instance, as a prosecutor you may be unable to argue sensibly that an alibi witness was mistaken about having been out of town with the defendant when a crime was committed. In such situations, you should explicitly acknowledge the "lying" inference.

b. "Falsus in Uno, Falsus in Omnibus"

A second issue concerns the range of a credibility attack. To what extent can you argue that an inconsistency or implausibility affects an adversary's entire story? To persuade a judge or juror that an adverse witness' entire story (or an adversary's overall story) is unworthy of belief, you generally need to stress the significance of the implausibility or inconsistency.

For example, assume that you are the defense attorney in the widely-publicized 1990's rape prosecution of William Kennedy Smith. The rape allegedly took place in the Kennedy Palm Beach estate. Prosecution witness Ann Mercer testified that her friend Patricia Bowman, the woman allegedly raped by Smith, told Mercer minutes after the attack that a rape had occurred. Cross examining Mercer, you elicited evidence that after hearing about the alleged rape, Mercer accompanied Smith throughout the dark house and grounds of the Kennedy estate, looking for Bowman's shoes. You consider this portion of the story implausible, and based on this implausibility want to urge the jury to disregard the entire rape story. You might argue as follows:

> "Recall Ms. Mercer's actions on the night of the supposed rape. Supposedly, as soon as Ms. Mercer arrives at the Kennedy estate, Ms. Bowman tells her friend Ms. Mercer about the rape. But Ms. Mercer admits that after hearing this, she went into the house with Mr. Smith

searching for Ms. Bowman's shoes. When they couldn't find the shoes in the house, she and Mr. Smith walked all over the dark grounds to the beach, looking for them.

"Ms. Mercer's story just doesn't make sense. Would she have walked all over a dark house and estate with Mr. Smith if she had just been told that Mr. Smith had raped her friend? Rape is an extremely traumatic experience. Wouldn't Ms. Mercer have wanted to get her friend away from the place where it happened as soon as possible? Use your common sense—do people leave friends alone at the scene of a rape while they go off in the dark to look for a pair of shoes with the alleged rapist? Moreover, wouldn't Ms. Mercer want to seek medical attention for her friend as soon as possible, and report the crime to the police?

"The only sensible conclusion you can reach is that the prosecution's case is a fiction. Ms. Bowman could not have told Ms. Mercer that she had been raped. Change this one fact, and everything makes sense. If Ann Mercer hadn't been told that a rape had occurred, it is perfectly reasonable for her to have gone off with Mr. Smith in search of her friend's shoes. Ms. Mercer would not have been in fear of Mr. Smith, nor would she have wanted to remove her friend from the house as soon as possible. Ms. Mercer's actions speak far louder than her words, and they tell you that no rape occurred. What is true is exactly what Mr. Smith told you: the intercourse was consensual."

By emphasizing the significance of the alleged implausibility, this defense argument gives the jury a basis for disbelieving the prosecution's overall story.

c. Arguments Supporting Credibility

The factors in the Credibility Model are pertinent to arguments attacking or supporting credibility. For an example, of how to develop an argument supporting credibility, assume that you represent Rodrigo Sanchez, the plaintiff who was struck by a truck driven by Don Nguyen, a building contractor. One of your witnesses, Melinda Moore, testified that she observed the collision and that Sanchez was in the crosswalk at the time he was struck by Nguyen's truck. Nguyen disputes Moore's testimony, and testified that the reason he struck Sanchez is because Sanchez suddenly ran out from between two parked cars, some distance down the road from the crosswalk. To support the credibility of Moore's testimony, you may make the following argument:

"The defendant has tried to attack the testimony of Melinda Moore. However, the circumstances clearly show that she was correct when she testified that Mr. Sanchez was in the crosswalk when he was struck by the defendant's truck. First, at the time of the accident Ms. Moore was driving a car and was stopped right next to the crosswalk, waiting for the light in her direction to turn green. She marked this diagram with this "x" to show you exactly where she was. Ms. Moore had no trouble seeing what happened, it was broad daylight and her view was unobstructed.

"And like we all often do when we're stopped at an intersection waiting for a light to change, Ms. Moore looked around. Maybe we don't always pay attention to what we're looking at, but in this case she had a particular reason to notice Mr. Sanchez. He was wearing a shirt that Ms. Moore had just bought as a present for her father. Think back to your own experiences—don't we all pay special attention when we notice someone wearing the same clothes that we're wearing or have just bought? Finally, remember that Ms. Moore has absolutely nothing to gain by testifying. She is neutral and unbiased, and came in here and told you exactly what happened. Every shred of evidence tells us that Ms. Moore is correct when she testified that Mr. Sanchez was in the crosswalk when the defendant ran into him."

Here, you combine several credibility factors into a single argument supporting a witness' credibility. They include ability to observe, reason to observe, and the witness' neutrality.

6. UNDERMINING SILENT ARGUMENTS

As you may recall (see Chapter 5), silent arguments result from improper considerations that may affect trial outcomes. For example, a jury's verdict may be influenced by a party's ethnicity or economic status. During closing argument you may try to undermine a silent argument when you believe that your client is its likely victim.

For example, assume that you fear that some jurors will disbelieve an important witness who testified on your behalf, because of the witness' low socio-economic status. To counter such an "argument," you might say something along these lines:

> "The plaintiff might argue that you shouldn't believe Sara's testimony, because Sara doesn't use two dollar words or wear fancy clothes. But we all know the old saying, 'you can't judge a book by its cover.' Use your common sense and think about what Sara said, not her speaking skills or the clothes she wore, and you will realize that her testimony is 100% accurate."

Note how in the course of countering the silent argument, you cleverly imply that it is the nasty adversary who would stoop so low as to rely on such an inappropriate argument.

Silent arguments often grow out of a juror's emotional reaction to evidence. Often you can respond effectively by acknowledging the emotion and dis-

tancing your client from it. For example, assume that
your client is charged with committing multiple child
molestations. You may acknowledge jurors' understandable emotional feelings as you caution against
their influence:

> "You have heard the testimony of children
> who have been subjected to brutal, repulsive
> acts. It has been at least as difficult and painful
> for my client Mr. Genghis to listen to as I am
> sure it has been for you. We do not in any way
> minimize the severity of their injuries. But
> please do not let your feelings for the children
> override your consideration of the evidence prov-
> ing that Mr. Genghis was not the person respon-
> sible for these terrible acts."

7. NORMATIVE AND "PSEUDO–NORMATIVE" ARGUMENTS

Normative legal elements require judges and jurors to evaluate parties' actions according to community norms or standards. That is, to determine
whether a driver's behavior was "unreasonable" or
whether a breach of contract was "material," a fact
finder implicitly evaluates the circumstances according to social norms.

Arguments about normative elements typically focus on the fairness or justness of a party's conduct,
the consequences that flowed from that conduct and
the possibility of alternative behavior. For example,
you might argue that a police officer's use of a baton

to subdue an arrestee was not reasonable because the arrestee wound up with a fractured skull, and because the officer had time to summon backup help before making the arrest.

Pseudo-normative arguments are a strategy for appealing to a judge's or juror's community values even when a factual dispute is purely historical. For example, assume that you contend that a defendant made a false statement or committed a murder. Analytically, the propositions are historical rather than normative. A judge or juror needn't make a normative judgment to decide either issue. Nevertheless, judges and jurors generally bring into the courtroom community values such as fairness, and a pseudo-normative argument explains why a historical outcome is fair and just.

For example, assume that in a personal injury case you have made a historical argument about the damages caused by a defendant's negligent conduct. Your pseudo-normative argument might go on to discuss the fairness of adequate compensation and the value of the principle that people should pay for the harms they cause. Similarly, in a copyright case you might argue that the public would be deprived of creative ideas if a few resemblances in stories constituted infringement.

8. THE BOTTOM LINE

Even if you've made your desired outcome clear from the outset of an argument (or case presentation), you should generally conclude with an explicit reference to your desired result. Depending on the extent to which you've previously discussed and defended your desired result, this portion of an argument can be as short as a sentence. For example, as a prosecutor you may state that "The evidence requires that you return a verdict of first degree burglary." Or, if you are a criminal defense attorney, you might assert that "The prosecution has failed to prove its case beyond a reasonable doubt, and you should return a verdict of not guilty."

It is not always in a client's interests to identify a specific desired verdict. As the defense attorney in a criminal case, for example, you may want to preserve the possibility of a not guilty verdict while being realistic about conviction of a lesser included offense. In such a situation, you might state your desired result in the alternative: "You should find the defendant not guilty of assault with a deadly weapon. At most the prosecution's evidence might support simple assault." (To repeat: many defense attorneys choose never to concede the possibility of conviction even on lesser charges.)

In civil cases, some jurisdictions forbid plaintiffs from making explicit arguments about the amount of damages for pain and suffering. In jurisdictions where you can mention specific numbers, you may not want to do so for fear of aiming too low. Even so, you can be fairly explicit about your desired result:

"Thus, the evidence amply demonstrates that the defendant fraudulently promised to produce a limited edition series of Great Law Professors trading cards. You should assess general damages in the sum of at least $175,000, and to punish the defendant for its fraudulent conduct impose punitive damages in the amount of at least $500,000."

When talking about your desired outcome, you may assure judges and jurors that the outcome not only is legally proper, but also it is fair and just. Decision-makers want to achieve justice.

E. ADDITIONAL ARGUMENT STRATEGIES

This section examines additional techniques for presenting persuasive closing arguments.

1. TWO–SIDED ARGUMENTS

Even if your formal fact finding has been limited to sorting out which child is telling the truth when both say, "the other one broke the cookie jar," you understand that an effective argument often describes both why one side is correct and the other is not. In like manner, you typically make two-sided arguments in support of your desired outcomes and in opposition to an adversary's contentions.

When you attack an adversary's *inferential* argument, you may rely on "except whens" in the record that undermine the adversary's desired inference. For example, assume that you are a prosecutor in a murder case. The police found a glove soaked with the victim's blood at the murder scene; when the defendant tried the glove on during the trial, it was about a size smaller than the defendant's hand. During its closing argument, the defense argued that the jury should conclude from the fact that the glove was too small for the defendant's hand that the defendant was not the murderer. You may attack this inference with the "except when" items of evidence that are part of the record. The two-sided argument may go as follows:

> "The defense has asked you to conclude that because the glove found at the murder scene was too small for the defendant's hand, the defendant is not the murderer. However, it has been over a year since the murder took place, and during almost that entire time, the glove has been kept in a refrigerated evidence locker. Remember the evidence you heard from a glove expert, who testified that the gloves would have shrunk about a size while they were in storage. Moreover, we introduced into evidence pairs of similar gloves that the police found in the defendant's home, and those gloves were of varying sizes. Thus, the fact that the glove seemed too small for the defendant when he tried it on during the trial in no way suggests that the defendant is innocent."

This attack on the defense argument relies on two "except whens:" the gloves having shrunk while in storage, and the defendant's owning gloves of various sizes. Re-stating an argument before you attack it, as in this example, tends to add force to your argument because you directly juxtapose the competing arguments.

Another strategy for attacking an adversary's *inferential* argument is to point out the weakness of the adversary's desired inference. For example, examine this argument that you might make as the prosecutor in the same murder case:

> "The defendant offered evidence that shortly after the time of the murder, he was chatting with a gardener a few houses away from his own house, where the murder took place. The defendant asks you to believe that if he had committed a murder, no way would he remain in the vicinity where the murder took place and talk to a gardener about tulips. I submit to you, ladies and gentlemen, that the defendant's argument makes no sense at all. Having committed a murder, the defendant might well have decided that the best way to throw suspicion on himself was to try to escape. For from suggesting innocence, I think you should view the defendant's remaining in the area and chatting with the gardener as additional evidence of his guilt."

Here, your attack is not based on additional items of evidence. Instead, you argue that circumstances do not support the defendant's desired inference, and even suggest that the same circumstances support the opposite inference.

You may also make two-sided *credibility* arguments. Assume that you represent the defendant in a personal injury case, and that the plaintiff has argued that a witness who provided favorable evidence for your client should not be believed because since the events took place, the witness and your client became friends. Your response to this attack on your witness' credibility may proceed as follows:

> "The plaintiff has argued that because the witness Mr. Adams and my client Mr. Jefferson have become friends since the accident, you shouldn't believe Mr. Adams. This argument has no merit. Mr. Adams and Mr. Jefferson were not friends when the accident took place, and they weren't friends an hour later when Mr. Adams told the investigating police officer exactly what he testified to under oath. Their friendship had no impact on Mr. Adams' obligation to give truthful and accurate testimony. Their friendship had absolutely no effect on Mr. Adams' testimony."

Making a two-sided argument may require you to *preempt* an adversary's argument. You preempt an argument when you have to argue before your adversary, and therefore have to respond to an argument before your adversary makes it. Preemption is a familiar argument technique, one you have probably used often. For example, perhaps as a teenager you made an argument such as,

> "Dad, I really ought to be allowed to borrow the car tonight. I haven't borrowed it in three weeks. I know you don't like me driving at night, but I'll be with Kevin and Hilary and they are both really experienced and careful drivers."

Here, you preempt by anticipating your father's "no night driving" argument, and responding to it before your father makes it. In the same way, you can preempt an adversary's argument at trial. For example, if in the personal injury example above you wanted to preempt the plaintiff's attack on Mr. Adams' credibility, you might have started out this portion of the argument by saying something like, "The plaintiff will no doubt argue that because the witness Mr. Adams and my client Mr. Jefferson have become friends since the accident, you shouldn't believe Mr. Adams. This argument has no merit. . ."

Exercise care when deciding to preempt. You do not want to spend more time attacking an adversary's potential arguments than promoting your own. Nor do you want to risk suggesting convincing arguments that neither the adversary nor a judge or juror would have thought of!

You can also make a two-sided argument by *inoculating* a judge or juror against accepting an adversary's desired conclusion. Inoculation is a strategy in which you acknowledge the validity of an argument while pointing out why it should not dictate the outcome of a case. Somewhat akin to "giving the devil his due," inoculation explains why a favorable verdict does not require that every issue be resolved in your client's favor.

For example, assume that you represent a defendant in a criminal matter. One of your arguments is that the arresting officer lied when the officer testified that your client confessed. To inoculate against the prosecution's argument that a police officer would not commit perjury to secure a conviction, you might make the following argument:

> "The prosecution correctly says that police officers are generally honest and wouldn't lie just to get a confession. Our justice system works because most police officers behave honestly. But the question you have to decide isn't how most police officers usually behave. The question is how a single police officer behaved in this specific case. And when you examine the evidence, you'll see why in this particular case the officer did not testify truthfully . . ."

This argument acknowledges the general validity of the prosecution's argument, but explains why its general validity does not dictate the outcome of the specific case.

2. ANALOGIES

Analogies are a powerful closing argument technique. Indeed reasoning by analogy has been fundamental to common law development. For example, in his famous *Palsgraf v. Long Island Railway* opinion, Justice Cardozo decided that a railroad was not liable when a platform guard negligently dislodged a package that exploded and the explosion caused a scale to fall over and injure a person standing on the platform. Cardozo analogized the unique platform events to a situation in which one person jostles another in a crowd and causes a bomb to fall and explode. Because for Cardozo liability would not exist in the second situation, neither should it exist for the railroad.

a. Developing Analogies

To develop persuasive analogies, follow a two-step process:

1. Consider the general category of which a case-specific event is but an example.

2. Identify a more familiar example that is part of the same general category.

You can use analogies to illustrate and add persuasiveness to any aspect of an argument. For instance, assume that you seek damages on behalf of a plaintiff who because of a congenital back defect suffered severe injuries in a minor fender-bender type of collision. You seek damages under the "take the plaintiff as you find her" legal principle. You might use an analogy to help explain the meaning of this principle to a jury. The specific rule is part of the general category of rules that in law and fairness make us liable for the injuries that we inflict through negligence. Finding an everyday illustration of this general category might produce an argument along these lines:

> "What does the law mean when it says that you take the plaintiff as you find her? Suppose you had three dolls, each of identical size and each dressed exactly alike. However, one doll is made of steel, another is made of wood, and the third is made of glass. If someone comes along and negligently knocks down and breaks the glass doll, you would want that person to pay for it. You wouldn't let the person avoid payment by claiming that no damage would have been done had the steel doll been knocked down. Paying for the harm you actually cause, that is the meaning of the principle that you take the plaintiff as you find her."

This analogy draws on people's everyday experiences with recompensing people for broken objects. The analogy thus helps a juror adopt a favorable attitude towards the rule that underlies your argument. Other familiar analogies for legal principles include:

- The *Burden of Proof*: "The judge will instruct you that we have to prove our case by a preponderance of the evidence. What does this mean? Assume that you have a balance scale and you place all of our evidence on one side of the scale and all of the defendant's evidence on the other side. If our side of the scale is heavier even by the weight of a single feather, we have proved our case by a preponderance of the evidence."

- Use of *Common Sense*: "The judge will instruct you that you can use your common sense when evaluating the evidence. To understand what this means, suppose that you saw someone walk into the courtroom wearing a wet raincoat. Your common sense would tell you that it was raining outside. No one needs to tell you that it was raining, your common sense allows you to draw an inference. And it is perfectly proper for you to draw such common sense inferences from the testimony you heard in this case."

- Effect of *Inconsistent Statements*: "The judge will instruct you that in considering the defendant's credibility, you may consider any inconsistent statements made by the defendant. What does this mean? Assume that you were planning on taking your family to a museum, and wanted to know if it would open on Monday. You call the museum, and the receptionist assures you that the museum will be open. The next day you call back, and the same receptionist tells you that it will be closed. This inconsistency would so destroy your trust in the receptionist that you would not know whether to go to the museum."

As Cardozo did in *Palsgraf*, you may also use analogies to influence a judge or juror's evaluation of evidence. For example, assume that you represent an allegedly negligent driver, and your client has testified that "I was driving extra carefully because I was carrying expensive kitchen cabinets in the back of my pickup." Generalizing, you might see this as an example of how "People drive carefully when they are transporting valuable objects." To provide a familiar analogy, you might argue:

> "You can well understand how carefully my client was driving. Perhaps you've never driven around with expensive kitchen cabinets in the back of a truck. But undoubtedly you've driven with other items you haven't wanted to break, whether glassware or even a carton of eggs that you're afraid might fall to the floor. You know that you instinctively drive more carefully when you are carrying objects you do not want to break."

A few suggestions for developing persuasive analogies:

- Never use analogies that put a judge or juror in an unfavorable light: "We have all had the experience of stealing candy from a baby."

- As a general rule, the shorter an analogy the better. Lengthy analogies—e.g., an analogy that includes a description of the labors of Hercules—are confusing and tend to deflect attention from the point you were trying to make in the first place.

- Determine familiarity according to a judge's or the jurors' likely background, not your own. An analogy to "the feel of moonrock between your toes" is unlikely to strike a responsive chord. While you may draw analogies from the Bible, the sports page, or television, make sure they will be familiar to your judge or jury.

- Develop "stock" analogies, particularly for legal principles such as the burden of proof that arise repeatedly. However, you'll need to adjust if you appear more than once before the same judge and you notice the judge mouthing an analogy along with you.

The persuasive power of an analogy that is "right on" was perhaps nowhere better illustrated than during the 1976 Republican Convention. Convention delegates favoring the nomination of Ronald Reagan wanted the delegates to adopt a rule requiring potential presidential nominees to name their vice presidential choices before the balloting for the presidential candidate began. Delegates favoring the nomination of Gerald Ford were opposed to the idea. During the debate, a convention delegate used the following analogy to illustrate her argument that it was unfair to change rules in the middle of the convention:

> "In South Carolina we have two sets of rules for the playing of checkers. Under one rule you must jump your opponent if you have the opportunity. Under the other, jumping the opponent is optional. However, there is one further rule that we always apply no matter which of the first two rules is being used. You can't change the rule about whether or not you have to jump in the middle of the game."

Perhaps aided by this analogy, Ford's followers defeated the proposal.

b. Responding to an Adversary's Analogy

Using an adversary's analogy against the adversary can be a dramatic and effective rebuttal technique. One rebuttal method is to attack an analogy's factual similarity. For example, if you represent the defendant in the "three dolls fender bender case," you may use the same analogy to make the point that your primary defense is the plaintiff's own negligence:

> "Counsel used the example of the three dolls to try to convince you that the defendant should pay for the plaintiff's injuries. We agree that if a person throws a rock against a piece of glass, he should pay for it. But that is not what happened here. Here, the piece of glass was thrown

against the rock, and the person holding the rock is not responsible for that."

A second rebuttal method is to accept the adversary analogy's factual fit, but use it to draw a different inference:

"Counsel talked about how people drive more carefully when they are carrying valuable cargo like children or fancy glass objects. If you think about it, counsel's own example explains exactly why the defendant drove carelessly—the defendant was so focused on those cabinets that the defendant was concentrating on the cabinets instead of on the road."

Pointing out that an analogy (like circumstantial evidence) can "cut both ways" is an effective method of deflating an adversary's argument.

3. LEGAL PRINCIPLES

At the time you deliver a closing argument to a jury, the judge undoubtedly will have already instructed the jury, or you will know the instructions that the judge will give after the arguments conclude. In either case, explaining critical instructions and demonstrating how your arguments connect between abstract legal principles and factual stories are usually important parts of a final summation.

a. The Burden of Proof

Some reference to the burden of proof is standard in nearly every legal argument, and even during introductory remarks. You may use analogies to illustrate its meaning, and defense attorneys frequently remind jurors of the plaintiff's/prosecutor's burden of proof at the beginning and the end of an argument. In addition, you may integrate references to the burden of proof into specific arguments.

For example, return to the auto accident case involving building contractor Don Nguyen's alleged careless driving. Section D above sets out plaintiff Rodrigo Sanchez's inferential argument based on evidence that Nguyen was talking on his cell phone about a problem on a remodeling job at the time of the accident. Integrating the burden of proof into that argument might produce the following:

> "We submit that the evidence demonstrates that the defendant was not paying attention to the road when he struck Mr. Sanchez. Remember that the defendant has admitted that he was on his cell phone at the time, talking about a big problem that had just arisen on a remodeling job site. Isn't it likely that building contractors such as the defendant who hear of a problem on a job site are going to be thinking about the problem as they drive? That's especially likely to be true when, as in this case, the contractor is in the vicinity of the job site when the call comes through and the problem is a large one that requires the

contractor's immediate attention. We know that the problem required the defendant's immediate attention because, as the defendant also admitted, the problem had to be handled before the project could continue and the defendant immediately changed course to head for the job site. Moreover, as the president of the company, the defendant had the most to lose if work was delayed. *Remember, this is a civil case, and to hold the defendant liable you only have to conclude that it is more probable than not that this phone call, together with all the other evidence, establishes that the defendant drove carelessly.* The defendant had lots of reasons to be thinking about the job site problem, and as a result was not paying attention to the road when he struck Mr. Sanchez."

Reminding jurors of the burden of proof is especially important when, as in the example above, you represent a civil plaintiff. Jurors who hear the words "burden of proof" often automatically think of the criminal standard of "beyond a reasonable doubt." Thus, an effective civil plaintiff's argument often explicitly and common-sensically explains the difference between the civil and criminal burdens.

b. Other Jury Instructions

Jury instructions would be a strong contender in any "Least Effective Form of Communication" contest. Voluminous, often abstract and usually read by judges with the enthusiasm of a dental patient reading a report recommending a root canal, jury instructions are more likely to confound than enlighten. Therefore, you typically should explain important instructions and relate them to your arguments.

For example, judges typically instruct jurors that circumstantial evidence is evidence from which an inference can be drawn. These words may mean little to visually-oriented jurors, who have never seen an inference. Thus, when relying on an inferential argument you may want to explain the instruction and its application. For example, a portion of the inferential argument above might go as follows:

> "Remember that the defendant has admitted that he was on his cell phone at the time, talking about a big problem that had just arisen on a remodeling job site. Now, Her Honor will shortly instruct you, and I paraphrase, that circumstantial evidence is evidence from which you can draw an inference. The term may be unfamiliar to you, but drawing inferences is perfectly proper and something we do all the time in daily life. An inference is simply a conclusion you reach based on information. For example, if you hear a report that an accident has occurred at midday on a main road, you will no doubt infer that it produced a traffic jam. This is exactly the kind of common sense reasoning you should use to infer that receiving the car phone call caused the defendant to drive carelessly. Isn't it likely that building contractors such as the defendant who

hear of a problem on a job site are going to be thinking about the problem as they drive? That's especially likely to be true when, as in this case . . ."

You may also explain the meaning of critical substantive rules, not only procedural rules such as those describing the burden of proof and inferential reasoning. For example, in a suit involving the sale of goods, you might discuss an instruction concerning damages as follows:

"The Judge will shortly instruct you that defendant GlueAll's breach of warranty caused Ms. Taylor's loss if that breach was a substantial factor in bringing about the loss. In other words, we must prove that GlueAll's mistakenly filling the tube with cake icing instead of adhesive was a substantial factor in causing Ms. Taylor's house to collapse. The term 'substantial factor' is critical. It means that for you to award damages to Ms. Taylor, we do not need to prove that GlueAll's mistake was the entire cause of the building's collapse, or even that it was the most important cause. As long as GlueAll's mistake was an important reason for the collapse, so long as it was more than a minor cause, more than an insubstantial factor, the law compels you to award damages to Ms. Taylor."

As you can see, explaining and illustrating jury instructions can be time-consuming. Therefore, you'll

typically have to limit discussion to the most important instructions.

F. ARGUMENTS IN BENCH TRIALS

To what extent should you modify a closing argument in bench trials? You generally need not modify
arguments' factual content. These arguments pertain
to unique historical events, and a judge's legal so-
phistication doesn't necessarily imbue a judge with
insights into historical interpretation. Thus, explicit-
ness, preemption, analogies and the other techniques
described above are typically as appropriate in bench
as in jury trials. On the other hand, in bench trials
you would not generally need to explain the meaning
of procedural and substantive rules, unless you want
to give an Olympics-hopeful judge practice in the Ga-
vel Throw.

In bench trials, a judge's comments and questions
often allow you to tailor arguments to the judge's
specific concerns. In jury trials, few jurisdictions allow jurors to pose questions, even in writing through
the judge. Thus, you are typically left to your judgment as to which issues jurors consider most significant.

G. ARGUMENT EXCERPTS: PEOPLE VS. O. J. SIMPSON (1995) AND CITIZENS OF ATHENS VS. EUPHILETUS (CIRCA 400–380 B.C.)

In 1995, actor and former football hero O. J. Simpson was prosecuted for murdering his ex-wife Nicole
Brown Simpson and her friend, Ron Goldman. Simp-

son was found not guilty in a nine month long "trial of the century" that was broadcast live on television to much of the world. (In a separate and non-televised 1997 civil trial, Simpson was found liable for the wrongful death of the two victims; the jury awarded millions of dollars in damages to their families.)

More than two millennia earlier, in a non-televised trial in Athens, Euphiletus was tried for murdering Eratosthenes. Euphiletus' defense was that the killing was justifiable because Eratosthenes had seduced Euphiletus' wife. Under Greek law at the time, the penalty for murder was death. However, if after the first day of trial Euphiletus believed that he would be found guilty, he could quit the trial and choose exile. Euphiletus did not choose exile, and delivered a closing argument that was written for him by Lysias, an advocate who was a forerunner of modern lawyers. The verdict is lost to history. For more information about the case and to read the closing argument in full, see Kathleen Freeman, *The Murder of Heracles and Other Trials from the Athenian Law Courts* (1991).

Excerpts from the arguments in these two criminal trials serve to illustrate many of the strategies described in this chapter. The excerpts from Euphiletus' argument also suggest that while much of the content of and cultural references and values embedded in closing arguments may have changed in 2500 years, rhetorical strategies have remained pretty much the same.

1. INTRODUCTORY REMARKS

Simpson. Co–Prosecutor Marcia Clark introduced her argument with such remarks as, "I'm sorry if I say things that you don't need to hear or . . . are already clear to you. Please bear with me because I am not a mind reader and I don't know. First I want to take the opportunity to thank you . . . from the bottom of my heart. . . You have made a tremendous sacrifice. You haven't seen your children enough. . . I apologize for that. . . But at the conclusion of all of our arguments, when you open up the windows and let the cool air blow out the smokescreen that has been created by the defense . . . you will see that the defendant has been proven guilty easily beyond a reasonable doubt. . . Now, I would like to start with the evidence. . ."

Defense attorney Johnnie Cochran Jr. began by telling the jurors that, "I'm not going to argue with you . . . what I'm going to do is to try and discuss the reasonable inferences which I feel can be drawn from this evidence. At the outset, let me join with the others in thanking you for the service that you've rendered. You are truly a marvelous jury, the longest serving jury in Los Angeles County . . . the final test of your service as jurors will not lie in the fact that you've stayed here more than a year, but will lie in the quality of the verdict that you render . . . one other group I should thank are our marvelous court reporters . . ."

Euphiletus began by telling the jurors that "I would give a great deal, members of the jury, to find you, as judges of this case, taking the same attitude towards me as you adopt towards your own behavior in similar circumstances. . . I shall expound my case to you in full from the beginning. . . In this alone lies my salvation, I imagine, if I can explain to you everything that happened."

2. ROADMAPS

Simpson. Near the outset of his final argument, defense attorney Cochran told the jurors that "I will address you first, and after I'm concluded—I will talk generally about the lay witnesses and overview of the evidence and what you've heard. I will try not to bore you. I'll strive to be honest in my discussions, to be relevant, to be concise of what we talk about here. When I'm finished, Mr. Barry Scheck will come before you and address some of the forensic issues. And then finally, after Mr. Scheck finishes, I'll come back and conclude. . ."

Euphiletus said, "What I have to prove, I take it, is just this: that Eratosthenes seduced my wife, and that in corrupting her he brought shame upon my children and outrage upon me. . . that I did not commit this act for the sake of money. . .nor for any other advantage except the satisfaction allowed by law. I shall expound my case to you in full from the beginning, omitting nothing, and telling the truth. In this alone lies my salvation."

3. ADVERSARY'S FAILURE TO OFFER PROMISED EVIDENCE

Simpson. Defense attorney Cochran told the jurors, "[Prosecutor] Darden did a good job in his argument, but one thing he tended to trip over and stumble over was when he started to talk about our case. . . First he stood up and started talking about the time line being at 10:15. Then he said, well. . . it may have been as late as 10:30 . . . You look back and see what Miss Clark promised you a year ago. 10:15, 10:15 was all they talked about, and they were going to use [as the time of the murders]."

4. USE OF VISUAL AIDS

Simpson. For her closing argument, prosecutor Clark prepared and referred to continuously a time-line chart depicting the prosecution's version of how events unfolded.

Responding to the prosecution's claim that a dark knit cap offered into evidence was part of Simpson's disguise, defense attorney Cochran put on the knit cap while arguing that "O. J. Simpson in a knit cap from two blocks away is still O. J. Simpson. It's no disguise."

Euphiletus' speech does not indicate the use of visual aids, but he used language that allowed the jurors to visualize the scene where the critical events took place: "Now first of all, gentlemen, I must explain that I have a small house which is divided into two. The men's quarters and the women's, each having the same space, the women's upstairs and the men downstairs."

5. PUFFING

Simpson. The defense accused police officer Mark Fuhrman of planting evidence and offered evidence that he had lied about not referring to African–Americans as "niggers." During closing argument, defense attorney Cochran called Fuhrman "a lying, perjuring, genocidal racist." Cochran also called Fuhrman the "personification of evil" and compared him to Hitler, "another man not too long ago in the world who had those same views."

Euphiletus told the Athenian jurors that "This punishment was inflicted not in my own interests, but in those of the whole community... Otherwise it would be far better to wipe out the existing laws and make different ones, which will penalize those who keep guard over their wives and grant full immunity to those who criminally pursue them." Of course, a verdict declaring that Euphiletus was wrong to kill Eratosthenes is a far cry from granting "full immunity" to seducers.

6. SILENT ARGUMENTS

Simpson. The defense could not explicitly argue that "you shouldn't convict Simpson because he's a celebrity sports hero." However, addressing jurors who might adopt a silent argument that someone of Simpson's stature would not commit murder, prosecutor Clark argued that "it's really kind of hard to believe that the man we saw in the movies and commercials could do this. But he did. And the fact that he did doesn't mean that he wasn't a great football player. It doesn't mean that he never did a good thing in his life. Nothing takes that away. That's still here. It will always be here. But so will the fact that he committed these murders."

Responding to a possible silent argument that a verdict of acquittal was tantamount to a vote against the police force, defense attorney Cochran argued: "This case is not-let me state it at the outset-about attacking the Los Angeles Police Department. We're not anti-police in making these statements. You're not anti-police. We all need the police ... But ... what all of us should have are honest, effective, non-biased police officers."

Euphiletus probably could not argue explicitly that Eratosthenes was a scoundrel and therefore deserved to die. But Euphiletus advanced this argument silently when he repeated what he was told by the messenger who told Euphiletus that his wife had been seduced: "The fact is, the man who is wronging you and your wife is an enemy of ours. Now if you catch the woman who does your shopping and works for you, and put her through an examination, you will discover all. The culprit is Eratosthenes from

Oea. Your wife is not the only one he has seduced—
there are plenty of others. It's his profession."

7. ANALOGIES

Simpson. Providing an analogy for how the jurors
should go about their fact-finding task, prosecutor
Clark said that "it is up to you, the jury, to weed out
the distractions, weed out the side shows, and determine what evidence is it that really helps me answer
this question (of who the killer was). And it is kind of
like the artist, the sculptor. Someone went to him
and said how do you make an angel. Well, I take a
piece of marble and I remove everything that is not
an angel. That is what you have to do."

Prosecutor Clark, arguing that reasonable doubt
doesn't require that every possibility be accounted
for: "I compare it to a jig-saw puzzle ... To know
what a jig-saw puzzle is depicting, if you're missing a
couple of pieces of the sky, you still have the picture
... So I kind of compare a jury trial to that because it
often happens that there are things that are not
shown to you... But those are like pieces of the sky,
you don't need them."

The prosecution offered evidence of DNA analysis
of blood found at the crime scene and in Simpson's
car and home to tie Simpson to the murders. The defense claimed that some blood samples were planted
by the police, while other samples were contaminated
by faulty police methods. Defense attorney Barry
Scheck analogized the police laboratory to "a black

hole," and used an analogy to illustrate the argument that problems with blood taken from a pair of socks justified the jurors' ignoring all the blood evidence: "If you find a cockroach in a bowl of spaghetti, do you then take every strand of that bowl of spaghetti to look for more cockroaches or do you just throw it away and eat no more?"

Defense attorney Cochran, implicitly warning the jurors against "mind set:" "In America you have to wait until you hear all the evidence. . . People are not making up their minds at the beginning. You don't decide a baseball game or a football game at halftime. You wait until the end."

Euphiletus argued that Athenian law allowed a man to kill an adulterer who seduced a concubine. Thus he should have a right to kill his wife's seducer, since concubines are less important than wives.

8. RESPONDING TO AN ADVERSARY'S ANALOGY

Simpson. Defense attorney Cochran, responding to co-prosecutor Christopher Darden's argument that Simpson was a "fuse" waiting to ignite: "This fuse he kept talking about kept going out. It never blew up, never exploded. There was no triggering mechanism . . . it was a nice analogy . . . let's look at this photograph (taken hours before the murders) . . . if you want to see how he looks while he is in this murderous rage, while this fuse is going on . . . where is the fuse now?"

9. CREDIBILITY ARGUMENT: *FALSUS IN UNO, FALSUS IN OMNIBUS*

Simpson. The defense offered evidence that a police officer who testified for the prosecution had made a false statement in a search warrant to search Simpson's home. Defense attorney Cochran argued, "You can't trust him. You can't believe anything he says, because it goes to the core of this case. When you are lying at the beginning you will be lying at the end. The Book of Luke talks about that. If you are untruthful in small things you should be disbelieved in big things."

Euphilitus. As the prosecutors of Euphiletus, Eratosthenes' family members sought to prove that Eratosthenes had run into a church, where Euphiletus would have had no right to kill him. Euphiletus responded that "you know as well as I do how wrongdoers will not admit that their adversaries are speaking the truth, and attempt by lies and trickery of other kinds to excite the anger of the hearers against those whose acts are in accordance with justice."

10. INOCULATION

Simpson. Police officer Mark Fuhrman was shown to have lied when he testified that he hadn't used the term "nigger." Acknowledging the legitimacy of the defense attack on Fuhrman's credibility while arguing that it shouldn't control the outcome, prosecutor Clark argued, "Just so it is clear. Did he (Fuhrman) lie when he testified here in this courtroom saying that he did not use racial epithets in the last 10 years? Yes. Is he a racist? Yes. Is he the worst the LAPD has to offer? Yes... In fact, do we wish that there were no such person on the planet? Yes. But the fact that Mark Fuhrman is a racist and lied about it on the witness stand does not mean that we haven't proven the defendant guilty beyond a reasonable doubt, and it would be a tragedy if . . . you found the defendant not guilty in spite of all that (evidence) because of the racist attitudes of one police officer."

11. INFERENTIAL ARGUMENTS

Simpson. Defense attorney Cochran's argument delineated the items of evidence that made it unlikely that Simpson would have committed murder on the day that Nicole Brown Simpson and Ron Goldman were killed: earlier in the day, he had attended a musical recital by one of his children, and shortly before the time of the murders had gone to McDonald's to get a hamburger. Cochran also argued that the fact that passersby testified that they did not hear dogs barking at the time the prosecution argued that the murders took place indicated that the prosecution's time line of events was incorrect.

Euphilitus. Arguing that in retrospect he should have realized that something was amiss, Euphiletus stated that though he wasn't suspicious, "It did seem to me, members of the jury, that she had done up her face with cosmetics, in spite of the fact that her brother had died only a month before."

The prosecutors claimed that Euphiletus set a trap for Eratosthenes by laying in wait in his house after having Euphiletus' servant go to Eratosthenes earlier in the day and tell him that the coast was clear. Euphiletus argued that the fact that a friend had dined with him on the night of the killing undermined this inference: "Ask yourselves whether, if on that night I had had designs on Eratosthenes. . . I should take a friend home to dinner. Surely Eratosthenes would have been less inclined to venture into the house. Further, does it seem to you probable that I would have let my guest go, and been left alone, without company? Would I not rather have urged him to stay, so that he could help me to punish the adulterer?"

12. TWO–SIDED ARGUMENTS

Simpson. Prosecutor Clark: "The defense . . . hint that the blood was planted . . . that multiple other bloodstains were contaminated and that somehow all the contamination only occurred where it would consistently prove that the defendant was guilty . . . If what they are saying is true then . . . why is it that the samples of blood they took from her pool of blood didn't come up with the defendant's blood type?"

13. PREEMPTION

Simpson. As evidence of Simpson's anger toward and motive to kill his ex-wife, the prosecution offered evidence of Simpson's earlier violent behavior towards his ex-wife. Prosecutor Darden: "I'm sure the defense is going to get up here at some point and say, that domestic violence evidence, it's irrelevant. They may say just because this defendant had some violence in his marriage, that it doesn't prove anything. Well . . . it's because when you look at all of that, it points to him."

14. THE RESULT

Simpson. Defense attorney Cochran: "Soon it will be your turn. You have the keys to his future . . . We believe you will do the right thing, and the right thing is to find this man not guilty on both of these charges."

Euphiletus argued that the laws not only approved his killing of Erastothenes but demanded it: "In my case the laws not only hold me innocent, but actually order me to take this satisfaction; but it depends on you whether they are to be effective or of no moment."

15. SEND A MESSAGE ARGUMENTS

Simpson. Defense attorney Cochran told the jurors that "Your verdict in this case will go far beyond the walls of Department 103 because your verdict talks about justice in America and it talks about the police and whether they're above the law and it looks at the police perhaps as they haven't been looked at very recently."

Euphiletus told the jurors that "This punishment [of Eratosthenes] was inflicted not in my own interests, but in those of the whole community. Such villains, seeing the rewards which await their crimes, will be less ready to commit offenses against others if they see that you too hold the same opinion of them . . . otherwise you will be granting such impunity to adulterers that you will encourage even burglars to declare themselves adulterers, in the knowledge that if they allege this reason for their action and plead that this was their purpose in entering other men's houses, no one will lay a finger on them."

16. PSEUDO–NORMATIVE ARGUMENT

Simpson. Defense attorney Cochran: "If we as the people don't continue to hold a mirror up to the face of America and say this is what you promised, this is what you delivered, if you don't speak out, if you don't stand up, if you didn't do what's right, this kind of (police mis-) conduct will continue on forever and we will never have an ideal society, one that lives out the true meaning of the creed of the Constitution or of life, liberty and justice for all."

Euphiletus: "This is the one crime for which, under any government, democratic or exclusive, equal satisfaction is granted to the meanest against the mightiest, so that the least of them receives the same justice as the most exalted."

H. ARGUMENT ANALYSIS: TO KILL A MOCKINGBIRD

In the classic book and film *To Kill a Mockingbird*, Atticus Finch takes on the perhaps hopeless task of defending black sharecropper Tom Robinson against a charge of raping a white woman, Mayella Ewell, in a small southern town in the 1930's. This section analyzes the rhetorical effectiveness of the film's version of Atticus' closing argument.

"I have nothing but pity in my heart for the chief witness for the State. She is the victim of cruel poverty and ignorance. But, my pity does not extend so far as to her putting a man's life at stake, which she has done in an effort to get rid of her own guilt. Now I say "guilt," gentlemen, because it was guilt that motivated her. She's committed no crime. She has merely broken a rigid and time-honored code of our society, a code so severe that whoever breaks it is hounded from our midst as unfit to live with. She must destroy the evidence of her offense. But, what was the evidence of her offense? Tom Robinson, a human being. She must put Tom Robinson away from her. Tom Robinson was to her a daily reminder of what she did.

Now what did she do? She tempted a negro. She was white and she tempted a negro. She did something that in our society is unspeakable: She kissed a black man. Not an old uncle, but a strong, young negro man. No code mattered to her before she broke it, but it came crashing down on her afterwards.

The witnesses for the State, with the exception of the sheriff of Lincoln County, have presented themselves to you gentlemen—to this

Court–in the cynical confidence that their testimony would not be doubted; confident that you gentlemen would go along with them on the assumption, the evil assumption, that all negroes lie; all negroes are basically immoral beings; all negro men are not to be trusted around our women, an assumption that one associates with minds of their caliber, and which is in itself, gentlemen, a lie–which I do not need to point out to you.

And so, a quiet, humble, respectable negro, who has had the unmitigated temerity to feel sorry for a white woman, has had to put his word against two white peoples. The defendant is not guilty. But somebody in this courtroom is.

Now, gentlemen, in this country our courts are the great levelers. In our courts, all men are created equal. I'm no idealist to believe firmly in the integrity of our courts and of our jury system. That's no ideal to me. That is a living, working reality!

Now I am confident that you gentlemen will review without passion the evidence that you have heard, come to a decision, and restore this man to his family.

In the name of God, do your duty. In the name of God, believe Tom Robinson.

Analysis

Atticus Finch's powerful closing argument stresses equality under the law and professes his faith that juries provide justice. However, the argument was probably better calculated to have an impact on viewers watching the film during the civil rights era of the 1960's than on the small town Southern jurors of the 1930's. While any defense that Atticus offered may have been doomed to fail, nevertheless his rhetorical strategies offer important lessons in trial advocacy.

Most noticeably perhaps, Atticus neglects to discuss the evidence. He attacks the credibility of Mayella (and her father Bob), but doesn't remind the jurors of the implausibility of their stories. Soaring oratory is not a substitute for evidentiary analysis.

Along with neglecting to attack the prosecution's evidence, Atticus fails to mention that the prosecution has to prove Robinson guilty beyond a reasonable doubt. Indeed, Atticus' last words ("believe Tom Robinson") suggest that the jurors have to believe Robinson in order to acquit him of rape. Atticus is in an uncomfortable yet familiar position. When defendants present their own version of what happened, defense attorneys need to emphasize the credibility of that version while at the same time reminding the jurors that the prosecution or plaintiff has the burden of proof. Atticus' last words unfortunately imply that the burden of proving what happened lay with Robinson.

Atticus misreads his audience when he refers to courts as "great levelers." The metaphor implies that a not guilty verdict puts the jurors on a par with Tom Robinson. The argument assumes the jurors capable of ignoring a social order in which the status of even the poorest white person is higher than that of a "negro." Immoral though that social order may be, a strategy that depends on jurors' willingness to set aside such deeply held beliefs is unlikely to succeed. The jurors have to live in the town after the trial. Like any advocate for an unpopular client, Atticus should try to offer the jurors a path for deciding the case in Robinson's favor without rejecting their way of life. (In a similar though less moralistic vein, Atticus' reference to "unmitigated temerity" might be lost on these poorly educated jurors!)

Atticus does offer the jurors a "theory of the case" that accounts for Mayella's false claim of sexual assault. Atticus' theory is rooted in psychology: Mayella needed to "get rid of her own guilt." As this is a possible inference from the evidence, Atticus does not violate the rule against arguing facts "outside the record" even though no psychologist testified. However, Atticus might have offered a more straightforward theory rooted in the testimony: realizing that her furious father Bob was watching from the window, Mayella cried rape in an effort to prevent her father from beating her for "kissing a black man."

While the fictional Atticus has to lose, might a real Atticus have been able to make a more effective closing argument? As for any attorney who represents an unpopular client, a real Atticus would look for an approach that offered the jurors a chance to rule in Robinson's favor without having to abandon their ingrained beliefs. Here are three possibilities:

* Atticus might take advantage of the southern jurors' likely anti-Yankee bias. That is, Atticus might argue that northerners unfairly attack southern justice. But this case allows the jurors to demonstrate that southern justice is alive and well by recognizing that Robinson's guilt has not been proved.

* Atticus might make a "silent argument" that puts Mayella outside the sexual code because it protects "virtuous" white women and therefore doesn't apply to Mayella, because she had on previous occasions lured Robinson onto her property.

* Atticus might argue on behalf of a conviction of a lesser included offense.

CHAPTER 13

ODDS AND ENDS

Intertwined with testimony and argument are the myriads of procedures and traditions that constitute the rituals of the adversary system. This chapter describes the most important of these rituals, but does not reveal which are "odds" and which are "ends." Life must have some mystery!

Many courtroom rituals reflect nothing more than local customs and practices, and often vary from one courtroom to another. For example, in one courtroom stepping into "the well" (the floor area between counsel table and the judge's bench) may be perfectly acceptable; in another, you may get a quicker hook than a bad vaudeville performer. Thus, always seek advice regarding a judge's procedural preferences from the court clerk or another attorney, or observe a judge in action before your case is scheduled. Otherwise, when you try a case you may end up feeling like the party guest who wonders why nobody else is in costume.

A. EXCLUDING (SEQUESTERING) WITNESSES

Judges issue sequestration orders in order to prevent witnesses from influencing each other's testimony. (See Federal Rule of Evidence 615) Sequestration orders typically:

- bar potential witnesses from the courtroom during trial to prevent them from hearing the testimony of other witnesses; and

- instruct witnesses not to discuss a case with other witness until both witnesses have completed testifying.

Some judges issue sequestration orders routinely, without prompting from attorneys. If not, you can make an oral request at the outset of a trial. Before celebrating a successful request, remember that the order will apply to both sides' witnesses.

Where do sequestered witnesses go? In short trials, to the corridor, or at least no further away than the cafeteria. In longer trials, most jurisdictions have "on call" subpoena procedures, which allow witnesses to carry on daily life outside the courthouse so long as they agree to and are able to appear in court on short notice.

Sequestration orders do not apply to parties. They may be paying dearly for their day in court, and should not have to miss a moment of it. Parties can derive some benefit from this privilege. By opting to testify last, parties can first hear what the other witnesses have to say. Attorneys who represent abstract entities, such as prosecutors, usually can designate a representative (e.g, an investigating police officer) to remain in court throughout testimony, even though that representative will testify.

B. STIPULATIONS

Stipulations are agreements between counsel. A stipulation cannot confer on a court powers that it does not have: e.g., "we stipulate that if convicted, the court shall order that defendant is to be tarred and feathered." Other than that, parties can stipulate to nearly any legal or factual issue. For example, parties can stipulate to the admissibility of evidence, to an expert's qualifications, and to the content of testimony.

Typically, attorneys arrange stipulations outside of courtrooms, and often before trials begin. You may inform judges of stipulations as soon as they are agreed to, or during trial at the time a stipulation becomes relevant. For example, you may advise a judge that both counsel have stipulated to an expert's qualifications when the expert is called to testify. Similarly, you may advise a judge that both sides have stipulated that a document qualifies as a business record at the time the document is marked for identification.

While oral stipulations are common, you may want to protect yourself against an adversary's sharp practices by reducing a stipulation to writing. In court, an attorney who lacks civility may try to back out of an oral stipulation by finding subtle ambiguities: "Your Honor, I did agree to stipulate that the animal on the premises had four legs, a tail, and barked. But I certainly did not intend to stipulate that it was a dog." If an unexpected disagreement prevents you from entering a stipulation into the record, you may suddenly find yourself in the middle of trial unprepared to offer evidence that you thought would be stipulated to.

Typical stipulations include:

- *Qualifications of an Expert.* You may stipulate that, e.g., "Dr. Broder is qualified to render a medical opinion." Indeed, when an adversary's expert is abundantly qualified, offering to stipulate to the expert's qualifications may prevent the adversary from parading the expert's honors and achievements before a jury. Judges, cognizant of time pressures, often try to persuade attorneys to accept such stipulations. However, you may want to resist an adversary's offer to stipulate to your expert's abundant qualifications. In such situations, you may argue that the impressive foundational information goes to the weight and not merely the admissibility of an expert's testimony, or that an expert's extensive training and experience have particular relevance to the factual propositions to which the expert's opinion relates.

- *Accuracy of Evidence.* You may stipulate that a fact or group of facts is true. For example, you may stipulate that, "All of the king's horses were at the wall," or that, "The chicken came first." Such stipulations are binding for the purposes of the litigation, and a judge will advise a jury to accept stipulated facts as true. Thus, you cannot attack the credibility of evidence whose accuracy has been stipulated to. At the same time, you can stipulate to the accuracy of evidence while retaining the right to question the *inference* that an adversary wants drawn from that evidence: "We did stipulate that all the king's horses were at the wall. But that in no way undermines our contention that the king was negligent. First, consider . . ."

- *Content of Testimony.* You may stipulate to the content of testimony without agreeing to its accuracy. For example, you may stipulate that, "If called and sworn, Ptolemy would testify that the sun and all the planets revolve around the earth." Even after that stipulation is made on the record, you could attack the accuracy of Ptolemy's testimony.

  You might ask an adversary to enter into a "content of testimony" stipulation to save time, to avoid having to ask for a continuance if a witness suddenly becomes unavailable, and perhaps to prevent inconsistencies that might appear if you called the various observers of an event as witnesses. You might accede to an adversary's request for such a stipulation to save time and to keep a very credible witness off the stand.

- *Foundational Matters.* In addition to an expert's qualifications, stipulations can obviate virtually every foundational showing in the world of evidence. For example, with respect to exhibits, attorneys often offer to "stipulate to yours if you stipulate to mine." Attorneys may also stipulate that an oral hearsay statement qualifies as a "spontaneous exclamation," or that a witness has personal knowledge. When you don't seriously contest a foundation, stipulating to admissibility is a useful way to save valuable court time.

C. MAKING OBJECTIONS

Objections are your means of enforcing (or more properly, asking judges to enforce) evidentiary principles. Since you may have less time to object to a question or an answer than the time interval between a traffic light turning green and the New York cabbie behind you honking, objections decisions may seem a daunting task. However, take solace in realizing that the risk of a trial's outcome turning on making or failing to make an objection is negligible. You will almost always know about and have time to research the admissibility of critical evidence before it is offered. The combination of crucial evidence and unanticipated evidentiary problems is rare.

1. MOTIONS *IN LIMINE*

A motion *in limine* is a request for a pretrial ruling on the admissibility of evidence. While the motion can be made by a party seeking a ruling that evidence is admissible, more typically a party makes a motion *in limine* to ask a judge to rule that an adversary's evidence is inadmissible. Motions *in limine* are often oral, though you may file a written motion accompanied by a trial brief.

Compared to resolving admissibility issues in mid-trial, motions *in limine* have a number of advantages. For example, if a judge grants your pretrial motion excluding evidence, your adversary cannot refer to the evidence during trial, and must instruct witnesses not to refer to it. By comparison, even if the judge sustains your mid-trial objection, jurors may hear the improper evidence. (Judges routinely admonish jurors to disregard improper evidence, but the effect of such admonishments is uncertain.) Moreover, you can plan more effectively for opening statement and direct and cross examination if a judge has already ruled with respect to important evidence. Finally, judges often delay ruling on motions *in limine*, hoping to make a more educated decision during trial. However, the fact that you made a motion *in limine* may add force to your objection when you renew it in mid-trial.

In criminal cases, a defendant's prior convictions are a frequent focus of defense *in limine* motions. Criminal defendants who might want to testify in their own defense may decide not to do so if a judge rules that their prior convictions are admissible for impeachment purposes under Federal Rule of Evidence 609. By making a motion *in limine* and perhaps obtaining a pretrial ruling on the admissibility of prior convictions for impeachment, a defense attorney can better prepare trial strategies. The hearing on a motion *in limine* may go as follows:

Def. Att: Your Honor, the prosecutor Ms. Abramowitz has advised me that should the defendant testify, she will seek to impeach the defendant with his prior robbery conviction for robbery. I've noticed this motion *in limine* prior to impaneling the jury to ask Your Honor to exclude the prior should the defendant testify.

Judge: Were you given adequate notice of the motion, Ms. Abramowitz?

Pros: Yes, Your Honor. I'm prepared to argue its admissibility.

Judge: I'll hear from defense counsel on the motion *in limine*.

Def. Att: Your Honor, my client is charged with drug trafficking. The circumstances leading to the charges are complex, and depending on how the government's evidence emerges it may well be critical for my client to testify and explain his remote and unwitting connection to the illegal activities. Allowing him to be impeached with the prior conviction, which occurred seven years ago when he was only 19, might prevent him from testifying and deprive the jury of important evidence. Reminding Your Honor that under Rule 609 the conviction is presumptively inadmissible, I ask that it be excluded should my client testify.

Judge: Counsel, are there any prior rulings you want me to consider?

Def. Att: Yes Your Honor.   (Defense Counsel refers to and discusses three appellate court rulings.)

Judge: Ms. Abramowitz, I'll hear from you.

Pros.: Thank you Your Honor. . .

Judge: I thank counsel for the fine arguments.   I will take the matter under submission and advise both parties before we start picking the jury tomorrow.   My tentative intention is to postpone a ruling on the motion until the close of the prosecution's case. Ms. Abramowitz, please be sure to advise your witnesses not to refer to the prior conviction and that it is not to be admitted in evidence unless I rule otherwise.

Motions *in limine* are equally appropriate in civil cases.   For example, a plaintiff in a "slip and fall" case may seek to offer evidence that another individual slipped at the same location as the plaintiff. The defendant may then notice a motion *in limine* to seek a ruling that evidence concerning the other individual is inadmissible under Federal Rule of Evidence 403.

2. TACTICAL AND ETHICAL CONSIDERATIONS

Especially in jury trials, objections can backfire even if they are sustained. Jurors may believe that an attorney who objects repeatedly is attempting to conceal damaging information. Prosecutors are particularly wary of such adverse inferences, and often are reluctant to object to defense evidence.

Moreover, you have an ethical responsibility to object only in good faith. You may not object in order to rattle a witness, to pay back an obstreperous opposing counsel, or to demonstrate your expertise by making an objection that allows you to cite a footnote in an obscure 19th century Paraguayan intermediate appellate court opinion.

As a result, you should in general object only when evidence is both improper and damaging to your claims. This is a judgment you will have to make on a case-by-case basis. For example, you may choose to let an occasional leading question or mention of irrelevant evidence go by without objection. On the other hand, if you suspect (perhaps based on behavior at a deposition) that opposing counsel is prone to rely repeatedly on improper leading questions, or that a witness is given to extemporaneous irrelevant answers, you may want to object from the outset of trial to each impropriety to convey your expectation that the judge will enforce the rules carefully.

A difficult tactical and ethical question can arise when you object in the hope that opposing counsel is unaware of an exception that you know exists. For example, you might object to hearsay in the hope that opposing counsel does not realize that the assertion qualifies as a declaration against interest. (Federal Rule of Evidence 804(b)(3)) Many attorneys would forgo objecting in these circumstances, unless the objection forces the adversary to offer evidence for a limited purpose. For instance, you might make a hearsay objection to an out-of-court assertion if you thereby force opposing counsel to offer it for the limited purpose of "effect on the hearer."

Finally, recognize that an objection may serve only to educate your adversary. For example, assume that you successfully object when an adversary constantly asks improper leading questions. All you may accomplish is to force the adversary into an open questioning style that enhances the credibility of the adversary's witnesses.

3. OBJECTIONS PROCEDURES

Objections should usually consist of nothing more than the word "objection" followed by the concise ground of objection. For example, you might state, "Objection, hearsay;" or, "Objection, the question calls for a narrative response." Most judges view "speaking" objections the same way they view speaking demurrers: with contempt. Thus, do not combine an objection with a lecture on, e.g., the importance of the hearsay rule to the democratic way of life. If a judge wants elaboration, count on the judge to ask for it.

Technically, a judge may overrule an objection if you state the wrong ground, or neglect to state any ground. (For example, "Objection, the question calls for inadmissible information" is an improper objection.) In practice, however, a judge may sustain an obvious objection before you get it fully out of your mouth. A judge may even sustain an objection for which, in the judge's opinion, you have chosen the wrong ground: "Well, I don't think the information is irrelevant, but it's hearsay under the reasoning of an obscure 19th century Paraguayan intermediate appellate court opinion. I'll sustain it on that ground."

The general rule is that you must object as soon as the ground for objection is apparent. Thus, you should:

- Object to an improper question after it is asked and before it is answered.

- Object to an improper answer as soon as you can, even if you have to interrupt a witness to do so. If the judge sustains (upholds) your objection, move to strike the improper testimony. For example, consider the following sequence:

Q: When did Rhoda arrive?

A: At eight o'clock, just after she knocked all the cookies a Girl Scout troop was trying to sell off the table.

Here, the ground for objection first appears in the answer. Depending on your reflexes, at some point after "o'clock" you would object that the remaining portion of the answer is "non-responsive" or "irrelevant" or "unfairly prejudicial." For the sake of the court reporter, first get the witness to stop talking (perhaps by standing up and saying, "Excuse me"), then state your objection. If the judge sustains your objection, you should "move to strike everything after eight o'clock" and ask the judge to instruct the jury to disregard the stricken testimony. Unless an improper answer is formally stricken, a judge or jury can consider it.

Do not thank a judge for an evidentiary ruling. Many attorneys habitually thank more people than the winner of a Best Picture Academy Award when a judge sustains an objection. "Thank you" is improper because it implies that the judge is doing a favor rather than making a ruling required by law. "Thank you" is even more improper, bordering on the contemptuous, following an adverse ruling.

If your objection is overruled (denied), in earlier days you would have had to "take exception" to the ruling to preserve the point for appeal. "Taking exception" was the legal equivalent of, "Oh, yeah? Wait until the appellate court hears about your ruling." Now, objections themselves preserve evidentiary points for appeal; you need not take exception to adverse rulings.

Do not immediately present additional argument to a judge who you believe has improperly overruled your objection. Ask for permission to argue by asking "to be heard further."

Finally, don't whine when making objections. Some attorneys object in voices that make it seem like their entire lives have been dogged by adversaries' improper evidence. Object in a professional and dignified tone of voice, as when you question witnesses or make final argument.

4. CONTINUING OBJECTIONS

You may make a "continuing" objection when a judge has overruled an objection that pertains to an entire line of inquiry. If the judge allows a continuing objection, you can forgo objecting to every question that pertains to the line of inquiry without running the risk that an appellate court will rule that you "waived the objection" by failing to object every time the area was raised.

For example, assume that you contend that all events that occurred after March 31 are irrelevant. This dialogue ensues:

Q: Turning your attention to April 1, where were you?

You: Objection, anything that took place after March 31 is irrelevant.

Judge: Overruled.

Rather than having to object to every question pertaining to events taking place after March 31, you may request a "continuing objection." Thus, this dialogue may ensue after the above ruling:

You: Your Honor, might I have a continuing objection to all questions and responses pertaining to events that occurred after March 31?

Judge: You may.

In addition to preserving the point for appeal, continuing objections save you from alienating a judge or jury with constant objections.

5. OFFERS OF PROOF

An offer of proof is an attorney's summary of expected testimony. When you are uncertain about the testimony that an adversary's witness is about to give and want to know whether an objection is appropriate, you may ask the judge to ask opposing counsel to make an offer of proof. For example, assume that your adversary asks, "Please tell us what was said in the June 8 conversation." You have little information about this conversation, and don't know what the testimony will be. If all or part of the answer will be objectionable, you prefer to know before the answer is given. That way, you can prevent a jury from hearing improper testimony in the first place rather than objecting and asking the judge to admonish the jurors to disregard testimony that they have already heard. Make a request for opposing counsel to make an offer of proof at the bench. If the judge grants the request, opposing counsel will briefly summarize the witness' expected testimony out of the jury's hearing. If testimony is objectionable, you can make the objection at the bench.

The burden may be on you to make an offer of proof when opposing counsel objects to testimony that you plan to offer. Unless it is clear from the record what the testimony will be, you have to make an offer of proof to provide the judge with an adequate basis for making a ruling. Otherwise, you cannot argue on appeal that the judge improperly prevented you from offering evidence.

For example, assume that you are a prosecutor and are prosecuting the so-called "kitchen sink bandits" for a residential burglary. (The defendants apparently sought to emulate the bumbling burglary team in the 1990 comedy film *Home Alone*.) Pursuant to Federal Rule of Evidence 404(b), you seek to offer "signature crime" evidence that the defendants also committed another burglary using the same unique method as in the charged burglary. When you call the "signature crime" witness to testify, the proceedings unfold as follows:

Q: Ms. Pesci, where do you live?

Def. Att: Objection Your Honor. The testimony that this witness will give constitutes improper character evidence, also I object that the testimony will be irrelevant and unfairly prejudicial.

Judge: Will both counsel please approach the bench. (With both counsel and the court reporter at the bench). Will the prosecutor please make an offer of proof as to this witness' expected testimony?

Pros.: Certainly Your Honor. Ms. Pesci will testify to the circumstances of a residential burglary that took place at her house just one week before the charged crime. Ms. Pesci will testify that she came home from a short trip to find that all the jewelry, small electronic items, silverware and many other personal possessions were gone from her home. In addition, rags had been stuffed into the drain of the kitchen sink and the water in the kitchen sink had been left running, so that the kitchen floor and the floors of adjacent rooms were covered with water. I will also prove through the testimony of Police Officer Krupke that Ms. Pesci's personal possessions were in the defendants' possession when Officer Krupke arrested the defendants in connection with the charged crime. I submit that the circumstances involving the burglary of Ms. Pesci's house are unique and nearly identical to the circumstances of the charged crime, and that her testimony is admissible as "signature crime" evidence under Rule 404(b).

Judge: Defense counsel, any response.

Def. Att: I object on the grounds previously stated Your Honor. (Argument omitted)

Judge: I'll admit the testimony pursuant to Rule 404(b). Prosecutor, please continue with Ms. Pesci's testimony.

An offer of proof can also be helpful in a "conditional relevance" situation. That is, if the relevance of evidence depends on testimony that you have not yet had a chance to offer, ask to make an offer of proof. If the judge agrees that the expected testimony makes the evidence relevant, the judge can admit it "subject to being connected up." Consider an example:

Q: What time did you awake that morning?

A: About 6 A.M.

Q: What did you do then?

A: I had breakfast.

Q: What did you have for breakfast?

Opp. Counsel: Objection, irrelevant.

Judge: Sustained.

Q: Your Honor, might I make an offer of proof? If permitted, the witness will testify that he cooked fresh grits for breakfast. He will further testify to the length of time it took for the grits to be cooked. The evidence will support my argument that the witness could not possibly have been at a meeting across town at 6:30 A.M., as opposing counsel Gambini contends.

Judge: The objection is overruled. You may inquire.

6. BEYOND OBJECTIONS

Objections are not always sufficient to protect your client from unfair prejudice. For example, an adverse witness may repeatedly refer to improper evidence, and an opposing counsel may barrage you with groundless objections or constantly ask improper questions. In such situations, consider asking the judge for remedies beyond sustaining individual objections. For example, you may ask the judge to:

- Instruct a runaway adverse witness to confine answers to questions. In an extreme situation, you may ask the judge to strike a witness' entire testimony.

- Warn obstreperous opposing counsel that the continued making of groundless objections will be dealt with by sanctions, including declaring a mistrial, awarding you costs and possible referral of the attorney to the state's licensing body for possible disciplinary action.

- Strike testimony that opposing counsel repeatedly and improperly tries to elicit through improper leading questions.

7. COMMON GROUNDS FOR OBJECTION

Objections typically are either *substantive* or *procedural*. Substantive objections pertain to the content of testimony; procedural objections concern the form of questions or answers. Common substantive objections include:

- *Objection, irrelevant.* (Federal Rule of Evidence 402) Irrelevant information wastes court time and is not logically connected to factual propositions.

Example: Houston is charged with petty theft. The prosecutor asks the store security guard, "Do people often try to steal merchandise?" The question is irrelevant because the actions of other people have no logical connection to Houston's guilt or innocence.

Sometimes, an adversary's argument as to why evidence is relevant can allow the adversary to preview a closing argument in front of the jury. Therefore, you may want to approach the bench to make an "irrelevant" objection.

- *Objection. probative value is substantially outweighed by the danger of unfair prejudice or confusion of the issues.* (Federal Rule of Evidence 403) Many judges permit this objection to be stated as *Objection, Rule 403.*

Examples: (1) A personal injury plaintiff offers a severed left leg into evidence. (2) A criminal defendant's prior conviction may unduly influence the jury's determination of whether the defendant committed the charged crime.

- *Objection, hearsay.* (Federal Rule of Evidence 801). Hearsay is an out-of-court assertion offered for the truth of its contents. The usual vice of hearsay is that a judge or juror cannot evaluate the credibility of the declarant.

Example: To prove that the defendant ran a red light, the plaintiff offers to testify that "A few days after the collision, I got a phone call from a woman who told me that she'd seen the accident and that the driver of the blue car [the defendant] had run the red light."

- *Objection, speculation; Objection, improper opinion; Objection, lack of personal knowledge.* (Federal Rules of Evidence 602, 701). Testimony concerning hypothetical situations or describing matters beyond a witness' ability to perceive is unreliable and invades the judge's or jury's province.

Examples: (1) "Why did the bear go over the mountain?" (A witness can only speculate as to the reason for another's actions.) (2) "If you had known what the spleen looked like, would you have removed it?" (3) "When your cellmate said that 'I'm going to beat her up as soon as I get out of here,' to whom was your cellmate referring?"

A "lack of personal knowledge" objection is also appropriate when you think that a witness is testifying based on hearsay. If in response to a lack of personal knowledge objection a witness admits that testimony is based on another person's out-of-court assertion, then you may make a hearsay objection.

- *Objection, lack of foundation.* (Federal Rule of Evidence 104). Evidence that fails to meet foundational requirements is unreliable. Since all evidence is subject to one kind of foundational showing or another (if only a lay witness' personal knowledge), an objection based on "lack of foundation" is the broadest possible ground of objection.

Example: Jordan offers a company document into evidence as a business record, but fails to offer foundational evidence demonstrating that the document was prepared in the ordinary course of business.

- *Objection, improper use of character evidence to prove conduct.* (Federal Rule of Evidence 404). Evidence is generally improper when its relevance depends on an inference concerning a party's propensity to engage in conduct.

Examples: (1) To prove that Larry was speeding, the adversary seeks to elicit Darryl's opinion that Larry tends to drive over the speed limit. (2) To prove that Andrea robbed a bank, the prosecution offers evidence that Andrea has committed two burglaries.

Procedural, or *form*, objections typically are addressed to a judge's discretion under Federal Rule of Evidence 611. Common "form" objections, some of which are also addressed in other chapters of the book, include:

- *Objection, vague; Objection, ambiguous; Objection, unintelligible.* A question is improper when its scope is so broad or uncertain that you cannot understand it or anticipate a witness' answer.

Examples: (1) "Please describe the nature of the event." (2) "When did you first become aware, with reference to the three meetings, that circumstances had changed but which on further reflection turned out to be mistaken?"

- *Objection, compound.* A compound question consists of multiple parts, creating uncertainty about which part a witness might answer. The problem usually arises during direct examination.

Example: "Please describe what happened during this meeting and then tell us what actions were taken afterwards."

- *Objection, calls for a narrative response.* Testimony is supposed to emerge in question/answer format, in large part to allow attorneys to anticipate and object to improper testimony. Questions that are framed so broadly that they invite witnesses to describe large chunks of information can therefore be improper. The problem usually arises during direct examination.

Example: "Please describe the events culminating in the invention of the hula hoop."

Witnesses sometimes launch into narrative responses to proper questions. When that occurs, you can interrupt a witness' answer to object that "the witness is narrating" or that "no question is pending."

- *Objection, asked and answered.* Attorneys who rehash testimony with the same witness waste court time. On direct examination multiple questions seeking the same evidence can also constitute an improper method of emphasizing portions of a story. And on cross examination, multiple questions on the same topic may constitute argumentative "badgering." However, judges often allow cross examiners to go over already plowed ground when witnesses are evasive.

Examples: Direct examination—"Ruth, please tell us again what happened when the robber came into the store." Cross examination-"I'll ask you for the third time, are you sure that it was the first cup of porridge that was too cold?"

- *Objection, assumes facts not in evidence.* A question is improper when an attorney makes an assertion as a precursor to a question. The form of the question does not allow a witness to respond to the attorney's assertion. The problem most commonly occurs during cross examination.

Example: "Doctor, with spiral fractures so readily apparent on x-rays, how come you didn't notice this one?"

- *Objection, argumentative.* Questions are argumentative when instead of asking for information they demand that witnesses respond to an attorney's conclusions or ask witnesses to give opinions about other witnesses' testimony. The problem almost always arises on cross examination.

Examples: (1) "Why shouldn't the judge believe the two other witnesses who saw things differently?" (2) "You don't want the jurors to infer from the fact that you were late for a meeting that you were speeding, do you?"

- *Objection, leading.* Leading questions are improper during direct examination because they allow attorneys to testify through the mouths of friendly witnesses, right? However, various exceptions may allow the use of leading questions during direct examination; see Chapter 7.

- *Objection, misquoting the witness/misstating the evidence.* When an attorney incorporates previous testimony in a new question, even subtle variations can alter a judge's or juror's perception of the testimony. The problem normally arises during cross examination. As with questions that assume facts not in evidence, the form of questions that misquote witnesses generally doesn't allow a witness to point out the alteration.

Example: On direct, a witness testified that he had just awakened and was *a bit groggy* when he heard a shot and saw the defendant run past his window. The cross examiner asks, "Now, when you're in your bedroom *pretty much out of it*, how much time goes by between the time you heard the shot and someone ran past your window?"

- *Objection, the witness failed to order fat free salad dressing on the side*. Actually, this is not a common ground of legal objection outside of California.

Handy-Dandy Summary of Common Objections
(Bring to trial or dinner parties)

Substantive objections

Irrelevant (Federal Rule of Evidence 802)

Probative Value Substantially Outweighed by Unfair Prejudice (Federal Rule of Evidence 403)

Hearsay (Federal Rule of Evidence 801)

Speculation or Improper Opinion (Federal Rule of Evidence 701); Lack of Personal Knowledge (Federal Rule of Evidence 602)

Lack of foundation (Federal Rule of Evidence 104).

Improper evidence of character to prove conduct (Federal Rule of Evidence 404).

Form objections (Federal Rule of Evidence 611)

Vague, Unintelligible, Ambiguous

Compound

Calls for a Narrative Response

Asked and Answered

Assumes Facts Not in Evidence

Argumentative

Leading

Misquotes the Witness

D. RESPONDING TO AN ADVERSARY'S OBJECTIONS

1. YOU CONCEDE THE POINT

You may realize that an adversary's objection to your question or to your witness' answer is well taken. For example, your witness' puzzled look may reveal the legitimacy of an adversary's "unintelligible question" objection; you may realize that you need to lay a further foundation; or you may agree that your witness' lengthy answer is improperly "narrative."

When you concede an objection to your question, you may either wait for the judge's ruling or offer to withdraw the question. By demonstrating your understanding of evidentiary rules, the latter tactic may lend force to your arguments on disputed evidentiary issues.

When you concede an objection to an answer, consider giving your witness a short, polite instruction if you think the witness is likely to repeat the error. For example, you may tell a witness who is prone to narration something like, "I know you're anxious to tell us everything you saw, but to be fair and help us understand your testimony, it's important for you to listen carefully and simply respond to what you're asked. Can you do that?" While your role during examination is supposed to be confined to asking questions, judges generally appreciate comments that further a trial's efficiency.

2. ARGUING OBJECTIONS

In general, do not argue an objection unless a judge invites you to do so. Not only is this proper procedure, but also the judge might be prepared to overrule the adversary's objection without the need for argument. If you want to comment on an objection, say something like, "Your Honor, might I be heard?" Use similar language if you want to ask a judge to reconsider an adverse ruling that you were unable to argue before the ruling.

3. OFFERING EVIDENCE FOR LIMITED PURPOSES

As you know, evidence is often admissible for one purpose but not for another. For example, an out-of-court assertion may admissible if limited to the issue of the hearer's "state of mind," and evidence of a "remedial measure" may be admissible if limited to the issue of ownership (Federal Rule of Evidence 407). In such situations, you may obviate an objection by incorporating the limited purpose into a question: "For purposes of state of mind only, please tell us what you heard Dumpty say just before falling off the wall." This tactic can both demonstrate your awareness of and willingness to follow evidence rules, and can avoid an objection that disrupts a witness' story.

4. THE ADVERSARY'S OBJECTION IS OVERRULED

Again, do not say "thank you" to the judge. And do not be so flush with victory that you neglect to get an answer to an objected-to question. If the witness does not recall the question, re-ask it or ask the judge to have the court reporter repeat it.

5. THE ADVERSARY'S OBJECTION IS SUSTAINED

Now, "thank you" is a real no-no! If you want to contest a ruling, you may ask to be heard. Unlike baseball umpires, judges sometimes do change their mind, especially if you can point out that a judge misapprehended the issue to which evidence relates.

If you are uncertain of the basis of a ruling, you cannot mend the problem with further foundational evidence. Therefore, you may want to ask for clarification: "Your Honor has sustained the lack of foundation objection. Might you inquire of counsel as to just what foundational element is lacking?" By artfully phrasing your request in this way, you take the judge off the spot and force opposing counsel to identify the missing foundation.

E. JUDGE OR JURY TRIAL?

Parties have the constitutional or statutory right to a jury trial in "serious" criminal cases and many types of civil cases. Nevertheless, juries are present in less than half of all U. S. trials. This section sets out factors that you and a client should consider when deciding whether to opt for a judge or jury trial.

The frequent importance of this decision, and the fact that you will usually have time to discuss it with clients in advance, means the decision is one that you should leave to clients after counseling whenever possible. ABA Standard for Criminal Justice 4–5.2 instructs criminal defense counsel that their clients have the right to make this decision, perhaps because in criminal cases defendants who opt for a bench trial have to personally waive their constitutional right to trial by jury.

Lawyers' "conventional wisdom" suggests a number of "default" selections. For example:

- Civil plaintiffs should lean towards jury trials, on the theory that jurors are likely to be more affected by a case's emotional aspects than judges and thus might be more inclined to award damages.

- Criminal defendants should also lean towards jury trials, because the rules generally requiring unanimous verdicts in criminal cases mean that one juror's not guilty vote can prevent a conviction. Moreover, a story that falls on the deaf ears of a judge who has "heard it all before" may impress a juror hearing it for the first time.

- Parties who rely on "technicalities" (e.g., a Statute of Frauds defense) are better off with judges, who have an institutional interest in enforcing rules that jurors may see as obstructions to justice.

- Parties whose cases are based on scientific evidence or are otherwise factually complex should opt for judge trials. Judges may be smarter than the average juror, and more likely to take a full set of trial notes. Moreover, you can "educate" judges before trial by filing trial briefs.

Do not use these bits of lawyer lore as anything more than starting points for deciding between a judge or jury. Among the other factors you should consider are these:

- Jury trials tend to be longer than judge trials, and therefore may entail greater expenses for clients. (A jury trial is also likely to impose greater costs on your adversary, perhaps increasing your case's settlement value.)

- Losing litigants may have to pay a "jury trial penalty." For example, a criminal defendant who puts forward what a judge considers to be a specious defense and who puts the system to the time and expense of a jury trial may (unofficially of course) pay for the impertinence with a harsh sentence. And a losing civil litigant may be taxed higher costs because jury trials tend to be more expensive than judge trials.

- Judges tend to enforce evidence rules more strictly in jury than in judge trials, perhaps thinking that they are less likely than jurors to be influenced by evidence of doubtful admissibility. At the same time, because judges necessarily become aware of information that they rule inadmissible, the possibility exists that a judge will be subtly influenced by information that jurors would never know about.

- The "one free bite" rule in effect in some jurisdictions (see, e.g., Cal. Code of Civ. Proc. 170.6) allows you to disqualify a judge who you and a client consider unacceptable, even though you cannot prove the judge's actual bias. By contrast, when you cannot show actual bias, rules strictly limit the number of potential jurors you can excuse.

- Judges often have "track records" in particular types of cases that you can investigate through sources such as computer data bases, other attorneys who have tried similar cases and even local legal newspapers that publish "judicial profiles" of sitting judges. You may also be able to gauge a judge's receptivity to your arguments by watching a judge conduct another trial. By contrast, background information about potential jurors is harder to come by, unless a client is able to pay a social science research company to conduct a community survey. (On the other hand, the potential ability to conduct a pretrial investigation of a particular judge may be worth little in localities where any of a large number of judges may be assigned to preside on the day set for trial.)

- If your adversary opts for a jury trial, you'll have one regardless of your and a client's preference.

- Once you and a client have decided on a judge or jury, you will need to comply with often-exacting local court rules. For example, to obtain a jury trial in a federal civil action you have to serve a jury trial request on your adversary no later than 10 days after the service of the last pleading. (Federal Rule of Civil Procedure 38–b). You may also have to deposit jury fees in advance of trial.

F. JURY *VOIR DIRE*

Jury *voir dire* (the term is Latin for "speak truth") refers to foundational questioning of potential jurors. Jury *voir dire* allows parties to take part in selecting a fair and impartial jury by excusing potential jurors who may be predisposed to the adversary. You have two avenues for excusing potential jurors:

Challenges for cause, which assert that a potential juror is legally disqualified from serving. For example, you can exercise a challenge for cause against potential jurors whose answers reveal actual bias or who appear to be too infirm to serve. You are allowed an unlimited number of challenges for cause.

Peremptory challenges, which permit you to excuse potential jurors based on your or a client's subjective belief that a potential juror harbors attitudes that predispose the juror to favor an adversary's arguments. Peremptory challenges are strictly limited in number. For example, 28 U.S.C. Sec. 1870 provides for only three peremptory challenges in civil cases; Federal Rule of Criminal Procedure 24 provides for three peremptory challenges in misdemeanor cases.

Traditionally, lawyers conducted *voir dire* questioning. However, to curtail the time devoted to *voir dire* by lawyers who used it improperly as an opportunity to argue their cases, judges now typically conduct the bulk of jury *voir dire*. Depending on a judge's practices, you may be limited to submitting written questions for the judge to ask, or you may be able to supplement the judge's questioning by putting your own questions to prospective jurors.

The same process of drawing inferences from circumstantial evidence that is so central to fact-finding at trial also plays a central a role in the jury *voir dire* process. Potential jurors' responses may not provide "direct evidence" of bias. That is, a potential juror may not say something along the lines of "I could never be fair in this case if it involves a drunk driver who caused serious injuries." Thus, when you ask a judge to excuse a potential juror for cause, your argument that a juror's answers indicate a lack of impartiality is often based on circumstantial evidence. Similarly, peremptory challenges are also based on circumstantial evidence, including not only a potential juror's answers to *voir dire* questions, but also a potential juror's background, demeanor, manner of dress and even choice of reading material.

For example, assume that you represent a defendant who is charged with shoplifting from an electronics store. A potential juror states that she works for a boutique clothing store. From this evidence, you may infer that the potential juror will be biased in favor of retailers, or will be prone to accept a security guard's testimony. If so, you may decide to exercise a peremptory challenge against this potential juror.

Just as when you prepare inferential arguments (see Chapter 3), you may seek out "especially whens" and "except whens" to help you assess the likelihood that a potential juror will accept a particular inference. For example, assume that you learn that the security staff at the potential juror's store has recently given a training course on how to identify shoplifters. You might infer that this experience would make it especially likely that the potential juror would believe a security guard's testimony. On the other hand, the potential juror might believe a security guard "except when" a couple of security guards in her store were recently fired for incompetency.

Unfortunately, you'll rarely have time during *voir dire* examination to thoroughly explore such topics, and you'll generally have to draw inferences based on incomplete data. Two strategies that may help you and a client make a more educated judgment are as follows:

- Ask open questions. When you encourage potential jurors to talk, they often reveal important information that you would not have thought to ask about. For example, you might ask the potential juror who works in a clothing boutique questions such as, "Tell me about your experiences with your store's security staff."

- In big-ticket trials, consider hiring a social science research firm to conduct community surveys and produce "profiles" of suitable jurors.

Lawyer lore is embarrassingly filled with stereotypes about the suitability of different social group members to serve as jurors. For example, people of German descent were often said to make good defense jurors. However, modern trial rules outlaw some of those stereotypes. For instance, challenges based on race and gender are forbidden. Anyway, in today's mobile and complex society, such broad social stereotypes are probably poor predictors of potential jurors' attitudes.

Judges rarely grant challenges for cause, even when an aspect of a potential juror's background gives rise to a strong inference of predisposition. So long as potential jurors insist that they can be fair to both sides, judges are likely to deny challenges for cause. For example, assume that you make a challenge for cause, asking the judge in the shoplifting case to excuse the clothing boutique employee from the jury. If the employee says something like, "I won't be influenced by my job; I can give both sides a fair trial," the judge will probably not excuse the employee for cause. To preserve your limited number of peremptory challenges, therefore, you may seek to prove through additional questioning that a potential juror who you believe is undesirable is legally disqualified from serving.

For example, assume that you represent the shop-lifting defendant, and together with your client have decided that the boutique clothing store employee is likely to be predisposed to the prosecution. To try to convince the judge to excuse the employee for cause, you may conduct *voir dire* questioning along these lines:

1. Q: Ms. Lynn–Sossin, you said that the fact that you work for a small clothing store will in no way influence you, correct?

2. A: That's right.

3. Q: I appreciate that. But just to follow up a bit more, can you briefly tell us about your experience with the store's security staff?

4. A: I've found them generally pretty reliable. Whenever a problem has arisen, they've dealt with it very quickly and professionally. They're well trained and don't let problems get out of hand.

5. Q: Is it fair to say that you're pretty impressed with them?

6. A: I'd have to say that's true.

7. Q: And in your experience the security guards you've worked with have been honest and reliable?

8. A: Yes.

9. Q: If you knew nothing about a person except that the person was a store security guard, how would that affect your belief in what the person had to say?

10. A: Well, I'd assume they were telling the truth, the same as other people I suppose. But I'd want to hear what everyone had to say before making a decision.

11. Q: But as compared to someone you knew nothing about, would you agree that the fact that a person was a store security guard would make you more inclined to believe that person's testimony?

12. A: I suppose it's possible, but I can be fair.

13. Q: Thank you, I appreciate your candor.

> **Comment:** At this point, you might challenge the potential juror for cause, arguing that she is predisposed in favor of the prosecution. If the judge refuses to excuse the juror, you and the defendant would then have to decide whether to exercise a peremptory challenge. If you have none remaining, or prefer to save them for other potential jurors, you might conclude by committing the juror to her promise of fairness:

14. Q: So Ms. Lynn–Sossin, if you're on the jury, you'll give both sides a fair trial. You won't believe or

disbelieve witnesses for either side based solely on their employment, correct?

15. A: That's right.

In the *voir dire* sample above, you sprinkle open questions into the voir dire examination (Nos. 3 and 9). By encouraging potential jurors to talk, you can often draw informed inferences from their choice of words, their body language, etc. about their suitability to sit as a juror. Though hard to convey in text, your manner should also be conversational and polite. You don't want to alienate people who might wind up as jurors—or the friends they leave behind on the jury if you excuse them!

Perhaps the two most basic rules of jury *voir dire* are these:

- *Prejudgment.* You cannot ask potential jurors to "prejudge a case." What this means is that you cannot ask potential jurors to reveal how they would decide a case under an assumed set of facts. For example, in a drunk driving case, you could not ask, "If you were satisfied that Mr. Chivas had only had one beer to drink before getting into his car, will you find that he was not under the influence of alcohol?"

- *Scope of questioning.* A general rule, not followed in all jurisdictions, is that the information you seek must be relevant to predisposition. This rule seeks to confine the scope of *voir dire* and protect the privacy of potential jurors by preventing attorneys from pursuing remote topics that might pertain only to a peremptory challenge, such as what TV programs a person watches or what books they read.

While you cannot ask potential jurors to prejudge cases in your favor, you can properly ask them not to prejudge cases against you. The key to this strategy is to phrase questions in such a way that they seek assurance that a potential juror is neither predisposed *in favor of* an adversary's arguments nor predisposed *against* your arguments.

For example, consider how you might use jury *voir dire* questioning to inoculate jurors against an adversary's arguments. To employ this strategy, confront potential jurors with evidence favoring the adversary, and seek assurance of open-mindedness despite that evidence. For example, assume that in the drunk driving case you will dispute the prosecution's evidence that your client Mr. Chivas had drunk three martinis before driving. You might ask:

> "Ladies and gentlemen, you'll probably hear testimony from a prosecution witness who claims that Mr. Chivas had drunk three martinis. Without listening to the evidence, do any of you think that you should accept that testimony simply because it comes from a prosecution witness?"

> "If you serve on the jury, you will all agree that it's wrong to prejudge any witness' testimony, and you promise to keep an open mind until you've heard all the evidence?"

Such questions are proper because a potential juror who refuses to promise to keep an open mind cannot legally serve on the jury. Of course, you expect potential jurors to make such promises. Your real purpose is an educational one.

During *voir dire* you might also seek to inoculate jurors against silent arguments. Assume that you represent a civil plaintiff suing a police officer for excessive force in making an arrest. A possible silent argument favoring the defendant officer is that "a conclusion that the force was excessive will deter police officers from adequately protecting citizens." During *voir dire*, you can surface the potential argument and seek a potential juror's agreement not to let it be determinative:

> "The judge will instruct you that in reaching your verdict, you shouldn't take into account the affect the verdict may have on other police officers. Will you be able to follow such an instruction?"

A juror who answered "no" would be subject to a challenge for cause. Thus, though your real purpose may be to educate and inoculate against a potential silent argument, the question is probably proper.

During *voir dire*, you can also educate jurors about legal rules by seeking jurors' agreement to obey them. For example, here is a question you might ask about the burden of proof:

> "The judge will instruct you that you cannot vote for conviction unless the prosecution proves its case beyond a reasonable doubt. Are you willing to follow that instruction?"

You would not reasonably expect a potential juror to answer anything other than "yes" to such a question. However, the question allows you to stress an argument while formally probing a potential juror's fitness to serve.

G. JURY INSTRUCTIONS

Jury instructions are the vehicle that judges use to inform jurors of the substantive and procedural rules that govern their deliberations. Traditionally, judges deliver jury instructions orally, usually at some length and with little enthusiasm. Jurors who are uncertain about the content or meaning of a rule then have to interrupt their deliberations, file back into the courtroom and ask for help. Increasingly, judges permit jurors to have the written instructions with them while they deliberate, though the practice risks the danger that jurors may focus too much on one instruction and overlook others that relate to or modify it.

Many instructions are "boilerplate," and judges take them from court-approved books of jury instructions. However, you can propose jury instructions that you've created. Potential sources for hand-crafted jury instructions include dictionaries, appellate court opinions, law review articles, and nutshell treatises.

One benefit of submitting instructions that you've prepared is that you can rephrase helpful instructions in "plain English" that jurors can understand. The language of many jury instructions makes insurance contracts seem entertaining, and you may facilitate jury understanding by preparing user-friendly yet accurate versions of rules.

You can also tailor self-prepared instructions to your case by substituting case-specific references for abstract language. For example, assume that a pattern jury instruction that a judge might give in a criminal case reads as follows:

> "Any person who carries concealed upon his person or concealed within any vehicle which is under his control or direction any pistol without having a license to carry such firearm is guilty of a misdemeanor."

Incorporating the evidence in a case, you may ask the judge to substitute this "tailored" instruction:

> "In order to convict Mr. Dillinger, the State must establish each of the following elements

> beyond a reasonable doubt: That Mr. Dillinger
> carried a revolver on his person when he at-
> tended the movie on May 6; that the revolver
> that Mr. Dillinger carried was completely con-
> cealed from view; and that Mr. Dillinger did not
> have a license to carry the revolver on May 6."

Anxious to avoid reversal, many judges prefer to give only pre-approved instructions. However, judges have discretion to give your proposed instructions so long as they conform to the law and the evidence.

H. SUBPOENAS

A subpoena is a court order requiring a witness to appear in court. A subpoena that directs a person to produce documents as well is a "subpoena duces tecum." In some jurisdictions, courts issue blank, pre-stamped subpoenas that you can complete and serve.

A good strategy is to subpoena even the friendliest of witnesses. If a witness you are counting on is ill or otherwise unable to attend when needed, the success of your request for a continuance may depend on your affirmative answer to the judge's question, "Is the witness under subpoena?" A friendly witness may regard a subpoena as an indication of distrust. How-ever, you can maintain rapport by assuring witnesses that the practice is routine, and even in the witness' best interests. For example, a subpoena can protect an employee who has to miss work to attend court.

Most jurisdictions have "on call" procedures, that allow witnesses under subpoena to go about their daily business until their testimony is needed.

I. PACKING FOR TRIAL

Your professionalism and proficiency at handling exhibits during trial can serve as silent arguments that your case is meritorious. Your presentation skills can affect the credence that judges and jurors give to your factual arguments, and that judges give to your evidentiary contentions. Thus, preparing for trial includes being sufficiently organized so that information and exhibits are available at your fingertips or at the click of a computer button.

A trial notebook is a traditional organizational tool, though one that is increasingly being supplanted or supplemented by laptop computers. A traditional trial notebook is a three ring binder in which documents are grouped and separated by differently colored index tabs. Your printed or electronic trial notebook may contain the following materials:

- *Copies of court papers*, such as pleadings, answers to interrogatories, trial briefs, pre-trial orders and written motions *in limine*. You may prepare separate sections for voluminous documents such as depositions.

- *Exhibits*. If you keep printed exhibits in an old-fashioned three ring binder, remember not to punch new holes in any exhibits that you plan to offer into evidence.

- A *Chronological Story Outline*, which consists of a timeline of crucial events and details.

- *Argument Outlines*, which comprise the items of evidence for each argument you rely on. To further the usefulness of argument outlines, you might annotate them by identifying the documents or witnesses that are the source of each item of evidence.

- *Direct Examination Outlines*, which list the important evidence you expect to elicit from each of your witnesses and which you can have in front of you as you conduct direct examinations. Direct examination outlines can also refer to the exhibits that you plan to offer during a witness' direct examination, and refer to any documents you can use to refresh a witness' recollection. (Some attorneys prepare actual "scripts" in question-answer format. Be aware that detailed scripts may impair your ability to respond to unexpected answers, and may cause you to focus on a script rather than on a witness and the judge or jury.)

- *Cross Examination Outlines*, which resemble direct examination outlines but list the important evidence you expect to elicit from adverse witnesses.

- *Opening Statement* and *Closing Argument Outlines.* These outlines should highlight what you plan to say without being so detailed that you will be tempted to read them. However, you may write out the exact text of an important jury instruction or of a witness' critical testimony.

- An *Exhibits List,* so you can keep track of which exhibits have been received into evidence. You may want to bring to court a list of all your expected exhibits. Checking off each as it is received into evidence is a good way to avoid the embarrassment of forgetting to offer an exhibit into evidence.

- *Jury documents.* Consider preparing an outline of topics you want to cover during jury voir dire. Also, you may have blank documents that are pre-numbered 1–12 (for 12 member juries) in which you record information pertaining to each juror.

- Copies of any *written stipulations.*

- *Witness information,* including subpoenas and data such as telephone and fax numbers for each witness. If you suddenly need to locate a witness who is "on call," this information may be very necessary.

- Downloaded copies of an astrophysics text and a brochure for an exclusive vacation getaway.

Tough they may have nothing to do with the subject matter of the trial, these materials may cause an adversary no end of worry.

J. MISCELLANEOUS CUSTOMS AND PRACTICES

1. SITTING AND STANDING

Unlike weddings, courtrooms don't come equipped with ushers. To find your place in an unfamiliar courtroom, look for the jury or witness box. Plaintiff's counsel table is usually the one closer to the jury or witness box. If you are still uncertain, ask the clerk or bailiff.

To show respect to the court, stand whenever you address a judge, whether you are making an argument or interposing an evidentiary objection. In many courtrooms, you are also required to stand behind a lectern while arguing or examining witnesses. In some courts you can remain seated while examining witnesses, but many attorneys prefer to stand up anyway.

You normally cannot approach a witness unless you have reason to do so, such as to point out a relevant portion of an exhibit. Ask the judge for permission to approach, unless the judge advises you that you need not bother to do so. Return to your "mark" when the reason for approaching a witness has expired.

2. PROMPTNESS

One of Murphy's unwritten laws is that the judge always takes the bench at the scheduled time when you are late. If for any reason you expect to be late, call the clerk promptly and give a realistic time for your arrival. Better yet, be on time.

3. APPROACHING THE BENCH

Ask to approach the bench whenever you want to make a statement or objection that you do not want a witness or jurors to overhear. Judges prefer bench conferences to the more time-consuming alternative of excusing jurors. Whenever a judge is likely to make an evidentiary ruling during a bench conference, or you or opposing counsel is likely to make statements you want on the record, request the court reporter's presence at the bench as well. Hope that the judge has a long bench.

4. CONVERSE IN THE TRIANGULAR

One of the stranger customs of trial is to address all comments to the judge, even though opposing counsel, the real target of your remarks, is standing right next to you. For example, assume that you want to inform a judge that opposing counsel is unfairly attempting to back out of a stipulation. Do not talk to counsel directly: "Why are you trying to get out of the stipulation we agreed to three days ago?" Instead, address the remark to the judge: "Your Honor, Ms. Boland agreed to this stipulation three days ago and now, after the witness has been excused, is suddenly attempting to withdraw it." (Fortunately, the custom is not pursued to its logical conclusion. The judge will not pretend that neither counsel can hear what the other said and repeat everyone's remarks!)

5. OBSERVE COURTHOUSE ETIQUETTE

Proper trial behavior extends beyond courtroom doors. Never discuss a case in a public area of the courthouse where you might be overheard. Public areas include elevators, corridors and bathrooms. In addition, avoid corridor conversations with jurors, as anything more than a smile and "good morning" might be interpreted as an attempt to influence the jury. (Either the judge or you should advise jurors that the attorneys are not being unfriendly, but simply following required procedures.) Of course, once a verdict is rendered, most jurisdictions allow you to discuss a case with any jurors who are willing to talk.

6. HANDLING CLIENT DISTRACTIONS

Some clients are wont to tug at their attorneys' sleeves in the middle of trial with proposed questions or arguments. One way to avoid this distraction is to furnish clients with an electronic or paper notepad and pen, advise the clients to record their thoughts, and promise to review what they've written before concluding testimony or argument. (This ploy will not work if the client is trying to tell you that your briefcase is on fire.) Another effective method that some attorneys use is to seat clients away from counsel table, perhaps even in the spectator area.

However, do not automatically regard all clients as potential distractions. Clients may assist you in a variety of ways, such as by:

- taking notes while you conduct direct examinations;

- alerting you to jurors' reactions to *voir dire* questioning and witness testimony;

Not only will such activities make a client feel involved in a case, but also your conferring with a client can serve as a silent argument that a client is responsible and trustworthy.

7. NOTE–TAKING

A trial task that will flood your mind with happy memories of student days is note-taking. A court reporter's recorded record is no substitute for a personal set of notes. For example, contemporaneous notes can help you make or respond to objections, frame cross examination questions without "misstating the evidence," and refer to specific testimony or an adversary's opening statement during your closing argument.

Note-taking may at first seem an impossible task: "I'm supposed to be alert for possible objections, observe jurors' reactions to testimony, watch out for inconsistencies with prior testimony, and take notes?" However, rather than being an extra task, note-taking may "keep your head in the game," helping you perform the other trial tasks.

K. THE TRICKS HALL OF FAME

By now, if you hoped to find in this book a collection of courtroom "tricks" guaranteed to win verdicts no matter what the validity of your arguments, you are no doubt sorely disappointed. As an apology, the book concludes with a few tricks that lawyers are said to have tried at one time or another. Some of them may be apocryphal, and in any event you should consider them only for whatever entertainment value they may have.

- *The Magic Cigar*. Clarence Darrow would draw attention away from an adversary's evidence by sticking a length of wire down the middle of a cigar. When he lit up, the wire caused the ashes to remain on the cigar. The jurors were so fascinated by the mysterious ashes that they paid no attention to the evidence. (A trick which manages simultaneously to violate ethical, evidence and health rules!)

- *Ripped van Winkle*. Listening to the direct testimony of an adverse witness who is providing devastating evidence, counsel leans back and appears to doze off, hoping to fool the jury into thinking that the testimony is of no consequence.

- *The Ancient Novice*. Finishing closing argument with an emotional appeal, the attorney humbly prays that the jurors will not hold the errors of a beginner against the client. The wily attorney is, of course, a veteran of 75 trials.

- *The Paper Chase.* In the middle of an aggressive cross examination, the attorney pauses, searches for and carefully studies a piece of paper. Holding the paper and smiling, the attorney asks, "Isn't it true that . . ." The shaken witness, assuming that the question is based directly on whatever is written on the paper, agrees to whatever the question asserts. The attorney then discards the previous day's shopping list. (In the film *Witness for the Prosecution* (1956), defense lawyer Sir Wilfrid Robarts reads from a piece of paper while cross examining Christine Helm, the key prosecution witness. Assuming that Robarts is mistakenly reading a letter that she wrote, Christine blurts out a damaging admission. Robarts then advises Christine that the piece of paper was a bill from his tailor.)

- *The Unreliable Informant.* Again in the middle of an aggressive cross, the attorney's associate rushes into the courtroom and whispers the latest stock market quotations into the attorney's ear. The attorney smiles and turns to the witness. The witness admits to anything in the next question.

- *The Fertile Octogenarian.* Sorry, wrong book.

- *William Fallon Gambits.* This flamboyant "mouthpiece for the mob" was one of the most notorious and successful attorneys through the first two decades of the 20th century, until alcoholism caused his untimely death. A biography of Fallon notes that he represented 126 defendants charged with homicide, and got each of them acquitted. (Fallon was the model for the character of defense lawyer Billy Flynn in the films *Roxie Hart* (1942) and *Chicago* (2002), and lawyer Vincent Day in *The Mouthpiece* (1932)). Two of Fallon's courtroom tricks include:

- Representing a defendant charged with first degree murder in front of a jury with a number of Catholics, Fallon instructed his client to conceal a rosary in his breast pocket while testifying. On a signal from Fallon, the witness caused the rosary to "accidentally" fall out of his pocket.

- Representing a defendant in a murder-by-poison case, Fallon swallowed the contents of the vial that the prosecution argued contained a deadly and fast acting poison. When Fallon calmly sat at counsel table and worked while the jurors deliberated, they decided that the defendant was not guilty. Fallon, who had drunk a stomach-coating liquid before swallowing the poison, then rushed to an empty room next door so that a doctor could pump his stomach. (*The Mouthpiece* depicts this dangerous and of course unethical strategy.)

- *Earl Rogers Gambits.* This Los Angeles attorney was a contemporary of Fallon, and equally flamboyant. Among his other clients, Rogers represented Clarence Darrow in Darrow's jury-bribing trial. Some of Rogers' courtroom tricks include:

- Representing an alleged thief who stole a ring worth only about $3.00, Rogers had the thief dress for court wearing fancy jewelry. The jury voted for acquittal, figuring that a rich man would not stoop to such a petty theft. After the trial, Rogers returned the items of jewelry to the pawnbroker from whom they'd been rented.

- Cross examining an eyewitness to the theft of a horse, Rogers engaged the witness in friendly conversation about farming. In the meantime, Rogers had the defendant quietly change places at counsel table with one of Rogers' associates, who had been seated in the spectator area of the courtroom. Asked to identify the thief, the witness pointed to the associate and the case was dismissed.

- In a murder case, a professional gambler was shot and killed by one of two young men with whom he was playing cards. Rogers' client was charged with the murder. The witness was the other young man, who said he stood by unafraid while the defendant drew a gun and shot the gambler. During closing argument, Rogers started screaming angrily. He suddenly drew a gun, and everyone in the courtroom, including the witness, ducked for cover or ran out the exits. The jurors voted for acquittal, figuring that the prosecution witness had lied about standing by unafraid. (The film *Criminal Court* (1964) depicts this trick.)

INDEX

References are to Pages

ABOTA, 10

ANALOGIES, 56, 115, 468, 519–525, 526, 530, 537–538

ARGUMENT–CENTERED NARRATIVES
Characteristics of, 3, 14, 22–30
Circumstantial evidence in, 5
Closing argument, 485
Cross examination, 286
Details, including, 26
Direct examination, 180, 209, 219
Emotional evidence, 29
Explanatory evidence, 25
Inferential evidence, 23, Chap. 3
Opening statements, 95
Persuasiveness of, 14
Settlement discussions, 7
Stories, see Stories
Thinking like a trial lawyer, 3
Truth and, 8
Two-sided, 513, 516, 541
Visual aids, 30

ARGUMENTATIVE QUESTIONS, 113, 246, 254, 259, 260, 285, 298, 326, 340, 572–575

ARGUMENTS
With others, very few

ATTORNEY–CENTERED QUESTIONING, 154, 156, 240

AUTHENTICATION
By content, 436, 440
Electronic records, 438, 440
Generally, 396, 399
Handwriting, 427
Inter-personal communications, 345
Reply doctrine, 437
Self-authentication, 434, 436, 438

"BEFORE AND AFTER" EVIDENCE, 5, 23, 223

BENCH TRIALS, 125, 530, 578

"BENTLEY" CASE, 356–357

BEST EVIDENCE RULE, 419–427

BIAS, 8, 51, 64, 66, 68–72, 81, 90, 200, 308, 464, 481, 504, 508, 536, 548, 581, 582

BLOCKS GAME, 28

BOOKEND EVENTS, 18

BOTTOM LINES, 66, 95, 101–102, 475, 498, 504, 511, 542

BURDEN OF PROOF, 31, 32, 98, 121, 124, 137, 498, 520, 523, 526, 546, 591

BUSINESS RECORDS, 372, 431

CHAIN OF CUSTODY, 408

CHARACTER EVIDENCE, 51, 76, 82, 173, 302–307, 360–369, 555, 564

CHRONOLOGY
Argument-centered narratives, 3, 180
Atypical, 183
Closing argument, reviewing during, 501
Cross examination, 287, 288, 320
Deviating from, 20–21, 184
Diagram, use to clarify, 418
Direct examination, 141, 180, 223
Experts providing, 470
Fact finding, 15
Front load technique, 185
Inferences, affecting, 15
Mini-chronologies, 184
Opening statements, 95, 107
Outlines of, 595
Separate, 107
Timelines to maintain, 17

CIRCUMSTANTIAL EVIDENCE
Argument-centered narratives, basis of, 5
Before and after, 5
Closing argument, 525
Credibility arguments, 6, 24
Cross examination, 257
"Except whens," 43
Expert witnesses, 469, 476
Factual propositions, 39, 45

Habit evidence, 362
Inferential arguments, 23, 34, 39, 223, 276, 316
Jury instructions, 528
Jury *voir dire*, 583
Normative arguments, 45
One question too many, 257
Opening statements, 114
Sexual assault cases, 368
Silent arguments, 120

CIVILITY, 9–12, 551

CLOSED QUESTIONS, 155–157, 188, 190

CLOSING ARGUMENT
Analogies, 519–525, 537, 538
Bench trials, 530
Bottom line, identifying, 498, 504, 511–513, 542
Burden of proof, reference to, 498, 526, 546
Content of, 496–499
Credibility arguments, 503, 516, 539
Delivery of, 494–496, 547
Everyday experience, relying on, 488
Evidence review, 500, 546
Examples and analyses, 530–548
Exhibits, use during, 496, 534
Eye contact, 495
Facts outside the record, 486
"*Falsus in uno. . .* " 505, 539
Generally, Chap. 12
Golden rule arguments, 493
Inferential arguments, 488, 502, 540
Inoculation technique, 517, 539

Introductory remarks, 497

Jury instructions, reference to, 498, 525–530

Lying or mistaken, 503

Normative arguments, 510

Nullification, 493

O.J. Simpson vs. Euphilitus, 530

Opening statement, adversary's failed promises, 534

Organization of, 499

Outline of, 596

Preempting adversary's argument, 516, 541

Pseudo-normative arguments, 510, 543

Puffing, 489, 535

Reviewing evidence during, 500

Roadmap of, 498, 533

Rules governing, 486–493

"Send a message" arguments, 492, 542

Silent arguments, addressing during, 491, 509, 535, 548

Strategies, 493

This is a really long list!

Two-sided arguments, 513, 516, 541

Vouching, 490

"CLOSING THE DOOR" TECHNIQUE, 333

COLLATERAL EVIDENCE RULE, 249, 303, 305, 309, 313

COMPETENCY TO TESTIFY, 142

COMPUTER RECORDS, 436

CONTINUING OBJECTIONS, 562

CONTRADICTION, 312

CONVERSATIONS, 19, 283, 345, 599

CREDIBILITY
Argument-centered narratives, 4, 24
Bias, 51, 64, 68–72, 81
Character for honesty, 51, 76, 82
Circumstantial evidence, 6, 24
Closing argument, 503, 516, 539
Demeanor, 51, 73, 82
Details, 25, 29, 105, 153, 181, 190, 225, 282, 283
Established facts, 51, 62, 80, 97
Everyday experience, 51, 52, 78
Expertise, 51, 67, 69, 81, 464
Explanations, 54, 61, 72
Factual propositions, 49
"*Falsus in uno. . .* ," 505, 539
Generally, Chap. 4
Impaired witnesses, 313
Importance of, 48
Important disputes, focusing on, 49
Internal consistency, 51, 58, 79
Leading questions, 171
Lying or mistaken, 66, 503
Model of, 51
Motive, *see* Bias
Opening statements, supporting in, 95, 114
Reason to observe or recall, 51, 72, 82
Relevance rule, 25
Source credibility factors, 51, 63
Specific vs. general, 64
Stipulating to, 552
Story credibility factors, 51, 52

"Taking the sting out" technique, 70, 122, 220, 226

Two-sided arguments, 516

CREDIBILITY MODEL, 50

CROSS EXAMINATION

Argument-centered, 286

Argumentative questions, 246, 259, 298, 326, 335, 340

Bias, 308–313, 481

Character evidence, impeachment with, 302–307

"Closing the door" technique, 333

Collateral evidence rule, 249, 303, 305, 309, 313

Contradiction, 312

Details, pursuing, 281, 283, 319

Emphasis strategies, 315

Established facts, questions based on, 267

Evasive answers, responding to, 323

Everyday experience, questions based on, 268

Expert witnesses, 480–484

Explanations, responding to, 327

Fishing, 244, 260–262, 280–286

Forgoing, 291, 321

Generally, Chap. 8

Good-faith belief, need for, 248, 303, 304

Highly safe questions, 263

"Hop, skip, jump" technique, 283

"I don't remember" answers, impeaching, 293

Impaired witnesses, 313

Inconsistent statements, impeachment with, 290–301

Leading questions, 240, 251

May and might answers, responding to, 327

Medium safe questions, 268

Mystique of, 240

"No, no, no" technique, 315

"Nose story," 242, 259

Objections, 340–343

Omissions impeachment, 299

"One-item" questions, 253

One question too many, 257

Open questions, 319

Order of questioning, 320

Outline of, 595

Pin down technique, 294, 298

Preparing witnesses for, 337

Prior statements, questions based on, 263–267, 290–301

Protecting your witness during, 340–343

Rehash of direct, 244

Safety model, 262

Sandbagging, 285

Scope of, 245, 343

Silent arguments, addressing during, 286, 289

This is another long list!

Tone of voice, 255

Ultimate conclusion questions, 316

Unavailable witness, statements of, 276

Unsafe questions, 280

"Why" questions, 255

"Your story" cross, 336

"CSI EFFECT," 196

CUSTOMS AND PRACTICES, 597

***DAUBERT* ISSUES,** 455

DEMEANOR
Background questions, aid to, 172
Closing argument, addressing during, 76
Exhibits as affecting, 75
Experts, 57
Field trips to aid, 73
Information overload, risks of, 75
Witness preparation, 74

DEMONSTRATIONS, 369, 443

DEMONSTRATIVE EVIDENCE, 63, 196, 344, 390

DEPOSITIONS
Argumentative question based on, 341
Civility, 9–11
Cross examination, 260, 264–267, 294–295
Direct examination, 218, 220
Exhibits, 404, 447
Experts, 451
Good faith belief, basis of, 304
Hostility of deponent, 164
Impeachment, source of, 58, 61, 218, 264, 291, 294–296
Objections based on behavior at, 558
Open questions based on, 320
Opening statements, 118, 130
Preamble, 296
Refreshing recollection, 352
Substantive evidence, testimony as, 264, 291
Timelines, 18

DETAILS

Advantages of, 26–28, 181

Character evidence, 303, 368

Cross examination, pursuing during, 281–283, 319

Diagrams, limitations of, 414

Direct examination, 140, 155–156, 181, 185, 188, 190, 193, 194–196, 219, 225

Excessive, risks of, 29, 104–106, 153

Opening statements, 104–106, 132

Opinion rule, 353

Stories, aspect of, 26

Timelines, including in, 18

Trial notebooks, 595–596

DIAGRAMS,

DIAGRAMS, 31, 74, 177, 196, 210, 225, 235, 390–392, 413–419, 447

DIRECT EVIDENCE,

DIRECT EVIDENCE, 6, 583

DIRECT EXAMINATION

Attorneys can't testify, 146

Atypical chronologies, 183

Background testimony, 140, 165, 172, 174, 209, 460

Children, questioning of, 142, 165

Client tasks, 150, 600

Closed questions, 155, 188

Competency of witnesses, establishing, 142

Concluding, 141, 170, 201, 210, 224

Cumulative witnesses, 228

"Do you recall" technique, 352

Emphasis techniques, 185

Established facts in, 63

Everyday language during, 237

Examples and analyses, 204–226
Exhibits, 196, 235
Expert witnesses, 158, 173, 231, 460–480
"Frontload" technique, 185, 219
Generally, Chap. 7
Gestures, clarifying, 197
Getting started, 172–180
Hostile witnesses, 164
Infirm witnesses, 165
Jargon, explaining, 226, 237, 470, 476, 480
Layered questioning, 188
Leading questions, 162–172, 176
Loops, 192
Mind set, 182
Mini-chronologies, 184
Multiple witnesses, 228–230
Narrative questions, 157, 176, 223
"No, no, no" technique, 190, 225
Offers of proof, 233
Open questions, 151–155, 188, 223, 471–472
Opinion testimony, 194–196, 469–480
Order of witnesses, 230
Outline of, 595
Partial stories, 229
Personal knowledge, establishing, 145
Points of reference, 192
Preparing witnesses for, 233–236
"Pseudo-narrative" questions, 160
Redirect examination, 202
Refreshing recollection, 166, 348–353
Re-opening, 204
Rules governing, 141–150

Scene-change questions, 179–180, 210
Scene-setting questions, 140, 175–180, 210
Silent arguments, addressing, 200, 223
Sitting and standing, 148
Specific vs. general credibility evidence, 64–65
"Taking the sting out" during, 70, 220, 226–228
Verbal tics, 238
"The Well," 148, 549

"DIT" INSURANCE CASE, 125

"DO YOUR RECALL" TECHNIQUE, 352

DYING DECLARATIONS, 385

EMBRYONIC ARGUMENTS, 39, 42

EMOTIONAL EVIDENCE, 29

EMPHASIS TECHNIQUES
Conclusions, 194–196
Cross examination, 315–319
Diagrams, 414
Direct examination, 185–196, 201
Exhibits, 196
"Frontload" technique, 185, 219
Layered questioning, 188
Loops, 192
"No, no, no" technique, 190, 315
Opinions, 194–196
Points of reference, 192
Repetition of testimony, 201
Ultimate conclusion questions, 316

"ESPECIALLY WHEN" TECHNIQUE, 40–42, 288, 503, 584

ESTABLISHED FACTS, 51, 62–63, 80, 97, 262, 267

ETHICAL CONSIDERATIONS, 9–12, 61, 117, 119, 228, 234, 236, 392, 454, 490, 558, 578

"EUPHILETUS" TRIAL, 530

EVASIVE ANSWERS, RESPONDING TO, 307, 323–327, 572

"EXCEPT WHEN" TECHNIQUE, 43, 483, 513–515, 584

EXCITED UTTERANCES, 378

EXCLUSION OF WITNESSES, 236, 549

EXHIBITS
Advantages of using, 30, 393–396
Authenticating, 399–401, 427–431, 436, 438, 440
Best evidence rule, 393, 419–427
Business records, 431
Chain of custody, 408
Closing argument, 496, 534
Computer records, 436
Demeanor, affecting, 74
Demonstrative vs. real, 30–31, 390–393
Diagrams, 31, 74, 177, 196, 210, 225, 235, 390–392, 413–419, 447
Direct examination, 196
Effective handling of, 404
Experts, 468
Facsimile exhibits, 407
Faxed documents, 437
Generally, Chap. 10

Handwritten documents, 427–431
Inscribed chattels, 423
Marking, 392, 394, 397–399, 406, 411, 430, 442
Opening statements, 111
Photographs, 411
Professionally prepared, 392, 447–448
Property of court, 402
Public records, 433
Publishing to jurors, 402–404
Recorded recollection, 441–443
Self-authentication, 434, 436, 438
Signed documents, 427–431
Sponsoring witness, 31, 396, 400, 403, 415, 418, 433, 437
Texts and tweets, 439
Trial notebook, including in, 596

EXPERT WITNESSES
Bias, 69, 464, 481
Compensation of, 451, 454, 481
Credibility, 68, 81
Cross examination, 480–484
Direct examination techniques, 460–480
Educational, 452, 471, 476
Established facts, source of, 62
Everyday experience to evaluate, 57
"Except when" cross examination, 483
Generally, Chap. 11
Hypothetical questions to, 458
Impeachment, 481
Inadmissible evidence, testimony to, 453
Inferential reasoning, 469

Jargon, 470, 476
Learned treatise cross examination, 484
Narrative answers, 454
Opinions, eliciting, 469–480
Personal knowledge, 452, 471
Principles, explaining, 467
Qualifications, 173, 457, 460–467, 481
Reliability of field of expertise, 455
Roles of, 450–452
Selecting, 64
Stipulations concerning qualifications, 457
Ultimate issue, opinions as to, 451, 459

EXPLANATORY EVIDENCE, 25, 54, 72, 202, 209, 210, 327

EYE CONTACT, 495

FACTUAL PROPOSITIONS
Arguments, focus of, 35, 42
Benefits of developing, 35
Closing argument, reference to, 499–501
Cross examination, 287
Defense perspective, 36
Defined, 35
Disputed elements, 39, 42
Elements, converting to, 35–39
Experts, stipulations to qualifications, 552
Historical, 43
Importance, evaluating, 49
Inferential arguments, 42
Marshaling evidence around, 35, 39
Normative legal elements, 45

FAXED DOCUMENTS, 437

FEDERAL RULES OF EVIDENCE
Authentication, 347, 399, 436
Best evidence rule, 393, 404, 419
Business records, 431
Character evidence, 65, 76, 173, 302, 360, 362, 363, 555, 556, 570
Competency of witnesses, 142
Exhibits, see Chap. 10
Experts, 67, 115, 140, 173, 449, 451, 452, 453, 455, 457–460, 470, 471
Form objections, 571
Foundations, 142, 168, 347, 369, 408, 419, 422, 423, 426, 427, 439, 455, 570
Habit, 362
Hearsay, 27, 58, 264, 290, 293, 372–389, 401,402, 431, 433, 484, 559, 569
Hostile witnesses, 119, 164, 231
Judges' control over proceedings, 114, 141, 158, 233, 571
Judicial notice, 62, 436
Leading questions, 162
Narrative questions, 571
Opinions, 115, 174, 195, 225, 353, 569
"Other acts," 365, 564, 570
Personal knowledge, 145, 419, 452, 569
Prior statements, 58, 290, 292, 293, 352
Public records, 433
Recorded recollection, 441
Redirect examination, 202
Refreshing recollection, 349

Relevance, 25, 26, 50, 173, 568
Remedial measures, 577
Sequestering witnesses, 549
Sexual assault cases, 368
Unfair prejudice, 30, 86, 233, 249, 303, 372, 413, 419, 443, 445, 448, 557, 568

FILM REFERENCES
Anatomy of a Murder, 15, 241, 260, 338
Chicago, 603
A Civil Action, 256
Criminal Court, 370, 605
A Few Good Men, 273
Home Alone, 564
Let Him Have It, 356
The Mouthpiece, 603
My Cousin Vinny, 55, 122, 237, 247, 333, 465, 473
Philadelphia, 135, 444
Reel Justice: The Courtroom Goes to the Movies, plug
Roxie Hart, 603
To Kill a Mockingbird, 87, 220–226, 543–548
Witness for the Prosecution, 2, 602
Young Mr. Lincoln, 268

FORFEITURE BY WRONGDOING, 387

GOLDEN RULE ARGUMENTS, 493

GOOD–FAITH BELIEF, 248, 281, 303

HABIT EVIDENCE, 362

HANDWRITING, AUTHENTICATING, 427

HEARSAY FOUNDATIONS, 372–387

"HILLMON" CASE, 32, 40, 78–83, 89

HOP, SKIP AND JUMP QUESTIONING, 283

HYPOTHETICAL QUESTIONS, 458

IMPLAUSIBLE TESTIMONY, 55, 268–276, 282, 331–333, 505–507

INCONSISTENT STATEMENTS
Analogy based on, 521
"I don't remember" responses, 293
Impeachment with, 290–301
Your witnesses' stories, 61
Pin down technique, 294, 298–299

INEBRIATION, FOUNDATION FOR, 357–360

INFERENTIAL ARGUMENTS
Bottom lines of, 66
Chronology, role of, 15–17
Closing argument, supporting during, 488, 502, 528, 540
Cross examination, supporting during, 287–288
Defendants', 36
Defined, 34
Direct evidence, credibility dependent on, 6
Embryonic arguments, 39
"Especially whens," 40–42, 288, 503, 584
"Except whens,"43, 483, 513–515, 584
Expert testimony, 469, 476
Factual propositions, use for developing, 35
Generally, Chap. 3
Implausible testimony, 55, 268–276, 282, 331–333, 505–507

Marshaling circumstantial evidence, 39
Normative, 43
Opening statements, 95
Stories, included in, 23
Strongest evidence, identifying, 39
Undermining, 42
Weak inference attack, 515

INOCULATION TECHNIQUE, 517, 539, 589

INTERNAL CONSISTENCY, 51, 58, 79

JUDGE OR JURY TRIAL, 578

JURY INSTRUCTIONS, 86, 498, 525–530, 591–593

JURY *VOIR DIRE*, 582–591

"KENNEDY–SMITH" TRIAL, 317, 505

LAYERED QUESTIONING, 188

LEADING QUESTIONS, 162–172, 251–255, 348, 558, 573

LEGAL ELEMENTS
Abstractness, 35
Converting to factual propositions, 35
Normative, 43–47

MARKING PROCESS, 392, 394, 397–399, 406, 411, 430, 442

MARSHALLING EVIDENCE, 35, 39, 97, 181, 210

MEDICAL HEARSAY, 380

"MENENDEZ" CASE, 271, 289

MERCY RULE, 363

MIND SET PHENOMENON, 182, 337, 538

MOTIONS *IN LIMINE*, 86, 117, 307, 554–557

MOTIVE, see Bias

NARRATIVE QUESTIONS, 157, 223

"NO, NO, NO" TECHNIQUE, 190, 315

NORMALIZING EFFECT OF STORIES, 15

NORMATIVE ARGUMENTS, 43–47, 510

NOTE–TAKING, 600

NULLIFICATION ARGUMENTS, 493

OBJECTIONS, 65, 113, 116, 141, 147, 148, 158, 161, 340–343, 554–578

OFFERS OF PROOF, 233, 563

"O.J. SIMPSON" CASE, 66, 88, 118, 530–543

ONE ITEM QUESTIONS, 253–255

OPEN QUESTIONS, 151–155, 223, 319, 584

OPENING STATEMENTS
Argument in, 93, 95, 103, 114–116, 137
Bench trials, 125
Body language, 110
Boilerplate, 113, 126
Bottom line, 95, 101–102
Chronology, 93, 107, 130, 132, 138
Closing argument, attacked during, 117, 534
Contents of, 92

Defense perspective, 98, 123
Details in, 104–106, 127
Everyday language, 107
Examples and analyses, 125–138
Eye contact, 110
Generally, Chap. 6
Goals of, 92
Inadmissible evidence, referring to, 116
"Mock" opening statements, 124
Motion *in limine,* 117
Outline of, 596
Over–promising, risks of, 117, 137, 534
Prima facie case, 121
Roadmap, 92, 93
Substantive rules, discussing, 94, 103, 129, 137
"The evidence will show," 112
Themes, 94, 99, 131, 135, 137
Unavailable evidence, referring to, 116, 119
Visual aids, 111
Voucher rule, 119
Weaknesses, volunteering, 121, 132

OPINION TESTIMONY, 174, 194–196, 353–357, 451–453, 459, 467, 469–480

OPPOSING PARTY STATEMENTS, 373–377

ORIGINAL WRITING RULE, see Best Evidence Rule

OTHER ACTS, 365

PERSONAL KNOWLEDGE, 145–146, 347, 353, 401, 452, 471, 570

PHOTOGRAPHS, 112, 391, 403, 411–413

PIN DOWN TECHNIQUE, 294, 298–299

POINTS OF REFERENCE, 192–194

PREEMPTION TECHNIQUE, 516, 530, 541

PREPARATION OF WITNESSES
Cross-examination, 337
Direct examination, 233

PRESENT SENSE IMPRESSIONS, 377

PRIMA FACIE CASES, 121

PRIMACY AND RECENCY, 113, 185, 201, 219, 475

PSEUDO–NORMATIVE ARGUMENTS, 510, 543

PUBLIC RECORDS, 433

PUFFING, 489, 535

REAL EVIDENCE, 26, 30, 390–392, 405–411

RECORDED RECOLLECTION, 441

REDIRECT EXAMINATION, 202

REFRESHING RECOLLECTION, 166, 348–353

"ROSENBERG ATOMIC SPIES" CASE, 89, 258, 309, 477

SAFETY MODEL FOR CROSS EXAMINATION, 262

SANDBAGGING, 285

SCENE–SETTING QUESTIONS, 140, 175–180, 210

"SEND A MESSAGE" ARGUMENTS, 492, 542

SEQUESTERING WITNESSES, 236, 549

SEXUAL ASSAULT CASES, 368

SIGNED WRITINGS, 426

SILAS DEANE STORY, 21

SILENT ARGUMENTS
Benefiting from, 84
Closing argument, 88–90, 491, 509, 535, 548
Cross examination, addressing during, 286, 289
Defined, 84
Direct examination, 85, 87, 200, 223
Generally, Chap. 5
Individualizing evidence, 87
Irrationality of, 84
Jury instructions, 86
Jury *voir dire*, 86, 590
Motions *in limine*, 86

STIPULATIONS, 457, 551–554, 596

STORIES
Defendants', 31
Details, role of, 26
Effectiveness of, 15, 93
Inference-driven, 21
Persuasiveness of, 14–17

SUBPOENAS, 593

SUBSTANTIVELY CRITICAL EVENTS, 22

"TAKING THE STING OUT" TECHNIQUE, 70, 122, 220, 226

TELEPHONE DIRECTORY DOCTRINE, 347

TEXTS AND TWEETS, 438

THEMES, 94, 99, 131, 134, 137

THINKING LIKE A TRIAL LAWYER, 3

TIMELINES, 17–21, 94

TRIAL NOTEBOOKS, 594

"TRIANGLE SHIRTWAIST FIRE" CASE, 59, 241

TRICKS HALL OF FAME, 601–605

TRUTH, 8, 61, 253

TWO–SIDED ARGUMENTS, 513–518, 541

ULTIMATE CONCLUSION QUESTIONS, 316–319

UNAVAILABILITY, 276, 381–385

VISUAL AIDS, 28, 30, 111, 393, 396, 496, 534

VISUAL LEARNING, 27, 393

VOUCHER RULE, 119–121, 490–493

"WHY" QUESTIONS, 255–257, 569

WITNESSES
Competency of, 142
Digressers, 154

Experts, see Expert Witnesses
Hostile, 164
Multiple, 228
Partisan, 153
Preparation to testify, 233, 337
Sequestering, 236, 549
Subpoenaing, 593
Unavailability of, 276, 381–385
Verbose, 153, 161, 572
Voir dire questioning of, 142
Witness-centered questioning, 152, 241

"YOUR STORY" CROSS EXAMINATION, 336–337

†